Accounting
for Non-Financial Managers

Revised Second Edition

John Parkinson

with

Charles Draimin

Captus Press

Accounting for Non-Financial Managers, Revised second edition

© 2007 by the authors and Captus Press Inc.

Captus Press Inc.
Mail: Units 14 & 15, 1600 Steeles Avenue West
         Concord, Ontario
         L4K 4M2
Tel: (416) 736–5537
Fax: (416) 736–5793
Email: info@captus.com
Internet: www.captus.com

Library and Archives Canada Cataloguing in Publication

Parkinson, John M.
    Accounting for non-financial managers / John Parkinson ; with
Charles Draimin. — Rev. 2nd ed.

Includes index.
ISBN-13 978-1-55322-173-9

    1. Accounting — Textbooks. 2. Managerial accounting — Textbooks.
I. Draimin, Charles, 1943– II. Title.

HF5657.4.P37 2007   658.15'11   C2007-904557-X

Canada We acknowledge the financial support of the Government of Canada through the Book Publishing Industry Development Program (BPIDP) for our publishing activities.

0 9 8 7 6 5 4
Printed in Canada

Contents

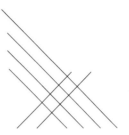

Chapter 1 Introduction **1**

    1.1 Accounting: Who Needs It? 2
    1.2 Scorekeeping. 5
    1.3 Attention Directing. 6
    1.4 Decision Making 6
    1.5 Financial Accounting, Management Accounting
         and Auditing 7
    1.6 Personal Financial Planning 8
    1.7 Summary 8
    Discussion Questions and Problems. 9

**Section 1 Financial Accounting
               for Scorekeeping** **13**

    Chapter 2 The Financial Statements **15**

        2.1 Introduction. 16
        2.2 The Objectives of Financial Reporting. 16
        2.3 The Accounting Equation 18
        2.4 Types of Financial Statements 23
        2.5 Characteristics of Accounting Information. 25
        2.6 Accounting Concepts 28
        2.7 Summary 30
        Appendix 2.1 The Mechanics of Accounting:
                    The Basics 31
        Self-Study Problems 67
        Discussion Questions and Problems. 70

    Chapter 3 The Income Statement **77**

        3.1 Introduction. 78
        3.2 Revenues 78
        3.3 Expenses 81

Table of Contents

3.4 Operating Income 88
3.5 Net Income 90
3.6 Retained Earnings 92
3.7 Earnings Per Share 94
3.8 Summary 94
Appendix 3.1 Example of an Income Statement 95
Appendix 3.2 Methods of Amortization 96
Appendix 3.3 Capital Cost Allowances and
 Deferred Taxes 99
Appendix 3.4 Example of a Statement
 of Retained Earnings 101
Appendix 3.5 The Mechanics of Accounting:
 The Income Statement 102
Self-Study Problems 121
Discussion Questions and Problems 125

Chapter 4   **The Balance Sheet (1):** *Assets* **135**
4.1 Introduction 136
4.2 Assets 138
4.3 Asset Turnover Ratio 150
4.4 Summary 151
Appendix 4.1 Example of a Balance Sheet 152
Appendix 4.2 Inventory Flow and Inventory
 Valuation Models 153
Appendix 4.3 Consolidation of Groups
 of Companies 157
Self-Study Problem 160
Discussion Questions and Problems 163

Chapter 5   **The Balance Sheet (2):** *Liabilities and Equity* . . . **169**
5.1 Liabilities 170
5.2 Equity 176
5.3 Summary 181
Appendix 5.1 Sarbanes-Oxley Act and Bill 198 182
Appendix 5.2 The Mechanics of Accounting:
 The Balance Sheet 183
Self-Study Problem 191
Discussion Questions and Problems 194

Chapter 6   **Statement of Cash Flows** **197**
6.1 Introduction 198
6.2 Cash from Operations 199
6.3 Cash from Financing Activities 201
6.4 Cash from and Cash Used in Investing Activities . . . 202
6.5 Change in Cash Balance 202
6.6 Interpreting the Statement of Cash Flows 203
6.7 Summary 204
Appendix 6.1 Example of a Cash Flow Statement 205
Appendix 6.2 The Mechanics of Accounting:
 Cash Flows 206
Self-Study Problem 215
Discussion Questions and Problems 217

Section 2   Budgeting for Planning & Control 223

Chapter 7   Budgeting 225

7.1   Introduction 226
7.2   Preparing the Budget for a Service Department 227
7.3   Preparing the Budget for a Production
      Department 231
7.4   The Master Budget 233
7.5   The Operating Budget 235
7.6   Cash Budgeting 242
7.7   Participation in Budgeting 245
7.8   Summary 246
Appendix 7.1 Budgeting Is Dead:
              Long Live Budgeting! 247
Self-Study Problems 249
Discussion Questions and Problems 253

Chapter 8   Budgetary Control 259

8.1   Control 260
8.2   Imposed and Participative Budgets 262
8.3   Responsibility and Control 263
8.4   Control in Organizational Sub-Units 264
8.5   The Balanced Scorecard 271
8.6   The Behavioural Aspect of Budgeting 273
8.7   Summary 274
Self-Study Problems 275
Discussion Questions and Problems 279

Chapter 9   Cost Behaviour, Break-Even, and
                Product Costing 283

9.1   Introduction 284
9.2   Cost Behaviour 284
9.3   The Break-Even Model 286
9.4   Product Costing 290
9.5   Over- and Under-Recovered Overhead 296
9.6   Summary 296
Self-Study Problems 298
Discussion Questions and Problems 302

Section 3   Financial Decision Making 309

Chapter 10   Analysis of Short-Term Decisions 311

10.1 Introduction 312
10.2 Differential Costs and Revenues: New Orders 312
10.3 Capacity Issues 314
10.4 Make or Buy 315
10.5 Sunk Costs 316
10.6 Committed Costs 316
10.7 Short-Term vs. Long-Term 316
10.8 Summary 317
Self-Study Problems 318
Discussion Questions and Problems 320

Table of Contents

Chapter 11 **Sources of Capital**. **325**

11.1 Introduction. 326
11.2 Common Shares. 326
11.3 Retained Earnings. 330
11.4 Preferred Shares. 330
11.5 Equity Capital 331
11.6 Debt 333
11.7 Debt, Risk, and Financial Leverage 335
11.8 Summary 339
Appendix 11.1 Risk and Return 340
Self-Study Problems. 345
Discussion Questions and Problems. 348

Chapter 12 **Long-Term Decision Making**. **353**

12.1 Introduction. 354
12.2 Strategic Analysis 355
12.3 Payback. 356
12.4 Return on Investment. 358
12.5 Present Value 361
12.6 Uncertainty 370
12.7 Summary 371
Self-Study Problems. 372
Discussion Questions and Problems. 375

Chapter 13 **Financial Statement Analysis** **379**

13.1 Introduction. 380
13.2 Liquidity. 382
13.3 Profitability 382
13.4 Debt 385
13.5 Efficiency 386
13.6 Market-Related Ratios. 387
13.7 Summary 389
Appendix 13.1 The Dupont Pyramid
of Operating Ratios 390
Self-Study Problem. 395
Discussion Questions and Problem 399

Section 4   Accounting for the Non-Profit Sector 401

Chapter 14 **Accounting for Non-Profit and
Governmental Organizations**. **403**

14.1 Introduction. 404
14.2 Non-Profit and Governmental Organizations 404
14.3 Accounting Techniques for
Non-Profit Organizations 409
14.4 Financial Accounting for Non-Profit Organizations. . . 410
14.5 Financial Statement Analysis 416
14.6 Evaluating Effectiveness and Efficiency in
Non-Profit Organizations 417
14.7 Budgeting and Budgetary Control 420
14.8 Summary 420

Appendix 14.1 Example of Financial Statements of
a Not-for-Profit Organization Prepared
Using Fund Accounting 422
Self-Study Problem. 432
Discussion Questions and Problems. 437

Glossary of Important Terms **445**

Index **463**

Student Self-Study Resource **471**

Introduction 1

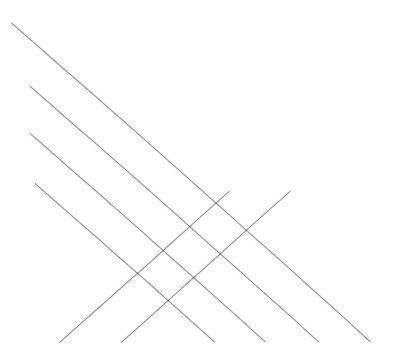

Learning
Objectives

After studying this chapter you should be able to explain:
→ Who needs to know about accounting
→ How accounting can be used to keep score
→ How accounting can be used for attention directing
→ How accounting can be used to support decisions

1.1   Accounting: Who Needs It?

The answer is that just about every manager needs it. This book will show why managers need to know about accounting, and will explain the language of accounting and some of the basic techniques. This book is not intended to cover the entire spectrum of accounting, nor is it intended to make accountants out of non-accountants. Its aim, rather, is to bridge the gap between accountants and other managers so that they can intelligently discuss topics of mutual importance. Consider the following three situations.

1.1.1   The Marketing Manager's Proposal

The marketing manager of a medium-sized company is in a meeting with the other managers of the company. He is proposing a marketing campaign to substantially increase product awareness. He is offering his audience the choice of several different ways of implementing the campaign. He is well into his presentation when one of the product managers asks,

"How will this appear in the financial statements?"

His answer may be along the following lines:

"Proposal *A* involves us buying a number of advertising trucks that would drive around the city with illuminated billboards. These purchases would appear in the balance sheet initially, and their amortization would appear in the income statement as expense. Proposal *B* involves renting advertising space on train and bus interiors, which would appear as an expense in the income statement, as incurred. Proposal *A* would initially reduce our liquidity ratios, and this may be a problem for investors, who will perceive us as a riskier investment. Proposal *B* would have minimal effect on liquidity ratios, but would, initially, reduce profits more. Both proposals are expected to increase profitability ratios in the medium term."

Alternatively, he may say,

> "Sorry, but I don't know enough about financial statements to answer you now. I will have to get back to you on that."

The first answer indicates that the marketing manager is familiar with the main financial statements, understands that different types of spending might get treated in different ways, and understands the implications for the users of financial statements. The second answer indicates that he does not fully understand the financial implications of the proposals he is making.

1.1.2   *The Human Resources Manager's Situation*

The human resources manager is called into her vice-president's office. The human resource department budget is overspent by 12% in the month of March, and the VP wants to know what went wrong. Her reply might be along these lines:

> "When I submitted the budget in October, it was quite clear that there were some uncertainties surrounding the issue of workload — issues over which I had no control. I indicated that the budget I had presented was contingent on the level of hirings and firings being approximately the same as in the previous year. As it happens, there has been a major reorganization in the Quebec region. The number of personnel we let go has increased by 50%, and hirings have also increased substantially. Given this change in workload, it is quite remarkable that we have been able to get by with only two additional staff members and an increase in spending of a mere 12%."

Alternatively, she may have to give some vague answer, such as

> "Well, we needed the extra staff because we were overworked,"

or

> "My assistant prepared the budget: I'll have to ask him and get back to you."

The first answer shows that she understands the way a budget is prepared and how it should be used as a control system. The second and third answers show that she knows neither.

1.1.3   *The Production Manager's Dilemma*

The production manager is proposing the purchase of a new packaging machine. The existing packaging machine is reaching the end of its useful life and needs to be replaced because it is prone to breaking down. Additionally, more modern machines can do more sophisticated packaging, such as integrated full-colour printing and shrink-wrapping. He proposes to spend $100,000 on a state-of-the-art packaging machine that will serve the company's needs for the next 10 to 20 years. The discussion is going well until someone asks if it is possible to lease the machine instead of buying it. His response may be along these lines:

> "Yes, leasing is a possibility. We have a leasing quotation from the supplier. Based on an expected useful life of 10 years, the present value of the lease payments would be $120,000. If we assumed a longer life, the present value of the lease costs would be even higher. So, outright purchase is a better economic alternative. Additionally, the VP of Finance informed me that we have adequate cash available for capital investment at this time, and the machine purchase will not strain liquidity."

Alternatively, he may explain that although leasing is a possibility, he has no basis for comparing a capital investment with a series of lease payments, so he cannot decide which is better.

The first answer shows that he is able to deal with the financial implications of his decisions, including consideration of the effect of his proposals on other areas (in this instance, finance and cash flow). The second answer indicates that he is not in command of the appropriate bases for making business decisions, even those within his area of direct control and supposed expertise.

The above three scenarios show that managers need to have a basic understanding of accounting reports and accounting-oriented decision processes. They need this so that they can appear as intelligent, well-informed members of the management team (general background), and so they can plan and control their own operating areas (budgetary control). Furthermore, they can deal with the financial implications of proposals they put forward (decision making).

Given the above hypothetical situations, as a manager, do you want to present yourself as someone who is informed and capable of making decisions appropriately? Alternatively, do you want to come across as a narrow specialist who understands his or her own discipline well, but has no knowledge of the wider issues of business? Today's business environment suggests that the role of the narrow specialist is decreasing; instead, managers are expected to be able to "talk" accounting as the universal language of business.

This book sets out to deal with situations like the ones faced by the managers above. Section 1 starts out with a description of the main financial statements that are used in external company reporting. It does not go into the detail of recording financial transactions, nor the minutiae of calculating the results. It does, however, show how the information flows through the system, and deals with the valuation and presentation of the amounts involved. Within each of the chapters in this section, financial ratios are used to explain the relationships between the accounting numbers. These ratios enable the interpretation of accounting data in ways that are meaningful to a wide variety of users.

Section 2 deals with the preparation of budgets and their use as controls. This is partially a number-crunching activity, but we also recognize that budgetary control has serious behavioural implications.

In the final section, Section 3, we look at accounting data as the basis for decision making. It covers both short-term operating decisions and longer-term capital budgeting decisions.

These three sections conform to one popular classification of accounting that divides accounting into scorekeeping, attention-directing, and decision-making roles.

1.2   Scorekeeping

When a company publishes its income statement and its balance sheet, it is engaged in scorekeeping. That is, the company is reporting to shareholders and other interested parties how well (or how badly) it has performed. These reports are about the past. The income statement covers a period of time that is now completed (the previous fiscal year). The balance sheet is a snapshot of the company at a point in time (usually the last day of the fiscal year).

Scorekeeping is an exercise in stewardship. Investors (and, to a lesser extent, creditors) have allowed the company the use of their resources. The company must, in return, report on what they did with those resources, and how well the investment has performed. With this information, existing investors and creditors can make informed judgments about how advisable it is to continue to be investors or creditors, or whether they should liquidate their holdings in this company and invest or lend elsewhere. In a similar fashion, potential investors and creditors will use the published financial statements to make judgments about whether they should invest or lend, and thus become actual investors or creditors of the company.

By *investor*, we mean the holder of the shares of a company. So, implicitly, we are referring to a limited liability company, the shares of which are listed on a stock exchange. These shares can be bought or sold at market prices by anyone who wants them. North America (particularly the United States and, to a lesser extent, Canada) is a world leader in individual investments in company shares. In other economies, it is more common for people to deposit surplus cash in a bank, or buy government securities.

By *creditor* we mean the holder of a company's debt, such as notes or debentures. These are lower risk than shares, and they usually yield a lower return. Like shares, however, they can be bought and sold in a public market, generally a specialized section of the stock market.

The limited liability company with shares listed and traded on a stock exchange is the obvious focus of a book such as this because most large organizations are formed with limited liability. There are also a number of large companies that are "private". Shares of private companies are not listed on any stock exchange. Other forms of business organization include sole proprietor, partnership, not-for-profit, and (in Canada) Crown Corporation. While there are no opportunities for buying and selling shares of such organizations, the idea of accounting as the language of business is just as relevant to them as to any publicly listed company. They also have to report their results to someone (owners, members, the government, etc.). Likewise, the attention-directing and decision-making sections following apply to their problems as well.

1.3 Attention Directing

One of the more powerful models of business is that of "management by exception". In this approach a company will go through a series of logically related steps to achieve its objectives:

Step 1:   Define the objectives.
Step 2:   Make plans that would, if achieved, accomplish the objectives.
Step 3:   Carry out the business operations in the plan.
Step 4:   Measure the results of operations.
Step 5:   Compare the results with the plans and the objectives.
Step 6a: If the objectives have been achieved, move on to the next iteration;
Step 6b: If the objectives have not been achieved, instigate corrective action, then move on to the next iteration.

Using this method, corrective action becomes necessary only when things have gone wrong; that is, when there is an exception. Routine activities that are carried out according to plan require no intervention. This cuts down on the amount of purely routine management, and enables management resources to be focused on areas where their use can actually achieve some improvement. Accounting has a major role in the process of defining what will be considered an exception, and in reporting exceptions as they occur.

A major part of organizational planning takes place through budget-setting and budget-approval processes. Only if the budget is capable of achieving the stated objectives and is accepted by all parties should it be approved.

Comparison between the budget and actual results reveals any gaps and should draw management's attention. Depending on the amount and the causes, management can then initiate informed corrective action.

1.4 Decision Making

The third role of accounting is to support decision making or problem solving. Decisions are the essence of business. When made correctly, they will ensure survival of the company and improve profitability. Conversely, when decisions are made incorrectly they will lead, sooner or later, to corporate failure.

As a general rule, decision making should incorporate the following steps:

Step 1:   Specify the problem or decision as precisely as possible.
Step 2:   Choose an appropriate decision technique.
Step 3:   Gather information.

Step 4: Use the information and the technique to make the decision.
Step 5: Implement the decision.
Step 6: Evaluate the outcome.

The basis upon which decisions should be made is not as clear-cut as it may seem. Non-accountants will refer casually to an idea such as "cost" as if it were unambiguous. To the accountant, however, there are as many definitions of *cost* as there are decision situations in which the term would be used. Should the cost be planned or actual? Should it be short-run or long-run? Should it be full cost or variable cost? Do the costs arise in the same time period, or do we need to incorporate the time value of money?

With respect to short-term decision making, we will start by examining the causes of costs, and in particular we shall focus on the modern idea of the "cost driver" — the underlying activities that cause costs to happen. Moreover, we will look at more established models such as the cost-volume-profit model, also at longer-term decision making through the "net present value" model.

1.5 Financial Accounting, Management Accounting and Auditing

Accounting is so large a subject that a number of specialisms have developed within it. The scorekeeping activities are referred to as financial accounting. Financial accountants are responsible for recording transactions, for measuring and for disclosure.

Recording transactions is increasingly a routinized, automated activity. When a customer goes through the checkout at a supermarket, when the utility employee zaps a wand at a meter, and in a hundred and one other situations, the transaction data is automatically recorded, and the accounting records on the computer are updated. It may not be long before manual entry of transactions is as outdated as using leather-bound ledgers and quill pens to keep records. However, as of this writing, a number of smaller businesses will still be entering data into the computer records by keying them in at a terminal.

Once the data are recorded, the next step is measurement. Judgment is called for to decide the effect of a transaction. Is the activity to which the transaction refers completed, or is there some residual effect that needs to be recognized as an asset/liability in the balance sheet? To answer these questions, the professional financial accountant has been trained to make appropriate value judgments based on generally accepted accounting principles (GAAP).

Finally, the information has to be communicated. The financial accountants will choose the most appropriate way of disclosing the information, so as to comply with the law and with GAAP, and to meet the needs of external users of financial statements.

Once the financial accountant has prepared the financial statements, an external auditor will review them and the records that support them.

The auditor is, formally, employed on behalf of the shareholders to safe-guard their interests. Although the auditor is paid by the company, the shareholders have the right to appoint/reappoint the auditor at the company annual general meeting. If the shareholders are dissatisfied with the auditor's work, they may vote against the appointment. In practice, this shareholders' right is more illusory than real; when the chips are down, management probably has more influence on the decision than the share-holders do.

Management accounting is an internal organizational activity. Its practitioners provide information almost exclusively to managers to assist them in their managerial activities, including the planning and control cycle, and also to support them in decision making.

1.6 Personal Financial Planning

All of the above refers in general to management and managers in organizations. There are also equally important uses for accounting information and accounting techniques in personal lives. There are specialized books that deal with these issues under titles such as *Personal Financial Planning*. Personal financial planning uses accounting information extensively. For example, when making a personal financial plan for the first time, one of the things you have to do is make a complete list of all your assets and liabilities — that is, a personal balance sheet. The difference between your assets and your liabilities is your personal wealth or equity. Also, when making choices about how much to invest in your savings so that you can afford to retire, the decisions are based on personal budgets and net present value techniques.

1.7 Summary

Accounting is the common language of business and is essential for communication in today's market-driven economy. It is necessary that all managers are familiar with the terminology, with the benefits of useful accounting information, and with some of the problem areas where accounting information is less helpful or less clear than it could be.

Accounting has a role in scorekeeping (how well the company has performed); in attention directing (what the managers should be paying attention to); and in decision making (the financial implications of business choices). Accounting is carried out by financial accountants and management accountants within the company, and external auditors on behalf of shareholders.

Discussion Questions and Problems

Discussion Questions

1. Who needs to know about accounting?
2. Why is accounting called the language of business?
3. What are the main uses of accounting information for managers?
4. Why does an investor need scorekeeping information?
5. What role does accounting have in the planning process?
6. How is control made possible by accounting?
7. What steps should be involved in decision making?
8. Why might the outcome of a decision be different from its expected outcome?
9. What are the main distinctions between financial accounting and management accounting?
10. What is the role of the auditor?

Problems

1. For each of the following situations identify the activity as being scorekeeping, attention directing or decision making, and explain why the situation fits into that category:

   - Loblaws receives a shipment of canned fruit from Ocean Fruit Inc. for sale in its stores, and records the amount owed to Ocean Fruit in its financial records.
   - Loblaws sells the canned fruit and records the cash received going into the bank.
   - Loblaws pay's Ocean Fruit Inc. and records the payment in its financial records.
   - Loblaws circulates a monthly profit report to its department managers.
   - Loblaws calculates the inventory of canned goods on hand and compares the actual inventory turnover ratio with the budgeted inventory turnover ratio.
   - Loblaws compares the profit markup on canned fruit from Ocean Fruit Inc. with that of Caribbean Canned Goods Co., and chooses to switch suppliers.
   - Loblaws uses the monthly departmental profit report to justify giving three of its managers a performance-related bonus.
   - Loblaws uses the budgeted profit for the year to justify expansion of the range of goods offered.
   - Loblaws has its annual financial statements audited by a firm of professional auditors.
   - Loblaws publishes its annual financial statements and circulates them to shareholders.

2. In respect of the Grange Company, identify the status of the following parties as investor, creditor, or neither:

   - Jim Jones owns 500 ordinary shares, which he bought for $20 each.

9

- Janice Jones, Jim's wife, is heir to his estate if he should die, and so she has the right to inherit his shares in Grange Co.
- Fred Boylestone is owed $25,000 for goods sold to Grange Co.
- Henry Pelham is the holder of a $100,000 debenture issued by Grange Co. This is due to be repaid in two years.
- Rene Sussex has sued Grange Co. for $15,000 for unlawful termination of employment. The case is to be heard next month.

3. On page 6 of the text there is a "six-step" approach that organizations should follow to achieve their objectives:

Step 1: Define the objectives.
Step 2: Make plans to accomplish the objectives.
Step 3: Carry out the business operations in the plan.
Step 4: Measure the results of operations.
Step 5: Compare the results with the plans and objectives.
Step 6a: If the objectives have been achieved, move on;
Step 6b: If the objectives have not been achieved, instigate corrective action, then move on.

Food Value Inc. (FVI) is a small chain of supermarkets that operates in the Oshawa area. The company has 10 stores and a head office. Identify the following activities according to this six-step approach:

- At the monthly management meeting the month's actual operating profit for each store is compared to its budgeted operating profit.
- In November the directors of FVI have an annual goal-setting and strategy meeting.
- The 10 stores sell groceries and other products to customers every day from 9:00 a.m. to 9:00 p.m.
- The Brant Street Store has made an operating profit of $165,000 for the month, which is $5,000 more than the budget.
- The Durham Mall Store has made an operating profit of $250,000. However, according to the budget, the operating profit should have been $275,000.
- Examination of the Durham Mall Store results shows that the store has too high an employee head count, and that this is the main cause of the profit shortfall. It is decided that no new employees will be hired until natural attrition has reduced the employee head count by 10%.
- Each of the 10 stores prepares a budget for the year and a business plan of what type of goods to stock.

4. The Hardy Co. is trying to find out its optimal store opening hours. The company has traditionally opened its retail hardware stores from 9:00 a.m. to 6:00 p.m., Monday to Saturday. However, the company finds that the "big-box" competitors (such as Home Depot) are open for longer hours, and management is concerned that the company is losing business. List the information the company will need to make a decision about extending the store opening hours.

5. In respect of a limited liability company:
   • Who appoints the auditor?
   • Who pays the auditor?
   • What is the auditor supposed to do?

6. In respect of a limited liability company:
   • Who records the financial transactions?
   • Who prepares the financial statements?
   • Who decides which financial statements will be published?
   • Who checks that the financial statements are correct?

7. The budget for Careful Insurance Brokers Inc. for the month of January was as follows:

Budgeted Income Statement
January

Insurance policies sold: gross premiums		$258,000
Commission on sale: 12.5%		$ 32,250
Less operating expenses:		
Wages & salaries	$10,000	
Employment-related expenses	2,500	
Rent expense	5,000	
Utilities	2,600	
Amortization	1,000	
Repairs & other expenses	1,450	
Total expenses		22,550
Budgeted operating profit		$ 9,700

At the end of January the actual results were as follows:

Actual Income Statement
January

Insurance policies sold: gross premiums		$250,000
Commission on sale		$ 35,000
Less operating expenses:		
Wages & salaries	$10,500	
Employment-related expenses	2,600	
Rent expense	5,000	
Utilities	2,900	
Amortization	1,000	
Repairs & other expenses	2,450	
Total expenses		24,450
Budgeted operating profit		$ 10,550

Comment on January's results, comparing them with the January budget. Should the management's attention be directed to this situation as one that needs its action?

8. You are the Human Resources Manager for a major appliance manufacturer. The collective agreement with the production employees will expire soon, and next month collective bargaining starts for the new agreement. List the information you would gather to enable you to be an effective member of management's team at the discussions.

Suppose that the negotiations failed to produce an agreement: the choice management faces is to cave in to the employee demands or to endure a strike. Describe how you would advise management to deal with that situation.

9. You are considering investing your retirement savings in shares of companies listed on the Toronto Stock Exchange. What information would you use to decide which companies to invest in? Where would you get the information?

10. Explain whether each of the following would be carried out by the financial accounting or management accounting personnel (or, possibly, neither):

- Keeping records of hours worked by hourly paid employees.
- Paying wages to sales staff.
- Advising on performance-related bonus payments to employees.
- Preparing operating budgets.
- Comparing monthly results with operating budgets.
- Recording amounts due from credit customers.
- Collecting amounts due from credit customers.
- Checking that goods have been received prior to payment for them.
- Checking the existence, ownership, and basis of valuation of long-term assets, such as production machinery.
- Investigating deviations from budgets.

1

Financial Accounting for Scorekeeping

Financial Accounting:

"Accounting is a service activity. Its function is to provide quantitative information, primarily financial in nature, about economic entities that is intended to be useful in making economic decisions, in making reasoned choices among alternative courses of action."

Accounting Principles Board Statements No. 4
"Basic Concepts of Accounting Principles Underlying
Financial Statements of Business Enterprises"
(New York, AICPA, 1970)

The Financial Statements 2

Learning
Objectives

After studying this chapter you should be able to describe:
→ The objectives of financial reporting
→ The accounting equation
→ The four main financial statements
→ The characteristics of accounting information
→ The main accounting concepts

2.1   Introduction

In the first chapter, we established the need for accounting, for score-keeping, attention directing, and decision making. We now go on to discuss the information financial accounting provides for scorekeeping. The set of financial reports that are produced for public use by a company consists of the following:

• the balance sheet
• the income statement
• the statement of retained earnings
• the cash flow statement

Each of these statements has a role; together, they provide a rich body of information about the organization. Each will be discussed in detail. First, though, we should establish what it is we are trying to achieve with these reports.

We will concentrate on the reporting process used by incorporated companies. Only incorporated companies are required to report externally. Other entities may choose to make their financial statements public, but they have no legal obligation to do so. The rules that are discussed in this chapter are those that apply to a company registered under the Canada Business Corporations Act. The rules that apply to a company incorporated under any of the provincial corporations Acts may differ slightly, but the main points are the same.

Not only is there a difference between publicly traded companies and other types of business entities in the way they publish information, there are also some differences in the reports themselves — mostly in the way owners' equity is treated. Those differences, however, will not be addressed here.

2.2   The Objectives of Financial Reporting

A company is incorporated under either the federal, or one of the provincial, Companies Acts. These acts, together with their associated administrative regulations, require the company to observe certain standards of financial reporting, in particular that

- the company must produce financial statements;
- the financial statements must be distributed annually to the shareholders;
- the financial statements shall consist of an income statement, a balance sheet, a statement of retained earnings, and a statement of cash flows;
- the statements should be prepared in accordance with the standards of the Canadian Institute of Chartered Accountants.

To elicit what the Canadian Institute of Chartered Accountants (CICA) requires, we have to look at their handbook. The CICA Handbook contains detailed provisions about the treatment of some, though far from all, of the elements of financial statements. For example, the valuation of inventories is discussed at length, but the calculation of sales revenue is not specifically addressed.

It is, therefore, clear that much of the detail of the way in which financial statements are prepared lies elsewhere. Such detail can be found in the professional knowledge that accountants have and use in their work on a day-to-day basis.

In addition to the handbook, the CICA has also published what it believes to be the underlying objectives of financial statements. According to the CICA, financial statements

- are prepared for the use of actual and potential investors and creditors;
- are for the use of those who make investing and lending decisions;
- should assist users to predict future cash flows.

There are at least two important deficiencies in the way the financial statements deal with the CICA objectives. First, only one of the four statements (see p. 16) actually deals with cash flows: the cash flow statement summarizes past cash inflows and outflows and shows their effect on the cash assets. By contrast, the income statement, the statement of retained earnings, and the balance sheet are all prepared using the accrual concept of resource flows. Where accrual accounting is used, cash flow reporting is replaced by reporting on wealth and changes in wealth. Second, all four statements refer to past events rather than expectations about the future.

For these two reasons, the linkage between the financial statements and the CICA objectives is somewhat weak. However, whatever their shortcomings, these financial statements are still important, and, in many instances, they are the only information publicly available, so we have to understand them.

The CICA statement of objectives is quite appropriate in the context of the shares of companies that are bought and sold by the general public through stock exchanges. It is also reasonable to state that the legal requirement for providing all shareholders with financial statements has a purpose. This purpose is to be found in the concept of *stewardship*.

The shareholders of the company do not take part in the day-to-day management. They appoint directors (and the directors, in turn, appoint managers) to carry out the actual work of management. This situation is sometimes referred to as the divorce of ownership and control. The financial statements provide some evidence of the extent to which the directors have exercised good (or, sometimes, bad) management. In other words, they enable shareholders to assess whether or not the directors have exercised their stewardship of the company assets effectively.

2.3 The Accounting Equation

Before we discuss any of the financial statements in any detail, it is necessary to introduce the accounting equation. The accounting equation is the logical structure that underlies the recording and reporting of financial results. It is normally expressed in terms of "debits" and "credits". A knowledge of the mechanics of debits and credits is not required for an understanding of accounting. All the same, those who have frequent dealings with accountants and accounting reports may find that some familiarity with debits and credits and the more technical vocabulary of accounting is useful. For those who are interested, an introduction to the basic ideas is presented in Appendix 2.1 of this chapter, and further details are provided in appendices to Chapters 3, 5, and 6.

All four financial statements are drawn from an accounting system based on the accounting equation. This is most evident in the structure of the balance sheet (a financial representation of the company at an instant of time). The balance sheet is essentially a detailed listing of

- what the company owns,
- what the company owes, and
- the owners' financial interest claim on the company

in a way that satisfies the following equation:

$$\text{ASSETS} \quad = \quad \text{LIABILITIES} \quad + \quad \text{OWNERS' EQUITY}$$

Each capitalized term in the equation represents the total value of all the items of that type that the company has a relationship to. In other words,

- ASSETS is the sum of the value of everything that the company owns;
- LIABILITIES is the sum of all the debt claims on the company (i.e., the sum of all the specific promises the company has made to pay monies to outsiders in the future); and
- OWNERS' EQUITY is the total value of the owners' financial claim on the company.

Thus, one way of looking at the accounting equation is that it is a representation of what the company OWNS on one side — total assets — and a representation of the total CLAIMS on those assets — total liabilities plus total owners' equity — on the other.

To make the nature of this equality clearer in a way that emphasizes the residual nature of the owners' claim, rewrite the accounting equation as follows. Subtract LIABILITIES from each side of the equation so it reads

ASSETS – LIABILITIES = OWNERS' EQUITY

The left-hand side is net assets, the net value obtained after the total claims of the debt holders are subtracted from the total value of the assets. If any transaction that affects the valuation of total assets or total liabilities such that the there is a difference between the two changes, then the valuation of owners' equity *must* also be adjusted to maintain the accounting equation.

The income statement, the statement of retained earnings and the cash flow statement are each summaries of changes in different parts of the accounting equation over a period of time, always respecting the rule that owners' equity is adjusted to reflect changes in net assets. In addition to the accounting equation and the rules for deriving from it the different accounting statements, there are a number of other rules involved in the accounting process, which are collectively called Generally Accepted Accounting Principles (GAAP). These will be discussed throughout Section 1 of this book.

Subject to the limitations of GAAP, financial statements can answer such questions as the following:

• What is the value of the company's assets at the end of the most recent financial year?
• What are the liabilities of the company at the end of the most recent financial year?
• What is the owner's equity (ownership claim) in the company, and how did it evolve in the year?
• How well did the company do this past year in its operations?
• How did the company get cash in the year, and how did it spend it?

Although these are independent questions and the answers are found on different parts of different statement, they are connected through the accounting equation.

Let us examine some simple transactions to see how they are handled by the accounting equation.

When a company is first organized, it has no assets, no liabilities, and no owners' equity. The accounting equation is satisfied since

$$\$0 \quad = \quad \$0 \quad + \quad \$0$$

As the company engages in transactions, the accounting equation will be used to record the effect of those transactions on the assets, the liabilities, and the owners' equity. In Appendix 2.1, the same transactions will be used to illustrate the mechanics of double entry accounting.

Transaction #1   The owners invested $25,000 in the company.

• Assets have increased by $25,000.
• Liabilities are unchanged.
• Owners' equity has increased by $25,000.

$$\text{ASSETS} = \text{LIABILITIES} + \text{OWNERS' EQUITY}$$
$$\$25,000 = \$0 + \$25,000$$

There is only one transaction (the owners invested $25,000 in the company). Note, however, that two separate aspects of the transaction have been recognized in the (revised) accounting equation. First, the company has recorded the fact that it now has $25,000 of assets. Second, the company has recognized that the source of that $25,000 was the owners' investment. The company not only has $25,000, it also has an obligation to the owners to account for the $25,000 they have invested.

It is this recording of the dual effect (on assets and equity, for example) that gives "double entry" bookkeeping its name.

The nature of the obligation to the owners is subtle. It is not a debt that has to be repaid, but the company is responsible for using the resources for the long-term benefit of the owners.

Transaction #2   The company borrowed $10,000 from a bank.

• Assets have increased by $10,000;
• Liabilities have increased by $10,000;
• Owners' equity is unchanged.

$$\text{ASSETS} = \text{LIABILITIES} + \text{OWNERS' EQUITY}$$
$$\$35,000 = \$10,000 + \$25,000$$

As with transaction #1, when transaction #2 was recorded, two aspects of the event were captured: (i) the assets were shown as increasing (they started at $25,000; they increased by $10,000; they became $35,000); and (ii) the source of that increase was shown by way of a matching increase in the liabilities. Again, as with transaction #1, the transaction was recorded using the accounting equation, and so the financial records of the company as a whole also continue to conform to the accounting equation.

Transaction #1 increased the owners' equity because the owners parted with some resources, which they let the company have. Transaction #2 did not change the owners' equity: assets increased, but liabilities increased by an equal amount; so the owners' equity (which is always equal to the net assets of the company) stayed the same.

Transaction #3   The corporation bought some inventory (goods for resale) for $8,000, which they paid for in cash.

• Assets (inventory) have increased by $8,000;
• Assets (cash) have decreased by $8,000;
• Liabilities are unchanged;
• Owners' equity is unchanged.

$$\text{ASSETS} = \text{LIABILITIES} + \text{OWNERS' EQUITY}$$
$$\$35,000 = \$10,000 + \$25,000$$

We recorded transaction #3 using the accounting equation, as we did with transactions #1 and #2. One asset has increased by $8,000, and another has decreased by $8,000. The total value of the assets has not changed, though the form of the assets has changed. As long as we accept that inventory that cost the company $8,000 is worth $8,000 (at least until we know something different), then the form in which the assets are held is far less important than their dollar total. There was no change in the liabilities; they remain at $10,000. There was no change in the net worth of the company, so owners' equity also remained unchanged.

Transaction #4   The company bought inventory (goods for resale) at a cost of $5,000. The vendor allows 30 days credit on the amount owing.

The accounting equation treatment of this transaction is as follows: assets (inventory) have increased by $5,000; liabilities have increased by $5,000. Once again, this is an exchange transaction where assets and liabilities of equal value are acquired, and owners' equity remains unchanged.

ASSETS = LIABILITIES + OWNERS' EQUITY
$40,000 = $15,000 + $25,000

Transaction #5   The company sold inventory to a customer for $7,000 in cash; the inventory had cost the company $4,000.

This is an exchange transaction where the value received ($7,000 in cash) is greater than the value surrendered ($4,000 of inventory). The difference represents an increase in the net assets of the business. This $3,000 is added to the owners' equity. Increases in net assets that arise from regular operations are, by definition, increases in the owners' equity in the business. Also, adding the $3,000 to owners' equity is the only way that the accounting equation can be kept in balance.

ASSETS = LIABILITIES + OWNERS' EQUITY
$43,000 = $15,000 + $28,000

Transaction #6   The company sold inventory to a customer on credit for $9,000; the inventory had cost the company $6,000.

Transaction #6 is similar to transaction #5, though not identical. In each case inventory has been sold, so in each case the asset inventory has to decrease. In transaction #5 the company clearly has the immediate benefit of the sale, as it now has an additional $7,000 of cash. In transaction #6 the $9,000 sale is represented by money owed to the company by the customer. A decision has to be taken as to what point in time this sale will be recognized. GAAP will recognize this as a completed sale and so will recognize the $3,000 increase in assets (or profit) at the time of the sale. This point will be developed more fully in Chapter 3, "The Income Statement". The $3,000 profit will, as with transaction #5, be added to owners' equity.

ASSETS = LIABILITIES + OWNERS' EQUITY
$46,000 = $15,000 + $31,000

Transaction #7 The customer, who had bought the goods for $9,000 on credit in transaction #6, paid for them. What a relief! The worry and uncertainty of having that money owed to the company is now over. The debt has been collected. Is the company any better off, though? We would suggest that it is no better off than before. An asset ($9,000 owed to the company by the customer) has been exchanged for an asset of the same monetary value ($9,000 in cash). There is no increase in the net assets and, therefore, there is no increase in the owners' equity. The company had already recognized the $3,000 increase in owners' equity when the sale was made. Recognizing it again at this point would be double counting. As a general rule, the benefit of a sale is recognized when the sale is made, which is not necessarily when the money is received.

$$\text{ASSETS} = \text{LIABILITIES} + \text{OWNERS' EQUITY}$$
$$\$46,000 = \$15,000 + \$31,000$$

Transaction #8 The company paid for the inventory it bought on credit ($5,000).

Assets (cash) have decreased by $5,000. Liabilities have decreased by $5,000. There is no change in the owners' equity because there is no change in the net assets.

$$\text{ASSETS} = \text{LIABILITIES} + \text{OWNERS' EQUITY}$$
$$\$41,000 = \$10,000 + \$31,000$$

Transaction #9 The company paid, in cash, interest of $100 on the bank loan.

Assets (cash) have decreased by $100, resulting in net assets having decreased by $100. Owners' equity has also fallen by $100. This is because the outflow of $100 has not resulted in the acquisition of an asset; rather, it measures an expense. An expense may be thought of as what happens when an asset expires and becomes worthless. There is, of course, a benefit. In this case, the benefit is that the company was allowed the use of a loan for a period of time. Expenses occur in many situations: payment of salaries and wages, rent of premises, fire insurance premiums, etc. In each case, the effect of incurring the expense is to reduce owners' equity.

$$\text{ASSETS} = \text{LIABILITIES} + \text{OWNERS' EQUITY}$$
$$\$40,900 = \$10,000 + \$30,900$$

Transaction #10 The owners decided to declare themselves a dividend (a cash payment out of profits). They paid themselves $1,000 in cash.

Assets (cash) have decreased by $1,000, resulting in net assets having decreased by $1,000. Owners' equity has fallen by $1,000.

$$\text{ASSETS} = \text{LIABILITIES} + \text{OWNERS' EQUITY}$$
$$\$39,900 = \$10,000 + \$29,900$$

The 10 transactions above cover the principles behind a lot of the transactions that financial statements have to accommodate. Note the following general points:

- Transactions that involve an exchange of assets and/or liabilities of equal value do not change the net assets of the company, and so do not alter owners' equity.
- Transactions that result in an increase in the net assets of the company result in an equal increase in owners' equity.
- Transactions that result in a decrease in the net assets of the company result in a matching decrease in owners' equity.

Note, too, that all transactions are recorded using the accounting equation. Because each transaction conforms to the accounting equation, the overall records of the company conform to the accounting equation.

2.4 Types of Financial Statements

2.4.1 The Balance Sheet

The balance sheet is a list, at a point in time, of the company's assets, liabilities, and owners' equity. (Yes, that is the same as the accounting equation.) The balance sheet is generally prepared once a year. Chapters 4 and 5 describe the balance sheet in detail. Because the balance sheet is a listing at a point in time, it has been compared to a snapshot or a still photograph of the company.

The balance sheet is used to get an idea of the type and value of the company assets, the amount and repayment dates of the company liabilities, and the net worth of the owners' equity investment.

2.4.2 The Income Statement

During the normal course of trade over a year, the company will probably engage in many transactions that affect the owners' equity. Every time a sale is made or every time an expense is incurred, the owners' equity either rises or falls. The income statement summarizes all these transactions over a one-year reporting period and reports on their overall effect. The net difference between the sales revenue generated and the total of all expenses is the net income or profit of the company for the year.

Because the income statement reports on the events of a period of time, it has been compared to a movie of the company. Although the income statement measures past income, it is used by investors and creditors to make informed judgments about how much income the company is likely to make in future years.

The income statement is described more fully in Chapter 3.

2.4.3 The Statement of Retained Earnings

This is a comparatively short statement that helps link the balance sheet and the income statement. One of the items on the balance sheet of any company is "retained earnings". The retained earnings represent income made on behalf of the owners but that has not been distributed to them by way of dividend. The retained earnings at the beginning of a year are increased by any net income (from the income statement) and decreased by any dividends paid that year. The remaining balance appears on the balance sheet at the end of the year. This information is reported in the statement of retained earnings.

The statement of retained earnings is described more fully in Chapter 3.

2.4.4 The Statement of Cash Flows

The statement of cash flows supplements the balance sheet and the income statement. It reports on the various sources of cash (cash from operations, cash from borrowing, cash from selling assets, cash from raising equity investment) and the various uses of cash (operating losses, repaying debt, buying assets, paying dividends). Because managing the organization's cash resources is so critical to corporate survival, it is as necessary to include this information for the use of investors and creditors.

The statement of cash flows is described more fully in Chapter 6.

2.4.5 Publication of the Financial Statements

Every year, at or before the company's annual shareholders' meeting, the shareholders must receive copies of the four financial statements. The directors are responsible for the preparation of the financial statements. At the shareholders' meeting, the shareholders will vote on whether or not to accept the financial statements. This applies to all companies, whether they are small and privately held (i.e., just a few shareholders) or public corporations that have their shares listed and traded on a stock exchange.

Except for small, privately held companies, the financial statements must also be filed with the director of the Canada Business Corporations Act.

Companies that have their shares listed on a stock exchange will also have a responsibility to file their financial statements with the stock exchange and, probably, with a provincial securities commission.

Unless the company is closely held (i.e., no public trading of shares) and the shareholders choose not to have an auditor, the company will also have an obligation to have its financial statements audited; that is, checked by a qualified auditor.

2.4.6 Using Financial Statements to Assess Profitability

The principal objective of most organizations is to make a profit. The dollar amounts of operating income and net profit after interest and taxes will be shown in the income statement. Judging whether or not these are adequate requires that they be compared with the assets. Large companies should produce large profits, while smaller companies need only produce modest amounts.

In reporting the income, it is quite normal to show operating income separately from net income. Operating income is the revenues less the operating expenses incurred in earning the revenues. It specifically excludes interest (which is a financing charge) and taxes (over which management has little control). Operating income is used to judge how well the assets of the business have been used. As such, it is a comment on management efficiency.

Net income is what is left after interest and taxes are deducted from operating profit. Interest paid is an expense that largely depends on the company's capital structure. A company financed entirely from equity capital will have no interest payments, but a company that is financed with a large amount of debt will have a high level of interest expense. Taxes are then deducted, and what is left over is the profit available for the equity shareholders to enjoy. The net income is a measure of how well the company did for its shareholders.

There are two ways of comparing company income to the resources used to generate it.

The ratio of operating income to total assets, or "return on assets" as it is often called, is used to assess the extent to which the assets have been efficiently utilized by management.

The ratio of net income to shareholders' equity is used to assess the effectiveness of the company as an equity investment. It is referred to as the "return on equity". It is also sometimes referred to as the "return on capital employed" or the "return on investment".

Exhibit 2.1 on page 26 shows how the return on assets and the return on equity ratios are calculated.

2.5   Characteristics of Accounting Information

When preparing financial statements, we want the information to be useful. It is not enough to say that the statements should be correct. There are a number of dimensions to the concept of correctness, and each needs to be considered under two important criteria: relevance and reliability.

2.5.1   Relevance

To be relevant, information has to be able to influence a decision or a belief.

Information that causes a bank to decide whether or not to make a loan would be relevant to that lending decision. Suppose a bank looks at the financial statements of a company and discovers that there is already an excessive amount of borrowing and that profits are low. As a result, it estimates that the chances of repayment of the proposed loan are low. The financial statements have provided relevant information. This is sometimes referred to as predictive value. By contrast, suppose that you happen to have a set of financial statements for a major clothing chain, and at the same time you want to buy a coat they stock. You are in possession of information (the financial statements), but it is not relevant to your purchasing decision. The decision to buy is based on factors such as

Exhibit 2.1:   Profitability Ratios

Didier Corporation Ltd. has the following summarized financial statements for 2006:

Didier Corporation Ltd.
Balance Sheet
As at December 31, 2006

Current assets	$200,000	Current liabilities	$110,000
		Long-term liabilities	130,000
Long-term assets	300,000	Total liabilities	$240,000
		Equity	260,000
Total assets	$500,000	Total liabilities and equity	$500,000

Didier Corporation Ltd.
Income Statement
Year Ended December 31, 2006

Sales revenue		$900,000
Operating expenses		800,000
Operating income		100,000
Interest expense	$13,000	
Income taxes	22,000	35,000
Net income		$ 65,000

Return on assets:

= operating income ÷ total assets

= $100,000 ÷ $500,000

= 20%

Return on equity (or Return on investment):

= net income ÷ shareholder's equity

= $65,000 ÷ $260,000

= 25%

Because the rate of interest on the borrowed money is less than the return on assets, the return on investment has been leveraged up from 20% to 25%.

the coat's price, availability, style, etc., and not on the financial health of the store.

Suppose an investor has shares in a company. At the year-end the directors send him the financial statements, and the investor is pleased to see that the company has made a reasonable net income, has adequate cash and other resources, and, in general, shows every sign of being well managed. The financial statements were relevant to the investor in supporting his belief that the directors were exercising good stewardship over the assets with which they had been entrusted. This is sometimes referred to as feedback value.

In both of the above situations the information was provided to the user in time for him or her to use it effectively. For example, it would be of no use to the bank to get the financial statements after making the loan. To be relevant, the information must be timely.

2.5.2 Reliability

Under the heading "Reliability" we refer to a number of aspects of "correctness". They include verifiability, representational faithfulness, neutrality, comparability and consistency.

Information should be verifiable. If a number of competent experts look at a set of financial statements' underlying data, they should agree on the accounting conclusions. A transaction might be the purchase of some production machinery. Most accountants would be able to agree that the money was spent and that it was spent on a long-term asset. That indicates verifiability. On the other hand, if those same accountants were to be asked over what period the asset should be amortized, there could be a range of acceptable opinions because this is a judgment call. The amortization expense is, therefore, less verifiable.

Information should have representational faithfulness. The intention of financial statements is to represent various events by means of their monetary values. Suppose a company buys some production machinery for $25,000 cash. If that was the whole of the transaction, then it would be representationally faithful. If, on the other hand, the company had traded in another machine with a realizable value of $10,000, the cash expenditure of $25,000 would not be representationally faithful. It would be better to record this transaction as the sale of the asset traded in (for $10,000) and the cost of the new machine as being $35,000.

Information should be neutral. Information sends strong messages to shareholders and other users. Some of these messages are positive, while others are negative. It is appropriate to have a balanced view: a view without a bias for either good or bad news. Information should not be reported selectively merely because it presents the view that management wants to demonstrate. Suppose a company is being sued by a customer for some fault in a product sold by them. At the same time the company is suing the supplier of that product, for the same underlying reason. An unbiased report would show both these legal actions and report the company's expectations about the outcome. To show only one legal action, or that the expected outcome is the success of one action and the failure of the other, would be biased. It would lack neutrality.

Information should be comparable. One of the requirements of financial reporting is that the company must report not only on the current year but also on the comparable data for the previous year. If the company has changed one of its accounting practices between the two years (e.g., by changing the number of years over which a machine is amortized), the data is no longer comparable.

Information should be consistent. The reason that the accounting data about amortization is not comparable is that it is inconsistent between the two years. Accounting treatments of events should be consistent. Where they are inconsistent, the nature of the change should be reported so that users may make adjustments in their interpretations and adjustments.

2.6 Accounting Concepts

In order to best pursue the accounting objectives, accountants have agreed on a set of principles that should be applied when accounting transactions are recorded and reported. These principles are more guides to action than they are absolutes. Indeed, some of them are in conflict, so judgment has to be used in their implementation. The concepts most frequently cited are as follows.

2.6.1 Business Entity

Whatever the legal structure, each business enterprise is considered to be a separate entity for accounting purposes. All the transactions relating to that entity must be recorded and reported, and those transactions extraneous to the entity should be excluded. In practice, this means, for example, that the share capital will be recorded in respect of a company, but other aspects of the shareholders' wealth, such as their personal assets, will not be included.

2.6.2 Historical Cost

Because the price actually paid (historical cost, or entry price) for an asset or an expense is objective and verifiable, it is considered superior to other valuations, and historical cost is the initial valuation of all transactions.

2.6.3 Going Concern

It is assumed that, in the absence of information to the contrary, the business will continue to exist. The implication is that assets will have their value in use as assets of a viable business (restricted to their historical cost), rather than some fire-sale price that they would fetch in a forced sale situation (which would be an exit price).

2.6.4 Periodicity

The life of a business entity is effectively unlimited. It does not die as would a person, and it may continue even though its shareholders pass away. It is assumed that partitioning this long life into yearly reports is a meaningful and useful exercise for the shareholders and other interested parties. Without periodicity, companies would present no periodic reports, and no one would know what was going on.

2.6.5 *Disclosure*

There are occasions where presentations in the reports might be misleading. The disclosure principle requires that any such situations be disclosed, generally by way of a "note" accompanying the financial statements. For example, suppose the company is being sued by a customer. The company may believe that the case will go in its favour, and so there are no cost implications and no expenses to report in the financial statements. However, the possibility that the case could be decided against the company should be disclosed in the notes to the financial statements.

2.6.6 *Conservatism/Neutrality*

In calculating income and in valuing assets, the conservatism concept requires that a somewhat biased approach be taken. If there has been a reduction in the value of an asset, that reduction is to be accounted for (shown as a loss). If there has been an increase in the value of an asset, however, its benefit should not be recognized until the benefit has been realized.

Since 2005 there has been a shift of emphasis. Conservatism is no longer so strictly applied. In its place has come a greater emphasis on neutrality. Neutrality means to present information, as far as is possible, free from any bias.

2.6.7 *Recognition*

The recognition (or realization) concept governs the point at which a transaction can be said to have happened. It would determine, for example, the rules about exactly when a sale has been made or an asset acquired.

2.6.8 *Matching*

The matching concept is necessitated by the periodicity concept. Periodicity splits the life of the entity into successive 12-month periods. Matching requires that the sales revenue realized in a period be reported in the same period and not in another. Matching also requires that the expenses reported be those that are incurred in the year the sales were recognized.

We will see these concepts being applied on the balance sheet and the income statement in the chapters that follow.

2.6.9 *Materiality*

Financial statement data should only consist of items that are large enough and important enough to be material to their interpretation; trivial amounts may be ignored.

2.6.10 *Constant Dollar*

It is assumed that dollars received or spent at any time are exactly equivalent to dollars received or spent at any other time. Where inflation is significant, this is untrue.

2.7 Summary

The company is required by law to publish financial statements consisting of the balance sheet, the income statement, the statement of retained earnings, and the statement of cash flows.

The objectives of publishing the financial statements are to assist investors and creditors in their investing and lending decisions, and to demonstrate good stewardship of the company assets by the directors.

The accounting equation (assets = liabilities + owners' equity) is the fundamental model used for recording all transactions and for reporting in financial statements.

Accounting information should be relevant. That is, it should have decision usefulness and be timely. Accounting information should be reliable. That is, it should be verifiable, representationally faithful, neutral, comparable, and consistent.

Accounting concepts used in the preparation of accounting reports include business entity, historical cost, going concern, periodicity, disclosure, conservatism, recognition, matching, materiality, and constant dollars.

Appendix 2.1
The Mechanics of Accounting:
The Basics

This appendix and corresponding appendices to Chapters 3, 5, and 6 present the mechanics of double-entry accounting. This is a six-step process carried out over a company's reporting period. The reporting period is typically one year, called the financial year, but it can be as short as one month for a large company. The process is referred to as the *accounting cycle* and the records it generates are the journal and general ledger, informally called the *books* of the company.

The Accounting Cycle

The six steps in the accounting cycle are as follows:

1. Identifying individual transactions and determining how they are to be recorded
2. Recording transactions as entries in the journal
3. Posting journal entries to the general ledger
4. Balancing the general ledger
5. Correcting, adjusting, and closing the books
6. Preparing the financial statements from the ledger balances

1. Identifying Individual Transactions and Determining How They Are to Be Recorded

This step is probably the most important one in the accounting cycle. The rules of accounting, Generally Accepted Accounting Principles (GAAP), determine what is an accounting transaction and what is not, and they also specify how transactions are to be accounted for. Getting these right requires both expertise and experience.

Although a business is engaged in numerous activities every day — both in internal operations and exchanges with those outside the company, such as customers, suppliers, owners, governments, etc. — only some of these events are considered *transactions* by the rules of accounting. A transaction is an event that is recorded in the books of the company. For example a typical sequence of events in a business is taking an order from a customer, shipping the order, invoicing the customer, and finally receiving a cheque from the customer in payment. Although each of these is a distinct and important step in making a sale, GAAP recognizes only the invoicing, shipping, and cheque receipt. As fundamental as getting the customer's order is to the sales process, it is *not* considered a transaction according to GAAP and is thus *not* recorded in the accounting system.

The manner in which a transaction is recorded is also subject to the rules of GAAP. Continuing the same example, if the sale of the goods is on typical commercial terms, the price will be agreed upon when the order is made. An invoice will be prepared and sent when the goods are shipped, specifying when payment is expected — typically within 30 days. The treatment of such a transaction is quite straightforward as we will see below. However, not all sales transactions follow normal commercial terms. Variations include conditions on the selling price that could lead to adjustment of the price depending on market conditions on the date of shipment; payment in advance, delivery later; and allowing the seller a very long time to pay. If special terms of sale apply, the accounting for the transaction may have to be adapted. For example, a software company advertises a radical improvement in one of its popular programs. The upgrade may be just what the market is waiting for and orders flow in from enthusiastic customers with cheques enclosed. As often happens in this business, programming difficulties delay shipments. Despite the difficulties, management will boast of the high rate of new "sales" (they have the orders and the money in hand, have they not?). According to GAAP, however, there is no revenue to record since the goods have not yet been delivered. (In Appendix 3.5, we will see how such transactions are properly recorded.[1])

2. *Recording Transactions As Entries in the Journal*

In a traditional accounting system, transactions are first recorded as entries in chronological order in the *journal*. The journal entry highlights the individual transaction and allows us to analyse it to ensure that it has been recorded in accordance with GAAP.

3. *Posting Journal Entries to the General Ledger*

The *account* is the basic building block of the accounting system. The complete set of all accounts for a company is called the *general ledger*. On a regular basis, the journal entries are *posted to* (copied into) these accounts. The general ledger is the core of the accounting system and is the basis for the preparation of the financial statements.

For the purposes of understanding the double-entry method, it is helpful for us to begin with a very simple framework. Accordingly, in this appendix we will start with a *one-write* system — in essence, the system used by computerized accounting systems, one that combines the journal entry and the posting to the general ledger. After we have established the basic framework, we will expand the system to include debits, credits, and journal entries.

4. *Balancing the General Ledger*

Periodically the general ledger must be balanced. In a computerized system, this is done with each transaction. In a manual system, balancing will be done less frequently but must be done before the books are closed at the end of the accounting period. Balancing the general ledger is a

---

[1] When accounting problems are uncovered in a company's financial statements, they are often related to the inappropriate recording of revenue.

purely mechanical exercise, but as an integral part of double-entry accounting, it protects against arithmetic bookkeeping errors.

By not permitting unbalanced entries, balancing is automatic in computerized systems. For this reason, the topic of balancing is not given much attention today. Still, understanding the nature of out-of-balance error is helpful in understanding how double-entry accounting works.

A balanced ledger is not necessarily correct, but being out of balance is a clear indication of error. The accounting significance of a single error is related to its size. For example, assume a company receives an invoice from its advertising agency for advertising services in the amount of $80,000. A cheque for the correct amount is written, sent, and recorded correctly. The expense, however, is incorrectly recorded as only $8,000. If independent records of cash and expense were maintained — what is known as a single-entry system — the discrepancy might never be discovered. The cash account will be correct and it will correspond with the bank statement. On the other hand, the advertising expense itself and total expenses on the income statement will be understated by $72,000. In a small company, this could give a very misleading impression of profitability. The strength of the double-entry accounting system is that the recording of the cash payment — the cheque — and the recording of the corresponding expense must be done together *and* must balance. If they do not, the periodic totalling of all the ledger balances will reveal the discrepancy. Knowing that an error exists is a necessary condition for correcting it. See Focus Box 2A1.1, "Finding an Out-of-Balance Error".

If there is a single unbalanced entry in the books, the out-of-balance discrepancy is a measure of the magnitude of the error. However, the converse is not necessarily true: an out-of-balance discrepancy does not always mean that there is a single error of that magnitude. The error — actually, errors — could be much larger. If there are two or more out-of-balance errors, large errors can partially offset each other, obscuring their significance. For example, assume there are two independent errors in an accounting system: the asset account, Buildings, is overstated by $500,000, and the revenue account, Sales, is overstated by $498,300. These two errors act in different directions and they almost cancel each other out, leaving only the small difference between the two of $1,700 as the observed error. Of course, we don't observe the underlying errors, so someone unfamiliar with accounting might conclude that the observed discrepancy of $1,700 was the full extent of the error. If the company had total assets close to $10 million, $1,700 would not be considered material and it would be reasonable to disregard the error. That would be a serious mistake: one error of half a million dollars would most certainly be considered material, and two independent errors of that magnitude would mean that the financial statements were seriously misleading.

5. *Correcting, Adjusting, and Closing the Books*

Apart from bringing an out-of-balance ledger into balance, there are other reasons why the ledger might need adjustment. One reason is to correct errors of valuation. Such errors usually arise at the identification or recording stage (step 1 or 2 above). Errors of valuation do not violate the accounting equation, but they are mistakes all the same and can result in

Focus Box 2A1.1: Finding an Out-of-Balance Error

In a computerized system, the balance in the ledger is effectively tested as the entry is made; if the entry is unbalanced, the transaction will not be accepted. Computers and accounting software are relatively inexpensive and widely used. Still, manual accounting systems are simpler to set up and will be more convenient for any operation that has relatively few transactions. Accounting students, of course, will also have to deal with manual accounting systems. Here are some simple procedures to help you find the cause of a single out-of-balance error when there are two columns of numbers, the totals of which should balance. In fact, beyond accounting, these procedures can be applied to any counting situation where there is a single error and where the magnitude of the discrepancy is known. The procedures are listed in order, the simplest ones first.

Begin by identifying the amount of the discrepancy and the total in each column. Then follow each of these rules in turn:

1. Look for the amount incorrectly posted or posted twice.
2. Scan the source documents for the amount that was not posted to a column.
3. If the error is an even number, look for half the amount in the columns.
4. Apply the rule of nine to the amount.

If none of these rules work, more detailed checking is required. First. check the addition of each column and then look for other arithmetic or posting errors.

These procedures are designed for a situation where there is a single error. Although they will not work if there are two or more errors, any close review of the system is likely to uncover errors. At some point only one will remain and then one of these procedures will work.

Here is an illustration. The two columns below are an example of what you might see if you find a balancing error. The example is consistent with a number of different underlying causes. Depending on which one it is, a different test will lead you to it.

18	13
9	12
5	4
11	8
19	7
62	44

Begin by identifying the amount of the discrepancy and the total in each column. The difference is 18 and the column totals are 62 and 44.

1. **Amount incorrectly entered.** Check first that the "18" in the left-hand column has not been posted there in error. If it shouldn't be there, the two columns will balance to 44. If this is not the problem, try step 2.
2. **Scan source documents for missing amount.** Look for another "18" in the source document that should have been posted to the right-hand column but has not been. If this is the problem, the two columns will balance to 62. If it is not, move to step 3.
3. **Half the error in the wrong column.** Check to see if the "9" in the left-hand column, which is half the error, should have been posted instead in the right-hand column. If that is the case, both columns would then balance with totals of 53. No success? Try step 4.
4. **Rule of nine.** This is a possibility if the discrepancy is divisible by 9, as it is here. If a discrepancy between two totals that should balance is divisible by 9, there is the possibility that there is a transposition error. In this case, for example, if the "13" at the top of the right-hand column should have been its transposition, "31", the difference is 18 and the two columns would in fact balance at 62. A transposition in a sum will always change the total by a number divisible evenly by 9. Thus 74 and 47 have a difference of 27, 649 and 946 have a difference of 297; the difference is always divisible evenly by 9. Satisfy yourself that 0, even if not explicitly written, also follows the rule: 101 is a transposition of 11, 100 of 10, 5000 of 50.

material misstatement in the financial statements. For example, if a credit sale is recorded, in error, as $150,000 instead of the correct $50,000, both the entry to revenue and the entry to accounts receivable will be overstated by $100,000. The error would normally be picked up when the customer remits a cheque in the correct amount of $50,000 and the discrepancy is investigated. However, if the transaction takes place late in the financial year and the receivable is not due until early in the next financial year, the current year's financial statements will be wrong: both sales revenue (on the income statement) and accounts receivable (on the balance sheet) will be overstated by $100,000. There are, of course, audit techniques that will find such errors since the balance owing from the customer (the account receivable) can be checked independently of the revenue. (This emphasizes the role and importance of the internal and external *audits* in ensuring the correctness of the accounts and the financial statements that are prepared from them.)

Books of account are permanent records, so when an incorrect entry is discovered, the original entry is not written over, erased, or removed. Rather, a second correcting entry is made as an *adjusting journal entry*. This was the practice when all books were kept in pen and ink and continues with computerized systems. Erasures in handwritten books were considered evidence of tampering. For the same reason, most computerized accounting systems do not permit an entry to be changed after it has been fully entered. The correction must be made as a new entry with a full explanation. The objective is to maintain an audit trail, to ensure that all entries, even incorrect ones, can be traced. If all valuation corrections and other changes are entered as adjusting journal entries, they are open to examination by the auditor.

At the end of each accounting period there is another class of adjusting journal entries to be made. These are not designed to correct errors, but they are non-routine. In most accounting systems, routine entries, including all transactions involving cash, all credit purchases and sales, and, in more sophisticated systems, the cost of goods sold, are made when some transaction takes place with a third party. Certain transactions, however, such as amortization, are a function of time only, and there is no event to trigger recognition; these are recorded periodically — at the end of the month or at the end of the financial year rather than on a day-to-day basis. In addition, in small companies, the cost of goods sold is not recorded for each sale. Instead, at the end of the accounting period, the inventory is counted and valued and only then is cost of goods sold calculated. All of these periodic transactions are entered into the accounts only at the end of each accounting period by means of *adjusting journal entries*. After the adjusting journal entries are made, the general ledger is balanced again, and the accounts are *closed*.

6. Preparing the Financial Statements from the Ledger Balances

At the end of an accounting period, the balances in the general ledger are used to prepare the financial statements: the balance sheet, the income statement, the statement of retained earnings, and the statement of cash flows.

Summary

The accounting cycle is the process of recording transactions in the company's books. A transaction is a single business event that is recorded in the accounting system. On a regular basis, journal entries are posted to the accounts in the general ledger. At the end of each accounting period the general ledger is brought up to date with adjusting journal entries, is balanced, and then closed. GAAP is the name for the set of rules that govern this process.

In the next section, the basics of double-entry accounting will be presented and illustrated using the 10 transactions presented in section 2.3 of this chapter. For the first three transactions, we will use a simplified double-entry system. We will then introduce the standard debit-credit method of double-entry accounting and use it to complete the remaining transactions.

Initially we will focus on steps 1 to 4 described above:

1. Identifying individual transactions and determining how they are to be recorded
2. Recording transactions as entries in the journal
3. Posting journal entries in the general ledger
4. Balancing the general ledger.

After all 10 illustrative transactions are recorded, we will show how end-of-period adjustments are made and how the books are closed (step 5), and, to complete the accounting cycle, how the financial statements are prepared from the ledger balances (step 6). In appendices to subsequent chapters we will use this framework to deal with the more complex transactions presented in those chapters.

A Simplified Double-Entry Accounting System

As we have seen, the accounting equation

ASSETS = LIABILITIES + OWNERS' EQUITY

forms the structure of the balance sheet. This equation in fact underlies the entire accounting system. For example, the general ledger, just as the balance sheet, has the same form as the accounting equation. When we speak of a "balanced ledger", we mean that the sum of the amounts in the asset accounts equals the sum of the amounts in the liability accounts plus the sum of the amounts in the owners' equity accounts. Moreover, to maintain this balance, each new transaction, which is to say each journal entry, must also be balanced in the terms of the same equation.

In traditional bookkeeping, transactions are first recorded in the journal in chronological order and are then posted (copied) one by one to the accounts in the general ledger. This method has certain advantages for division of labour and for filing, particularly in large, manual systems. However, for the purposes of demonstrating how the system works, it is more useful initially to combine these two steps and write the transactions directly into the accounts arrayed in the form of the accounting equation.[2] After the basic principle is established using this framework, we will move to the standard format of journal entries followed by postings to accounts in the general ledger.

We will begin by defining the basic accounts. There is an account for every class of *asset*, *liability*, and *owners' equity*. In this appendix, account names will be indicated by the use of an initial capital letter — for example, Cash, Accounts Receivable. We will start with a skeleton set of accounts and expand it as necessary. The first accounts are the main *asset* accounts:

Account	Description
Cash	Primarily money on deposit at a bank; also includes cash on hand
Inventory	Goods purchased for resale
Accounts Receivable	Amounts due from customers for goods they have purchased from the company on credit
Fixed Assets	Assets, such as furniture, machines, cars and trucks, building, land, that are purchased for use over several years rather than for resale

Similarly, there are accounts for each different type of *liability*, or debt, such as the following:

Account	Description
Bank Loan	The obligation to repay a loan taken from the bank
Accounts Payable	The obligation to pay money in the future to suppliers from whom the company has purchased goods on credit

A *sole proprietorship* will normally have only one *owners' equity* account on the balance sheet. However, in a *partnership* or an *incorporated company*, owners' equity is divided into different accounts, representing differing legal or accounting aspects of the owners' claim. The example in section 2.3 did not make these distinctions, but now that we are demonstrating actual accounting procedures, they will be necessary. Since most business organizations are incorporated, this will be the form we will use. In an incorporated company, a distinction is made between invested capital and earned capital and thus there are always at least these two owners' equity accounts, usually called, respectively, *Share Capital* and *Retained*

---

2 This, essentially, is how a computerized accounting system works. Even in a computerized system, however, the information is typically printed in journal entry form or in ledger account form for internal analysis and reporting purposes.

Earnings. Also, since the owners are called shareholders, the entire owners' equity section of the balance sheet is called *shareholders' equity* rather than owners' equity. We will continue to use the term *owners' equity* when referring to the owners' interest in general terms, but the term *shareholders' equity* will always be used when we are referring specifically to the equity section of an incorporated company.

Account	Description
Share Capital	The portion of the shareholders' equity (the claim of shareholders) that arises when new investment is made — i.e., when shares are issued by the company in exchange for assets, usually cash, paid in by the shareholders. Share capital is reduced only in the rare circumstance that shares are cancelled or redeemed. This can happen when a company is reorganized after seeking bankruptcy protection or when it is wound up.
Retained Earnings	That portion of the claim of shareholders that increases as the company operates profitably and is reduced when dividends are paid as losses are incurred.

An important objective of financial accounting is the measurement of the company's operating success, its profitability, in the period. Rather than measure profit directly, transaction by transaction, it is more convenient and informative to measure separately the components of profit, namely, *revenue* and *expense*, for each transaction throughout the accounting period, using accounts with the same names, and then calculate profit (or, as accountants prefer to call it, *net income* or *earnings*) only at the end of the accounting period. Looked at in terms of the basic accounting equation, Revenue and Expense, like Net Income, are measures of *change* in owners' equity. *Revenue* is defined as the gross increase in owners' equity from operations — for example, the period's sales at selling price. *Expense* is the gross decrease in owners' equity necessary to generate revenue — an example would be all the costs incurred necessary to make the period's sales. Netting these two basic gross measures of operations — revenue less expense — gives *net income* (assuming that revenue exceeds expense; if expense exceeds revenue, the net of the two is called *net loss* or, more simply, *loss*).[3]

Account	Description
Revenue	The gross increase in owners' equity from operations
Expense	The gross decrease in owners' equity from operations

---

[3] *Net income* or *net loss* are simply the names for the difference between revenue and expense. One or the other will appear as the bottom line on the income statement, but neither exists as an account in the general ledger. (In some traditional accounting books, a single account called Profit and Loss was used as part of the process of closing the books.)

There are several things to note about Revenue and Expense. First, although Revenue and Expense are treated as individual accounts in this appendix, in practice, they each represent *sets* of accounts. A company will normally have one or more particular kinds of revenue, depending on what it actually does to generate it: for example, if the company generates its revenue by selling goods, it is called *Sales Revenue* (or more simply, *Sales*); revenue from selling a service would be either *Service Fees* or *Consulting Fees*, depending on its nature; revenue from real estate is *Rental Revenue*; and revenue from lending money is called *Interest Revenue*.[4] Accounting for revenue, both by line of activity and in total, allows us to keep track of different aspects of the company's business.

All companies will have a number of expense accounts, such as *Salaries*, *Cost of Goods Sold*, and *Amortization*. Keeping separate accounts of expenses, measures of the various costs incurred to earn revenue of the period, is a prerequisite for gauging the efficiency of operations.

Second, although revenue and expense accounts do not appear on the balance sheet, they are nonetheless ledger accounts, sub-accounts of Retained Earnings. Since these accounts are part of the balance in the Retained Earnings account, they have a direct effect on the balance sheet.

The third point is important for understanding how the financial statements are linked. Because revenue and expense are defined in the context of double-entry accounting, there is a corresponding change in an asset or a liability each time revenue or expense is recognized. We will call these changes in assets or liabilities *resource flows*. Resource flows occur in a business for different reasons. Some are simple exchanges — one asset is exchanged for another (buy a building for cash) or an asset is acquired in exchange for debt (take a bank loan). Revenue and expense transactions are different. They are not resource flows themselves; rather, they indicate that the particular resource flow represents a change in the ownership claim — a change in owner's equity — from business operations. We can illustrate this distinction as follows. A merchandising company sells goods for cash. In double-entry terms, this is cash inflow/revenue. Calling this particular cash inflow *revenue* is how the accounting system tags it as an operating resource flow — a resource flow that affects owners' equity. As well, there is another resource flow in a sales transaction — the outflow of the goods that are transferred to the customer. This is the expense part of this transaction. In double-entry terms, this is an inventory outflow/cost of goods sold expense. Calling this asset outflow *expense* is how the accounting system tags the transfer of goods to the customer as an operating resource flow. The goods were transferred for the purpose of earning revenue. Hence the name of the expense — Cost of Goods Sold. Other expenses are not tied to particular revenue transactions, but they are expenses of the period nonetheless. Office supplies and labour, for example, are measures of resources used to earn revenue. In the former, a par-

---

[4] Sometimes you will see such revenue accounts referred to as *Income* — for example, "Rental Income" or "Interest Income". This can be confusing. In business accounting uses, *income* is properly a net concept (revenue less expense), and you should avoid using it as an alternative term for revenue.

ticular asset is used up (office expense); in the latter, a flow of services is used up. We can think of the asset labour being created and used instantaneously, but because the company buys it as it is used, we measure the implicit liability to pay the wages as the labour service is used. This is the resource flow tagged as expense. In double-entry terms, this is wages payable/wage expense. (There will be a cash outflow when the wages are actually paid later. This is illustrated in the next paragraph.)

Non-operating resource flows are transactions that involve only assets and liabilities. For example, if a company buys a building for cash, there is an outflow of the asset, cash, in exchange for the inflow of another asset, the building. There is no effect on owners' equity. Another example is the cash inflow that would result if the company were to borrow money: cash is received in exchange for the issuance of debt (the promise to repay the loan with interest in the future); there is again no immediate effect on owner's equity. (Interest expense, the operating cost of borrowing, will be a reduction of owners' equity (i.e., an expense), but only as it accrues in the future.) In the wage example above, the operating transaction is the use of the labour (the expense) and recognition of the wages payable (the operating resource flow). When the workers are paid subsequently, there are non-operating resource flows: cash is transferred to the workers, and the liability (the obligation to pay them) is extinguished.

Dividends is a single account in a class of its own. Dividends (the account name is often written in the plural) is the reduction of Retained Earnings that occurs when assets — normally cash — are distributed to owners *as a result of successful operations* (i.e., after income has been earned). Dividends must not be confused with expenses. Although dividends, like expenses, reduce Retained Earnings, dividends are not a measure of the cost of earning revenue and therefore are *not* an expense.

Account	Description
Dividends	The decrease in Retained Earnings when profits are distributed as cash (or other assets) to shareholders

Like the Revenue and Expense accounts, the Dividends account is a sub-account of Retained Earnings. All the sub-accounts — Revenue, Expense, and Dividends — are temporary accounts, and they are closed at the end of each accounting period to Retained Earnings.

There are other features of accounts that we will need, but we will introduce them as required.

As we proceed, there are three important points to bear in mind:

1. **Money.** All transactions are recorded in money terms; in Canada, that usually means in Canadian dollars. We must be careful to distinguish between the asset money — which we call *cash* to minimize confusion — and money as a measure of value. It is important to remember that, in accounting, the dollar is being used primarily as a unit of *value*. Thus, money valuation is a feature of all accounting transactions, but money as cash is part of a recorded transaction

only if cash actually changes hands. To avoid mistakes many beginners make, think twice before concluding that because every transaction is measured in money terms, one-half of every double-entry transaction must involve cash. The account Cash is involved in a transaction only if the asset cash has increased or decreased.

Because the term *money* has so many meanings in business discourse, it is best to avoid the use of the word as much as possible except in a clear valuation sense, as in the phrase "money measurement". Finally, because all figures in the accounts are in dollar terms, by convention the dollar sign is not used in the journal or the general ledger.

2. **Balancing entries involving more than two accounts.** Because of the double-entry nature of accounting, each transaction must affect at least two accounts and the entry must be *balanced*. What this usually means is that an entry of the same dollar value amount will be made in each of two accounts. If three accounts are affected, the sum of the dollar value of the entries in two accounts must equal the dollar value of the entry in the third account (and similarly in the rare case that four or more accounts are affected). Examples given below will make this clear.

3. **Chronology.** In accounting, chronology is important. In these examples we will identify each transaction with a transaction number in the first column to indicate chronological order. If these were actual transactions, each one would be dated instead. All the transactions illustrated in this appendix are assumed to have taken place over the month of December 2007. The identification of the period is necessary for the preparation of the financial statements (see pp. 64 and 66).

Entering the Transactions

For the next step, we construct the general ledger in the form of a spreadsheet, reflecting the underlying accounting equation. The accounts are placed under the appropriate section heading of the accounting equation. Asset accounts are on the left-hand side of the spreadsheet, liability and shareholders' equity accounts are on the right-hand side. In Table 2A.1, there are four accounts. (The two that are named Cash and Share Capital are needed for the first transaction; others will be added as we proceed.) Each account is divided into two columns, one representing *increases* to the account, the other representing *decreases*. Note the difference in the labelling of increases and decreases in these two accounts. *If the account is an asset, increases are on the left side of the account and decreases are on the right side*. For accounts on the other side of the accounting equation, the convention is reversed. *If the account is a liability or owners' equity, increases are on the right side and decreases are on the left*. These conventions are maintained in all accounting systems.

Normally the transaction would be written up first in the journal on an entry-by-entry basis. This is the procedure we will in fact follow starting with transaction #4 on page 48, but right now, however, since we are familiar with the basic accounting equation that the general ledger in a spreadsheet form reproduces, it is more convenient to write each transaction directly into the ledger. Although they are not in the standard journal form, each line in the spreadsheet can in fact be read as a journal entry.

Table 2A.1

#	Assets				Liabilities		Shareholders' Equity	
	Cash						Share Capital	
	increase	decrease	increase	decrease	decrease	increase	decrease	increase

Transaction #1

Having set up the ledger in this form, we can now make the first entry into the accounts. To set the stage, recall that initially there are no assets, no liabilities, and no owners' equity; the basic accounting equation is satisfied since both sides are equal to zero. In the first transaction, the owners contribute $25,000, which we will assume to be cash. The increase in the asset Cash is evident, but double-entry accounting means that there must be a corresponding change elsewhere — a change that, together with the increase in cash, maintains the equality of the accounting equation. If we saw only $25,000 cash being received by a company without knowing the reason, we would not know if this was the result of (1) a *decrease* of another asset (an exchange), (2) an *increase* in a liability (borrowing of money), or (3) an *increase* in shareholders' equity (revenue or share issue). In this particular case we know that the cash is being received because the shareholders are making their initial capital contribution, and therefore we can identify the balancing change as an increase in shareholders' equity, specifically, an issue of shares that represents the shareholders' claim.[5]

We can summarize the transaction as follows:

The asset account, Cash, increases by $25,000.
The shareholders' equity account, Share Capital, increases by $25,000.

This being the first entry, it is written on the first line following the account headings, as shown in Table 2A.2. There are, of course, two parts to the entry. Taking the cash part first, we note that Cash is an asset account, so the increase in cash is represented by a sub-entry in the Cash account. For the other part of the entry, we see that Share Capital is a shareholders' equity account, so the increase in share capital, the issuance of shares, is written on the right side of that account.

---

[5] In an incorporated company, *shares* represent the owners' claims. The number of shares issued when the company is first organized is essentially arbitrary. What is important is the *relative* number of shares each owner holds. It will be proportional to his or her investment.

Table 2A.2

#	Assets				Liabilities		Shareholders' Equity	
	Cash						Share Capital	
	increase	decrease	increase	decrease	decrease	increase	decrease	increase
1	25000							25000

After the two parts of the entry are made, there is a positive balance of $25,000 in the asset account, Cash, and a positive balance of $25,000 in the shareholders' equity account, Share Capital. The ledger balances: total assets are $25,000 and total liabilities and shareholders' equity are also $25,000. Although the general ledger is not a balance sheet as such — a balance sheet is a formal document that must show the company name, statement title, and date, and satisfy certain other requirements — it is easy to see how a balance sheet could be drawn up from the information we have in the general ledger at this point. Normally, a balance sheet is drawn up only at end of an accounting period. Still, if the entries for the period are complete and correct, drawing up the balance sheet and the other financial statements at any time is a relatively straightforward exercise.

Transaction #2   The company has raised its initial capital from its shareholders. This is a shorthand way of saying that it acquired assets in the form of cash by issuing shares. (The cash will be used to buy other assets.) Having done this, it is now in a position to raise the additional funds necessary to begin operations by taking a loan from the bank. Again, the asset acquired is assumed to be in the form of cash, but the corresponding claim is a liability — an obligation to repay the principal amount of the loan as well as interest at agreed-upon rates and times[6] — rather than a permanent ownership claim like share capital. We need to create a new account, Bank Loan, as shown in Table 2A.3.

We can summarize the transaction as follows:

The asset account, Cash, increases by $10,000.
The liability account, Bank Loan, increases by $10,000.

The entry for transaction #2 is written on the line following transaction #1. Again, this being double-entry accounting, there are two parts. As in transaction #1, the increase in cash is represented by a sub-entry of $10,000 in the Cash account. For the other half of the entry, we know that Bank Loan is a liability account, so the increase in the liability, Bank Loan, is written on the right side of that account.

---

[6] These details, as important as they are, are not shown here, but a record of the terms of the loan would, of course, be kept.

Table 2A.3

#	Assets				Liabilities		Shareholders' Equity	
	Cash				Bank Loan		Share Capital	
	increase	decrease	increase	decrease	decrease	increase	decrease	increase
1	25000							25000
2	10000					10000		
account balances	*35000*					*10000*		*25000*

The entry itself is balanced: a $10,000 increase in assets balances a $10,000 increase in liabilities and shareholders' equity (although in this entry only a liability account was affected). Moreover, even though two account balances have changed, the general ledger itself remains balanced. In the third row we confirm this by taking an interim balance of the ledger. (To distinguish balances from entries, balances are written in italics and the row is shaded.) Balancing involves the following steps:

(i) finding the balance in each account (if there were decreases in any of the accounts, the decreases would be netted against the increases to come to the account balance)
(ii) adding up the balances in the asset accounts (there is just one such balance here)
(iii) adding up the balances in the liability and shareholders' equity accounts
(iv) comparing the totals in (ii) and (iii) to ensure that they are equal.

In this case, the asset side of the ledger totals $35,000 (Cash only), which is equal to the $35,000 in liabilities and shareholders' equity ($10,000 and $25,000, Bank Loan and Share Capital, respectively).

Transaction #3 In transaction #3, the company uses $8,000 of its cash to buy inventory. We need to add another account, Inventory, as shown in Table 2A.4.
The asset account Cash *decreases* by $8,000. This is the first example of a reduction of an account.
The asset account Inventory increases by $8,000.
This entry is written on the line immediately below the interim balance that we took after transaction #2. In this case, since the asset account Cash is being decreased, there is right-side entry in this account. Inventory is increased, so the entry is on the left side.
Because there are entries on both sides of the Cash account, when we strike a balance, we need to do it in two steps. First, each column is sub-totalled ($35,000 and $8,000); then the two columns are netted against each other with the difference ($27,000) being placed as the account balance in the column with the larger subtotal. Since there were more increases to the cash account than decreases, the balance in this case is a net increase. There is an equal and opposite change in the Inventory account so total assets have not changed. There is, of course, no change at

all on the other side of the ledger and thus the entry is balanced. (If you compare the balancing that followed transaction #1 with the balancing that followed transaction #2, you will see that there is no particular relationship between the changes in the account balances following a transaction and the overall balance in the ledger [total assets, total liability, and shareholders' equity], which may or may not change. The overall account groups totals have no special significance here; all that matters is that the general ledger remains balanced.)

Table 2A.4

#	Assets				Liabilities		Shareholders' Equity	
	Cash		Inventory		Bank Loan		Share Capital	
	increase	decrease	increase	decrease	decrease	increase	decrease	increase
1	25000							25000
2	10000					10000		
account balances	*35000*					*10000*		*25000*
3		8000	8000					
column subtotals	*35000*	*8000*						
account balances	*27000*		*8000*			*10000*		*25000*

Debits and Credits

At this point we generalize what we have learned so far and then make a change in terminology. This will allow us to formalize the process of balancing the ledger accounts and, more important, to write journal entries.

The division of accounts into a left side and a right side and its connection to balanced entries is an extension of the basic accounting equation. As we have seen, a left-side entry in an asset account *increases* it; but a left-side entry *decreases* a liability or shareholders' equity account. The effect is the opposite for a right-side entry. We also see that a full entry — the representation of a complete transaction that maintains the equality of the basic accounting equation — involves both a left-side entry *and* a right-side entry of equal value. Thus, in transaction #1, an increase in the asset cash, which is a left-side entry, is paired with an increase in shareholders' equity, which is right-side entry. Both have the same value. Transaction #2 is similar, but the right-side entry represents an increase in a liability rather than shareholders' equity. Transaction #3 affects only asset accounts. The left-side entry is the increase in the asset Inventory, and the right-side entry represents the *decrease* in the asset Cash. Again, both have the same value.

We can summarize this graphically. On the left in Figure 2A.1 we list the significance of left-side entries in different accounts, and on the right, the significance of right-side entries. To keep things uncluttered, we show only account groups, assets (A) and liabilities or equities (L/E).

A left-side entry can represent an increase in an asset (+A) or a decrease in a liability or an equity (including an expense and dividends) (–L/E).[7]

A right-side entry can represent an increase in a liability or an equity (including revenue) (+L/E) or a decrease in an asset (–A).

Bars connect all possible combinations of a left-side entry and a right-side entry, such as {+A •▬• + L/E} and {+A •▬• –A}. These combinations and *only* these combinations of equal value entries satisfy the basic accounting equation. Combinations of entries listed on the same side of the figure, such as {+A and –L/E} in the left-hand column, or {+L/E with –A} in the right-hand column, do *not* satisfy the equation. Similarly, a pair of two identical entries such as {+A and +A} on the left, or {+L/E and +L/E} on the right, do not satisfy the basic accounting equation. Put another way, every possible transaction that satisfies the basic accounting equation involving two accounts can be described by one of the four linked combinations.

Figure 2A.1

Left-side entries   **Right-side entries**

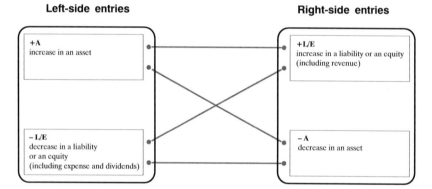

We can illustrate this framework using the three transactions we studied above. Transactions #1 and #2 are both examples of the first combination represented by the top bar: the increase in the asset Cash is combined with an increase in Shareholders' Equity (#1) or with an increase in the liability Bank Loan (#2). Transaction #3 is an example of the second combination represented by the bar sloping down to the right: the increase in the asset Inventory matches a reduction of another asset. We will see examples of the other combinations following.

The rule, then, for recording transactions is as follows:

> **To maintain the basic accounting equation, every accounting transaction must have a left-side entry and a right-side entry of equal value.**

---

[7] We haven't seen an example of the latter yet, but if you guessed that a liability or equity is *reduced* by a left-side entry, you are correct.

There is one more step, and this is purely terminological. Instead of referring to left-side entries and right-side entries, accountants use the terms *debit* entries and *credit* entries, respectively. We can redo the figure using the debit–credit terminology, as shown in Figure 2A.2:

Figure 2A.2

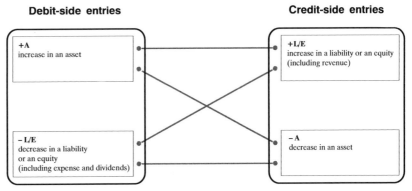

The rule is now written as follows:

To maintain the basic accounting equation, each accounting transaction must have a *debit entry* and a *credit entry* of equal value.

As shown in Table 2A.5, instead of writing *increase/decrease* for each set of asset account columns, or *decrease/increase* for each set of liability and shareholders' equity account columns, *every* account will be labelled in the same way: *debit* (abbreviated *Dr*) for the left-hand column, and *credit* (abbreviated *Cr*) for the right-hand column. If we redo the general ledger up to transaction #3 using debits and credits, we see that nothing has changed except the headings of the columns, which are now identical for each account: *debit* for the left column, *credit* for the right column.

The process of balancing is unchanged, except that now the account balances are labelled *debit* and *credit* as the case may be, rather than *net increase* and *net decrease*. In a balanced general ledger, total debit balances equal total credit balances, as we can verify in Table 2A.5: total debit balances, all in the asset section, are $35,000; total credit balances, all in the liabilities and shareholders' equity section, are also $35,000. You should note, however, that debit account balances will not always be associated with assets, nor credit balances with liabilities. (We will see examples following.) All that is required for a balanced ledger is that total debit balances equal total credit balances. You can satisfy yourself that even though debit balances do not all correspond only to asset accounts, or credit balances only to liability and shareholders' accounts, if total debit balances equal total credit balances, this is equivalent to saying that total assets equal total liabilities and shareholders' equity from a balancing point of view.

Table 2A.5

#	Assets				Liabilities		Shareholders' Equity	
	Cash		Inventory		Bank Loan		Share Capital	
	Dr	Cr	Dr	Cr	Dr	Cr	Dr	Cr
1	25000							25000
2	10000					10000		
account balances	35000					10000		25000
3		8000	8000					
column subtotals	35000	8000						
account balances	27000		8000			10000		25000

The Language of Debits and Credits

The word *debit* means simply "an entry on the left side of the ledger"; *credit* means, similarly, "an entry on the right side of the ledger". In addition to being the technical terms used in standard accounting systems, the terms *debit* and *credit* offer us a convenient shorthand method of expression. Instead of saying "there is an entry of 25,000 on the left side of the account Cash" that recorded an increase of cash, we say simply "there is debit to cash of 25,000". The words can also be used even more concisely as verbs: "Cash is debited by 25,000", or the bookkeeper might be told to "debit cash 25,000". (The word *dollars* or the dollar sign is always understood.)

By extension, *debit* and *credit* refer to balances as well as entries. As we have seen, an asset account normally has its *balance* on the left side; a liability or shareholders' equity account normally has its balance on the right side. Thus, we call a balance on the left side a *debit balance*, and a balance on the right side a *credit balance*. Bear in mind that if an account has a balance on an unexpected side, it may have to be reinterpreted. Thus, if Cash (the company's record of its bank account) has a credit balance (normally Cash has a debit balance), the company does not have "money in the bank"; rather, it owes the bank money — it has an overdraft.

We will now show how debits and credits allow us to record transactions as standard journal entries. We will also introduce revenue and expense accounts using the language of debits and credits. After we have done this, we will explore why we use debits and credits along with other related questions. We begin by recording transaction #4.

Transaction #4   In transaction #4, the company purchases an additional $5,000 worth of inventory. In this case, however, payment is not made in cash, but instead the company agrees to pay the supplier in 30 days. The deferred payment is called *buying on credit* by the buyer and *selling on credit* by the seller, and the particulars of the arrangement — quite a common one in business transactions — are called *credit terms*. The word *credit* derives from the Latin *credere*, "to believe or to trust" — the Latin word is the source of both the bookkeeping term and the name of the business transaction. In this case, the buyer, the company for which we are keeping the books, will in fact record the liability as a credit in ledger to the account Accounts Payable, but we should resist using this as a mnemonic device; if the company were to "sell on credit", it would record the expected future receipt as a *debit* to the asset account Accounts Receivable (which is exactly what the supplier in this particular example is doing). Thus, two uses of the term *credit* are closely related, but meanings are quite distinct and they should not be confused.

To summarize:
The asset account, Inventory, increases by $5,000.
The liability account, Accounts Payable, increases by $5,000.

We need to add a new account — Accounts Payable, a liability account, as shown in Table 2A.6.
Now that we know that the asset increase is called a debit and that the liability increase is called a credit, we can write this transaction as a standard journal entry:

		[Dr]	[Cr]
Date			
[Dr]	Inventory {asset}	5,000	
[Cr]	Accounts Payable {liability}		5,000

Transaction #4: Purchase from X Co. Ltd., terms, 30 days.

Leaving aside the date and the narrative (the detailed description of the transaction) at the end, this is read,

"Debit Inventory 5,000; credit Accounts Payable 5,000"

The important pieces of information in the journal entry are the date, the account names and amounts, and the positions of the account names and amounts. The indenting indicates whether an account is being debited or credited. The abbreviations in brackets, [Dr] and [Cr], in the first column under the date and at the top of the debit and credit columns are optional. The account types {asset, liability, etc.} in curly brackets are included in these appendices for teaching purposes only. They do not appear in regular journal entries.

The journal is a chronological record of transactions. As the name implies, journal entries are written up daily as they occur. The information in the journal is subsequently posted to the relevant accounts in the general ledger. These postings are not necessarily made daily, but all the period's journal entries must be posted before financial statements are prepared. Of course, in computerized systems, the initial entry is made in real time and the posting is done simultaneously.

Table 2A.6

#	Assets				Liabilities				Shareholders' Equity	
	Cash		Inventory		Bank Loan		Accounts Payable		Share Capital	
	Dr	Cr	Dr	Cr	Dr	Cr	Dr	Cr	Dr	Cr
1	25000									25000
2	10000					10000				
3		8000	8000							
4			5000					5000		
column subtotals	35000	8000	13000			10000		5000		25000
account balances	27000		13000			10000		5000		25000

Notice again that the general ledger remains in balance: debit account balances total 40,000 (27,000 + 13,000); credit account balances total 40,000 (10,000 + 5,000 + 25,000).

(To keep the ledger uncluttered we have deleted the balances we struck after transaction #2. These were for information only at that time and their removal now changes nothing. This practice will be continued as we proceed.)

Transaction #5 Up to this point, all transactions have involved only accounts that appear on the balance sheet. Transaction #5 is what is called a *revenue transaction*. It involves activities through which the company earns a profit. In this transaction, as shown in Table 2A.7 on page 53, we see an example of *revenue* (i.e., the company sells goods for $7,000) and *expense* (i.e., the goods sold cost the company $4,000).

In the description in section 2.3, transaction #5 was presented as an increase in net assets of $3,000, representing a corresponding increase in owners' equity. In terms of the simplified accounting equation used in section 2.3, this is correct. In terms of debits, credits, and ledger accounts, the story is a little more involved. This net increase in owners' equity represents increases in components of profit: revenue and expense. However, since there will probably be other revenues and expenses of the business before the end of the accounting period, it would be inappropriate to label the $3,000 as the profit just yet. (As it happens, there is both revenue and expense in transaction #6 as well as additional expenses in subsequent transactions.) Profit is the difference between *all* the revenues and *all* the expenses of the period. In fact, the accounting process acknowledges that the measurement of profit is tentative until we have come to the end of the accounting period. Until we close the books, there is no explicit measure of profit in the general ledger. All we see now are some of its components — in this case just sales revenue and cost of goods sold expense (COGS). The process of calculating and recording profit must wait until the accounting period is over and all the other revenues and expenses have been recorded.

A sales transaction is typically recorded in two separate steps: in the first step, the revenue is recorded (5a); in the second, the associated expense is recorded (5b).

Transaction #5a — Sales Revenue

This is a simple cash sale. Revenue, the gross increase in shareholders' equity from operations, is represented by an inflow of cash.

To summarize:
The asset account, Cash, increases by $7,000.
The revenue account, Sales Revenue, increases by $7,000.

An increase in the asset Cash is recorded by a debit of $7,000. The increase in the revenue account Sales Revenue is recorded by a credit of $7,000.

We represent this transaction in journal entry form as follows:

		[Dr]	[Cr]
Date			
[Dr]	Cash {asset}	7,000	
[Cr]	Sales Revenue {SE — revenue}		7,000

Transaction #5a: Sale of goods to Y Co. Ltd., for $7,000 cash.

To emphasize that revenue accounts are sub-accounts of retained earnings and therefore part of shareholders' equity, these entries will be labelled {SE — revenue} in the journal entries. Similarly, expense entries will be labelled {SE — expense}.

Transaction 5b — Cost of Goods Sold

This transaction records the *direct* expense of this particular sale. The cost is the using up (transfer out to the customer) of the goods that have been sold. Whereas the sale is recorded at the selling price, the cost of the goods sold is recorded at the cost price, which will normally be lower. Establishing the actual value of the cost of the goods sold can become a little complicated; we will look at it in more detail below. In this case, we will accept that the cost of this particular sale is $4,000 and leave to later the discussion of the techniques for establishing cost of goods sold.

To summarize:
The asset account, Inventory, decreases by $4,000.
The expense account, Cost of Goods Sold, increases by $4,000.

An expense, even though it is read as a positive number, is a *reduction* of equity. A reduction of equity is represented by a debit. The other side of the transaction is the actual reduction of the asset Inventory. This is the credit.

We represent this transaction in journal entry form as follows:

		[Dr]	[Cr]
Date			
[Dr]	Cost of Goods Sold {SE — expense}	4,000	
[Cr]	Inventory {asset}		4,000

Transaction #5b: Cost of goods sold to Y Co. Ltd. (Transaction #5a)

We can now post both entries to the general ledger and then check the balance. We need to create new accounts in the ledger. These are in fact sub-accounts within Retained Earnings: Revenue — Sales, and Expense — Cost of Goods Sold. (See Table 2A.7 on the next page.)

Having struck a balance in each account, we can balance the general ledger. Debit account balances — now found on both sides of the ledger — total 47,000 (34,000 + 9,000 + 4,000). Credit account balances also total 47,000 (10,000 + 5,000 + 7,000 + 25,000). Notice that we have left the two sub-accounts of Retained Earnings, Revenue — sales and Expense — cost of goods sold, with credit and debit balances, respectively. The process of profit measurement is as yet incomplete. Only when the books are finally closed at the end of the period will all the revenue and expense accounts (there would normally be a number of them) be closed, and net income — i.e., profit — calculated. We will demonstrate this procedure at the end of this appendix.

It is worth pausing at this point to consider the meaning and importance of using debits and credits.

What Do Debit and Credit Mean?

In accounting, the words *debit* and *credit* are just shorthand terms — they have no significance other than "left side of the ledger" and "right side of the ledger". In everyday language, however, these words have other connotations. It is important not to confuse these usages. Although the words *debit* and *credit* are often used in an evaluative way in everyday language, in accounting they have a purely technical meaning. Debits are not bad, nor are credits good. If a building is purchased, the asset account must be increased; this is done by "debiting" the account Building, which will normally have a debit balance. Debits are what increase asset accounts, and an asset account with a positive balance has a debit balance. But with every debit, there is a credit; if the building is purchased for cash, at the same time Building is debited, the account Cash is credited, which is simply another way of saying that the account Cash was reduced. None of these transactions imply in any way that the company is worse off. In fact, the transactions simply record trading of assets — cash for building.

Consider a different situation. If the building had been purchased entirely "on credit" — in other words, the money to purchase the building was borrowed — the debit entry would be the same as before, but now, instead of crediting Cash, we would credit Mortgage Loan Payable. *Credit* in this case means the recognition of a liability. It is a different way of financing the purchase and has different implications for future cash management, but in itself, the credit has no moral or judgmental significance.[8] A third method of financing the purchase of the building might be (if the seller would accept it) to pay for the building by issuing new shares. Issuing shares involves a credit entry simply because an increase in shareholders' equity is recorded by a right-side entry. In none of these cases can we say that the company is *ipso facto* better or worse

---

[8] Of course, these other meanings of *debit* and *credit* have some relationship to the accounting terms. Still, strictly speaking, in accounting *debit* and *credit* mean no more than "left side" and "right side".

Table 2A.7

#	Assets				Liabilities				Shareholders' Equity							
	Cash		Inventory		Bank Loan		Accounts Payable		Retained Earnings						Share Capital	
									R/E		Revenue —Sales		Expense —COGS			
	Dr	Cr	Dr	Cr	Dr	Cr	Dr	Cr	Dr	Cr	Dr	Cr	Dr	Cr	Dr	Cr
1	25000															25000
2	10000					10000										
3		8000	8000													
4			5000					5000								
5a	7000											7000				
5b				4000									4000			
column subtotals	*42000*	*8000*	*13000*	*4000*		*10000*		*5000*				*7000*	*4000*			*25000*
account balances	*34000*		*9000*			*10000*		*5000*				*7000*	*4000*			*25000*

off because of what the debits or credits record. In fact, in every recorded transaction, total debits equal total credits: that is the nature of double-entry accounting.

Why Should Non-accountants Learn about Debits and Credits?

Why should non-accountants learn double-entry accounting using debits and credits? The short answer is that double-entry accounting underlies all business accounting, and understanding double entry means that you will be less intimidated by financial reports. All standard systems, including all computer systems designed for business use, use standard double entry. While it is true that you don't need to understand double-entry accounting to read a set of financial statements, familiarity with the system has undoubted advantages. Understanding debits and credits is a large part of understanding the language of accounting. Modern financial statements are increasingly complex. A basic accounting course is not going to make us experts; but even if we don't understand a particular transaction or some aspect of statement presentation, a familiarity with basic debits and credits puts us in a better position to follow the explanations of accountants and make intelligent interpretations.

We can now complete the remaining transactions in section 2.3, balance and close the ledger, and show how the financial statements are prepared.

Transaction #6 As noted in section 2.3 of the text, transaction #6 is very similar to transaction #5. The amounts are different, of course; moreover, transaction #5 is a cash sale and this sale has been made on credit. In practical accounting terms, the difference in the terms of sale is reflected solely in the asset account debited: it was Cash in transaction #5, and will be Accounts Receivable in this transaction. As explained in section 2.3, under GAAP, credit sales are normally recognized as completed sales and we will follow that convention here. This question is explored in more detail in Chapter 3.

Again, this sales transaction is recorded in two separate steps, as illustrated in Table 2A.8 on page 56: in the first step, the revenue is recorded (6a); in the second, the associated expense is recorded (6b).

Transaction 6a — Sales Revenue

This sale is a credit sale, a sale "on account". The increase in shareholders' equity is represented by a claim on the customer for a *future* payment of cash. It is not a receipt of cash now, so it is *not* an increase in the account Cash. The account representing a claim for a future payment is Accounts Receivable.

To summarize:
The asset account, Accounts Receivable, increases by $9,000.
The revenue account, Sales Revenue, increases by $9,000.

An increase in the asset, Accounts Receivable, is represented by a debit of $9,000. The increase in the revenue account, Sales Revenue, is represented by a credit of $9,000.

The journal entry is as follows:

		[Dr]	[Cr]
Date			
[Dr]	Accounts Receivable {asset}	9,000	
[Cr]	Sales Revenue {SE — revenue}		9,000

Transaction #6a: Sale of goods to Z Co. Ltd., for $9,000 on account, terms, 30 days

Transaction 6b — Cost of Goods Sold

As in transaction #5b, transaction #6b records the *direct* expense of the revenue earned in transaction #6a. The expense is the expired cost of the asset transferred to the customer — the cost of the goods that have been sold.

To summarize
The asset account, Inventory, decreases by $6,000.
The expense account, Cost of Goods Sold, increases by $6,000.

We represent this transaction in journal entry form as follows:

		[Dr]	[Cr]
Date			
[Dr]	Cost of Goods Sold {SE — expense}	6,000	
[Cr]	Inventory {asset}		6,000

Transaction #6b: Cost of goods sold to Z Co. Ltd. (Transaction #6a)

We can now post entries #6a and 6b to the general ledger. We need to create one new account in the ledger: Accounts Receivable. (Accounts Receivable is an asset account. The account name is written in the plural since we normally have more than one account receivable. At this point, of course, there is just the one.) We have not verified that the general ledger balances, but you should do that yourself as an exercise. (See Table 2A.8 on the following page.)

We will write the journal entries for transactions #7 through #10 before posting them to the general ledger in Table 2A.9 on page 59.

Transaction #7 This is the collection of the receivable created when we made the sale in transaction #6a.

To summarize:
The asset account, Cash, increases by $9,000.
The asset account, Accounts Receivable, decreases by $9,000.

An increase in the asset Cash is represented by a debit of $9,000. The decrease in the asset account Accounts Receivable is represented by a credit of $9,000.
The journal entry is as follows:

		[Dr]	[Cr]
Date			
[Dr]	Cash {asset}	9,000	
[Cr]	Accounts Receivable {asset}		9,000

Transaction #7: Collection of accounts receivable from to Z Co. Ltd. (Transaction #6a)

Table 2A.8

#	Assets						Liabilities				Shareholders' Equity								
											Retained Earnings							
	Cash		Accounts Receivable		Inventory		Bank Loan		Accounts Payable		R/E		Revenue —Sales		Expense —COGS		Share Capital	
	Dr	Cr	Dr	Cr	Dr	Cr	Dr	Cr	Dr	Cr	Dr	Cr	Dr	Cr	Dr	Cr	Dr	Cr
1	25000																	25000
2	10000							10000										
3		8000			8000													
4					5000					5000								
5a	7000													7000				
5b						4000									4000			
6a			9000											9000				
6b						6000									6000			

Transaction #8   This is the settlement of the liability (Accounts Payable) incurred in transaction #4: purchase of inventory on account.

To summarize:
The liability account, Accounts Payable, decreases by $5,000.
The asset account, Cash, decreases by $5,000.

An decrease in the liability Accounts Payable is represented by a debit of $5,000. The decrease in the asset account Cash is represented by a credit of $5,000.
The journal entry is as follows:

		[Dr]	[Cr]
Date			
[Dr]	Accounts Payable {liability}	5,000	
[Cr]	Cash {asset}		5,000

Transaction #8: Settlement of account payable to X Co. Ltd. (Transaction #4)

Transaction #9   This is the payment of bank loan interest. As explained in section 2.3, interest is an expense. The account is called Interest Expense to distinguish it from Interest Revenue, which doesn't appear here but can arise.

To summarize:
The expense account, Interest Expense, increases by $100.
The asset account, Cash, decreases by $100.

An increase in the expense Interest Expense is represented by a debit of $100. (Remember, an expense represents a *decrease* in Retained Earnings.) The decrease in the asset account Cash is represented by a credit of $100.
The journal entry is as follows:

		[Dr]	[Cr]
Date			
[Dr]	Interest expense {SE — expense}	100	
[Cr]	Cash {asset}		100

Transaction #9: Interest on bank loan for the period.

Transaction #10   The company has had a period of profitable operations, and the directors have decided to pay the owners a cash dividend. There are actually two stages to this transaction: the declaration of the dividend by the board of directors, and later, after the list of shareholders is updated, the payment. In this case, both stages are recorded as one transaction.

To summarize:
The dividend account, Dividends, increases by $1,000.
The asset account, Cash, decreases by $1,000.

An increase in the dividends account Dividends is represented by a debit of $1,000. (Remember, dividends reduce Retained Earnings.) The decrease in the asset account Cash is represented by a credit of $1,000.

57

The journal entry is as follows:

		[Dr]	[Cr]
Date			
[Dr]	Dividends {SE — dividends}	1,000	
[Cr]	Cash {asset}		1,000

Transaction #10: Declaration and payment of a dividend of $1,000.

Now we can post the four last transactions and balance the ledger. We need to create two new accounts in the ledger: Interest Expense and Dividends. Interest Expense is in fact another sub-account within Retained Earnings and it will be included here in the column headed Expenses. (See Table 2A.9.)

In balancing the ledger, notice that two of the accounts have fallen to zero: the account receivable was collected and the account payable paid. You can verify that the ledger balances: total debits = total credits = $51,000.

At this point we will make one additional entry, one that was not made in section 2.3, but that is the type of entry that would normally be made at the end of the period.

A standard accounting system is designed to recognize and record, as they take place on a day-to-day basis, all transactions involving cash; most systems will record credit purchases and credit sales as well. In general, any standard business transaction that involves an organization or individual outside the company will trigger an accounting entry. Transactions #1 through #10 are good examples of the sorts of entries that a standard accounting system will capture as they occur.

When we come to the end of the accounting period, however, any event that is deemed to affect the balance sheet or income statement according to GAAP must be recorded. This includes events that have not yet triggered an accounting entry because cash has not been involved and no invoice has been received or sent. For example, imagine that the period covered by transactions #1 to #10 is one month and the books must now be closed. At the beginning of this period, we hired an office assistant on a part-time basis. The agreement was that she was to be paid a monthly salary of $900 for this work, to be paid to her one week after the end of each month. At the end of this accounting period, she has worked for one month but will not be paid until another week has passed. According to GAAP, the cost of the work she did — $900 — is an expense of the past month. No payment has been made (an invoice would not normally be sent by the employee in a salary relationship), so there has been no event to trigger an entry. Standard accounting practice provides for such time-based transactions through the use of *adjusting journal entries* (AJEs). The following are some examples of transactions that would be handled by adjusting journal entries:

• Recognizing an expense for part of a billing period that covers two accounting periods (this is called an *accrued expense*, or simply *an accrual*). The salary example above is in effect an example of such an accrual.

Table 2A.9

#	Assets						Liabilities				Shareholders' Equity									
											Retained Earnings								Share Capital	
	Cash		Accounts Receivable		Inventory		Bank Loan		Accounts Payable		R/E		Revenue —Sales		Expenses		Dividends			
	Dr	Cr	Dr	Cr	Dr	Cr	Dr	Cr	Dr	Cr	Dr	Cr	Dr	Cr	Dr	Cr	Dr	Cr	Dr	Cr
1	25000																			25000
2	10000							10000												
3		8000			8000															
4					5000					5000										
5a	7000													7000						
5b						4000									4000					
6a			9000											9000						
6b						6000									6000					
7	9000			9000																
8		5000							5000											
9		100													100					
10		1000															1000			
column subtotals	51000	14400	9000	9000	13000	10000		10000	5000	5000				16000	10100		1000			25000
account balances	36900		0		3000			10000	0								1000			25000

- Recognizing revenue for part of a billing period that covers two accounting periods (another *accrual* — in this case, an *accrued revenue*).

- Recognizing that a payment made for something that is of the nature of an expense and was so accounted for when paid but is not an expense *this period*, is *deferred* to the next period. (An example would be a payment for six months rent paid two months before the end of the accounting period. The whole payment is often charged to expense at the time of payment, a common practice since the payment is of the nature of an expense. However, this treatment is correct only if the part of the payment that will be an expense in the next period is removed from this period's expense by means of an AJE.)

- Recognizing that a payment received for something that we will deliver in the next period is not counted as revenue this period but is *deferred* to the next period. (An example was described on page 32.)

- Cost of goods sold for any business that does not record inventory change for each transaction.

- Amortization.

All of these periodic transactions are identified at the end of each accounting period following a review of operations, contracts, and policies, and then entered into the accounts by means of an adjusting journal entry (AJE).

We will make the AJE for the *salary accrual.*

Adjusting Journal Entry — Accrual of Salary Expense

The assistant's salary has been earned by her for work done in the past month even though it has yet to paid. The value of her labour has been used up in the month and so, like interest in transaction #10, it is an expense for the period. It is normally called Salary Expense.

To summarize:
The expense account, Salary Expense, increases by $900.
The liability account, Salary Payable, increases by $900.

An increase in the expense Salary Expense is represented by a debit of $900. The corresponding increase in the liability account, Salary Payable, is represented by a credit of $900. Salary Payable is very similar to Accounts Payable; for this reason, the two liabilities will be combined and the account simply renamed Payable.

The adjusting journal entry is as follows:

		[Dr]	[Cr]
Date			
[Dr]	Salary expense {SE — expense}	900	
[Cr]	Payable {liability}		900

Adjusting journal entry: accrual of unpaid salary expense

See Table 2A.10.

Table 2A.10

#	Assets						Liabilities				Shareholders' Equity									
	Cash		Accounts Receivable		Inventory		Bank Loan		Payables		R/E		Revenue —Sales		Expenses		Dividends		Share Capital	
	Dr	Cr	Dr	Cr	Dr	Cr	Dr	Cr	Dr	Cr	Dr	Cr	Dr	Cr	Dr	Cr	Dr	Cr	Dr	Cr
1	25000																			25000
2	10000							10000												
3		8000			8000															
4					5000					5000										
5a	7000													7000						
5b						4000									4000					
6a			9000											9000						
6b						6000									6000					
7	9000			9000																
8		5000							5000											
9		100													100					
10		1000															1000			
AJE										900					900					

Closing the Books

We assume now that the one adjusting journal entry was all that was necessary and that the books are thus up-to-date and in accordance with GAAP. We begin the closing process by balancing the accounts. These balances will be used to draw up the financial statements. Before continuing, you should confirm that the general ledger itself is balanced. (See Table 2A.11.)

Closing the books does three interrelated things:

1. It calculates the profit or loss for the period and carries it to retained earnings.
2. It sums the dividends for the period and carries that number to retained earnings.
3. It leaves all the temporary accounts — Revenue(s), Expense(s), and Dividends — with zero balances, ready to begin the next period.

The method we use records two closing journal entries, one for revenues and expenses and one for dividends, which are then posted to the general ledger.

Closing Journal Entry — Revenue and Expense Accounts

We have opened one revenue account, Sales Revenue, and three expense accounts, Cost of Goods Sold, Interest Expense, and Salary Expense. The entry to close the revenue and expense accounts is purely mechanical: the Sales Revenue account is simply debited with the amount of its final balance of 16,000, and each of the expense accounts are credited with the amounts of their final balances, 11,000 in all. Since revenue exceeds expenses — the company has made a profit for the period — the balancing entry to Retained Earnings is a credit of 5,000. Had there been a loss, expenses would exceed revenue, and the balancing amount would have been a debit.[9]

The closing journal entry is as follows:

		[Dr]	[Cr]
Date			
[Dr]	Sales Revenue {SE — revenue}	16,000	
[Cr]	Cost of Goods Sold {SE — expense}		10,000
[Cr]	Interest Expense {SE — expense}		100
[Cr]	Salary Expense {SE — expense}		900
[Cr]	Retained Earnings {SE — R/E}		5,000

Closing journal entry: revenue and expense

---

[9] In this particular case, this is the first month of operations for the company and the opening balance of Retained Earnings is zero. After closing the books, Retained Earnings would have a debit balance. Negative Retained Earnings is call Deficit. If an incorporated company has deficit, it is normally illegal to declare a dividend.

Table 2A.11

#	Cash Dr	Cash Cr	Accounts Receivable Dr	Accounts Receivable Cr	Inventory Dr	Inventory Cr	Bank Loan Dr	Bank Loan Cr	Payables Dr	Payables Cr	R/E Dr	R/E Cr	Revenue—Sales Dr	Revenue—Sales Cr	Expenses Dr	Expenses Cr	Dividends Dr	Dividends Cr	Share Capital Dr	Share Capital Cr
1	25000																			25000
2	10000							10000												
3		8000			8000															
4					5000					5000										
5a	7000													7000						
5b						4000									4000					
6a			9000											9000						
6b						6000									6000					
7	9000			9000																
8		5000							5000											
9		100													100					
10		1000															1000			
AJE										900					900					
Balances	*51000*	*14100*	*9000*	*9000*	*13000*	*10000*		*10000*	*5000*	*5900*				*16000*	*11000*		*1000*			*25000*
	36900		*0*		*3000*			*10000*		*900*							*1000*			*25000*

Closing Journal Entry — Dividends Account

The balance in the Dividends account is closed to Retained Earnings in the same way as the revenue and expense accounts. In this case there was only one dividend declared but in practice there might be up to four declared in the year. The closing entry transfers the final debit balance in the Dividends account to Retained Earnings, which has the effect of reducing its balance.

The closing journal entry is as follows:

		[Dr]	[Cr]
Date			
[Dr]	Retained Earnings {SE — R/E}	1,000	
[Cr]	Dividends {SE — dividends}		1,000
	Closing journal entry: dividends		

Once the closing entries are posted, the general ledger is balanced for the last time. This *post-closing trial balance*, the closing entries, and other information in the ledger are used to prepare the financial statements. (See Table 2A.12.)

Preparing the Financial Statements

To complete the accounting cycle, we prepare financial statements: Income Statement, Statement of Retained Earnings, Balance Sheet, and Statement of Cash Flows. Further discussion, including the interpretation of these statements, will be the subject of the next three chapters. What is important to note now is the importance of form. Even though all of the information contained in the financial statements can be found in the ledger and journal, these last, the "books", are the internal records of the company. These four financial statements constitute the only *formal* financial record of a company's operations and its financial position.

Example Co. Ltd.
Income Statement
for month ended December 31, 2006

Revenue		
Sales		$16,000
Expense		
Cost of goods sold	$10,000	
Interest	100	
Salary	900	11,000
Net income		$ 5,000

Example Co. Ltd.
Statement of Retained Earnings
for month ended December 31, 2006

Net income	$ 5,000
Less Dividends	1,000
Closing balance	$ 4,000

Table 2A.12

#	Cash Dr	Cash Cr	Accounts Receivable Dr	Accounts Receivable Cr	Inventory Dr	Inventory Cr	Bank Loan Dr	Bank Loan Cr	Payables Dr	Payables Cr	R/E Dr	R/E Cr	Revenue—Sales Dr	Revenue—Sales Cr	Expenses Dr	Expenses Cr	Dividends Dr	Dividends Cr	Share Capital Dr	Share Capital Cr
1	25000																			25000
2	10000							10000												
3		8000			8000															
4					5000					5000										
5a	7000													7000						
5b						4000									4000					
6a			9000											9000						
6b						6000									6000					
7	9000			9000																
8		5000							5000											
9		100													100					
10		1000															1000			
AJE										900					900					
Balances	51000	14100	9000	9000	13000	10000		10000	5000	5900				16000	11000		1000			25000
Trial Bal.	36900		0		3000			10000		900				16000	11000		1000			25000
Close R/E												5000	16000			11000				
Close Div.											1000							1000		
Post-closing Trial Bal.	36900				3000			10000		900		4000	0	0	0		0			25000

Example Co. Ltd.
Balance Sheet
as at December 31, 2006

Assets

Cash		$36,900
Inventory		3,000
		$39,900

Liabilities & Shareholders' Equity

Liabilities		
Salary payable	$ 900	
Bank loan	10,000	
Total liabilities		$10,900
Shareholders' Equity		
Share capital	$25,000	
Retained earnings	4,000	
Total shareholders' equity		29,000
		$39,900

Example Co. Ltd.
Statement of Cash Flows
for month ended December 31, 2006

Cash from operations	
Net income	$ 5,000
Add: decrease in non-cash working capital	7,900
	$12,900
Cash from financing activities	
Cash from issuing shares	$25,000
Cash used for dividends	(1,000)
	$24,000
Change in cash balance	$36,900

You should satisfy yourself that you understand how the information in the general ledger at the end of the period (Table 2A.12) has been used to prepare the first three financial statements shown above. (The balances in the revenue and expense accounts [before closing] are used to draw up the income statement. The net income figure from the income statement along with the balances in the dividend and retained earnings accounts are used to create the statement of retained earnings. The post-closing trial balance provides the figures for the balance sheet.) The fourth financial statement, the statement of cash flows, is also based on information from the general ledger, but the relationship is not so simply described. In Appendix 6.2 we will learn a technique for taking information from the books — or, more directly, from the first three financial statements — to construct the statement of cash flows for the period.

Self-Study Problems

1. Charley Farley went into business on October 1, 2005, by opening a doughnut shop. He carried on the business in a rented store in downtown Orillia. At the end of December, he realized that he would have to pay income tax on the business profits, but he had no idea how much profit he had made. He has asked you to advise him how much income to report for the three months he has been in business.

   He has presented you with his bank statements and a pile of invoices and receipts. The following is a summarized list of payments and receipts for the three months.

   Receipts paid into bank account:

1.	Owners' equity	$ 50,000
2.	Bank loan	$ 55,000
3.	Cash sales	$146,500

   Payments made out of bank account:

4.	Suppliers	$104,500
5.	Wages	$ 12,000
6.	Rent	$ 20,000
7.	Utilities	$ 5,000
8.	Insurance	$ 4,000
9.	Equipment	$ 99,000
10.	Repayment of bank loan	$ 4,000

   Required
   (a) Enter the summarized transactions into the accounting equation, and show the balance of assets, liabilities, and equities after each transaction. Assume, for now, that transactions 4, 5, 6, 7, and 8 all reduce owners' equity.
   (b) As at December 31, 2005, the assets total $102,000 according to the accounting equation. What are those assets?

2. The financial statements of Ozark Outfitters show an operating income of $100,000 and a net income of $75,000. Total assets are $1 million, liabilities are $500,000, owners' equity is $500,000.

   Required
   (a) What is the return on assets?
   (b) What is the return on equity?

3. Bombardier Inc. reported operating income of $1,700 million and net income of $391 million for the year ended January 31, 2002. The company's total assets were $27,753 million and owners' equity was $4,090 million as at January 31, 2002.

   Required
   (a) How much were the total liabilities as at January 31, 2002?
   (b) What was the return on assets for the year?
   (c) What was the return on equity for the year?

4. Continue with Problem #3: for the year to January 31, 2004, the operating income for Bombardier Inc. was $246 million, and there was a net loss (for the shareholders) of $89 million. Total assets were $25,569 million, and liabilities totalled $22,319 million.

Required
(a) How much was the shareholders' equity as at January 31, 2004?
(b) What was the return on assets for the year?
(c) What was the return on equity for the year?

Solutions

1. (a)

		Assets	=	Liabilities	+	Owners' Equity
1.		$ 50,000	=		+	$ 50,000
2.		55,000	=	$55,000	+	nil
		$105,000	=	$55,000	+	$ 50,000
3.		146,500	=	nil	+	146,500
		$251,500	=	$55,000	+	$196,500
4.		–104,500	=	nil	+	–104,500
		$147,000	=	$55,000	+	$ 92,000
5.		– 12,000	=	nil	+	– 12,000
		135,000	=	$55,000	+	$ 80,000
6.		– 20,000	=	nil	+	– 20,000
		$115,000	=	$55,000	+	$ 60,000
7.		– 5,000	=	nil	+	– 5,000
		$110,000	=	$55,000	+	$ 55,000
8.		– 4,000	=	nil	+	– 4,000
		$106,000	=	$55,000	+	$ 51,000
9.	–99,000 +	99,000	=	nil	+	nil
		$106,000	=	$55,000	+	$ 51,000
10.		– 4,000	=	– 4,000	+	nil
		$102,000	=	$51,000	+	$ 51,000

(b) The assets consist of:

Cash at bank	$ 3,000
Equipment	99,000
Total	$102,000

2. (a) Return on assets:

= operating income ÷ total assets
= $100,000 ÷ $1,000,000
= 0.1 (or 10%)

(b) Return on equity:

= net income ÷ owners' equity
= $75,000 ÷ $500,000
= 0.15 (or 15%)

3.   (a)   Accounting equation:

> Assets = Liabilities + Owners' equity
> $27,753 million = Liabilities + $4,090 million
> Total liabilities = ($27,753 – $4,090) million
> Total liabilities were $23,663 million

    (b)   Return on assets:

> = (operating income ÷ total assets)
> = ($1,700 million ÷ $27,753 million)
> = 0.061 (or 6.1%)

    (c)   Return on equity:

> = net income ÷ owners' equity
> = $391 million ÷ $4,090 million
> = 0.096 (or 9.6%)

4.   (a)   Accounting equation:

> Assets = Liabilities + Owners' equity
> $25,569 million = $22,319 million + Owners' equity
> Owners' equity = ($25,569 – $22,319) million
> Owners' equity was $3,250 million

    (b)   Return on assets:

> = (operating income ÷ total assets)
> = ($246 million ÷ $25,569 million)
> = 0.0096 (or 0.96%, i.e., less than 1% p.a.)

    (c)   Return on equity (or Return on investment):

> = net income ÷ owners' equity

As there was a net loss, this is not a meaningful calculation.

Discussion Questions and Problems

Discussion Questions

1. It is 1997, and you are thinking about investing in Inco Ltd., a Canadian mining and resource company that is (as of 1997) proposing to open one of the richest metal ore mines in the world, in Voiscy's Bay, Labrador. List the information available to you as a potential investor, its source, and its degree of usefulness to your investment decision.

2. As a shareholder of Abitibi-Price Consolidated Inc., a Canadian pulp and paper processor, list the information the company will give to you and assess its relevance and reliability.

3. For some time you have been concerned about the environment. In January of the current year your uncle died and left you 500 shares of the Ford Motor Company. What can you do to make yourself more comfortable about the relationship between Ford, you and the environment?

4. Banks and trust companies regularly provide mortgage loans to home buyers. What financial information do they require before making their lending decisions? What additional steps do they take to make sure their loans are safe?

5. Owners' equity is described as the residual in the accounting equation. Explain what this means in terms of assets and liabilities. If you are the owner of 10 shares in Bell Canada Enterprises Inc., what is your entitlement to the owners' equity on the balance sheet?

6. When an asset is acquired, it is valued at cost because of the historical cost accounting principle. Under what circumstances would this be inaccurate, and what steps should be taken to make the balance sheet show the correct value?

7. The matching concept requires that expenses be reported in the period that received the benefit of the expense, and not in the period when the cash was paid out. Where in the balance sheet would the effect of this be reported?

8. Where in the financial reports would the financial outcome of an ongoing litigation be reported?

9. Does an audit improve the relevance, or the reliability, of financial reports?

10. What does the term *residual interest* mean when it is applied to common shares?

Appendix 2.1

11. What is a transaction? How does a transaction differ from an event?

12. What is a journal entry? What is the relationship between a journal entry and a transaction? Between a journal entry and an event?

13. What is an account?

14. What is the general ledger?

15. What is a debit?

16. What is a credit?

17. Are debits better than credits?

Problems

1. The following is a list of financial statements; briefly describe the content of each one:

    • The income statement
    • The balance sheet
    • The statement of retained earnings
    • The statement of cash flows

2. As a shareholder in a company listed on the Toronto Stock Exchange, briefly describe your rights in respect of financial statements.

3. You want to buy a condominium for $200,000. You have the deposit of $50,000 and enough additional cash resources to pay for the lawyers' fees and closing costs, but you need a mortgage of $150,000. You intend to approach your bank for the loan. Consider the following list and explain how each item may be useful or not useful in your loan application (use the criteria of relevance and reliability):

    • A list of your personal property, such as clothes, furniture, and electronic equipment, including the cost of each item
    • Your bank statements and returned cheques for the past six months
    • A letter from your employer attesting that you have worked there for three years, and stating your salary as $60,000 per year
    • The names of your uncles and aunts who may leave something to you in their wills
    • A professional valuation of your sailboat, for $125,000
    • Your university transcript showing that you are a solid B student
    • A list of the shares you own and their market prices

4. Tom goes into business as a computer repair consultant on January 1. The following independent transactions take place during his first month of operations. Show how each would be dealt with by the accounting equation (show the $ increase or decrease in assets, liabilities, and owner's equity for each transaction separately):

    • Tom opens a bank account for the business by transferring $10,000 of his personal savings into a company bank account.
    • Tom negotiates a line of credit from his bank of $25,000. He does not actually take the money, but it is there for him to spend if he wants to.
    • Tom buys a truck and some computer repair equipment for a total of $22,000. He pays $2,000 out of the bank account and takes $20,000 from the line of credit.
    • Tom buys repair materials and spare computer parts for $2,500, paying from the bank account.
    • Tom buys repair materials and spare computer parts for $3,000, agreeing to pay the supplier within two weeks.

- Tom visits a total of 14 customers, and charges each of them a flat fee of $150 for computer repair, which they pay, and which Tom puts in the bank.
- Tom carries out a major system overhaul for his local supermarket: they agree to pay him $1,000 next month.
- Tom carries out a computer repair for a friend who pays him $50: Tom keeps the money to buy gas and groceries.
- Tom pays the suppliers the $3,000 they are owed.
- Tom checks his inventory of spare computer parts and discovers that he has used exactly half of them.
- Tom checks his inventory of spare computer parts and discovers that one of the motherboards has been damaged, and is no longer fit for use: it had cost $100.

5. Tom goes into business as a computer repair consultant on January 1. The transactions that take place during his first month of operations are shown in Problem #4 above. Show how they would be dealt with in (i) the income statement; and (ii) the balance sheet.

6. The accounting equation for Samantha's Sportsware was as follows on June 30:

Assets		
Cash	$ 2,000	
Inventory	15,000	
Owed by customers	1,000	
Rent deposit	2,000	$20,000
Liabilities		
Owed to suppliers	$10,000	
Owner's equity		
Samantha	10,000	$20,000

Show the accounting equation for Samantha's Sportsware after each of the following transactions (or summaries of transactions):

- July 1: Collected $700 of the money owed by customers.
- July 5: Bought additional inventory for resale for $7,500, on one-month's credit terms.
- July: Sold goods that had cost $10,000 for $18,000 cash.
- July 31: Paid $2,000 for August rent.
- July 31: Paid $1,500 for July utilities.
- July 31: Tried to collect the remaining $300 owed by customer, but the customer had run away!
- July 31: Paid the suppliers the $10,000 owed to them at the beginning of the month.

7. For each of the following independent situations, decide whether it (i) increases owners' equity, (ii) decreases owners' equity, or (iii) leaves owners' equity unchanged:

- Harriet, an architect, designs a building for a client and bills the client $55,000.

- Thomasina, a computer consultant, carries out a system upgrade for a client. She charges the client $15,000; she had to buy software for $8,000 and employ a helper for $2,000.
- Dick, a retailer of foods, buys inventory for resale for $5,000. His normal markup is to add 80% to cost to get his target selling price.
- Dick, a retailer of foods, has goods for resale marked at $9,000 selling price. The goods had cost him $5,000. Due to some discolouration he had to sell them for $4,500.
- Harriet, an architect, pays her helper, Judy, one month's wages of $2,500.

8. Sly Sam runs a second-hand car outlet. He boasts to you that he is worth a million dollars. He has worked this out by taking the number of cars on his lot (100) and multiplying it by the average sticker price ($10,000).

   In what ways is Sam's estimate of his wealth reliable and relevant?

9. Williams Hosiery makes women's stockings. The total assets of the company at the end of the most recent year were $750,000, which were represented by owners' equity of $600,000 and liabilities of $150,000. Sales for the year were $400,000; cost of goods sold and operating expenses totalled $250,000, leaving operating income of $150,000. Interest was $10,000 and taxes were $50,000, leaving net income of $90,000.

   Required
   (a) What was Williams Hosiery's return on assets %?
   (b) What was Williams Hosiery's return on equity %?

10. Gertrude runs a mobile snack bar that drives round to building sites and sells coffee and snacks. Her snack truck cost her $37,000 just recently, and she has inventory that cost her $3,000. Each year she expects to make $50,000 for her time and effort, plus a 10% return on her investment.

    How much operating income does Gertrude expect to make each year?

11. For each of the following situations state which of the accounting concepts is being used (it is common for more than one accounting concept to be relevant in a given situation):

    - Jennifer, who operates a delivery service, keeps a careful record of the distance she drives for business deliveries and the distance she drives for personal journeys.
    - Anne, who is a potter, calculates her income and expenses for each month, to see if her business is still worthwhile.
    - Randi, who is a dress designer, has a considerable inventory of dress materials. When she calculates the value of her inventory at year-end she assumes that she will be able to use it in future designs.

- Hermione, who is a manufacturer of gold jewellery, calculates the value of her inventory at its materials cost, as it could always be melted down and re-used; she excludes the design and manufacturing costs.
- Jennifer, who operates a delivery service, calculates amortization on her delivery truck as 20% of its original cost each year, even though she hopes it will last seven years before requiring replacement.

12. Sly Sam, a second-hand car retailer, is being sued by a customer for $100,000 for an accident caused by a faulty vehicle that he sold in August. The court case will be heard in next February. Sly Sam has not included the $100,000 in his liabilities as at December 31.

Required
(a) Is Sly Sam correct to exclude the $100,000 from his liabilities?
(b) If the $100,000 were to be included in his financial statements, in which statement, and under what heading would it appear?
(c) What accounting concepts apply?
(d) How should Sly Sam have treated the $100,000 in his financial statements?

13. Here are the financial statements for Barry's Biscuits Inc.

Barry's Biscuits Inc.
Balance Sheet as at December 31

Current assets			Current liabilities	$ 50,000
Cash	$ 5,000		Long-term debt	200,000
Inventory	95,000		Total liabilities	$250,000
	$100,000			
Long-term assets	650,000		Shareholders' equity	500,000
Total assets	$750,000		Total liabilities & equity	$750,000

Barry's Biscuits Inc.
Income Statement for the year ended December 31

Sales revenue	$800,000
Operating expenses	600,000
Operating income	$200,000
Interest & taxes	80,000
Net income	$120,000

Required
(a) What was Barry's Biscuits return on assets %?
(b) What was Barry's Biscuits return on equity %?

14. The return on assets and the return on equity both measure the profitability of an organization. In what ways are they different, and who is likely to be the user of each ratio?

15. Explain the relationship between the accounting equation and the balance sheet.

Appendix 2.1

16. Prepare journal entries for each of the events described in Problem #7.

17. Using the simple increase-decrease spreadsheet framework, record the first three events described in Problem #4. [Hint: not all of these events are transactions.]

18. Using the information provided in Problem #4, complete the six-step accounting cycle for Tom's Computer Repair for January 20xx. Use debits and credits, and organize your answer in the following three stages:

    (a) Identify and record the transactions as journal entries (accounting cycle, steps 1 and 2).

    (b) Post the journal to the general ledger. Use the spreadsheet form provided on next page — the first transaction is entered. Add as many extra rows as necessary to complete the post-closing trial balance. See the completed spreadsheet in Table 2A.6 for a model (accounting cycle, steps 3, 4 and 5).

    (c) Use the information from the completed spreadsheet to prepare (i) an income statement for the month, and (ii) a balance sheet as at the end of the month, both in good form (accounting cycle, step 6).

19. Using the information in Problem #6, complete the accounting cycle for Samantha's Sportsware for July 20xx in the same manner as you did for Tom's Computer Repair in Problem #18 above. [Hint: the opening balances in the general ledger on July 1, 20xx, are the closing balances of June 30. Thus, in part (b) below, the first row of the spreadsheet must include the balance (debit or credit as appropriate) for each account on the June 30 balance sheet (ignore the totals).]

    (a) Identify and record the transactions as journal entries.

    (b) Post the journal to the general ledger. Lay out the general ledger in spreadsheet form and complete it up to the post-closing trial balance.

    (c) Use the information from the spreadsheet to prepare (i) an income statement for the month and (ii) a balance sheet as at the end of the month, all in good form.

#	Assets								Liabilities				Owners' Equity					
	Cash		Accounts Receivable		Supplies Inventory		Fixed Assets		Bank Loan		Payables		Retained Earnings				Tom, Capital	
													Revenue		Expense			
	Dr	Cr	Dr	Cr	Dr	Cr	Dr	Cr	Dr	Cr	Dr	Cr	Dr	Cr	Dr	Cr	Dr	Cr
1	10000																	10000

The Income Statement

3

Learning
Objectives

After studying this chapter, you should be able to describe and work with the following elements of the income statement:
→ Revenues
→ Cost of goods sold and expenses
→ Operating income and net income
→ Calculation and use of profitability ratios
→ Calculation of retained earnings
→ Calculation of earnings per share (EPS)

3.1   Introduction

In Chapter 2 we introduced the four main financial statements: the balance sheet, the income statement, the statement of retained earnings, and the statement of cash flows. In this chapter we shall look at the income statement in greater detail.

In the early days of accounting, the emphasis was on the balance sheet, which shows the "wealth" of the owner(s) at a point in time. More recently, to meet the information needs of investors in companies, the emphasis has shifted to the income statement. The income statement reports changes in wealth over a period of time, typically one year.

The changes in wealth that the income statement reports are the net effect of revenues the company has generated and expenses it has incurred. Expenses are deducted from revenues, to leave the bottom line, which is a figure of net income, or profit. If the expenses exceed the revenues, a loss will be reported.

Both revenues and expenses are calculated according to the matching principle. That is, only the revenues earned in the period (no matter when the money was received) and the expenses that were consumed in the period (no matter when they were paid for) are counted. This idea of matching is effected through accrual: moving revenues and expenses from one period to another to reflect real resource flows. Accrual/matching is the principal difference between the income statement and a list of payments and receipts.

3.2   Revenues

3.2.1 Sale of Goods and Services

Revenues are resources that flow into the company. They increase the value of the company and, hence, increase the owners' equity. Revenues arise mostly as a result of selling goods or services to customers.

The dollar value of any individual sale is seldom in dispute as it will be clearly stated on the invoice. The time period when revenue should be recognized is more subjective. Let us consider a company with a one-year reporting period from January to December.

The most straightforward situation is where the entire transaction is completed within the year. That means the goods are sold, the cash is collected, and all obligations under the contract of sale are completed within the calendar year. In this simple situation, the sale would be recognized in the year. This is typical of a retail store that sells on a cash basis, especially if, like Honest Ed's in downtown Toronto, there is a sign on the door that reads, No Refunds, No Exchanges. Less straightforward situations will occur where some aspect of a transaction falls outside the year: either occurring before the start of the year, or after the end of the year. When that happens, the matching principle requires that an accrual be made to move a part of the transaction forward or backward in time.

The most common accrual is in respect of credit sales. Credit sales are common in many business situations. Typically, credit terms are for 30 days, after which the invoice value is payable in full.

The resource flow that the accrual accounting/matching process is most interested in locating is the period when the goods were sold. That is generally taken to be the point when, legally, ownership of the goods passes from seller to buyer. In a retail store, that point is when the goods are delivered and payment is made. In a business-to-business situation, it is

Focus Box 3.1:   Revenue Recognition — Fred's Fabrics Inc.

Fred's Fabrics Inc. retails fabrics and prepares the income statement each year for the 12 months ended December 31.

In December, cash sales were $60,000.
The entire $60,000 was recognized as realized revenue for the year.

In the same month, a further $15,000 was sold on credit.
The $15,000 would also be recognized as a realized sale even though the cash had not been received.

So far, for December, a total of $75,000 ($60,000 + $15,000) has been matched to the current accounting year and recognized as sales revenue.

Because of the sale of this $75,000 of goods, matching requires that the related cost of the inventory be treated as an expense. If the cost of inventory was exactly $50,000, then an expense (cost of goods sold) of $50,000 would be recognized. The gross profit on these sales would be $25,000 ($75,000 – $50,000).

Because there is some risk that some or all of the $15,000 may not be received, it would also be necessary to recognize a bad debt expense. This would be the expected value of uncollectible accounts in respect of the $15,000. If, historically, Fred's Fabrics has experienced losses of 10% of its accounts receivable, then a bad debt expense of $1,500 ($15,000 × 10%) would be recognized.

more likely to be when the goods are delivered. There are some special circumstances where it may be at another point, depending on the nature of the contract between the buyer and the seller.

The revenues for the sale of all goods sold in a given year will be recognized as revenues of that year, even if they have not been paid for.

This raises another problem: what happens if the customer fails to pay? The matching principle requires us to recognize this possibility even if, at the time we are preparing the income statement, we do not have all the information to know which customers will prove problematic. We would, therefore, "accrue" an allowance for bad debts, based on past experience. That would create an expense (bad debt expense) that is matched with the time period.

Some sales are incomplete when initially made. A publisher, for example, sells books to bookstores, but the bookstore has a right to return some or all of the shipment if the books don't sell as well as expected. To take credit for all the sales at the time of delivery would be misleading, so a percentage of expected returns has to be held back in reporting sales. Another example is the sale of a new car, which will have a warranty (say 50,000 km or three years). While the full value of the car as sold may be treated as revenue, the expected costs to be incurred under warranty should be treated as an expected future payment, but a current expense, and matched by making it an expense in the same year the sale was recorded. So, in both of these examples the invoice (and even the cash received) may be an overstatement of the eventual net sales revenue.

Here's another example. Suppose you pay a subscription to a magazine and you are entitled to 12 issues. At the end of the financial year, your subscription may still have three months to run. The magazine should defer one quarter of your subscription to the following year's revenue. (See Focus Box 3.2.)

Suppose a builder has a contract to construct a new office block. It may take more than a year to complete, so work will be carried out that covers more than one accounting period. A very conservative approach would be to wait until the building is complete and handed over to the client, and then recognize the revenue at that point. A more reasonable approach would be to estimate the revenue earned in each period based on the percentage of the contract completed.

The fundamental question, in each case, is, What would the sales revenue be, for the accounting year, if we had full knowledge of all the eventual outcomes? In the absence of full knowledge we make reasonable assumptions. In cases of doubt, we exercise conservatism so that revenues are not over-reported.

3.2.2   *Other Revenues*

Other, non-sale, situations that give rise to revenues would include

- interest revenues from bank deposits, GICs, etc.
- rent revenues
- commission revenues

These are not, typically, important sources of revenues for the company.

**Focus Box 3.2:   Revenue Recognition
— Peerless Publishers Inc.**

Peerless Publishers Inc. publishes books and magazines. They prepare their financial statements for the year to December 31 each year.

During 2005, they sold books to bookstores at an invoiced price of $500,000 per month, every month. Because of the terms of trade, the bookstores were allowed to return up to 10% of the books they had bought on credit if they remained unsold. They could exercise this right for up to six months, after which no further returns were allowed.

December 31, 2005:	
Total sales for 2005: $500,000 × 12 months	$6,000,000
Less potential returns: $500,000 × 6 months × 10%	300,000
Net sales recognized in year 2005	$5,700,000

The $300,000 reserve against returns would be treated as a liability as at December 31, 2005.

In 2006, the $300,000 reserve, less the value of any actual returns of these books, would be recognized as revenue.

During 2005, Peerless Publishers received a total of $400,000 from subscriptions to magazines. It is estimated that half of the magazines for the paid subscriptions had been sent to the subscribers during the year. The other half represented issues to be sent during 2006.

December 31, 2005:	
Total received for magazine subscriptions	$400,000
Less half for issues not yet sent	200,000
Net sales recognized in 2005	$200,000

The $200,000 would be classified as deferred revenue and treated as a liability as at December 31, 2005.

In 2006, when the outstanding issues were all sent out, the $200,000 would be recognized as revenue.

3.3   Expenses

Expenses are the opposite of revenues. They decrease equity. In measuring the net income we try to match the expenses with the revenues of the accounting period. The same problem that we dealt with in respect of revenues exists for expenses: the cash flow may not be a perfect guide to the resource flow we want to recognize. This means that we will have to make the same sort of adjustment, shuffling expenses from one period to another to get a good match.

Expenses are many and varied. They include items incurred directly in relation to the sale of goods, such as the cost of the goods sold in a retail store, or the cost of manufacturing the goods sold in a production plant.

In respect of these direct costs, we can see the link between the revenue-generating process and the associated costs incurred, and matching the two is relatively straightforward. Expenses will also include the many operating costs of the company other than cost of goods sold, such as wages, rent, utilities, etc.

3.3.1 Cost of Goods Sold and Inventory

When a company purchases inventory for resale, the transaction is revenue-neutral. One asset (cash or its equivalent) has been exchanged for another asset (inventory) of equal value. As long as they still have the inventory, no change in equity occurs. When the inventory is sold, it creates revenue, and it also reduces the asset inventory. This reduction in inventory value is recorded as an expense, called cost of goods sold.

Depending on the type of record-keeping system in use, it may be possible to capture the cost of goods sold at the time of the sales transaction. This would always happen where the goods were valuable and, specifically identifiable (a car or a washing machine, for example). It would also happen in a supermarket, where the bar code on a product passing through the checkout would trigger the recording not only of the sale but, also, the cost of goods sold (it would also feed into inventory records and re-ordering routines).

Where goods are of relatively small individual value, simpler systems that do not capture cost of goods sold as the sale takes place may be used. In these situations, the cost of goods sold is found indirectly. First, goods purchased during the year are added to the opening inventory. Then, the closing inventory is deducted. The balance is the cost of goods sold. (See Focus Box 3.3.)

**Focus Box 3.3:   Calculating the Cost of Goods Sold
— Greg's Gas Ltd.**

Greg's Gas Ltd. deals in gas, and all purchases in 2005 were made at a price of $0.40 per litre. They had 10,000 litres of regular gas on hand at the start of 2005. During 2005 they bought 250,000 litres. A total of 260,000 litres was available for sale during the year. Had they sold it all, the cost of the entire 260,000 litres would have become cost of goods sold. As it happened, at the end of 2005 they had 20,000 litres in inventory. The cost of goods sold would be the cost of 240,000 litres sold to customers during the year.

Opening inventory (January 1, 2005)	10,000 litres @ $0.40	$ 4,000
Gas purchased (during 2005)	250,000 litres @ $0.40	100,000
Available for sale	260,000 litres @ $0.40	$104,000
Less closing inventory (as at December 31, 2005)	20,000 litres @ $0.40	8,000
Cost of goods sold in 2005	240,000 litres @ $0.40	$ 96,000

Focus Box 3.4:   Gross Profit % — Greg's Gas Ltd.

Greg's Gas Ltd. sold 240,000 litres of regular gas in 2005, which had a cost of $0.40 per litre. Sales revenue for regular gas totalled $135,000.

Sales revenue	$135,000	100.00%
Cost of goods sold (240,000 × $0.40)	96,000	71.11
Gross profit margin	$ 39,000	28.89%

Selling price is usually cost plus 60%. Selling price should have been $0.64 per litre, and the gross profit margin should have been exactly 37.5% of the selling price. Some of the controls have been lax. The sale of gas should be more carefully controlled to ensure that it does not happen again.

Control of the cost of goods sold is carried out in a number of ways. One method is through the gross profit (or gross margin) to sales ratio. Because the relationship between the cost of goods sold and the selling price is known, the gross profit to sales ratio should be precise. If the actual gross margin is lower than expected, then something has gone wrong. (See Focus Box 3.4.)

Suppose the selling price is re-established by adding 100% to the cost. Selling price thus becomes 200% of cost. A cost of $0.40 will result in a selling price of $0.80, with the gross profit 100% of the cost. Expressed differently, both the cost and the gross profit are 50% of the selling price. If the gross profit falls below 50% of the selling price, an unplanned loss has occurred. This might be due to evaporation, theft, temporary selling price reductions, or a range of other causes. If the difference is significant, it should be investigated and corrective action should be initiated.

The cost convention tells us that inventory is recorded at cost in the first instance. If the inventory becomes impaired in some way, then the conservatism convention tells us that its value should be reduced. Suppose some of the inventory deteriorates and becomes unsaleable. The value of the inventory should be written down to reflect this, and the amount of the writedown becomes an expense. (See Focus Box 3.5.)

The inventory may also lose value for reasons external to the organization. Suppose inventory has been bought at a cost of $5,000. Because of a world oversupply, the market price has fallen. The same inventory could now be replaced for a lesser amount. The conservative treatment requires the value of the inventory would be reported in the balance sheet at the lower of its cost and the market (replacement) cost.

In summary: when inventory is bought, it is an asset. Until it is used, it will appear on the balance sheet as an asset, recorded at cost. If market value falls below cost, the inventory value will be reduced to market value. When it has been sold, it will be reported in the income statement as an expense, and it will no longer appear on the balance sheet as an asset.

Focus Box 3.5: Inventory Valuation at the Lower of Cost or Market Value — Greg's Gas Ltd.

Greg's Gas Ltd. had 20,000 litres of regular gas in inventory as at December 31, 2005. This had a cost of $0.40 per litre. Due to world oversupply of oil, on December 31, 2005, the wholesale price of gas fell from $0.40 to $0.35 per litre.

Cost of regular gas in inventory (20,000 litres @ $0.40) $8,000
Replacement value (20,000 litres @ $0.35) $7,000

Greg's Gas Ltd. would show the value of its inventory of regular gas as $7,000 (its replacement cost) rather than $8,000 (its actual cost), using the "lower of cost and market value" (or LCM) rule.

Reducing the value of closing inventory by $1,000 has the effect of increasing the cost of goods sold by $1,000. This, in turn, reduces income by $1,000.

	Litres	Actual cost	Lower of cost or market value
Opening inventory as at January 1, 2005	10,000	$ 4,000	$ 4,000
Gas purchased during 2005	250,000	100,000	100,000
Gas available	260,000	$104,000	$104,000
Closing inventory as at December 31, 2005	20,000	8,000	7,000
Cost of goods sold in 2005	240,000	$ 96,000	$ 97,000

3.3.2 Overhead Expenses

In addition to the cost of goods sold, expenses also include overhead costs such as

- wage and salary expenses;
- payroll-related expenses (e.g., employers' pension plan and employment insurance contributions);
- establishment expenses (taxes, rent, utilities, repairs, etc.);
- marketing expenses (advertising, sales commissions, etc.);
- research and development expenses; and
- financing expenses (e.g., interest).

Here the matching process is done indirectly. Most of these overhead expenses cannot be directly linked to any particular revenues. Instead, they are more commonly linked to the passage of time. Matching for these expenses is done by matching the time period to when the revenues were earned, rather than to the revenues themselves.

Take utilities, for example. (See Focus Box 3.6.) For the most part, the electricity bills paid in the year will be for electricity consumed in the year and, therefore, they are expenses for the current year. At the end of the year, there may be an unpaid invoice for electricity. That invoice should be included as part of the current year's electricity expense. Moreover,

---

Focus Box 3.6:   Accrued Expenses — Allan's Advertising Inc.

Allan's Advertising Inc. is an advertising agency. The agency prepares its financial statements on a calendar year basis. On January 1, 2005, the agency owed $1,100 for electricity consumed in 2004, but not yet paid for. During 2005, they paid electricity bills each month, and the total amount paid in the year was $6,800. As at December 31, 2005, there was an unpaid invoice for $950 covering use up to December 15, 2005. The agency also estimates that electricity used in the second half of December 2005, but not yet billed, would be $500.

Accrued electricity expense at January 1, 2005	$(1,100)
Cash paid in 2005	6,800
Unpaid invoice for use up to December 15, 2005	950
Accrued electricity use from December 16 to 31, 2005	500
Electricity expense for 2005	$ 7,150

The expense of $7,150 is now matched to the consumption of electricity during 2005.

---

the invoice may only cover consumption up to December 15, as recorded by the meter reading. Electricity consumed between December 15 and 31 should be estimated and accrued, so that it, too, becomes an expense of the current year. Assuming the same process was carried out at the end of the previous year, the electricity expense reported this year would not include the amount owed at the start of the year.

This process of examining the payments and judging whether or not they accurately represent the expense incurred in the year should apply to every expense category.

Sometimes the adjustment will go the other way. Rent or insurance contracts, for example, are often paid in advance, and the expense has to be reduced by the amount of the prepayment. This, in turn, will be added to the "prepaid expense", an asset on the balance sheet. (See Focus Box 3.7.)

In general, we use "accruals" to adjust cash payments to reflect the resource flows and to match expenses to time periods. If the company has incurred an expense, but not yet paid for it, add the accrued expense to the payments. If the company has paid for an expense, but not yet used it up, deduct the prepaid amount from the payments.

3.3.3   *Amortization (Depreciation)*

When a long-term asset, such as a piece of machinery, is bought, the historical cost principle implies that no expense has yet occurred. The asset cash has been exchanged for the asset machinery, both having equal value. Over time, the machine will be used in the operations of the business. Eventually, it will become worn out and worthless. Although the asset

---

Focus Box 3.7:   **Payments in Advance**
— Allan's Advertising Inc.

On September 1, 2005, Allan's Advertising Inc. agreed to rent an office for $2,400 per month. The agreement was for five years, with first and last month's rent due on September 1, 2005.

Payments were made as follows in 2005:

September 1	$ 4,800	(first and last month's rent)
October 1	2,400	
November 1	2,400	
December 1	2,400	
Total paid	$12,000	

Rent expense for 2005 should be reported as $9,600 (4 months × $2,400). The remaining $2,400 should be shown on the balance sheet as the asset "rent paid in advance".

---

is long-term, its life is not infinite. Over the span of its useful life, it is necessary that the cost be written off as expense in some orderly fashion. This process is called amortization or depreciation. (Some years ago the Canadian Institute of Chartered Accountants decided that the term *amortization* would be the exclusive term for this concept. Despite this, many organizations continue to use the term *depreciation*.) The most straightforward way to calculate amortization is to assume that the net cost is to be written off in equal annual instalments. Any anticipated salvage or sale value will be deducted from the cost, and the balance divided by the number of years the asset is expected to be in operation, to arrive at the annual expense.

Suppose Harry's Haulage Ltd. buys a truck for $100,000. (See Focus Box 3.8.) On day one, they have exchanged an asset (cash) worth $100,000 for another asset (the truck), also worth $100,000.

This transaction creates neither revenue nor expense. As time goes by, the asset truck will be used up, and the $100,000, eventually, will all become expense. Amortization will allocate the $100,000 to the periods to which it should be matched.

Suppose the company intends to use the truck for four years and then sell it for $24,000. The amount that has to be amortized is $76,000 ($100,000 – $24,000). This will be spread over the four years as a $19,000 ($76,000 ÷ 4) amortization expense each year.

In the balance sheet, the truck will be reported as having a cost of $100,000. From that cost the accumulated amortization to date will be deducted. At the end of year one, the written-down value will be $81,000 ($100,000 – $19,000). At the end of year two, the written-down value will be $62,000 ($81,000 – $19,000). At the end of year three, the written-down

Focus Box 3.8:   Amortization — Harry's Haulage Ltd.

The amortization for Harry's Haulage Ltd.'s new truck, using straight-line amortization, is calculated as follows:

Initial cost	$100,000
Expected life	4 years
Expected terminal value	$24,000

The annual amortization is ($100,000 – $24,000) ÷ 4 = $19,000 per year.

Year	Amortized Expense	Accumulated Amortization	Written-Down Value
2005	$19,000	$19,000	$100,000 – $19,000 = $81,000
2006	$19,000	$38,000	$100,000 – $38,000 = $62,000
2007	$19,000	$57,000	$100,000 – $57,000 = $43,000
2008	$19,000	$76,000	$100,000 – $76,000 = $24,000

Over four years, $76,000 of expired cost is written off as amortization expense, with the expectation that the truck will be sold at the end of 2005 for $24,000.

value will be $43,000 ($62,000 – $19,000). At the end of year four, the written-down value will be $24,000 ($43,000 – $19,000). At this point the company could do a number of things.

The truck could be sold for $24,000, as per the original plan. If that is the case, the $24,000 realized will be an exact match for the written-down value, and there will be no effect on the income statement.

Quite possibly, the truck could be sold for a higher amount, say, $40,000. This will result in a gain on sale of $16,000. Or, the truck could be sold for less than $24,000, say, $20,000 and result in a loss on the sale of $4,000. Gains and losses have to be brought into the income statement as revenues and expenses, respectively; but, in reality, they are an admission that the original amortization estimate was incorrect.

Other amortization models also exist. Declining balance amortization applies a constant percentage rate to each year's written-down value. The effect is a higher amortization charge in the earlier years of the asset's life, and lower rates in later years. Suppose this truck were to be amortized using a rate of 30% on the declining balance. The amortization expense would be different from the previous example. It would be $30,000 in year one (30% of $100,000), $21,000 in year two (30% of $70,000), $14,700 in year three (30% of $49,000), and $10,300 in year four (30% of $34,300) with numbers rounded to the nearest hundred dollars. By the end of year four, the written-down value has become $24,000, as before.

The truck could also be amortized on the basis of use. If it is assumed that the truck will run 500,000 km over its life, then the rate of $0.152 per km could be charged as amortization. ($0.152 is the $76,000 net cost divided by 500,000 km.) The effect would be to charge amortization expense according to how heavily the truck was used each year.

3.3.4 *Bad Debt Expense*

When sales are made on credit, there is some uncertainty as to whether or not the customers will pay. Most customers pay (eventually), but some turn into bad debts. When looking at revenue recognition (section 3.2), we made it clear that the sales should be recognized when the legal title of the goods is passed to the customer. Good matching requires that we recognize an estimated amount of bad debt expense related to those sales in the same year that the sales are recognized.

The bad debt expense will be an estimate relating to future events, of which the precise details are unknown. (See Focus Box 3.9.) Past history is often a good guide to the amount of bad debt expense that would be prudent to recognize. Suppose the bad debts have worked out to be between 2% and 3% of all unpaid accounts each year for the past 10 years. Recognition of bad debt expense in the amount of 3% of the current year's accounts receivable would be prudent and reasonable. We do that by creating a bad debt expense of 3% of the accounts receivable and a matching allowance for doubtful debts.

There is a difference between the bad debt expense and most other expenses. The majority of expenses are identified because there is a transaction involved, normally, a payment for the expense. This transaction is then adjusted through the accruals process to represent the actual resource flow that should be recognized as expense. In the case of the bad debt expense, there is no transaction. We create the expense without any payment being involved. To recognize an expense in the absence of a payment requires that we create an allowance for doubtful debts on the balance sheet. The allowance for doubtful debts is a *contra-asset account* and is deducted from the accounts receivable to which it refers. By doing this, it reduces the accounts receivable to their net realizable value.

In the next accounting period, when the actual bad debts come to light, they can be written off by deducting them from the bad debt provision. This means that we can adjust the accounts receivable to accommodate the actual bad debts discovered, without making any additional expenses in the income statement of the "current" year. This is good matching.

3.4 Operating Income

Operating expenses are deducted from revenues to reveal the operating income of the organization. Operating income is a measure of how well the organization did in its chosen line of business. The operating manager is held responsible for this figure. Operating income is monitored through the use of ratios.

Focus Box 3.9: Bad Debts Expense and Bad Debt Provision — Mike's Motor Repair Shop

It is December 31, 2005, and Mike's Motor Repair Shop is preparing its annual financial statements for its first year of operation. Mike has made a list of the money owed to him by customers. There are 125 customers on the list, and the total amount of the outstanding invoices is $27,000. Looking down the list he can identify three problem customers, whose accounts total $2,000. One has gone bankrupt, one has skipped town, the third has complained that the work has not been done properly and has refused to pay. In addition to these, Mike thinks it would be prudent to assign 2% of the remaining receivables as an allowance for doubtful debts.

2005 Income Statement

Bad Debt Expense:	
3 customers whose accounts are specifically identified as bad debts	$ 2,000
2% on the balance of receivables [2% × ($27,000 – $2,000)]	500
Bad debt expense for 2005 (as per income statement)	$ 2,500

2005 Balance Sheet

Receivables:	
Accounts receivable (net of the $2,000 of specific bad debts written off)	$25,000
Less: Allowance for doubtful debts	500
Net realizable value	$24,500

At the end of January 2006, Mike's accounts receivable amounts to $30,000. Two customers have defaulted upon their obligations and failed to pay for work, amounting to $400, that was done in 2005. This $400 can be taken away from the allowance for doubtful debts without further recourse to the income statement, or the balance sheet.

January 31, 2006:	
Accounts receivable, prior to recognizing bad debts	$30,000
Less: Allowance for doubtful debts (no change from December 31, 2005)	500
Net realizable value	$29,500

The $400 of identified bad debts is then removed from both the receivables and the provision.

January 31, 2006:	
Accounts receivable, after recognizing bad debts ($30,000 – $400)	$29,600
Less: Allowance for doubtful debts ($500 – $400)	100
Net realizable value	$29,500

As can be seen, the net realizable value is the same ($29,500) in both cases.

3.4.1   Gross Profit Ratio (or Gross Profit to Sales Ratio)

The gross profit ratio, or gross margin %, is the gross profit (revenues less cost of goods sold) expressed as a percentage of the revenues. So, if a company (say, Shugamai's Styles Inc. in Exhibit 3.1) has revenues of $1 million and gross profit of $500,000, it has a 50% gross profit ratio. In managing retail outlets, this is a critical control number and is carefully checked against expectations and against what the competition is earning.

3.4.2   Return on Sales Ratio (or Operating Profit to Sales Ratio)

The return on sales ratio is the operating profit (revenues less both cost of goods sold and operating expenses) expressed as a percentage of the revenues. So, if Shugamai's Styles Inc. has revenues of $1 million and operating profit of $100,000, its return on sales ratio is 10%. This is a useful measure of overall performance for virtually every company.

3.4.3   Return on Assets Ratio

To get a sense of how much the operating profit is in relation to the assets employed, we calculate the return on assets ratio. This is the operating income divided by the operating assets (frequently taken to be the total assets). So, if a company has operating income of $100,000 and total assets of $500,000, it has earned a 20% return on assets. (See Exhibit 3.1.)

3.5   Net Income

Financing charges, such as interest expense, are deducted from the operating income, as are income taxes. The result is the net income of the company. If Shugamai's has sales of $1 million, operating income of $100,000, interest expense of $25,000, and income taxes of $40,000, its net income is $35,000.

3.5.1   Net Income to Sales Ratio

To understand how much of each sale's dollars remains as income, we can calculate the ratio of net income to sales.

$35,000 ÷ $1,000,000 = 3.5%.

3.5.2   Return on Equity Ratio (or Return on Shareholders' Equity Ratio)

Net income can be compared with the owners' equity to give the return on shareholders' equity ratio. Suppose that the total liabilities and equity equals $500,000, and the liabilities are $300,000. Owners' equity is then $200,000, and the ratio of net income to owners' equity is $35,000 ÷ $200,000, which is 17.5%.

Exhibit 3.1: Profitability Ratios

Shugamai's Styles Inc.
Income Statement December 31, 2005

Sales revenue	$1,000,000
Cost of goods sold	500,000
Gross profit	$ 500,000
Expenses	400,000
Operating profit	$ 100,000
Interest and tax expenses	65,000
Net income	$ 35,000

Shugamai's Styles Inc.
Balance Sheet as at December 31, 2005

Current assets			Liabilities	
Cash		$ 20,000	Trade payables	$100,000
Accounts receivable		75,000	Long-term liabilities	200,000
Inventory		105,000		$300,000
		$200,000		
Long-term assets				
At cost	$650,000			
Accumulated amortization	350,000			
		300,000	**Shareholders' equity**	200,000
		$500,000		$500,000

Gross profit to sales ratio:

= (gross profit ÷ sales) × 100%
= ($500,000 ÷ $1,000,000) × 100%
= 50%

Operating profit to sales ratio (return on sales ratio):

= (operating profit ÷ sales) × 100%
= ($100,000 ÷ $1,000,000) × 100%
= 10%

Return on assets ratio:

= (operating profit ÷ total assets) × 100%
= ($100,000 ÷ $500,000) × 100%
= 20%

Net income to sales ratio:

= (net income ÷ sales) × 100%
= ($35,000 ÷ $1,000,000) × 100%
= 3.5%

Return on shareholders' equity ratio:

= (net income ÷ shareholders' equity) × 100%
= ($35,000 ÷ $200,000) × 100%
= 17.5%

3.6   Retained Earnings

Retained earnings is a classification that appears on the balance sheet as part of owners' equity. It is a recognition that net income has been made, but that the net income has not been paid out to its ultimate owners: the shareholders. If nothing were ever given to the shareholders, then retained earnings would be the accumulated net income of the company from its inception to date. Conversely, if all the net income is paid to shareholders as dividends each year, then retained earnings will be zero.

The most common situation is that neither of the above happens. The amount paid as dividends is most likely to be some of the net income, but not all of it. The directors like to give shareholders back something on their investment, but prudence dictates that they not give it all. As a result, the category Retained Earnings on the balance sheet tends to get larger each year.

3.6.1   *Statement of Retained Earnings*

The statement of retained earnings is a required report for companies. It picks up the opening balance of retained earnings in the balance sheet at the start of a year and adds in the net income for the year. It then deducts dividends paid and any other transactions that reduce retained earnings. The remaining balance is the retained earnings at the end of the year.

One of the features of laying out the statement in this style is that the amount of dividend that is legally possible is highlighted. Companies may only pay dividends out of net income (i.e., current net income), or retained earnings (accumulated undistributed net income). The intermediate total of $355,000 for XYZ in Focus Box 3.10 is the maximum amount legally distributable as dividend. Other considerations, such as cash availability and the need for investment funds, generally mean that the dividend payout is substantially less than the maximum that is legally distributable.

The relationship of the dividend to the net income for the period may be expressed as a dividend payout ratio (i.e., dividend ÷ net income). A company that paid a dividend of $250,000 out of current earnings of $500,000 is said to have a payout ratio of 50%.

There are some other transactions that are reported in the statement of retained earnings, mostly concerned with the ramifications of issuing or retiring shares, but these are rarer and not usually of prime importance.

There are a number of permissible layouts to this statement. In some presentations the statement is separate. Many companies tack it onto the end of the income statement, so that it is presented as a seamless continuum. Exhibit 3.2, showing the income statement and statement of retained earnings for Canadian Tire, does exactly that. In this example, you will also notice the statement is used to report the effect of changing the company's accounting standards, and the repurchase of some shares.

Focus Box 3.10: Statement of Retained Earnings and Dividend Payout Ratio

On the balance sheet of XYZ Inc. the accumulated retained earnings from earlier years, as at December 31, 2004, was $220,000. During 2005, the net income was $135,000. A cash dividend of $100,000 was paid. At the end of 2005, the retained earnings were $255,000. The statement of retained earnings would report that information as follows:

XYZ Inc.
Statement of Retained Earnings
for the Year Ended December 31, 2005

Retained earnings as at December 31, 2004	$220,000
Add: Net income for the year	135,000
	$355,000
Less: Dividend paid	100,000
Retained earnings as at December 31, 2005	$255,000

Dividend payout ratio:
= (dividend ÷ net income) × 100%
= ($100,000 ÷ $135,000) × 100%
= 74%

Exhibit 3.2: Income Statement and Statement of Retained Earnings — Canadian Tire

Canadian Tire
Statement of Earnings and Retained Earnings for 2005
($ million)

Gross operating revenue	$7,774
Less: Operating expenses and interest	7,254
Operating income (after interest, before taxes)	$ 520
Less: Income taxes	190
Net income	$ 330
Add: Retained earnings at start of year	1,547
	$1,877
Less: Cost of repurchase of shares	(17)
Dividends paid	(47)
Retained earnings at end of year	$1,813

Focus Box 3.11: Earnings Per Share

Jones Co. had earnings of $6 million in 2005. There were 500,000 shares in issue at December 12, 2005. There is a $100,000, 6% debenture that could be converted into 200,000 common shares.

Earnings per share:

= net income ÷ number of shares in issue
= $6,000,000 ÷ 500,000
= $12 per share

Fully diluted earnings per share:

= (net income + interest saved on conversion)
  ÷ (number of shares potentially in issue)
= ($6,000,000 + $6,000) ÷ (500,000 + 200,000)
= $8.58 per share

3.7 Earnings Per Share

At the end of either the income statement or the statement of retained earnings, most companies will also report a calculation of earnings per share (EPS). This is a statistic widely used by analysts when they attempt to value shares. The proposition is that a share's intrinsic value is the earnings the company makes on behalf of that share. The greater the number of shares in existence (for a given amount of net income), the less each one is worth.

A company that reports a net income of $5 million and has 500,000 common shares in issue will report an EPS of $10 ($5,000,000 ÷ 500,000). Even though the earnings may not be paid out as dividend, it is assumed that ploughing the profits back into the company will have beneficial long-term growth effects and will, eventually, result in larger dividends being paid to shareholders.

Many new companies reward their employees with the issue of shares, or options to buy shares, instead of cash. Issuing shares dilutes the EPS for all shareholders. The existence of obligations to issue new shares at some future date will also reduce the EPS. To ensure full disclosure, a "fully diluted" EPS is reported, as well as the basic EPS. This is the EPS that would exist if all the extra shares were issued. (See Focus Box 3.11.)

3.8 Summary

The income statement summarizes all the operating revenues and expenses to show the operating income. From that, interest and taxes are deducted to calculate the net income. Revenues, expenses, and time periods are matched with one another through the use of accruals.

Appendix 3.1
Example of
an Income Statement

Wendy's International, Inc. is famous not only in respect of the Wendy's hamburger chain; the company also owns Tim Horton's, which operates mainly in Canada. The income statements produced below were prepared from information on page 25 of the company's "10-K" report, which has to be filed under U.S. law. The complete report is available on the Wendy's International Web site: **www.wendys.com** or at **www.wendys-invest. com/fin/10k/wen10k05.pdf**

Wendy's International, Inc. and Subsidiaries
Consolidated Statements of Income
($ million)

		Year Ended		
		January 1, 2006		**January 2, 2005**
Revenues:				
Retail Sales		$3,028		$2,936
Franchise revenues		755		700
Total revenues		$3,783		$3,636
Costs and expenses:				
Cost of sales	$2,004		$1,900	
Restaurant operating costs	682		669	
Operating costs	172		168	
Administrative expenses	322		284	
Amortization	200		178	
Other expenses	26	3,406	210	3,409
Earnings before interest and tax (operating income)		$ 377		$ 227
Interest expense		39		43
Earnings before tax		$ 338		$ 184
Income taxes		113		132
Net income		$ 225		$ 52
Earnings per share (basic)		$1.95		$0.46
Earnings per share (diluted)		$1.92		$0.45
Dividends per share		$0.58		$0.48

Appendix 3.2
Methods of Amortization

There is more than one pattern of amortization expense. In this appendix, we shall discuss the three commonly used models: the straight-line amortization method, the declining balance method, and the units of production method.

It should be recognized that the management of a company has some choice here. GAAP requires the cost of long-term assets to be amortized over the life of the asset, but GAAP does not specify what amortization model must be used. Therefore, managers can elect to use any rational amortization policy. Of course, once they have made that selection, they are expected to stick with it, so that the financial statements are comparable. They are also expected to disclose the amortization policies and rates, so that users can judge the effects of this policy choice.

The Straight-line Amortization Method

In the straight-line model the cost (net of any expected salvage or disposal value) is divided by the expected life of the asset to give an equal annual amortization instalment.

= (cost – disposal) ÷ number of years
= annual amortization expense

Example: Acto purchased a new filling machine on January 1, 2003, for $100,000. They expected to use it for five years and then sell it for $8,000.

Straight-line amortization:

= ($100,000 – $8,000) ÷ 5 years
= $18,400 per year

Total amortization expense over five years:

= $18,400 × 5
= $92,000

Declining Amortization Balance Method

Under the declining balance amortization method, the annual amortization amount is a percentage of the asset's written-down value as at the beginning of the year. Because the percentage is being applied to a steadily reducing amount, the amortization expense is less each year. To get to a similar end point as the straight-line method, declining balance amortization has to start with a higher amortization expense, and the annual expense becomes less and less toward the end of the asset's life.

> **Example:** If Acto used the declining balance amortization method on the new filling machine it purchased for $100,000 on January 1, 2003, and they still expected to use it for five years and then sell it for $8,000, the amortization would be calculated as follows:

Declining balance amortization @ 40% per annum:

Cost on January 1, 2003	$100,000
Amortization 2003: 40% × $100,000	40,000
Written-down value as at December 31, 2003	$ 60,000
Amortization 2004: 40% × $60,000	24,000
Written-down value as at December 31, 2004	$ 36,000
Amortization 2005: 40% × $36,000	14,400
Written-down value as at December 31, 2005	$ 21,600
Amortization 2006: 40% × $21,600	8,640
Written-down value as at December 31, 2006	$ 12,960
Amortization 2007: 40% × $12,960	5,184
Written-down value as at December 31, 2007	$ 7,776*

* (which is approximately equal to $8,000)

An advantage of declining balance amortization is that it sometimes represents a better matching of the decline in an asset's value than the straight-line method. Also, it is a better match with Canada Revenue Agency's (CRA) ideas on amortization (for a note on this topic, see Appendix 3.3 to this chapter).

The disadvantage is that it is a little more complex to calculate and that you get a different amortization expense each year, so it is untidy.

In general, to achieve a similar total amortization effect over the life of the asset, a declining balance amortization rate has to be about twice the straight-line amortization rate. In the example above, the straight-line rate is 20% (1 ÷ 5 years = 20%), while the declining balance rate is 40%.

Units of Production Amortization Method

The units of production method of amortization is intended for those assets where a measurement of the amount of work produced is possible. This would include motor vehicles (measured by kilometres travelled), production machines (measured by hours run or tonnes processed), mines and gravel pits (measured by tonnes extracted), woodlots (measured by board feet of lumber won). In the units of production method, an attempt is made to exactly match the expense with the activity.

The total activity over the life of the asset is estimated. This is used to divide the cost to give a rate per unit. Each year, the number of units processed is multiplied by the rate to get the amortization expense.

Example: Assume Acto's newly purchased, $100,000 filling machine is expected to fill 92 million bottles over its five-year life, and will have a resale value of $8,000. The amortization expense, using the units of production method, will be calculated as follows:

Amortization rate:

= $92,000 ÷ 92,000,000 fills
= $0.001 per fill

Actual usage of the filling machine and related amortization expense is:

2003	25 million fills	$ 25,000
2004	25 million fills	25,000
2005	20 million fills	20,000
2006	15 million fills	15,000
2007	7 million fills	7,000
Total amortization over five years:		$ 92,000

Purchase of Machine on January 1, 2003	$100,000
Amortization 2003: 25 million fills × $0.01	25,000
Written-down value as at December 31, 2003	$ 75,000
Amortization 2004: 25 million fills × $0.01	25,000
Written-down value as at December 31, 2004	$ 50,000
Amortization 2005: 20 million fills × $0.01	20,000
Written-down value as at December 31, 2005	$ 30,000
Amortization 2006: 15 million fills × $0.01	15,000
Written-down value as at December 31, 2006	$ 15,000
Amortization 2007: 7 million fills × $0.01	7,000
Written-down value as at December 31, 2007	$ 8,000

Summary

Each of these three amortization methods results in the same or similar total amortization expense ($92,000) being charged over the five-year life of the asset. The overall effect in the long term is, therefore, immaterial. However, the different methods do report different operating profits year by year. The difference lies in the allocation of expense to different years. In general, the three methods can be characterized as follows:

• The straight-line method is most straightforward.
• The declining balance method writes off the expense sooner, so it is more conservative. (It defers income to the later years of the asset's life.)
• The units of production method is most precise.

Appendix 3.3
Capital Cost Allowances and Deferred Taxes

Companies pay taxes on their income. Under GAAP, the reported tax expense is the tax that would be due if the company paid tax on its reported profit. If the reported net income were precisely the same as the taxable income, there would be a neat matching of the actual tax paid and the tax expense. However, such neatness rarely happens. In general, the amount on which a company is assessed for taxes is different from the amount of its reported net income.

There are two broad classes of difference: permanent differences and timing differences. A permanent difference is the result of some rule that says an amount reported as income or expense in the income statement is not subject to tax (or, in the case of an expense, not allowable against tax). Permanent differences result in a change in the tax expense compared to that based on the current year's income.

A timing difference, on the other hand, is an item that is shown in the income statement in one year, but that will be assessed or allowed for tax in a later year.

One of the principal timing differences is the treatment of amortization. Because amortization rates (what percentage is used) and amortization models (the choice between straight-line and declining balance methods, for example) are both within the choice of management, the CRA rejects such amortization expense reporting by the company and replaces it with its own version, which is referred to as CCAs, or capital cost allowances.

CCAs are a set of allowances at prescribed rates that companies are allowed to charge in lieu of amortization. They are mostly declining balance rates, though a few are based on the straight-line method.

Some sample CCA rates are:

100%: Class 12 — miscellaneous tools or utensils costing less than $200;
 30%: Class 10 — automotive equipment and data processing equipment;
 25%: Class 9 — electrical generating equipment;
 20%: Class 8 — machinery and equipment not elsewhere described; and
  4%: Class 1 — buildings (straight-line).

So, when a company is being assessed to taxes, the amortization expense is eliminated from the income statement and replaced by the CCAs.

The effect of this (and other adjustments to the taxable income) is that the tax paid is no longer the same as the tax expense as calculated according to GAAP. Companies go to considerable pains to ensure that they do not pay any more taxes than they have to, and that they pay those they have to as late as possible. They will actively manage their affairs so as to first reduce the tax payable, and where that is not possible, defer the tax payable to a later date. It is therefore likely that the GAAP-based tax expense will be higher than the tax actually paid in any given year.

The difference between the tax expense and the actual tax paid is referred to as deferred tax. It is tax that is not due at the time of the balance sheet, but that may, eventually, become due at some unspecified later date. We use the words "may become due" because it is by no means certain that the tax will ever be paid. This, in turn, has led to a degree of controversy over how deferred taxes should be reported.

On the one hand, there are those who say that deferred taxes are a liability, of which the timing may be uncertain, and even remote, but from which there is no escape. They would, therefore, have deferred taxes reported on the balance sheet as a liability: probably in the long-term liabilities section. This is the treatment required by the Canadian GAAP.

On the other hand, there are those who say that the historical evidence is that most companies have put off paying these deferred taxes indefinitely, and they are likely to continue to do so. If this is true, the logical way of reporting deferred taxes is to treat them as part of equity. They may have to have some special treatment within equity to show that they are not distributable (and cannot be paid out as dividends to shareholders), but they are not liabilities because they are so unlikely ever to be paid as tax.

Let's say Energen Inc. has reported earnings of $108,000, and its basic tax rate is 35%. Included in the reported income are the following:

- $10,000 of dividends received from Canadian companies that are tax-exempt
- $2,000 of hospitality expense that is not tax-allowable
- $30,000 of amortization expense

You are also told that the total CCAs claimable are $50,000.

Reported earnings	$108,000	
Less: Non-taxable income	(10,000)	These are permanent
Add: Non-allowable expense	2,000	differences
Reported income for tax expense	$100,000	
Tax expense (35%)	$ 35,000	

Reported income for tax assessment	$100,000	
Add: Amortization expense	30,000	These are temporary
	$130,000	differences
Less: CCAs	(50,000)	
Taxable income	$ 80,000	
Tax payable (35%)	$ 28,000	

On the balance sheet, this would be reported as:

Current liability: tax payable	$ 28,000
Long-term liability: deferred taxes	7,000
Tax expense for the year	$ 35,000

Appendix 3.4
Example of a Statement
of Retained Earnings

Wendy's International, Inc. is not only famous in respect of the Wendy's hamburger chain, they also own Tim Horton's, which operates mainly in Canada.

The statement of retained earnings reproduced below was prepared from information on page 30 of the company's "10-K" report, which has to be filed under U.S. law. The complete report is available on the Wendy's International Web site: **www.wendys.com**

Wendy's International, Inc. and Subsidiaries
Consolidated Statements of Retained Income ($ million)

	Years Ended	
	January 1, 2006	January 2, 2005
Beginning balance	$1,701	$1,704
Net income	224	52
Dividends paid	(66)	(55)
Closing balance	$1,859	$1,701

Appendix 3.5
The Mechanics of Accounting:
The Income Statement

In this appendix we present an introduction to accounting for operating transactions: the debits and credits of revenue and expense. In addition to the basic journal entries to record revenue and expense, this appendix will cover such issues as accounting for deferred revenue, inventory, accruals and deferrals, amortization, and bad debt expense. The treatment emphasizes the linkage between adjustments to revenue and expense on the income statement and changes in the balance sheet accounts.

Revenue

Basic Revenue and Expense

The basic revenue and related transactions are illustrated in Focus Box 3.1: Revenue Recognition — Fred's Fabrics Inc. The transactions described involve cash and credit sales, cost of goods sold, and bad debt expense. We show the entries for the sales and cost of goods sold here and defer the discussion of bad debt expense to later in this appendix.

We saw cash and credit sales transactions in Appendix 2.1, but we repeat them here as a review. We will also take this opportunity to formalize the writing of journal entries. There will be a box for each entry or set of entries with column headings Date, Accounts/Description, Dr, and Cr. (See Table 3A.1.) Each new transaction will be indicated by a date in the first column. In the second column will be the names of the accounts affected — accounts to be debited will be left-aligned, accounts to be credited, indented. In the third column is the dollar amount of debit entries; in the fourth column, the dollar amount of credit entries.

Usually, there is only one debit line in a journal entry, but if there are any more accounts to be debited in the entry these will be written in the same manner immediately following the first debit line. Credit lines follow the debit lines, the account name indented in the second column, followed by the dollar amount in column four. Usually, there is only one credit line in an journal entry, but if there are more credit lines, these will be written immediately after the first credit line. The last line of the entry is the description, left aligned in column two. We will continue to label the accounts by their nature, such as {asset}, {SE — revenue} though it should be remembered that this is a pedagogical device only; these labels are not used in regular journal entries.

If there is a series of entries written together, a space followed by a date indicates a new entry.

The entries for sales and cost of goods sold are as follows in Table 3A.1.

Table 3A.1

Date	Accounts/Description	Dr	Cr
① Dec. 31/0X	Cash {asset}	60,000	
	Sales Revenue {SE — revenue}		60,000
	December cash sales		
② Dec. 31/0X	Accounts Receivable {asset}	15,000	
	Sales Revenue {SE — revenue}		15,000
	Credit sales in December		
③ Dec. 31/0X	Cost of Goods Sold {SE — expense}	50,000	
	Inventory {asset}		50,000
	Cost of goods sold in December		

We will comment on the three transactions in Table 3A.1 and then post them to the ledger accounts.

1. A revenue transaction always has the same form. The debit indicates the resource flow: this can be an increase in an asset (usually cash or accounts receivable) or a decrease in a liability. The credit is to a revenue account: this indicates that this particular resource flow is an increase to owner's equity from operations.

2. The credit to the revenue account does not distinguish between cash sales and credit sales. Under normal circumstances, a sale "on credit" is concluded only after the seller has satisfied itself that payment will be received as promised. This is one of the tests of realization, the basis for calling a transaction "revenue". Once it is decided that the transaction is revenue, no distinction is made in the revenue account; credit and cash sales are treated identically. Of course, the cash or credit nature of the transaction is recorded in the journal entry, and that might even be copied into the ledger, but when the entries to Sales Revenue are totalled, there is one combined total for cash and credit sales and this is what is reported as sales for the period. No doubt some credit sales will not be collected, but there is a separate procedure to account for expected bad debts. We will examine this at the end of this appendix.

3. There are a number of ways of recording cost of goods sold. Depending on the system used, either the cost of goods sold is measured directly, or it is arrived at indirectly by adjusting the carrying cost of inventory to the actual value. In either case, the entry is as follows: debit Cost of Goods Sold, credit Inventory. We will look more closely at the different methods used below.

Now we can post these entries to the accounts. This step is identical to what we did in Appendix 2.1 of Chapter 2 except that now, in the interests of simplicity, we show only the accounts that are affected by the entries being made. For these three journal entries, five different ledger accounts are affected. They are Cash, Accounts Receivable, Inventory, Sales Revenue, and Cost of Goods Sold. Because only a selection of ledger accounts are shown, there is no need to present them in spreadsheet form. Instead, we arrange them separately in a convenient order on the page. Since the accounts are now separate, we can simplify them, drawing only a top line under the account name and a centre line separating debits from credits. Drawn in this way, each one is called a **T-account**. A T-account is a simplified representation of a general ledger account. All T-accounts have the same form:

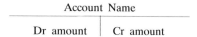

We can now lay out the five accounts affected by these three transactions on Table 3A.1 and post the entries:

Cash			Accounts Receivable			Inventory		
2005			**2005**			**2005**		
	X	X		X	X		X	X
① ∣	60,000		② ∣	15,000		∣ ③		50,000
	X	X		X	X		X	X
to B/S	**A** ∣		to B/S	**B** ∣		to B/S	**C** ∣	

Sales Revenue			Cost of Goods Sold		
2005			**2005**		
		X		X	
∣ ①		60,000	③ ∣	50,000	
∣ ②		15,000			
to I/S		**D**	to I/S	**E** ∣	

Xs have been added to represent other entries that have been or will be made to these accounts. In addition, we have indicated final account balances with bold letters: **A, B, C**, etc. These year-end balances, which incorporate the three entries we have made, will appear in the financial statements. The final balances in the asset accounts — Cash, $A; Accounts Receivable, $B; and Inventory, $C — appear on the balance sheet (B/S). They are not underlined because they are carried forward as the opening balance in the account in the next period. The final account balances in Sales Revenue, $D and Cost of Goods Sold, $E, show on the income statement (I/S). These balances are double-underlined to indicate that these accounts are closed at the end of the period and reopened with zero balances in the next period.

One point that must be emphasized is that because this is double-entry accounting, any change or correction of one number in the books will, in general, affect *both* the balance sheet and the income statement. If, for example, a customer draws to our attention an error in a sales invoice and we agree that he owes us $200 less, not only is Accounts Receivable on the balance sheet lower by that amount, but Sales Revenue in the period must also be $200 less. Similarly, if, after a review of the records, we realize that final inventory was not $C but instead $3,000 less (i.e., $C – $3,000), not only would the inventory figure on the balance sheet at the end of December be $3,000 lower, the Cost of

Goods Sold on the income statement would be $3,000 *higher* (and net income would be $3,000 lower). You should follow through the effect of revising the journal entries to satisfy yourself that all these changes would occur. We will see further examples of this phenomenon in the illustrations that follow.

Issues in Revenue Recognition

The journal entry for a revenue transaction is quite straightforward. It is always "debit asset (or liability), credit revenue". The problems that arise in accounting for revenue are not in the form of the transaction, but rather in knowing exactly *when* a resource flow that has some of the characteristics of a revenue transaction actually *becomes* a revenue transaction. We call this the question of *revenue recognition*. Consider, for example, Focus Box 3.2: Revenue Recognition — Peerless Publishers Inc. There are two issues illustrated here: one is how to account for books sold with a limited right to return unsold books; the other is the treatment of magazine subscriptions paid in advance. In both cases, there is a question of timing: how much revenue is recorded in this period and how much in the next. We will begin by examining the *principle of revenue recognition* and then show, in each case, how an examination of the transaction in the light of this principle helps us establish the correct accounting treatment.

The Principle of Revenue Recognition

A sale is made when a company and a potential buyer agree on the terms of the sale, the goods are delivered, and payment is made. To be more precise, the *earnings process* is considered to be complete when the following three criteria are satisfied:

1. There is an arm's length transaction defining the terms of the exchange.
2. The ordered goods are delivered to the buyer.
3. The seller receives the agreed amount of cash, an asset of equivalent value or an enforceable claim to cash or equivalent asset.

The first criterion means that we must have an agreement on the terms of the sale made at arm's length. There are two aspects to this — an agreement to complete the transaction and the notion of arm's length. An *agreement on terms* implies that both parties have concluded that they cannot do better under the circumstances and that they intend to carry out the transaction. *Arm's-length agreement* means that the two contracting parties are pursuing independent interests. The seller is trying to get the highest possible price; the buyer, to pay the lowest possible price. If the two parties are not independent — for example, a business owner selling to his wife or son, a company buying from its subsidiary — the agreement is not considered arm's length. The terms of a non-arm's-length agreement — the price, most notably — cannot be assumed to reflect the market value and cannot be relied upon as being fair.

The second and third criteria appear self-evident: the buyer must enjoy the benefit of the good or service and the seller has the benefit of the proceeds of the sale. Generally the situation itself is obvious: either the customer has the goods or he does not; he has paid or he has not. Sometimes, however, conditions on delivery or the nature of payment mean that it is not always clear that these two criteria are both satisfied. Not surprisingly, when questions arise about the validity of a company's revenue recognition policies, we typically find that an unorthodox interpretation of one or more of these criteria has been made.

But even aside from questions of interpretation, the fact that there are three independent criteria for the completion of the earnings process means that what appears to be a revenue transaction is not yet one because not all the criteria have been satisfied. There are of course many situations we are familiar with in which all three criteria are satisfied simultaneously. For example, a customer comes into a store, selects a product marked with a price, pays cash to the store owner, and leaves with her purchase. The earnings process is complete and the store recognizes the revenue for that particular transaction at that moment. This is true even if the customer pays with a debit card (cash is exchanged electronically rather than physically), or uses a credit card (through agreements both the customer and the merchant have made with the credit card issuer, the merchant has an enforceable claim for payment against the credit card issuer, which in turn has an enforceable claim for payment against the customer).

Although the simultaneous satisfaction of the three criteria defining the completion of the earnings process is common, it can happen that the three criteria are *not* all satisfied at the same time. When they aren't, there is a question as to when and how revenue is realized in the books of the seller. There are a number possibilities, each with its own recognition solution. We will examine two of them here. Consider first a customer who tells a merchant that he likes a particular household accessory but that he is not sure that it is the right colour for his room. The store owner tells him to pay for it, take it home, and try it; if it works, he keeps it; if not, he has a week to return the piece for a full refund, no questions asked. There is payment, there is delivery, but there is not a sale. The price is not an issue — it has been agreed upon and a payment made; the customer has the goods — there has been delivery. But all this is conditional: only when the customer agrees to keep the goods can revenue be realized by the seller. If the customer returns the product, his payment is returned. There was no sale and no revenue was realized.

The second possibility that we will examine is deferred delivery. A customer comes into the store in late December 2005, near the end of the store's financial year, and describes the product she wants. The store owner says that he can get it on special order. The customer agrees to pay the full price at the time of order to facilitate the transaction. She pays (cash, debit card, or credit card) and leaves with an invoice for goods "to be delivered in four to six weeks". It would be natural to speak of this as a sale. In all likelihood both the customer and store owner would see it this way as it is only a matter of time until the goods are delivered, the more so if it is agreed that the price is final. Still, from an accounting point of view, timing is an issue. The sale cannot be recognized in 2005 because the goods have not yet been delivered. Delivery is expected to be made in the next accounting period, but, regardless, the revenue will not be recognized until delivery is made. The situation is similar to the second Peerless Publishers example, which brings us back to Focus Box 3.2 on p. 81.

Returns

The right to return unsold merchandise is a particular feature of the book publishing business. Interest in books can be very short-lived. If a customer wants a particular book, she is generally not inclined to wait if it is sold out. She may get another book, she may go elsewhere, or she may just forget the idea entirely. To ensure that its newly published books will be available when customers are ready to buy, the publisher gives an incentive to booksellers to order more, rather than fewer, books by agreeing to take back a percentage of unsold books up to some months later. In this way the publisher and the bookseller share the risk of overstocking. Some books, of course, do sell out, others do not, but which ones do and which ones do not is unpredictable. As a rule, however, the publisher expects booksellers to take advantages of the 10% returns policy.

The objective of this accounting exercise is to ensure that sales revenue for the year is an accurate reflection of revenue transactions actually completed in 2005. Peerless Publishers has gross sales in 2005 of $6 million; this is the first entry. However, we know not all these sales will be completed. The next entries account for returned books.

Assume that books are not returned until the very end of the six-month return period. To make this example a little more realistic, assume also that the returns policy has been in effect for sales since January 1, 2005. (The example in Focus Box 3.2 implicitly assumes that the policy has been in effect only since July 1, 2005.) The new assumption explains the second entry on the following page — a transaction was not part of the discussion in Focus Box 3.2. This transaction records returns from sales made in the first six months of 2005. Books billed by Peerless at $300,000 (6 × $500,000 @ 10%) in this period would have to have been returned by the end of December 2005, and so this amount is debited to Sales Returns. Sales Returns is considered a (negative) revenue account rather than an expense account since the debits to this account represent a direct reduction or correction of revenue. An argument could be made to call this an expense account; the effect would be the same. The important thing is sales returns are treated as a reduction of gross revenue on the income statement. The credit in the second entry is to Accounts Receivable to reflect the reduction in the receivables from the bookstores that are returning the books.

The third entry is an adjusting journal entry, an accounting estimate for books expected to be returned out of shipments in the period July to December 2005. The debit is again to Sales Returns and the amount is again $300,000 since sales in the second half of the year were at the same level as in the first half. However, in this entry the credit is to a liability account since there have been no actual returns yet. The balance in the account Liability for Book Returns will appear in the liability section of the balance sheet dated December 31, 2005.

We can follow events through into the new year. Beginning January 2006, the returns for sales made after July 1 begin to be received. Again, for realism let's assume that Peerless's books were especially popular in the fall of 2005 and that our estimate of 10% returns was over-conservative. If only 8% of sales were actually returned, how do we deal with the 2%? As they are received, the customers' accounts will be credited (fourth entry, 2006 financial year). Since $300,000 worth of returns have been accounted for in the adjusting journal entry and matched to sales of 2005, the debits in entries recorded in 2006 reduce the liability. If books with a selling price totalling only $240,000 are returned (6 × $500,000 @ 8%), the liability is reduced to $60,000, not to zero. But if we know the rest of the books were sold and that there is no further liability, the account must be reduced to zero. We deal with this by debiting the Liability account by the full $300,000 and crediting the balance not represented by returns — $60,000 worth — to Sales Revenue in 2006. The $60,000 is in reality a correction of the estimate we made at the end of December 2005, but our books have been closed and the amount must be credited to 2006 sales. In general, GAAP requires that any correction of a previous year's revenue or expense estimate is credited (or debited, as the case may be) to the current year's revenue or expense. This is done to encourage accurate estimates and to minimize revisions of previously published financial results.

Date	Accounts/Description	Dr	Cr
① Jan.–Dec. 05	Accounts Receivable {asset}	6,000,000	
	Sales Revenue {SE — revenue}		6,000,000
	Gross book sales 2005		
② Jul.–Dec. 05	Sales Returns {SE — revenue}	300,000	
	Accounts Receivable {asset}		300,000
	Actual returns for book sales Jan.–Jun. 2005		
③ Dec. 31/05	Sales Returns {SE — revenue}	300,000	
	Liability for Book Returns {liability}		300,000
	AJE — estimates sales returns		
④ Jan.–Jun. 06	Liability for Book Returns {liability}	300,000	
	Accounts Receivable {asset}		240,000
	Sales Revenue {SE — revenue — 2006}		60,000
	Actual sales final returns re: 2005		

We will post these entries to the T-accounts and then show the relevant sections of the 2005 financial statements.

	Accounts Receivable				Liability for Book Return	
2005				**2005**		
	X	X			X	X
① | ②	6,000,000	300,000				300,000
	X	X		| ③		300,000
to B/S	XX			**to B/S**		300,000
2006				**2006**		
| ④		240,000		④ |	300,000	
	X	X				0

	Sales Revenue			Sales Return	
2005			**2005**		
| ①	6,000,000		② |	300,000	
			③ |	300,000	
to I/S	**6,000,000**		to I/S	**600,000**	
2006			**2006**		
| ④	60,000		X |		

Peerless Publisher's Inc.
Partial Income Statement
for year ended December 31, 2005

Sales Revenue	
Gross	$6,000,000
Less Sale Returns	600,000
Net	$5,400,000

Peerless Publisher's Inc.
Partial Balance Sheet
as at December 31, 2005

Current Liabilities	
Liabilities for Book Returns	$300,000

Deferred Delivery

Some goods or services are paid for when they are ordered, but delivery takes place over an extended period. Peerless's magazine subscriptions are a good example. Peerless sells $400,000 worth of subscriptions in 2005 but only half are delivered in this financial year. The revenue for half the issues must thus be postponed or *deferred*. The $200,000 for the magazines delivered in 2005 is credited to Sales Revenue in the year; the $200,000 received in 2005 for magazines to be delivered in 2006 is a liability at the end of 2005 (see the first journal entry below). Note that Deferred Revenue is not a revenue account but a liability account. The liability is the obligation to supply magazines to subscribers in 2006.

In 2006, as the magazines are published and delivered, the liability is reduced as the balance is effectively transferred to Sales Revenue in 2006 (see the second journal entry below).

Date	Accounts/Description	Dr	Cr
① Jan.–Dec. 05	Cash, Accounts Receivable {assets}	400,000	
	Sales Revenue {SE — revenue}		200,000
	Deferred Revenue {liability}		200,000
	Subscriptions received 2005		
② Jan.–Dec. 06	Deferred Revenue {liability}	200,000	
	Sales Revenue {SE — revenue — 2006}		200,000
	Prepaid subscriptions delivered 2006		

109

	Cash, Acc. Rec.			Deferred Revenue	
2005			**2005**		
	X	X		X	X
①	400,000			①	200,000
	X	X			
to B/S	XX		to B/S		**200,000**
2006			**2006**		
				②	200,000
	X	X			

	Sales Revenue	
2005		
	①	200,000
to I/S		**200,000**
2006		
	②	200,000

Expense

Cost of Goods Sold

In the past, keeping track of the day-to-day movements of inventory was only worthwhile if the individual items, such as cars or jewellery, were valuable enough. Now the use of bar coding and information technology make a *perpetual inventory system* advantageous for many merchandising operations. In such cases, the inventory account is adjusted for all movements of goods in and out of stock, and the goods sold expense is recorded for every sale.

A purchase of goods on account costing $5,000 on September 3, 2005, with a $300 delivery charge and 6% GST[1] would be recorded as follows:

Date	Accounts/Description	Dr	Cr
① Sep. 3/05	Inventory {asset}	5,300	
	GST Due {liability}*	318	
	Accounts payable {liability}		5,618
	Purchase X Co., invoice #1234		

* Whether GST Due is an asset or a liability depends on the balance. In principle, one might have one account for GST paid {asset} and another for GST due {liability}; but at period end, one will be netted against the other, and typically, the amount due will exceed the amount paid since the volume of sales normally exceeds purchases.

Notice that delivery is as much a part of the cost of the goods as is the invoice price. In practice, the invoice cost and the delivery charges

---

[1] On October 31, 2007, Finance Minister Jim Flaherty announced a further cut to the GST. Effective January 1, 2008, the GST will be 5%.

might be segregated in separate accounts for analysis purposes (Purchases, Transportation In), but by the end of the accounting period the balances of the delivery account would be transferred to the Inventory account. Note also that because of strict rules for accounting for GST and other sales taxes, GST (due or paid) would be segregated from trade payables and accounts receivable.

If half of this shipment were sold for $4,500 one week after it was purchased, in addition to the revenue transaction there would be an entry in a perpetual inventory system recognizing the cost of goods sold:

Date	Accounts/Description	Dr	Cr
② Sep. 10/05	Accounts Receivable {asset}	4,770	
	Sales Revenue {SE — revenue}		4,500
	GST Due {liability}		270
	Sale to AA Co., sales invoice #5678		
③ Sep. 10/05	Cost of Goods Sold {SE — expense}	2,650	
	Inventory {asset}		2,650
	COGS, sale to AA Co., sales invoice #5678		

The entries in the general ledger accounts affected would look like this:

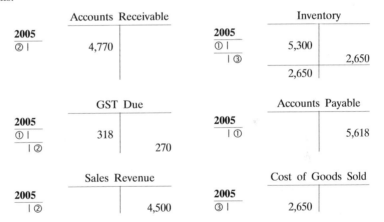

In the traditional *periodic inventory system*, costs (debits) still accumulate in the inventory account as purchases are made in exactly the same way they were recorded in the perpetual system (i.e., transactions #1). In all inventory systems, purchases are always accounted for as they are made. The receipt of an invoice will trigger the entry. In addition, the company wants to ensure that there is an accounting record to check against the receipt of the goods before payment is made.

The difference in accounting treatment in the periodic system is at the time of sale. In this case, only the sale is recorded (i.e., transaction #2). In other words, under the periodic system only the first two transactions would be recorded at the time they occurred. The cost of good sold would be recorded at the end of the accounting period (as is in fact developed on the following page).

We assume that the year-end is December 31. In a period inventory system there must be a physical count of inventory in the company's warehouse at the end each financial year. (Periodic physical inventory counts are usually taken in perpetual systems as well as a check on the record system, but they can be done at any time, not necessarily at year-end.) This physical count is then costed, item by item, taking account of other purchase costs, such as transportation-in cost, to arrive at the *cost of closing inventory*. (In this connection a flow of costs must be assumed — see Appendix 4.2.)

Let us assume that the cost of closing inventory on December 31, 2005, is $350,000. This same exercise would have been done at the previous year-end. Assume that the inventory cost then was $280,000. Satisfy yourself that this year's opening inventory must be the same as last year's closing inventory. Finally, assume that total inventory purchases in 2005 were $640,000. We do the following calculation to find Cost of Goods Sold:

Opening inventory	$280,000
Purchases	640,000
Cost of Goods Available for Sale	$920,000
Less: Closing inventory	350,000
Cost of Goods Sold	$570,000

An adjusting journal entry simultaneously records Cost of Goods Sold and reduces the Inventory account to the correct value.

Date	Accounts/Description	Dr	Cr
Dec. 31/05	Cost of Goods Sold {SE — expense}	570,000	
	Inventory {asset}		570,000
	AJE: Cost of Goods Sold		

We now post this entry to the general ledger. We have not shown the journal entries for purchases or sales. These would have been recorded on a day-by-day basis as they occurred throughout the year. We show only the summary entries to Cash & Accounts Receivable, Inventory, Accounts Payable, Sales Revenue, GST Due, and Cost of Goods Sold. Cash and Accounts Receivable are combined here for convenience, and GST Due represents the net of GST paid and GST collected as normally done in practice. (Sales Revenue, both cash and on account, is assumed to be $975,000 for 2005.) Recall that the opening balance in the Inventory account is not the result of an entry for that amount; it is simply the previous year-end Inventory Account balance brought forward.

Cash & Accounts Receivable			Inventory	
2005		**2005**		
975,000		Opening inventory	280,000	
		Purchases	640,000	
		AJE COGS		570,000
			350,000	

Accounts Payable			Sales Revenue		
2005			**2005**		
		640,000			975,000

Cost of Goods Sold			GST Due		
2005			**2005**		
	570,000			38,400	
					58,500

Note: GST Due includes GST paid (Purchases × GST % = $640,000 × .06 = $38,400) and GST collected (Sales × GST % = $975,000 × .06 = $58,500).

Inventory Allowances

Inventory records are kept on a cost basis. Normally, these same costs are the basis for the reporting of inventory on the balance sheet and cost of goods sold on the income statement. Occasionally, however, it happens that purchase prices fall by year-end, and the cost of replacing the inventory would be lower than the actual costs incurred. When this occurs, GAAP requires that the value of the inventory on the balance sheet be reduced to the replacement cost. (Note that *replacement cost* refers to the current market price at the year-end. It is not a question of whether the company has paid these lower prices for any of its inventory or even plans to do so. It is most likely, in fact, that most of the company's inventory was purchased at the older, higher costs. If all or most of its inventory had been purchased at the new, lower price, the question of replacement cost being less than the actual price would not arise.)

Focus Box 3.5 on p. 84 illustrates this situation. The journal entry helped explain why the "write-down" of inventory increases expense and reduces net income. If an asset account, Inventory, is overvalued, some of the asset — the *value* of the asset, to be precise — must have expired. And recall that "expired asset" is a definition of expense.

Date	Accounts/Description	Dr	Cr
Dec. 31/05	Cost of Goods Sold {SE — expense}	1,000	
	Inventory {asset}		1,000
	AJE: Reducing inventory to market price.		

Often the inventory records are left at cost — $0.40 a litre in this case — especially if the price decline is considered to be temporary. In such a situation, the adjustment to the Inventory is done by crediting an *allowance account* rather than reducing the Inventory account. This allowance, what is known as a "contra-asset" account, is deducted from the asset Inventory and only the net amount is reported on the balance sheet. The debit to Cost of Goods Sold is the same as in the previous journal entry. The financial statements will be the same in either case, the direct write-down or the allowance method. The difference is in the underlying records and particularly in the Inventory accounts. Allowance accounts are commonly used in accounting for bad debts as well — see following.

113

Date	Accounts/Description	Dr	Cr
Dec. 31/05	Cost of Goods Sold {SE — expense}	1,000	
	Allowance for Inventory Reduction {asset}		1,000
	AJE: Lower of cost and market price, allowance method		

Overhead Expenses

Cost of goods sold is a direct expense. The revenue is earned because goods are delivered to customers; the matching process starts with this physical transfer. As section 3.3.2 explains, in the case of overhead expenses there is no direct relationship between the use of the resources and the revenue: it is, rather, a case of matching the use of resources to the financial year. Typically, the accounting system will record the payments for the resources. Proper matching of expenses, however, requires that we look at the invoices to ensure that expense reflects the resources used in the period rather than the resources paid for in the period. This involves *accruing* expenses that have been incurred but not yet recorded and *deferring* expenses that have been paid but not yet used.

Accruals. The electricity example in Focus Box 3.6 is a typical accrual. We will show the journal entries, but the story is best understood by following the sequence of posting in the T-accounts.

The first entry is the accrual, entered as an adjusting journal entry on December 31, 2004, to correct the electricity expense for 2004. The accountant would find this information either by examining the invoice in January before she closed the books, or by telephoning Hydro to determine unbilled electricity usage to December 31, 2004. The second entry, a composite of entries made throughout 2005, records electricity invoices received in the year (excluding the $1,100 that we already recorded in the accrual of December 31, 2004). This entry includes the last invoice received, for usage up to December 15, 2005, which was still unpaid at year-end. Note that the debit is to 2005 electricity expense. We know that this is not the full expense for the year, but the year-end accrual, the final entry, will correct it. The third entry records electricity payments for the year, including the $1,100. The last entry is the 2005 accrual — the half a month's electricity usage from December 15 to December 31, 2005.

Date	Accounts/Description	Dr	Cr
Dec. 31/04	Electricity Expense [2004] {SE — expense}	1,100	
	Accounts Payable {liability}		1,100
	AJE: Electricity expense accrual		
Jan.–Dec. 05	Electricity Expense [2005] {SE — expense}	6,650	
	Accounts Payable {liability}		6,650
	Electricity invoices 2005 (net of 2004 accrual)		
Jan.–Dec. 05	Accounts Payable {liability}	6,800	
	Cash {asset}		6,800
	Cash payments to Hydro 2005		

Date	Accounts/Description	Dr	Cr
Dec. 31/05	Electricity Expense [2005] {SE — expense}	500	
	Accounts Payable {liability}		500
	AJE: Electricity expense accrual		

Cash

2004		
	X	X
to B/S	XX	
2005		
	X	X
2005 payments		6,800
to B/S	XX	

Accounts Payable

2004	X	X
2004 accrual		1,100
to B/S		**1,100**
2005		
2005 invoices (net of $1,100)		6,650
2005 payments	6,800	
2004 accrual		500
to B/S		**1,450**

Electricity Expense

2004	
2004 accrual	1,100
to B/S	**1,100**
2005	
2005 invoices	6,650
2004 accrual	500
to I/S 05	**7,150**

Deferrals. An accrual corrects expense by recognizing an expense that has not yet been recorded. A deferral has the opposite effect. It postpones (defers) to the next period a good or service that has been paid and charged (debited) to expense this period. (Revenues can also be accrued and deferred. We saw an example of deferred revenue in the case of Peerless Publishing.) The need for deferral usually arises because a payment, or part of a payment, is made in advance of the use of goods or services. The rent example in Focus Box 3.7 is a typical deferral. In addition to paying each month's rent at the beginning of that month, the lessee is required by the lease agreement to pay the last month's rent (in this case five year's hence) at the beginning of the lease. Because almost all the rent payments are expense in the period they are paid, the accountant adopts the policy of debiting the rent payments as expense. At December 31, 2005, she must remember, however, to defer the last month's rent that was paid in September. The deferral, an adjusting journal entry, debits the amount to an asset account, Rent Paid in Advance or Prepaid Rent, which is shown on the December 31, 2005, and successive balance sheets until 2009. It will be expensed in 2010 as the August rent. (There will be no rent payment that month.)

Date	Accounts/Description	Dr	Cr
Sep. 1/05	Rent Expense {SE — expense}	4,800	
	Cash {asset}		4,800
	Rent first and last months: Sep. 05 and Aug. 10		

Date	Accounts/Description	Dr	Cr
Oct. 1/05	Rent Expense {SE — expense}	2,400	
	Cash {asset}		2,400
	Rent October 2005		

[Similar entries recording rent payments are made Nov. 1 and Dec. 1, 2005.]

Dec. 31/05	Rent Paid in Advance {asset}	2,400	
	Rent Expense {SE — expense}		2,400
	To defer August 2010 rent paid in advance		

	Cash				Rent Paid in Advance	
2005				**2005**		
	X	X		2005 deferral	2,400	
Sep. payment		4,800		**to B/S**	**2,400**	
Oct. payment		2,400				
Nov. payment		2,400				
Dec. payment		2,400				
to B/S	**XX**					

	Rent Expense	
2005		
Sep. payment	4,800	
Oct. payment	2,400	
Nov. payment	2,400	
Dec. payment	2,400	
2005 deferral		2,400
to I/S	**9,600**	

Amortization

Amortization (sometimes called *depreciation*) is the process of expensing a long-term asset over its estimated useful life. In the example in section 3.3.3 and Focus Box 3.8, Harry's Haulage purchases a new truck early in 2005 for $100,000. The truck has an estimated useful life of four years and an expected salvage value of $24,000. The amortizable (or depreciable) cost is $76,000, which the company has decided to amortize on a straight-line basis. If the financial statements are prepared annually, an entry will be made at the end of each year to amortize 25% of the amortizable cost, which is $19,000. The first set of entries are written on the assumption that Harry's keeps the truck until the end of 2008, at which point it disposes of it at its net book value (the amortized cost of the truck on its books at that point — $24,000).

Date	Accounts/Description	Dr	Cr
Jan. 1/05	Truck {asset}	100,000	
	Cash {asset}		100,000
	Purchase of truck		

Date	Accounts/Description	Dr	Cr
Dec. 31/05	Amortization Expense {SE — expense}	19,000	
	Accumulated Amortization {asset}		19,000
	Amortization of truck 2005		

[Identical entries recording amortization are made on December 31, 2006, December 31, 2007, and December 31, 2008.]

Dec. 31/08	Cash {asset}	24,000	
	Accumulated Amortization {asset}	76,000	
	Truck {asset}		100,000
	Sale of truck at net book value		

Cash

2005	X	X
truck purchase		100,000
	X	X
2008		
truck sale	24,000	

Truck

2005		
truck purchase	100,000	
to B/S 2005	**100,000**	
2006		
to B/S 2006	**100,000**	
2007		
to B/S 2007	**100,000**	
2008		
truck sale		100,000
to B/S 2008	**0**	

Accumulated Amortization

2005		
amortization		19,000
to B/S 2005		**19,000**
2006		
amortization		19,000
to B/S 2006		**38,000**
2007		
amortization		19,000
to B/S 2007		**57,000**
2008		
amortization		19,000
truck sale	76,000	
to B/S 2008		**0**

Amortization Expense

2005		
amortization	19,000	
to I/S 2005	**19,000**	
2006		
amortization	19,000	
to I/S 2006	**19,000**	
2007		
amortization	19,000	
to I/S 2007	**19,000**	
2008		
amortization	19,000	
to I/S 2008	**19,000**	

Amortization expense of $19,000 is recorded each year. In essence, we are recognizing that the cost of the asset, truck, is expiring at that rate. Note, however, that the credit of $19,000 is not to the truck account itself but to the contra-asset account, Accumulated Amortization. The reason for not crediting the asset account itself is that readers of the financial statements want to know the scale of the long-term assets — remember, physically they are not disappearing; amortization simply allocates their cost to expense over their useful lives. On the balance sheet we see both the original cost of the truck as well as its net book value, as the following partial balance sheet at the end of 2007 shows:

Harry's Haulage Ltd.
Partial Balance Sheet
as at December 31, 2007

Long-term assets		
Truck, at cost	$100,000
Less accumulated amortization	57,000
Net book value	$ 43,000

In the example above we happened to sell the truck after four years at exactly its estimated salvage value. If we were able to sell it for $40,000, the final entry would read as follows:

Date	Accounts/Description	Dr	Cr
Dec. 31/08	Cash {asset}	40,000	
	Accumulated Amortization {asset}	76,000	
	Truck {asset}		100,000
	Gain of sale {SE — revenue}		16,000
	Sale of truck for $40,000		

The debit to Accumulated Amortization and the credit to the Truck account are unchanged — both these accounts must be brought to zero since the asset has been sold. Following GAAP, the difference between the proceeds and the net book value of the truck is treated as a gain on sale in 2008 even though, as pointed out in the chapter, in fact it represents a correction of the original estimated salvage value. You should satisfy yourself that if the truck were sold for $20,000, instead of the credit to the Gain of Sale account, there would be a debit to the expense account, Loss on Sale, of $4,000.

Bad Debt Expense

Companies offer credit terms to their customers because it is convenient for both parties to separate buying and selling from paying and collecting. As well, being able to buy on account is standard practice in many industries.

While no business would knowingly sell to a customer who cannot pay, at the same time experience tells us that some customers do default. Proper matching of expenses to sales requires that the loss be expensed in the period the sale was recognized. We do this using the "*allowance method*".

The allowance for bad debts, like any other accrual, involves a debit to expense matched by a credit to an asset (or to a liability). Accounts Receivable is the relevant asset in this case, but, as we saw in the accounting for Inventory, there are detailed records of receivables from individual customers that must agree with the balance in the general ledger account. Thus, apart from everyday transactions, such as the receipt of a payment from a customer, we should credit Accounts Receivable only if we "write off a particular account" — that is, declare it non-recoverable and remove it from the detailed list. This is the reason we use the allowance method for recognizing bad debts: it permits us to reduce the asset based on some statistical assessment of probable defaults without actually crediting the asset account itself.

We can illustrate this using the example of Mike's Motor Repair Shop in Focus Box 3.9. In this case, we see examples of both direct write-offs and of the allowance method. In 2005, his first year of operations, Mike identifies three accounts, let us say, Mr. A, Ms. B, and Mr. C, totalling $2,000, that are not worth pursuing for payment. In the first adjusting journal entry below, Mike writes off these three accounts from both Accounts Receivable and from his list of debtors. The debit is to bad debt expense.

However, Mike knows that it is likely that there will further uncollectible accounts among the $25,000 of receivables remaining. After discussing the matter with his accountant, he estimates that 2%, $500, is a reasonable allowance. This is the second adjusting journal entry. Again, the debit is to bad debt expense, but because no particular accounts have been identified as bad and no accounts are written off, the credit is to a contra-asset account, Allowance for Doubtful Debts (alternatively, Allowance for Doubtful Accounts).

Date	Accounts/Description	Dr	Cr
Dec. 31/05	Bad debt expense {SE — expense]	2,000	
	Accounts Receivable {asset}		2,000
	AJE: To write off as uncollectible the accounts of A, B, and C.		
Dec. 31/05	Bad debt expense {SE — expense]	500	
	Allowance for Doubtful Debts {asset}		500
	AJE: Bad debt expense 2005.		

These entries are posted to T-accounts on page 120. The effect on the income statement and the balance sheet can been seen in Focus Box 3.9 on page 89.

Now that we are using the allowance method to estimate bad debt expense, subsequent write-offs have no effect on the net value of accounts receivable, nor do they affect bad debt expense directly. We can confirm this by considering the treatment of two receivables that are deemed uncollectible in January 2006. Ms. D and Mr. E owed Mike's Repair Shop $400 for work done in 2005. It is clear to Mike that he will not collect this money, and he has decided to write off these two accounts. Since a general provision was made for such an eventuality, the write-off is against the contra-asset account, Allowance for Doubtful Debts. There is no effect on the net value of Accounts Receivable, and the Bad Debt Expense account is not involved.

Date	Accounts/Description	Dr	Cr
Jan. 30/06	Allowance for Doubtful Debts {asset}	400	
	Accounts Receivable {asset}		400
	AJE: To write off as uncollectible the accounts of D and E.		

Since Accounts Receivable and the contra-account, Allowance for Doubtful Debts, are both reduced by the same amount, net accounts receivable does not change. (See Focus Box 3.9.)

Although bad debt expense is not affected by this transaction, there is an indirect effect at year-end when the bad debt estimate is made by taking a percentage of the year-end accounts receivable, as Mike does. Assume that Mike's gross accounts receivable at the end of 2006 are $40,000. Assume also that he continues the practice of having his year-end allowance be 2% of receivables. The allowance must be $800; but since there is already a balance in the Allowance account, the entry, and the year's bad debt expense, is only $700.

Date	Accounts/Description	Dr	Cr
Dec. 31/06	Bad debt expense {SE — expense]	700	
	Allowance for Doubtful Debts {asset}		700
	AJE: Bad debt expense 2006.		

Indirectly, then, the write-off does affect the bad debt expense. Satisfy yourself that had we written off more than $400 in January, the debit to Bad Debt Expense at year-end would have been higher, and had we written off less, it would have been lower.

	Accounts Receivable				Allowance for Doubtful Debts	
2005			**2005**			
	X	X				
	27,000					
write off A, B & C		2,000	bad debt expense 2005			500
to B/S 2005	**25,000**		to B/S 2005			**500**
2006			**2006**			
write off D & E		400	write off D & E		400	
	X	X	bad debt expense 2006			700
to B/S 2006	**40,000**		to B/S 2006			**800**

	Bad Debt Expense	
2005		
write off	2,000	
bad debt expense 2005	500	
to I/S 2005	**2,500**	
2006		
bad debt expense 2006	700	
to I/S 2006	**700**	

Self-Study Problems

1. Charley Farley went into business on October 1, 2005, by opening a doughnut shop. He carried on the business in a rented store in downtown Orillia. At the end of December, he realized that he would have to pay income tax on the business profits, but he had no idea how much profit he had made. He has asked you to advise him how much income to report for the three months he has been in business.

   He has presented you with his bank statements and a pile of invoices and receipts. The following is a summarized list of payments and receipts for the three months.

   Receipts paid into bank account:

1.	Owners' equity	$ 50,000
2.	Bank loan	$ 55,000
3.	Cash sales	$146,500

   Payments made out of bank account:

4.	Suppliers	$104,500
5.	Wages	$ 12,000
6.	Rent	$ 20,000
7.	Utilities	$ 5,000
8.	Insurance	$ 4,000
9.	Equipment	$ 99,000
10.	Repayment of bank loan	$ 4,000

   You are given the following additional information:
   (a) The cash received from sales was $161,500. Charley Farley took $5,000 each month from the cash sales for his own living expenses before paying the balance into the bank.
   (b) Charley has a coffee delivery arrangement with a nearby office. He delivers the coffee daily; they pay him weekly. At the end of December they owed him $500.
   (c) The $104,500 paid for supplies is not exactly the amount used: Charley owes suppliers another $5,000, and there is inventory on hand that had cost him $1,500.
   (d) The $20,000 paid for rent consists of $5,000 per month payment for October, November, and December, plus the "last" month of the lease of $5,000.
   (e) In addition to the $5,000 paid for utilities, another $1,000 is owed.
   (f) The insurance premium of $4,000 gives him cover from October 1, 2005, to September 30, 2006.
   (g) Amortization expense on the equipment should be taken as $9,000 for the three months to December 31, 2005.

   [Note: This is a continuation of Self-Study Problem 2.1 on page 67. You may need to refer back to that problem to help in doing this one.]

Required
(a) Prepare an income statement for Charley Farley for the three months to December 31, 2005.
(b) What was the ratio of gross profit to sales?
(c) What was the ratio of operating profit to sales?

2. Fanatical Fitness is a health club. At the start of 2005 there was a liability on their balance sheet of $200,000, representing the unused balance of members' subscriptions paid in 2004 but extending into 2005. During 2005 they sold $1,800,000 of new subscriptions. At the end of 2005 the amount of subscriptions that customers had paid in advance was $500,000.

Required
How much membership revenue should Fanatical Fitness recognize for 2005?

3. Fenella's Fashions had inventory on hand that cost $27,500 on January 1, 2005. During the year the owners bought goods for resale at a cost of $450,000. Inventory on hand at December 31, 2005, cost $56,000.

Required
(a) What was the cost of goods sold for 2005, based on the information given above?
(b) The closing inventory had a cost of $56,000. If you were told that it would be sold in the normal course of trade during 2006 for somewhere between $120,000 and $130,000, in what way would you change the cost of goods sold for 2005?
(c) The closing inventory had a cost of $56,000. If you were told that it had a market value of only $43,000 due to changes in styles and colours, what would be the cost of goods sold for the year?
(d) Which accounting principles/concepts are relevant to your answers to (a), (b), and (c) above?

4. Farmer Giles has bought himself a new hay baler. It cost $30,000. He plans to use it for 15 years and then abandon it in the corner of his 40-acre field with all the other worn-out farm implements.

Required
(a) How much amortization expense should he report for the baler each year?
(b) The day after he bought the baler, a new, better model was introduced at a cost of $25,000. How does this affect the amortization calculation?
(c) If it had been his intention and expectation to use the baler for five years and then sell it for $15,000, how much would the annual amortization expense be?

5. Go back to the information provided in Problem #1. Prepare a statement of owners' equity for Charley Farley for the three months ended December 31, 2005.

Solution

1. (a)

Charley Farley's Donut Shop
Income statement for the three months
ended December 31, 2005

			%
Sales revenue:			
Cash banked	$146,500		
+ withdrawals	15,000		
+ owed by customer	500	$162,000	100.0%
Less Cost of goods sold:			
Paid to suppliers	$104,500		
+ owed to suppliers	5,000		
− closing inventory	(1,500)	108,000	
Gross profit (or gross margin)		$ 54,000	33.3% (b)
Less Expenses:			
Wages	$ 12,000		
Rent ($20,000 − $5,000 prepaid)	15,000		
Utilities ($5,000 + $1,000 owed)	6,000		
Insurance ($4,000 − $3,000 prepaid)	1,000		
Amortization	9,000	43,000	
Operating profit		$ 11,000	6.8% (c)

2.

Subscriptions paid in advance at January 1, 2005	$ 200,000
Add: Subscriptions sold in 2005	1,800,000
	$2,000,000
Less: Subscriptions paid in advance at December 31, 2005	500,000
Revenue recognized in 2005	$1,500,000

3. (a)

Opening inventory	$ 27,500
+ Goods purchased	450,000
Goods available for sale	$477,500
− Closing inventory	(56,000)
Cost of goods sold (COGS)	$421,500

(b)   No adjustment is necessary; cost of goods sold is still $421,500. We never anticipate profit; we wait until it is realized.

(c)   The closing inventory must be valued at the lower of cost or market value: $43,000.

Opening inventory	$ 27,500
+ Goods purchased	450,000
Goods available for sale	$477,500
− Closing inventory	43,000
Cost of goods sold	$434,500

As a result, operating profit will be reduced by $13,000.

(d)   The matching principle and the cost principle are used in (a), (b), and (c); additionally, the conservatism concept is used in (b) and (c).

4. (a) Straight-line amortization:

$$= (\text{cost} - \text{scrap value}) \div \text{number of years}$$
$$= (\$30,000 - \$0) \div 15$$
$$= \$2,000 \text{ per year}$$

(b) No change: the baler has been bought to use, not to trade, so the cost principle is used to value it (do not use the lower of cost or market value for long-term assets).

(c) Straight-line amortization:

$$= (\text{cost} - \text{scrap value}) \div \text{number of years}$$
$$= (\$30,000 - \$15,000) \div 5$$
$$= \$3,000 \text{ per year}$$

5.

Charley Farley
Statement of Owners' Equity for the three months
ended December 31, 2005

Owners' equity as at October 1	nil
Add: Cash invested	$50,000
Add: Net income for the period	11,000
	$61,000
Less: Withdrawals	15,000
Owners' equity as at December 31, 2005	$46,000

Discussion Questions and Problems

Discussion Questions

1. What is the purpose of the income statement?
2. The income statement provides a link between successive balance sheets: how does it do this?
3. Why is the income statement prepared for a one-year period, unlike the balance sheet, which is prepared at a point in time?
4. Which is more useful to the shareholder, the income statement or the balance sheet? Which is more useful to the creditor?
5. Explain what is meant by revenue matching in the income statement.
6. Give a practical example of matching expenses against a time period.
7. In calculating cost of goods sold, explain how the inventory adjustment makes matching possible.
8. What happens when the historical cost concept is in conflict with the conservatism concept?
9. What is the purpose of the allowance for bad and doubtful debts?
10. What is the accounting principle that underlies the amortization calculation, and how is this achieved by the amortization expense?

Problems

1. V.G.Styles operates an architecture practice in Cambridge, Ontario. In 2005 the following occurred:

   - 27 clients had used V.G.Styles's services to design buildings. The total invoiced to customers in the year was $978,000 for jobs completed.
   - During the year a total of $980,000 was collected from clients. This included $20,000 in respect of work that was carried out in 2004. At the end of 2005 clients owed V.G.Styles $18,000.
   - Of the $18,000 owed by clients at the end of 2005, one customer who owed $8,000 vowed he would never pay as his house had been designed back-to-front, and he was tired of sleeping in the kitchen.
   - Normally V.G.Styles expects bad debts to be 10% of amounts owed (other than those specifically identified as problematical).
   - Five developers had requested quotations for new project architecture jobs. At the end of 2005 V.G.Styles had received acceptance on four of the quotations. The company had started working on two of the jobs (priced at $50,000 and $20,000, respectively) but had not yet started on the other two (priced at $15,000 and $28,000, respectively). The two jobs started were approximately half-finished by December 31, 2005.

   Required
   (a) Calculate the sales revenue for 2005.
   (b) Calculate the bad debt expense for 2005.
   (c) Describe all the accounting principles that apply to this situation.

125

2. Grabbit, Sue & Runne is a legal partnership, specializing in personal accident cases. During 2005 the following occurred:

   - Cash collected from 2004 and earlier cases: $500,000. (#1)
   - Cash collected from 2005 cases: $2,400,000. (#2)
   - Cash deposits collected from clients whose cases will be dealt with in 2006: $250,000. (#3)
   - Total cash collected: $3,150,000. (#4)
   - At the end of 2005 clients had unpaid accounts owed to the law firm of $650,000. (#5)

   Required
   Calculate the practice's revenue for 2005.

3. Marsha Miller operates a computer store. Most sales are for cash, so there is no problem identifying sales revenue. Cash sales in 2005 were $565,000. However, at the end of 2005, there were two customers who had ordered new computers and who had each paid a deposit of $250, which had been included in the takings banked of $565,000. The new computers were expected to be received in January, and would then be sold for $1,250 each. There was also one customer who had definitely decided to buy a second-hand laptop for $600, and who had asked that it be laid away for her to buy in January; she had not paid a deposit.

   Required
   Calculate Marsha Miller's sales revenue for 2005.

4. Sonya Bates runs a dollar store in Oshawa. On average the items she sells for $1 each cost her $0.75 each. The following data apply to 2005:

Opening inventory at January 1, 2005	$ 7,500
Inventory items purchased during 2005	$150,000
Closing inventory at December 31, 2005	$ 22,500
Sales revenue for 2005	$175,000

   Required
   (a) Calculate the cost of goods sold.
   (b) Calculate the gross margin.
   (c) Calculate the gross margin as % of sales.
   (d) Is there a problem with the gross margin %?
   (e) Is there a problem with the closing inventory?

5. Marsha Miller runs a computer store. On September 1, 2005, she took out a one-year life insurance policy on her own life at a cost of $6,000, and a one-year "all risks" business policy at a cost of $18,000. She expects to be able to renew both policies on September 1, 2006.

   Required
   (a) Will both insurance policies be included in the business operating expenses? (State which accounting concepts apply.)

(b) For the all-risks business policy calculate the insurance expense for 2005.

(c) For the all-risks business policy calculate the insurance expense paid in advance at December 31, 2005.

(d) For the all-risks business policy calculate the expected insurance expense for 2006.

6. Carolyn Jantzen operates a haulage company. Her truck expense details include the following:

• Licence fees paid in advance as at January 1, 2005 (2 months): $500;
• Licence fees paid in 2005: $3,000;
• Licence fees paid in advance as at December 31, 2005 (one month): $600.

Required
Calculate the licence fee expense for 2005.

7. Cotti Industries is a manufacturer of food products. During 2005 the company paid the following bills for electricity:

Date paid	Amount	Bill for
31/1/2005	$27,000	3 months to December 20, 2004
30/4/2005	$20,600	3 months to March 20, 2005
31/7/2005	$12,500	3 months to June 20, 2005
31/10/2005	$15,300	3 months to September 20, 2005
Total	$75,400	paid in 2005

The bill for the three months to December 20, 2006, is $27,900.

Required
Calculate the following:
(a) the amount owed for electricity as at January 1, 2005;
(b) the electricity expense for 2005;
(c) the amount owed for electricity as at December 31, 2005.

8. Cotti Industries had an accrual (amount owed) for wages of $500,000 on January 1, 2005. During 2005 a total of $3,400,000 was paid as wages. As at December 31, 2005, wages owed amounted to $250,000.

Required
Calculate the wages expense for 2005.

9. Cranx Inc. had accrued wages of $850,000 on January 1, 2005. During 2005 a total of $6,750,000 was paid as wages. The wages expense for 2005 was $6,900,000.

Required
Calculate the wages accrued as at December 31, 2005.

10. Cotti Industries bought a new cookie-dough mixer on January 1, 2005, at a cost of $15,000. The company expects to be able to use it for 10 years, and then it will be discarded with no residual value.

    Required
    Using the "straight-line" amortization method calculate the annual amortization for 2005.

11. Cranx Inc. bought a new printing press for its publishing business on January 1, 2005, at a cost of $580,000. The company expects to use it for five years, and then its expected resale value will be $130,000. Cranx Inc. uses the straight-line amortization method.

    Required
    (a) Calculate the annual amortization expense for years 2005 through 2009.
    (b) If the press is sold on December 31, 2005, for $500,000, what will be the gain or loss on disposal?
    (c) If the press is used for five years and then is disposed of for $80,000, what will be the gain or loss on disposal?

12. Hunter Co. had sales of $5,000,000, a gross margin of $2,000,000, an operating income of $700,000, and net income of $250,000. Comparable companies have a gross margin ratio of 35% and an operating income as % of sales ratio of 12.5%.

    Required
    (a) Calculate the gross margin as % of sales ratio.
    (b) Calculate the operating income as % of sales ratio.
    (c) Calculate the net income as % of sales ratio.
    (d) Is Hunter Co. doing well or doing poorly?

13. Hack Inc. had sales of $1,000,000, gross profit of $700,000, operating profit of $160,000, and net income of $125,000. Total assets were $2,000,000 and owners' equity was $500,000. Investors in this type of business expect a return on equity of 20%.

    Required
    (a) Calculate the return on assets ratio.
    (b) Calculate the return on shareholders' investment ratio.
    (c) How well is the company doing?

14. National Co. had retained earnings of $1 million at the beginning of 2005. During 2005 the company made net income of $500,000. At the end of 2005 the company paid a dividend of $200,000. At the end of 2005 there were 10,000 common shares.

    Required
    (a) Prepare the statement of retained earnings for 2005.
    (b) Calculate the earnings per share.
    (c) Calculate the dividend payout ratio.
    (d) What was the dividend per share?

(e) What is the maximum 2005 dividend National Co. could legally pay?

15. As at December 31, 2005, the total assets of Greco Co. were $1 million. The liabilities and equity were as follows:

Trade payables	$100,000
Short-term bank loan	$ 50,000
Long-term bank loan	$ 75,000
15% Convertible debenture	$200,000
8% Preferred shares	$150,000
Retained earnings	$125,000
30,000 Common shares	$300,000

This was after the company had made net income of $250,000 in 2005, and had paid a dividend of $50,000. The 15% convertible debentures could be converted into 20,000 common shares by the debenture holders at any time they chose.

Required
(a) Show how the statement of retained earnings would look, so that it resulted in the balance of retained earnings of $125,000 at the end of the year.
(b) Calculate the dividend payout ratio for the common shares.
(c) How much interest was paid on the 15% debentures?
(d) Calculate the earnings per share for the common shareholders.
(e) Calculate the fully diluted earnings per share for the common shareholders.

16. Renoir Inc. had an EPS of $10 in 2005. The dividend payout ratio was 75%. Auguste, who owned 20% of the common shares in Renoir Inc., received a dividend cheque for $75,000.

Required
(a) Calculate the dividend paid to each common share.
(b) Calculate the number of shares Auguste owned.
(c) Calculate the total number of common shares in Renoir Inc.
(d) Calculate the net income for 2005.
(e) If the balance of retained earnings as at January 1, 2005, was nil, what was the balance of retained earnings as at December 31, 2005?

17. Van Deisel Ltd. had retained earnings at the beginning of 2005 of $18 million. During 2005 the company made operating income of $9 million, paid interest on loans of $2 million, and income taxes of $3 million. A dividend of $2 million was paid on the common shares. Changes in accounting standards caused the company to revise its pension obligations, and this resulted in a reduction of the retained earnings brought forward at the beginning of 2005 of $800,000. The company bought some of its own common shares in the stock market and retired them. Because the purchase price was higher than the balance sheet amount, this resulted in a reduction of retained earnings of $200,000.

Required
Prepare the statement of retained earnings for 2005.

18. You are given the following statement of retained earnings for Turner Inc.

Turner Inc.
Statement of Retained earnings for the Year Ended
December 31, 2005

Retained earnings as at January 1, 2005	$400,000
Net income for the year 2005	100,000
	$500,000
Dividends on common shares	250,000
Retained earnings as at December 31, 2005	$250,000

Required
(a) Was it legal to pay the dividend of $250,000?
(b) Was it a good idea to pay the dividend of $250,000?

19. The Church Co. had the following items relating to its 2005 income statement:

Closing inventory	$250,000
Amortization expense	$ 25,000
Goods purchased for resale	$500,000
Income tax expense	$ 50,000
Interest expense	$ 25,000
Opening inventory	$200,000
Sales revenue	$950,000
Wages expense	$100,000
Rent expense	$ 50,000

Required
(a) Prepare an income statement for 2005 in good form.
(b) Calculate the gross margin as % of sales.
(c) Calculate the operating income as % of sales.
(d) Calculate the net income as % of sales.
(e) If the shareholders expect a return of 12.5% on their investment, what is the maximum amount that the shareholders' equity can be?

20. The following transactions occurred for Rodney's Retail in January:

- Cash sales totalled $200,000. (#1)
- Credit sales totalled $80,000. (#2)
- Cash received on account of credit sales of earlier months totalled $50,000. (#3)
- Typically 2% of credit sales are uncollectible. (#4)
- Goods purchased for resale totalled $150,000. (#5)
- Opening inventory as at 1/1/2005 was $25,000. (#6)
- Closing inventory as at 31/1/2005 had a cost of $20,000. (#7)
- Due to deterioration and water damage the market value of the closing inventory as at 31/1/2005 was only $15,000. (#8)

- Wages expense for the month was $28,000. (#9)
- In addition to the wages at the end of January, Rodney owes staff $2,000 for performance-related bonuses. (#10)
- Rent and utilities expense for the month was $15,000. (#11)
- Amortization expense for the month was $2,000. (#12)
- New equipment was ordered, received, and paid for: $50,000. (#13)

Required

Prepare an income statement for January 2005 in good form.

21. Company A started up its business on January 1, 2001. In the five years to December 31, 2005, it made a net income of $1 million per year. No distributions (dividends) were paid. What is the accumulated retained earnings as at December 31, 2005?

22. Company B has been in operation for some years. As at January 1, 2005, it had retained earnings of $5 million. During 2005 a dividend of $10 million was paid. Net income (after interest and taxes) for 2005 was $18 million. What was the balance of retained earnings as at December 31, 2005?

23. Company C had a balance of retained earnings as at January 1, 2005, of $500,000. During 2005, the company had revenues of $10 million, operating expenses of $5 million, interest expense of $1 million, and income taxes of $2 million. A dividend of $2 million was paid in 2005. Prepare a statement that shows the operating income, the net income after tax and interest, and the retained earnings at the end of 2005.

24. Company D has a balance of retained earnings as at January 1, 2005, of $750,000. During 2005, the company had a net loss of $200,000. No dividend was paid in the year. What was the balance of retained earnings at the end of 2005?

25. Company E had a balance of retained earnings of $10 million as at January 1, 2005. During 2005 the company made operating income of $4 million, and paid $750,000 in interest and $1,250,000 income tax. The company paid a dividend of $2 million. Changes in accounting standards relating to pensions caused the company to revise the retained earnings of earlier years, and this resulted in a $200,000 reduction in retained earnings. The company bought some of its own shares through the stock market and retired them. Because the purchase price was different from the share price in the balance sheet, this led to a charge on retained earnings of $100,000. Prepare a statement of retained earnings for the year 2005.

26. Company F has a net income of $500,000. There are 500,000 common shares in issue, and options exist that would increase common shares by 100,000. If the options were exercised there would be a saving of $40,000 interest expense. Calculate the basic and fully diluted EPS.

Appendix 3.5

27. Refer to Problem #2 on page 126.

Required
(a) Write journal entries for the information given.
(b) Set up T-accounts for the following four accounts: Cash, Accounts Receivable, Deferred Revenue–Deposits, and Revenue–Legal Services. Assume that the opening balance of Accounts Receivable is $500,000.
(c) Post the journal entries you have written in response to (a) and incorporate the other information provided.
(d) In the Accounts Receivable account, enter the amount necessary to balance it. To which account would the other side of the entry be made? Complete the entry.
(e) Write out the full journal entry required in (d).
(f) What is the firm's revenue for 2005?

28. This is a comprehensive question that covers the accounting cycle from events to preparation of financial statements for Rodney's Retail Ltd. for the month of January, 20xx. If you need guidance or examples, refer to Appendix 2.1

Required
(a) Set up the following ledger accounts for Rodney's Retail Ltd. with opening balances where indicated. You can use a computer spreadsheet program such as Excel using Table 2A.6 in Appendix 2.1 as a model. If you prefer to do the problem on paper, set up the general ledger as a set of T-accounts as in the previous problem. You will need the account names for the journal entries in part (b) and you will complete these ledger accounts in part (c).

Account	Dr	Cr
Cash	70,000	
Accounts Receivable	55,000	
Allowance for Doubtful Debts		3,000
Inventory	25,000	
Equipment	500,000	
Accumulated Amortization		38,000
Accounts Payable		130,000
Wages Payable		4,000
Share Capital		300,000
Retained Earnings		175,000
Sales		
Cost of Goods Sold		
Bad Debts		
Wages		
Rent and Utilities		
Amortization		
Dividends		
	650,000	650,000

Note that the accounts are in balance sheet order. The first six are asset accounts, including two contra-asset accounts. The next two are liability accounts (Accounts and Wages Payable), followed by two equity accounts (Share Capital and Retained Earnings). These 10 accounts are all the balance sheet accounts, and the opening balances are as of January 1, 200X (and the same as the balances on the balance sheet prepared the day before, December 31 of the previous year). The next six accounts are the revenue and expense accounts: one revenue account, Sales, and five expense accounts. The last account is dividends. Because they are used to account for activity in the period, the revenue and expense accounts and the dividend account all start the period with zero balances.

(b) Write journal entries for the transactions presented in Problem #20 on page 130 using the accounts names listed above. Assume that the goods purchased for resale (5th bullet point) were purchased on account, and that the wages (9th bullet point) and rent and utilities (11th bullet point) were paid in cash in January. In addition, add the following three transactions:
- Cash paid on account for December purchases totalled $130,000.
- Cash paid to discharge end of December wages payable, $4,000.
- Dividend paid in cash at the end of January, $60,000.

It is not necessary to label the accounts as {asset}, {liability}, etc.

(c) Post the journal entries to the ledger accounts.

(d) Balance the ledger and then close the books. Write two entries, one to close revenue and expense to retained earnings, and the second to close dividends to retained earnings, and then post them to the ledger.

(e) Use the information from the ledger to prepare (i) an income statement for the month ended January 31, 200X, (ii) a statement of retained earnings for the month, and (iii) a balance sheet as at January 31, 200X, all in good form.

The Balance Sheet (1): Assets

4

Learning
Objectives

After studying this chapter you should be able to list and explain the following components of the balance sheet:

→ Current assets (cash, accounts receivable, inventory)
→ Long-term assets and amortization.

You should also be able to assess efficiency through asset turnover ratios (receivables, inventory, total assets).

4.1   Introduction

In Chapter 2 we introduced the four main financial statements: the balance sheet, the income statement, the statement of retained earnings, and the cash flow statement. In this chapter we shall look at the balance sheet in greater detail.

The accounting equation (assets = liabilities + owners' equity) is the fundamental model for recording and reporting transactions. The balance sheet is laid out in the same way as the accounting equation. The assets (the left-hand side of the accounting equation) are listed and totalled. The liabilities and the equities (the right-hand side of the accounting equation) are listed and totalled. The two totals are agreed to show that the accounting equation is in balance. It is, therefore, a list showing a point in time: what a company owns, what it owes, and what owners' equity remains.

The balance sheet is laid out with a format that focuses on the term of both assets and liabilities. The assets that are most readily realizable are listed first, and at the end of the list are the assets that the company will be realizing either not at all, or only after a long delay. Likewise, the liabilities are listed, with those that are immediately payable first and those with a long timeline last.

This ordering of the assets and the liabilities helps the user to assess the liquidity of the company, and the probability of the company's being unable to pay its debts. (See Exhibit 4.1.)

The dollar values that appear on the balance sheet are those that are recognized by the accounting equation when transactions occur: i.e., the historical cost. In general, this will give a fair idea of their value, but there are at least two problems with the historical cost approach.

First, the transactions are an incomplete record of the events that are important to the company. There are plenty of events that make the company richer or poorer but that are not captured by transactions, and so go unrecorded. These would include actions by competitors and unusual successes or failures of the company's activities. (See examples in Focus Boxes 4.1 and 4.2.)

Exhibit 4.1: The Balance Sheet

The balance sheet lists items in order of liquidity:

ASSETS	**Everything the company owns**
Current assets:	realizable within one year
Cash	available immediately
Short-term investments	realizable quickly
Accounts receivable	collectible within two months
Inventory	saleable and therefore convertible into receivables within a couple of months
Long-term assets:	those that will be used indefinitely in the course of operating the business

LIABILITIES	**Everything the company owes**
Current liabilities:	payable within one year
Trade payables	payable within a month or at most two months
Short-term debt	payable within one year
Long-term liabilities:	payable beyond one year
OWNERS' EQUITY	**Owners' equity is what is left over**
	the owners cannot insist on their equity being repaid

Focus Box 4.1: Bayview Hardware and the Competition

In 1984, on Bayview Avenue in Toronto there was a shopping centre with a hardware store. The hardware store was independently owned and operated, and had been there for over 20 years. The hardware store was successful and had provided a reasonable living for its owner operator. In 1985, one of the major hardware franchises opened up a competing store across the road. Because of the franchise's ability to buy in bulk, it was able to offer more competitive prices. The franchise could also offer its customers more choice because of its ability to carry more inventory centrally. Also, because of the franchise's national TV advertising campaign, it could attract customers effectively. Within a year the independent hardware store had closed its business.

The opening of the competing franchise store was not a transaction as far as the independent hardware store was concerned, so it was never recorded anywhere in the company's balance sheet, yet it drove the store out of business.

The second problem with the historical cost approach is that it sometimes misrepresents the value of assets or liabilities. The true value of an asset or the true value of a liability may be understated or overstated by its historical cost. The accounting concept of conservatism is a major influ-

---

Focus Box 4.2:   Jose Lopez Moves to Volkswagen

In 1993, Volkswagen recruited Jose Lopez as a manufacturing executive for its car plants. The company recruited him from General Motors, where he had been credited with turning around the production and inventory management, making GM much more profitable than it would otherwise have been. Volkswagen expected that he would be able to work the same magic in its plants.

Since there was no transaction with a dollar value involved, the addition of this dynamic executive would not be recorded on the Volkswagen balance sheet (nor would GM record his loss).

Despite this, it is frequently said that the employees are any company's most valuable asset.

---

ence on how we deal with such issues. If the historical cost of an asset is higher than its value in use, conservatism requires that we reduce the historical cost to a more reasonable amount, and if the historical cost of a liability is an understatement, conservatism requires that we increase it to its likely actual future cost. Assets that are undervalued and liabilities that are overvalued by the historical cost approach are not increased, which is an application of conservatism.

We shall see applications of these adjustments below in respect of current assets, such as accounts receivable and inventories, and in respect of the amortization of long-term assets.

4.2   Assets

An asset is anything that is valuable and is owned by the business. In order for the asset to appear in the balance sheet, it must have been acquired at a measurable cost (because of the historical cost basis used in valuation).

When carrying out an audit, the auditors will seek to establish the existence, the ownership, and the basis of valuation of the business assets. The existence of assets is established by physical inspection, counting, etc. For example, the auditors will probably attend when the company staff counts the inventory at the year-end.

The ownership is established by looking at the paper trail. For example, the registration documents for a car show who the owner is, and the auditor would expect to see them.

The basis of valuation is where the accounting expertise comes in: assets are normally valued at their original cost, less any amortization. The auditor would check that the amortization rate is reasonable, considering the nature of the asset.

On the balance sheet, assets are grouped into current assets and long-term assets.

4.2.1   Current Assets

The first grouping of assets on the balance sheet is current assets. An asset is defined as current if its term is one year or less. That means that within a year it is likely to be realized (or is available for realization). Assets with terms longer than one year are classified separately as long-term assets.

Realization means different things in respect of different assets. Cash is always taken to be a current asset because it may be spent immediately. Realization of receivables means collection of the money owed. Realization of inventory means using it in the manufacture of goods, or selling it.

Note that the one-year cut-off is somewhat arbitrary. There is no magical difference between a receivable that is due in 364 days and one due in 366 days. Yet one is treated as a current asset, and the other is treated as a long-term asset. However, some cut-off has to be made, and one year ties in with the idea of an annual reporting cycle (normally, balance sheets are prepared at one-year intervals, and the income statement covers one year).

4.2.1.1   Cash

Cash is the most readily available current asset. It is immediately available for the payment of any company obligation, such as paying a debt that is due, or a recurrent expense, such as payroll. Because of its immediate availability, it comes first in the list of current assets.

The balance sheet does not distinguish the form in which cash is held. Traditionally, cash means notes and coin, but for the balance sheet, money in a chequing account is treated as cash, too. Money in any bank account that is immediately available would be treated as cash.

Money in a term deposit would not be treated as cash, as there is a waiting period before it is available. Because the interest rate on a term deposit is significantly higher than the one (if any) on a chequing account, the company will want to pay particular attention to balancing the objective of making the most out of the available resources against both the objectives of staying liquid, and of appearing liquid on the balance sheet.

All the various sites (till balances, floats, chequing accounts, etc.) where cash is held would be added together to give one total figure of cash to appear on the balance sheet.

4.2.1.2   Short-term Investments

Short-term investments are relatively liquid and easily realizable assets. If the company has a cyclical pattern of operations, it may have a temporary surplus of funds. Rather than tie those funds up by investing them in plant, or using them up by paying the shareholders a dividend, the company can put the money into a term deposit, or buy money market certificates, or even shares of other companies. In each case, the asset is one that has either a fixed date of maturity in the near future, or there exists a well-established market where it can be bought or sold at any time.

Note that it is the intention of the company as to the holding period that determines whether or not an asset is a short-term investment. An investment in the shares of a company may be a short-term investment. If the plan is to sell those shares in three months, when the cash is needed for some purpose, it is short-term. An investment in the shares of the same company that was made for strategic reasons and with the intention to hold these shares indefinitely would be a long-term investment. Short-term investments usually earn interest.

4.2.1.3   *Accounts Receivable (or Receivables)*

Sales of goods to customers are frequently made on credit terms. (See Focus Box 4.3.) The customer takes the goods (or services), but does not pay for them immediately. The customer is expected to pay according to the "terms of trade". These may vary from one industry to another, but a credit period of 30 days is common.

Thirty days may be the requested credit period, but sometimes customers stretch their payments to longer periods. In extreme cases, customers may lose the privilege of credit sales and be put on a "cash with order", or "cash on delivery" basis. Companies are reluctant to do this, however, as it makes selling more difficult. There is often a difference of opinion between the sales force, who want to sell as much as possible and who will want to use credit terms as a customer inducement, and the accounting department, who only want to allow credit sales to customers who pay on time.

The worst customers do not pay ever. When the credit sale is first made, a receivable arises. It is not known for certain whether the customer will settle the debt or not. While most customers pay eventually, some credit sales generally turn into "bad debts". When the balance sheet is

---

**Focus Box 4.3:   Receivables Turnover Ratio
and Receivables Collection Period**

Continental Containers has a receivables balance of $10,000 as at December 31, 2005. Sales for the year 2005 were $73,000.

Receivables turnover ratio:

= annual sales ÷ end of year receivables
= $73,000 ÷ $10,000
= 7.3 times per year

Receivables collection period (days' sales in receivables):

= end of year receivables ÷ (single day's sales)
= end of year receivables ÷ (annual sales ÷ 365)
= $10,000 ÷ ($73,000 ÷ 365)
= 50 days

The company is turning over its receivables 7.3 times each year, or, alternatively, the company is collecting its receivables in 50 days, which is a little less than two months.

---

drawn up, it is unclear which accounts are good and which are bad. The balance sheet accommodates the expected bad debts using an "allowance for bad and doubtful debts".

The bad debt expense was introduced in the previous chapter. Because the bad debt expense has been recognized without any transaction to support it, a matching quasi-liability (or "contra-asset") has to be created, called the "allowance for bad and doubtful debts". This provision is deducted from the historical cost of the receivables, reducing them to their expected eventual collectible cash value.

How well the company is managing receivables may be assessed through the receivables turnover ratio. In this ratio, the receivables at the end of the year are compared to the sales for the year. Companies with low receivables will have a high turnover ratio. Companies that are slow in collecting their receivables will have a low turnover ratio.

A similar conclusion can also be attained by dividing the receivables by the amount representing the single days' sales. This shows how many days' sales the receivables represent.

There are no absolute standards about how high the receivables turnover should be: it will be affected by the terms of trade. The trend of the ratio over time is probably as important as the ratio itself. A company that has increased its receivables turnover ratio (e.g., 6.0 last year to 7.3 this year) is collecting its debts more quickly and, all other things being equal, is becoming more efficient.

4.2.1.4 *Inventory*

Inventory represents assets that are owned by the company and that have been bought for resale or for use in production.

In a service organization, inventory will probably be trivially small. This is because such organizations have neither goods for resale nor raw materials for manufacture. An architect's office, for example, might have only paper and drawing supplies as its inventory.

In a merchandising company, the inventory will be the goods bought for resale: that is, all the stock on the shelves, plus goods kept in stockrooms and warehouses, ready for sale.

In a manufacturing company, inventory will consist of three separate classes. There will be inventory of raw material, awaiting use in the production process; there will be inventory of products that are partway through the production system (work-in-process inventory); and there will be inventory of finished goods, awaiting sale.

Inventory has to be both counted and valued. Counting establishes the quantities involved and is normally not controversial: inventory is either there or not. Valuation puts a dollar value on the things that are there and is much more problematic.

Because of the "historical cost" principle, the value of inventory is taken to be what it cost to buy it. In a merchandising company, and in respect of the raw materials in a manufacturing company, this is relatively straightforward. Valuing finished products in a manufacturing company, however, is more complex.

One of the valuation issues is that of making appropriate inventory flow assumptions. If inventory is always bought at the same price, then it really does not matter which units of goods purchased have been used up (e.g., sold) and which units are still in inventory. If the prices at which inventory is bought are different, then we have to make some decisions about the inventory flows and their related cost flows. There are a number of possible methods, including specific identification, average cost, first-in-first-out, last-in-first-out. We shall not go into the details of any of these here since they are discussed in Appendix 4.2. Suffice it to say that depending on which assumption is made about how the inventory flows through the system, inventory may have a higher or a lower value placed on it.

This is important from the perspective of both the balance sheet and the income statement. If closing inventory has a relatively high value attributed to it, then the cost of goods sold will be lower. This, in turn, raises operating income and net income. Conversely, if inventory has a lower valuation, cost of goods sold will increase, and operating income and net income will decrease.

Inventory Valuation in Manufacturing Companies: Variable Cost vs. Full Cost

In a manufacturing company, it is necessary to value raw materials. It is also necessary to value both work-in-process and finished goods, and that presents a special problem in respect of the treatment of fixed costs. Tracing the direct materials and direct labour that have been used to produce inventory is normally straightforward, through the use of cost records. The same cost records will also be used to allocate overhead to inventory (overhead allocation is covered in Chapter 9).

The allocated overhead will be a mix of variable cost and fixed cost. Variable overhead includes such costs as electricity and supplies. It fluctuates according to the level of activity. Fixed overhead, on the other hand, is not affected by changes in the volume of production.

Everyone would agree that inventory should carry its fair share of variable overhead because the production of the inventory caused the overhead to be incurred. Including the fixed overhead is, however, more problematic.

Fixed overhead includes such costs as rent, property taxes, amortization, supervisory salaries, etc. However, the argument for including them in inventory valuation is not as strong, even though incurring these costs provided the production capabilities that enabled production.

While these fixed overhead costs have clearly expired, goods manufactured during the same period may have been sold or they may remain in inventory. If the goods are still in inventory, there is a choice: the choice to treat the associated fixed overhead as an expense of the current period, or to treat it as inventory value. If the latter is selected, the associated costs will get carried forward on the balance sheet. They will become an expense in a future accounting period when the goods eventually get sold. This is, therefore, an important choice, for it has the effect of moving expense from one period to another, thus changing net income in both periods.

One perspective on these costs is that they were incurred to provide production capacity during a period of time. Once that time period has expired the costs should be expensed. Even if inventory that was made during the time period exists, these "period" costs confer no benefit on any future time period, and so it is improper to carry it forward. Inventory is valued at variable cost. This is referred to as "variable" or "direct" costing. All other things being equal, it will result in a lower income in the current period, and increased income in the subsequent periods.

The alternative perspective on these costs is that the full cost of goods produced in the current period should include a fair share of manufacturing costs, including fixed manufacturing costs. If they are in inventory at the end of the period, then that full cost is to be carried forward, and only expensed when the goods are sold. This is referred to as "full" or "absorption" costing. (See Focus Box 4.4.) All other things being equal, full costing has the effect of increasing current income (by deferring cost) and reducing future income by the same amount.

In either case, the effect is not to change the total amount of net income reported but to change its allocation to accounting periods.

Focus Box 4.4: Inventory — Variable vs. Full (Direct vs. Absorption) Inventory Valuation

Terri's Tools manufactures a comprehensive line of machine tools. One of the new products for 2004 was a 1.5-metre drill press. The drill press has been costed out as follows:

	Cost per unit
Direct materials	$ 500.00
Direct labour	750.00
Variable manufacturing overhead	500.00
Total variable cost	$1,750.00
Fixed manufacturing overhead	750.00
Total cost	$2,500.00

In 2004 the company made 100 of these drill presses, of which 80 were sold and 20 remained in inventory. In 2005 the company made 50. During 2005 Terri's Tools sold all 70 of the presses available and discontinued production, having developed a better model.

	Using variable (direct) costing	Using full (absorption) costing
31/12/2004: Inventory value	$35,000 (20 @ $1,750)	$50,000 (20 @ $2,500)

If direct costing is used, inventory value on the balance sheet (and net income) for 2004 will be $15,000 lower than if full costing had been used. As a result, net income for 2004 will be $15,000 lower, having fixed manufacturing overhead all expensed in 2004.

That effect will be reversed the following year (2005). In 2005 the opening inventory valued using direct costing will be $15,000 lower, and net income will be $15,000 higher.

Focus Box 4.5: Inventory — Lower of Cost or Market Price

Mike's Motor Sales had two vehicles in inventory at the end of January 2006. The Pontiac Firebird cost $15,000, and the Mazda Protegé cost $12,000. Due to its rarity value, the Pontiac's replacement cost would have been $2,000 higher than its $15,000 cost. Due to a temporary excess supply of the model, Mike could have replaced the Mazda for as little as $9,000.

	Cost	Market price	Lower of cost or market price
Pontiac Firebird	$15,000	$17,000	$15,000
Mazda Protegé	12,000	9,000	9,000
Inventory value on balance sheet			$24,000

Inventory Valuation: Lower of Cost or Market Price

Once the cost has been determined, a further comparison is done between the cost and the market price. If the market price is less than the cost, then the inventory value for the balance sheet is reduced to that level. Note that if the market price is higher than cost, the inventory value is not increased. This is described as valuing inventory at the "lower of cost or market price". (See Focus Box 4.5.) Market price can mean the replacement price, or can mean the price the goods will be sold for.

The lower of cost or market price rule is an example of conservatism in accounting. Conservatism implies taking the hit immediately if a loss is apparent but not anticipating any profit before it is realized.

Inventory Turnover Ratios

How well the company is managing its inventory may be assessed through the inventory turnover ratio. In this ratio the inventory at the end of the year is compared to the sales for the year. (See Focus Box 4.6.) The company that has low inventory will have a high turnover ratio. The company that is slow in selling its inventory will have a low turnover ratio.

A similar conclusion can be attained by dividing the inventory by the amount of a single day's sales. This shows how many days' sales the inventory represents.

4.2.1.5 Other Current Assets

Any assets with a term of one year or less that do not fall under the headings Cash, Short-term Investments, or Receivables would be listed as "Other Current Assets". The most common of these is the "prepaid expense". (See Focus Box 4.7.)

When the company has an expense, the contract sometimes calls for paying the bill before receiving the services. A heating system mainte-

**Focus Box 4.6:   Inventory Turnover Ratio
and Days' Sales in Inventory**

Continental Containers has an inventory total of $7,300 as at December 31, 2005. Sales for the year 2005 were $73,000.

Inventory turnover ratio:

= sales for the year ÷ inventory at year-end
= $73,000 ÷ $7,300
= 10.0 times per year

Days' sales in inventory:

= inventory at year-end ÷ (sales ÷ 365)
= $7,300 ÷ ($73,000 ÷ 365)
= 36.5 days

The company is turning over its inventory 10 times each year, or, alternatively, it is selling its inventory every 36.5 days, which is a little more than one month.

Focus Box 4.7:   Prepaid Expense

Boxer Balloons started business on April 1, 2005. The company paid an annual business insurance premium of $2,000, on April 1. When the company prepared its financial statements as at December 31, 2005, the company recognized the following:

• Nine months of the premium (April through December 2005) had been used up, and so $1,500 should be treated as an expense and recorded in the income statement.

• Three months of the premium (January through March 2006) was still unused, so a prepaid expense of $500 should be reported as an asset (a short-term asset) on the balance sheet.

nance service contract, for example, might specify a quarterly payment, in advance, of $200. If, at the end of an accounting period, some of this maintenance time is not yet expired, the company would recognize that as an asset called Prepaid Expense. Deposits are also found under this heading.

4.2.1.6 *Total Current Assets*

The total of the current assets is always shown on the balance sheet.

The cash assets are stated as cash values. The receivables are stated as realizable values (i.e., gross amount owing, less allowance for bad and doubtful debts). The inventories are stated at the lower of cost or market price. This is a consistent approach. Because they are going to be realized, all the current assets are stated at cost or at realizable, or exit values: what they are expected to bring in when, as expected, they are disposed of. This contrasts with the long-term assets, where the historical cost is more dominant in the valuation.

Showing the total of current assets facilitates the calculation of the liquidity ratios, which compare the current assets against the current liabilities they have to pay.

4.2.2   *Long-term Assets*

Assets the company intends to hold for periods longer than one year are listed under the heading Long-term Assets (sometimes called Fixed Assets). The general intention is that they will be used in the company business to generate sales. Because the intention is to hold the long-term assets indefinitely, it is not so important to indicate their relative liquidity. Instead, major sub-headings that identify the different classes of long-term assets are generally presented in this order: land, buildings, plant and equipment, intangible assets, and investments in associated companies.

4.2.2.1   *Land*

Land owned by the company is an asset that has no effective time horizon. The land may be owned by the company forever (unless the company sells it). The historical cost (what was paid for it) is used as the value. Given the nature of money, inflation, and property markets, it may be that this understates the land's market value. Because of the conservatism principle, any such increases in value are ignored. Conversely, if the land has suffered a drop in value, the conservatism principle requires that the reduction in value be recognized and the balance sheet value reduced accordingly. Consequently, the longer the time between the acquisition of the land and the balance sheet date, the wider any discrepancy between market price and cost is likely to be.

4.2.2.2   *Buildings*

Land, which lasts forever, should be kept separate from the buildings that stand on the land. Unlike land, buildings deteriorate over time, and that has to be recognized in the financial reports. If land is bought separately, and the buildings are then constructed on the land, it is relatively easy to keep the cost of the land separate from the cost of the buildings. If, as is common, land and buildings are purchased together, it becomes necessary to apportion the cost between the two.

Suppose a company were to buy a building for $800,000. (See Focus Box 4.8.) Its expected economic life is 20 years, and it will have no residual value. The entire $800,000 must be charged as an amortization expense of $40,000 per year for each of the next 20 years.

Focus Box 4.8:   Amortization of Building

Harry's Video Store has just bought a building and the land it stands on for $1 million. The appraised value of the land is $200,000 and of the building is $800,000. The building was built five years ago and had, at that time, a 25-year expected useful life. It therefore has another 20 years of expected life at this time. The cost ($800,000) will be amortized in 20 equal instalments of $40,000 per year over the useful life.

Balance Sheet

Year 1:	Cost	$800,000	
	Less accumulated amortization	40,000	$760,000
Year 2:	Cost	$800,000	
	Less accumulated amortization	80,000	$720,000
Year 3:	Cost	$800,000	
	Less accumulated amortization	120,000	$680,000

And so on for each year, until the written-down value is reduced to zero:

Year 20:	Cost	$800,000	
	Less accumulated amortization	800,000	$ nil

Note that by the end of year 20 the asset's value has been completely written off by way of 20 amortization charges of $40,000 each (20 × $40,000 = $800,000). Even though written down to zero value on the balance sheet, the asset is still owned by the company and may even continue to have some use. It will continue to appear in the balance sheet (as an asset with nil value) as long as it continues in use. Only when its use is discontinued will it be taken out of the balance sheet.

Effectively, having an asset on the balance sheet with a value of $0 means that the amortization was too aggressive and the asset written off before its useful life was over.

4.2.2.3   *Plant and Equipment*

One of the largest categories in most balance sheets is plant and equipment. This covers the various items that the business needs to operate, including production machinery, office equipment, computers, motor vehicles, hand tools, furniture, retail store fixtures, computing hardware, software, passenger cars, trucks and so on. For purposes of calculating amortization, they will probably be grouped into a number of different subcategories, with the assets in each category being amortized on a common basis. Like buildings, plants and equipment are recorded at cost initially, and will gradually be retired through the amortization process. Because of the nature of the assets, it is probable that plant and equipment would be written off over much shorter time periods than the buildings, but the principle is the same. (See Focus Box 4.9.)

Focus Box 4.9:   Amortization Rates at Sara Lee

Sara Lee is a conglomerate that has interests in a range of consumer products. The company's financial statements for 1994 reported its assets as being amortized as follows:

> "Property is stated at cost, and depreciation is computed using principally the straight-line method at annual rates of 2% to 20% for buildings and improvements, and 4% to 33% for machinery and equipment."

Focus Box 4.10: Amortization — Plant and Equipment

Terri's Tools has just bought a new delivery truck. The cost was $60,000. The company expects to keep the truck for two years. At the end of two years, Terri's Tools will sell it and replace it with a new one. The expected selling price in two years is $40,000.

Cost	$60,000
Expected selling price	40,000 (residual value)
Total loss in value over two years	$20,000
Annual amortization charge	$10,000 ($20,000 ÷ 2)

The general formula for (straight line) amortization is as follows:

   (cost – residual value) ÷ number of years = annual amortization charge

In the balance sheet the net "written-down value" of an asset is as follows:

   initial cost of the asset – (sum of all amortization expense for that asset to date)

Other patterns of amortization exist. Suppose you buy a new truck. (See Focus Box 4.10.) It is probable that the major element of amortization occurs in the initial years of the truck's life, while the later years should bear a lesser charge. This can be achieved by calculating amortization as a constant percentage of the written-down value (declining balance amortization). It is also possible to relate amortization to use (units of production amortization). If you assume the truck will last for 200,000 km, you could charge 1/200,000 of the cost to each period when a kilometre was travelled. (These amortization methods are described in detail in Appendix 3.2.)

4.2.2.4   *Intangible Assets*

Some assets have similar characteristics to plant and equipment (in that they are owned and used over a long time period), but they have no physical form. These are called intangible assets, and would include things like patents, trademarks, and goodwill.

Focus Box 4.11: Patents at Xerox Copiers

When the Xerox Corporation developed its photocopying method, the company patented the design. No one else had the technology to carry out the task, so Xerox had a monopoly of the market. The cost of acquiring and registering that patent was an asset on Xerox's balance sheet.

The value on the balance sheet was probably a major understatement of the true value of the company's monopoly position, but its cost was all the historical cost convention would permit recording.

Patents and Trademarks

These represent a legally enforceable right to a particular process or product. A patent is normally granted for a new invention, which the developer registers to safeguard his right to exploit. (See Focus Box 4.11.) A patent lasts for 17 years under Canadian law.

A trademark is the legally enforceable uniqueness of a product. Competitors are allowed to produce similar, but not identical products. Thus, Pepsi-Cola competes against Coca-Cola, but Pepsi cannot call its product "Coke". It has been estimated that if Coca-Cola lost the right to the name, the bottle shape, and all the other trappings of its product, it would cost the company about $83 billion to replace the brand, the image, and the product recognition in the mind of the public. Again, the accounting model only permits the recognition of the cost of the trademark, not its replacement value. The $83 billion does not appear anywhere on the corporate balance sheet because its value has been built up gradually, over time, and the cost has been written off as expense along the way. If another company were to buy the Coke brand though, that cost could appear on its balance sheet.

Goodwill

When one company buys the assets of another company, the net assets acquired are valued. There are three possible relationships between the value of the net assets acquired and the purchase price.

If the purchase price is the same as the net value of the assets, the assets will be recorded at their valuations, and no problem exists.

If the valuation of the assets is more than the purchase price, the price is prorated over the assets, and they are all reduced in value proportionately.

If the value of individual assets is less than the purchase price, the buying company is said to have bought "goodwill". Goodwill is recognition that the earning power of the purchased company (because of things such as employees, brands, and reputation) is greater than the sum of the individual values of its assets. Goodwill is an intangible asset and appears on the balance sheet as such.

Focus Box 4.12: Total Assets — General Motors

Though not the world's largest corporation, General Motors is certainly one of the big boys. Its total assets at the end of 2005 were over $475 billion (US). This is an almost incomprehensible burden of management responsibility, and it raises serious issues about how such a huge quantity of assets can be effectively managed.

Goodwill appears only when a company has been bought. Instead of amortization, goodwill is periodically subjected to an "impairment" test, and any deficiency is written off at that time.

4.2.2.5   *Total Assets*

When all the above assets are added together, the total represents all the assets the company has control over. This total is used by analysts to get an objective measure of the size of the company. The greater the total assets, the larger the company, and so the greater the profit it should make. (See Focus Box 4.12.)

4.3   Asset Turnover Ratio

The extent to which assets have been used efficiently or inefficiently is measured by the asset turnover ratio. This is calculated by dividing the sales revenue by the total asset figure (see Focus Box 4.13). An organiza-

---

Focus Box 4.13: Asset Turnover Ratio

The efficiency with which the assets have been used to generate sales can be measured using the asset turnover ratio.

Philomena's Fashions had total assets of $500,000 at the end of 2004 and $550,000 at the end of 2005. Sales in 2004 were $5,000,000, and $6,600,000 in 2005. Assets have increased (by 10%), but sales have increased even more (32%).

Asset turnover ratio:

= sales ÷ total assets

2004: $5,000,000 ÷ $500,000 = 10 times
2005: $6,600,000 ÷ $550,000 = 12 times

The company is turning over its assets more quickly in 2005, indicating that it is more efficient, all other things being equal.

---

tion that uses a large amount of assets to create its sales is less efficient. The organization that requires the smallest asset base is the most efficient. Assets are there for the purpose of creating sales revenue: the smaller the asset base for any given level of sales, the better the organization is managing its assets. There are two reasons for this.

First, a larger asset base means that more money has been invested by the owners. For any given level of profit, a larger asset base will lead to a lower return on equity (and profit is driven by sales volume). Second, assets create costs: a larger asset base means more plants, more machinery, more vehicles, etc. All of these have to be operated by people, and that leads to a higher wage expense as well as other operating expenses.

The passenger vehicle industry across the world is plagued by overcapacity. The industry has relatively low asset turnover ratios. It is no surprise that we regularly hear announcements by the big auto manufacturers that they are closing plants. They are trying to improve their asset turnover ratios.

4.4   Summary

In this chapter we have dealt with how the balance sheet reports the assets of the business. The assets are broadly divided into two groups: the current assets (cash, receivables, inventory, etc.) and the long-term assets (plant, vehicles, real estate, intangibles, etc.). Current assets are expected to be going through a continuous process of realization and replacement, whereas long-term assets are generally owned over the long term and are bought to be used rather than to be sold.

When deciding the dollar amounts that will go on the balance sheet, the assets must be owned in the first place, and then they must be valued. Current assets are valued conservatively: that is, they are valued at the lower of their cost, or their market value. Long-term assets are typically valued at cost, less an allowance (accumulated amortization) for the proportion of their cost that is expired.

Appendix 4.1
Example of a Balance Sheet

Wendy's International, Inc. is not only famous in respect of the Wendy's hamburger chain, the company also owns Tim Horton's, which operates mainly in Canada. The balance sheets reproduced below were prepared from information on the company's "10-K" report, which has to be filed under U.S. law. The complete report is available on the Wendy's International Web site: **www.wendys.com**

Wendy's International, Inc. and Subsidiaries
Consolidated Balance Sheet ($ million)

	As at			
	January 1 2006		January 2 2005	
Assets				
Current assets				
Cash and equivalents	$ 393		$ 176	
Accounts receivable, net	139		127	
Notes receivable, net	12		12	
Deferred income tax	29		27	
Inventories	63		56	
Other	120	$ 756	60	$ 458
Long-term assets				
Property and equipment, net	$2,326		$2,350	
Notes receivable, net	15		13	
Goodwill, net	129		167	
Deferred taxes	6		7	
Intangible assets, net	42		42	
Other assets	166	2,684	161	2,740
Total assets		$3,440		$3,198
Liabilities and Shareholders' equity				
Liabilities:				
Current liabilities				
Accounts payable	$ 188		$ 197	
Other current liabilities	395	$ 583	491	$ 688
Long-term liabilities		616		594
Total liabilities		$1,199		$1,282
Deferred taxes, commitments and redeemable securities		183		200
Common Stock	$ 12		$ 12	
Capital in excess of stated value	406		406	
Treasury stock* and other	(218)		(403)	
Retained earnings	1,859	2,059	1,701	1,716
Total liabilities and shareholders' equity		$3,441		$3,198

* Treasury stock consists of the company's own shares purchased on the open market.

Appendix 4.2
Inventory Flow and Inventory Valuation Models

As discussed throughout Chapter 4, inventory has to be both counted and valued. Counting establishes the quantities involved. Counting is a matter of fact: either the inventory is there, or it is not. Valuation puts a dollar value on the inventory. Unlike counting, the valuation process is negotiable. Depending on the assumptions we make, we will get different answers to the question, "How much is the inventory worth?" These assumptions focus on the pattern of how inventory flows through the system.

In situations where the price per unit of inventory is the same at all points through the year, it makes no difference what assumptions we make about inventory flow: they all give identical results in terms of operating profit and the inventory value on the balance sheet. In situations where the price per unit of inventory changes, different inventory flow assumptions will result in different inventory valuations and different reported operating profit. Changing prices are more likely than steady prices, so this is an area where we should spend some time understanding the implications of how we record values in the accounting system.

Four possible cost-flow approaches will be dealt with: specific identification, first-in-first-out, last-in-first-out, and weighted average cost.

Specific Identification

If inventory consists of things that have substantial individual value and unique characteristics allowing items to be separately recorded, then the specific identification method may be suitable. (See Focus Box 4A2.1.) This method would apply to inventory such as household appliances, computers, etc. — each of which has a unique identification serial number. The cost of each item is recorded. If the item is still in inventory, its cost is recorded as inventory value and will appear on the balance sheet. If the item is sold, its cost is transferred out of inventory, and into an account called Cost of Goods Sold, which will appear as an expense on the income statement.

Identical or Similar Goods

In many cases, goods purchased for resale are identical with, or very similar to, goods already in inventory, and the purchases and the existing inventory become mixed together. It may be impossible or impractical to discover which specific goods have been sold and which are still on hand. Three possible patterns of usage can be considered. We could assume that

Focus Box 4A2.1:   Inventory Valuation — Specific Identification

Mike's Motor Sales has five used vehicles in inventory at the start of January:

Make and Model	Cost
Ford Mustang	$10,000
Pontiac Firebird	15,000
GM half-tonne truck	7,000
Mazda Protegé	12,000
Toyota Tercel	11,000
Total	$55,000 (a balance sheet asset as at January 1)

By the end of January, the Ford, the GM, and the Toyota have all been sold; the Pontiac and the Mazda are still in inventory. No further vehicles have been bought. Specific identification of inventory would report the following:

Cost of goods sold
($10,000 + $7,000 + $11,000) $28,000 (an income statement expense for January)

Inventory
($15,000 + $12,000) 27,000 (a balance sheet asset as at January 31)

Total accounted for $55,000

the first goods bought were the first ones used; we could assume that the last goods bought were the first ones used; or we could assume it appropriate to average out the inventory and the purchases because they were mixed randomly.

FIFO Model

In a "first-in-first-out" (FIFO) system, the assumption is that, although the goods are not different, because of the way they are delivered, stored, or used, it is reasonable to assume that those bought earliest get used soonest. This implies that the flow-through of cost to the cost of goods sold account consists of goods that were bought less recently than the goods that remain in inventory. While the expense account in the income statement is valued at the earlier price, the inventory account on the balance sheet is valued at the more recent price. (See Focus Box 4A2.2.)

LIFO Model

In some circumstances, the inventory flow may be that the goods sold are those most recently acquired — i.e., a last-in-first-out (LIFO) system. Therefore, inventory becomes that which was acquired the earliest. This is a pattern, however, that is rarely observed in practice. (See Focus Box 4A2.3).

Focus Box 4A2.2:   Inventory — FIFO

Mike's Gas Station has a convenience outlet attached. Among the products it sells are bread and milk. Because both bread and milk deteriorate over time, the cartons they are delivered in always state on the instructions to "sell old stock first". So, when the new stock is put on the shelf, the new stock is put at the back, and the old stock is put at the front. When customers pull the milk or bread off the shelf, they are buying the older stock, and the inventory is always the newer goods.

At the beginning of May the inventory of one litre, 2% milk was 20 packets, each having a cost of $1.10. During the month of May there were eight deliveries, each of 100 packets. The first six deliveries were invoiced at $1.10. For the last two deliveries the price went up to $1.20. At the end of the month the inventory was 10 packets.

		Packets	Price	
Inventory at May 1		20 × $1.10		$ 22.00
+ Goods purchased in May	6 × 100 =	600 × $1.10		660.00
	2 × 100 =	200 × $1.20		240.00
Goods available for sale		820		$922.00
– Inventory at May 31		– 10		
Total units sold in May		810		
Cost of goods sold (810 units)	20 + 600 =	620 × $1.10	$682.00	
	190 =	190 × $1.20	228.00	910.00
Inventory at May 31	820 – 810 =	10 × $1.20		$ 12.00

Focus Box 4A2.3:   Inventory — LIFO

Mike's Gas Station sells engine oil. This product has a long shelf life, and the packaging design is not frequently changed. Price, however, may change occasionally. When new inventory comes in it is loaded at the front of the display case, and old inventory is pushed to the back. Customers who pick oil off the shelves are buying the most recently purchased inventory.

There were 50 half-litres of 10W/30 oil in inventory at the end of April, and they had cost $2 each. In the month of May, there was a delivery of oil that included 200 half-litres of 10W/30, at a cost of $2.50 each. During the month 150 half-litres were sold, and there were 100 in inventory at the end of the month.

	Units	Price		
Inventory at May 1	50 × $2.00			$100.00
Purchase during May	+ 200 × $2.50			500.00
Available for sale	250			$600.00
– Inventory at May 31	– 100			
Total units sold in May	150			
Cost of goods sold (150 units)	150 × $2.50			375.00
Inventory at May 31 (250 – 150 = 100)	50 × $2.50	$125		
	50 × $2.00	100		$225.00

It is generally included in accounting textbooks because of a peculiarity of the U.S. tax laws. In the United States, companies are allowed to

---

Focus Box 4A2.4: Inventory — Weighted Average

Mike's Gas Station sells gas. The regular gas tank holds 20,000 litres, and there are deliveries whenever stocks fall to a level of 5,000 litres. The price Mike's pays for gas depends on world gas prices, which can change for every delivery. Once in the tank, of course, all the existing gas is mixed with the new delivery. There were 10,000 litres of regular gas in inventory on May 1, at a cost of $0.55 per litre. Deliveries of 15,000 litres (to fill up the tank) were made on the 1st, 15th, and 22nd of the month, at costs of $0.55, $0.60, and $0.54, respectively. There were 6,000 litres in the regular gas tank at the end of May.

Inventory at May 1	(10,000 × $0.55)	$ 5,500.00
Delivery, May 1	(15,000 × $0.55)	8,250.00
Delivery, May 15	(15,000 × $0.60)	9,000.00
Delivery, May 22	(15,000 × $0.54)	8,100.00
Total	55,000	$30,850.00
Weighted average	$30,850 ÷ 55,000 = $0.56091	
Total units sold	55,000 – 6,000 = 49,000 litres	
Cost of goods sold	49,000 × $0.56091	$27,484.59
Inventory as at May 31	6,000 × $0.56091	3,365.46
Total accounted for	55,000 × $0.56091	$30,850.05

---

use LIFO to value inventory as a way of giving them a tax break in times of rising prices. This situation does not apply to Canada, and LIFO is not used by Canadian companies.

Weighted Average Model

In many situations, new purchases are mixed with existing inventory, and it becomes impossible to separate them. The only reasonable inventory valuation would be averaging the inventory values. (See Focus Box 4A2.4.)

The pattern of inventory flows is a matter of fact. The question of whether to use that actual inventory flow as the model for the accounting resource flow is a separate decision. Perhaps surprisingly, GAAP does not absolutely require the inventory flow assumption used for financial accounting be the same as the inventory flow pattern that happens in reality. Of the various inventory flow assumptions, the most common one used in Canada is FIFO.

In times of steady prices, the differences between the methods are small or non-existent. In times of rapidly changing prices, the difference in operating profit caused by using different valuation models will be substantial. The choice of valuation model is, therefore, potentially an important decision.

Appendix 4.3
Consolidation of Groups of Companies

When one company owns a few shares of another company, it is an investment (either short- or long-term, depending on the facts) that appears at cost (or market value, if less) on the balance sheet. Where the shareholding is large, rather than treating them as two separate companies, it may be more sensible to treat both companies as a single economic entity. This is done through a process called consolidation.

In consolidation, the cost of acquiring the shares of the subsidiary company is replaced, on the balance sheet of the holding company, by the assets and liabilities of the subsidiary company.

The consolidated income statement will be the sum of the income statements of the holding company and the subsidiary company. Their revenues and expenses are added together. As a result, the income becomes the sum of the incomes of the two companies.

An exception to this is where the holding company and the subsidiary have traded between each other. In order to reflect the idea that the consolidated accounts are the results of the composite economic unit, intercompany sales and purchases are eliminated from both income statements, and any unrealized profits on intercompany sales are eliminated.

Mike's Motor Sales Inc. is a wholly owned subsidiary of Mike's Motors Inc. In preparing the balance sheet of Mike's Motors Inc., there is an asset, Investment in Mike's Motor Sales Inc., of $25,000. Consolidation would replace that $25,000 with the actual assets and liabilities (but not the equity) of Mike's Motor Sales Inc. The new title of the balance sheet would be "Consolidated Balance Sheet of Mike's Motors Inc. and Its Subsidiary" (see next page).

Minority Interest: Goodwill on Consolidation

Where all the shares in the subsidiary company are owned by the holding company, the consolidation process consists of adding all the assets and liabilities of the subsidiary to the assets and liabilities of the holding company and adding the two income statements together.

Even where the holding company owns less than 100% of the subsidiary, it may still be necessary to consolidate them. Canadian accounting practice requires the consolidation of companies where 50% or more of the shares are held, or where as little as 20% of the shares are held if the holding company can effectively control the subsidiary (e.g., by having the power to appoint the directors of the company).

Mike's Motors Inc.
Balance Sheet as at December 31

Assets

Current assets

Cash	$ 2,000	
Receivables	45,000	
Inventory	23,000	$ 70,000

Long-term assets

Equipment at cost	$50,000	
Less: Accumulated amortization	30,000	$20,000
Investment in Mike's Motor Sales Inc.		25,000	45,000
Total assets		$115,000

Liabilities and Equity

Current liabilities

Trade payables	$ 5,000
Bank loans	25,000
	$ 30,000
Long-term liabilities	20,000
Total liabilities	$ 50,000
Shareholders' equity	65,000
Total liabilities and equities	$115,000

Mike's Motors Sales Inc.
Balance Sheet as at December 31

Assets

Cash	$ 5,000
Receivables	0
Inventory	24,000
Total assets	$ 29,000

Liabilities and Equity

Trade payables	$ 4,000
Shareholders' equity	25,000
Total liabilities and equities	$ 29,000

Mike's Motors Inc. and Its Subsidiary
Consolidated Balance Sheet as at December 31

Assets

Current assets

Cash ($2,000 + $5,000)	$ 7,000	
Receivables	45,000	
Inventory ($23,000 + $24,000)	47,000	$ 99,000

Long-term assets

Equipment at cost	$50,000	
Less: Accumulated amortization	30,000	20,000
Total Assets		$119,000

Liabilities and Equity

Current liabilities

Trade payables ($4,000 + $5,000)	$ 9,000
Bank loans	25,000
	$ 34,000
Long-term liabilities	20,000
Total liabilities	$ 54,000
Shareholders' equity	65,000
Total liabilities and equities	$119,000

In situations where the subsidiary company is less than 100% owned, we have to recognize that there is some part of the net assets that is not owned by the holding company. This is done by showing an item on the balance sheet called Minority Interest.

Another issue is where the amount paid for the shares by the holding company is not precisely equal to the balance sheet value of the net assets of the subsidiary. Where the net assets exceed the cost of the shares, we will show "gain on consolidation" in the equity of the consolidated balance sheet. Where the cost of the shares exceeds the net assets of the subsidiary, we will show an asset Goodwill in the consolidated balance sheet.

In the previous example, suppose the $25,000 that Mike's Motors Inc. paid for shares in Mike's Motor Sales Inc. had bought Mike's Motors Inc. not 100%, but only 60% of the shares. Two items would now have to be recognized: first, the 40% minority interest in the net assets of the subsidiary (40% × $25,000 = $10,000); second, the goodwill of $10,000. Goodwill is calculated as follows:

Net assets of subsidiary ($29,000 – $4,000)	$ 25,000
Less: Minority interest	10,000
Holding company's interest	$ 15,000
Amount paid	$ 25,000
Goodwill ($25,000 – $15,000)	$ 10,000

Mike's Motors Inc. and Its Subsidiary
Consolidated Balance Sheet as at December 31

Assets

Current assets		
Cash	$ 7,000	
Receivables	45,000	
Inventory	47,000	$ 99,000
Long-term assets		
Equipment at cost	$50,000	
Less: Accumulated amortization	30,000	
	$20,000	
Goodwill	10,000	30,000
		$129,000

Liabilities and Equity

Current liabilities		
Trade payables	$ 9,000	
Bank loans	25,000	$ 34,000
Long-term liabilities		20,000
Total liabilities		$ 54,000
Shareholders' equity	$65,000	
Minority interest	10,000	75,000
		$129,000

Instead of amortization, goodwill is periodically subjected to an "impairment" test, and any deficiency is written off at that time.

Self-Study Problem

1. Charley Farley went into business on October 1, 2005, by opening a doughnut shop. He carried on the business in a rented store in downtown Orillia. At the end of December, he realized that he would have to pay income tax on the business profits, but he had no idea how much profit he had made or what his assets and liabilities were. He has asked you to prepare a balance sheet.

   He has presented you with his bank statements and a pile of invoices and receipts. The following is a summarized list of payments and receipts for the three months.

   Receipts paid into bank account:

1.	Owners' equity	$ 50,000
2.	Bank loan	55,000
3.	Cash sales	146,500
		$251,500

   Payments made out of bank account:

4.	Suppliers	$104,500
5.	Wages	12,000
6.	Rent	20,000
7.	Utilities	5,000
8.	Insurance	4,000
9.	Equipment	99,000
10.	Repayment of bank loan	4,000
		$248,500

   You are given the following additional information:
   (a) The cash received from sales was $161,500. Charley Farley took $5,000 each month from the cash sales for his own living expenses before paying the balance into the bank.
   (b) Charley has a coffee delivery arrangement with a nearby office. He delivers the coffee daily; they pay him weekly. At the end of December they owed him $500.
   (c) The $104,500 paid for supplies is not exactly the amount used: Charley owes suppliers another $5,000, and there is inventory on hand that had cost him $1,500.
   (d) The $20,000 paid for rent consists of payment for October, November, and December's rent of $5,000 per month, plus the "last" month of the lease of $5,000.
   (e) In addition to the $5,000 paid for utilities, another $1,000 is owed.
   (f) The insurance premium of $4,000 gives him coverage from October 1, 2005 to September 30, 2006.
   (g) Amortization expense on the equipment should be taken as $9,000 for the three months to December 31, 2005.
   (h) The bank loan is on a five-year term.

   [Note: This is a continuation of Self-Study Problem 3.1 on page 121. You may need to refer back to that problem (and even Self-Study Problem 2.1 on page 67) to help in doing this one.]

Required

(a) Prepare a balance sheet for Charley Farley as at December 31, 2005.
(b) Given that the sales for the year were $162,000, what are the receivables turnover ratio and the receivables collection period?
(c) Given that the sales for the year were $162,000, what are the inventory turnover ratio and the days' sales in inventory holding period?
(d) Given that the sales for the year were $162,000, what was the total asset turnover ratio?

Solution

1. (a) Cash account summary:

Cash banked	$251,500	
Owner's withdrawals	15,000	
Total receipts		$266,500
Bank payments	$248,500	
Owner's withdrawals	15,000	
Total payments		263,500
Cash balance		$ 3,000

Charley Farley
Balance Sheet as at December 31, 2005

Assets

Current assets:		
Cash	$ 3,000	
Receivables	500	
Inventory	1,500	
Prepaid rent	5,000	
Prepaid insurance	3,000	$ 13,000
Long-term assets:		
At cost	$ 99,000	
Less: Accumulated amortization	(9,000)	90,000
		$103,000

Liabilities and Equity

Current liabilities:		
Trade payables	$ 5,000	
Accrued utilities	1,000	$ 6,000
Long-term debt (bank loan)		
($55,000 – $4,000)		51,000
Total liabilities		$ 57,000
Owners' equity:		
Cash introduced	$ 50,000	
Add: Net income	11,000	
Less: Withdrawn	(15,000)	46,000
		$103,000

(b)   Receivables turnover ratio:

$$= \text{sales} \div \text{receivables}$$
$$= \$162{,}000 \div \$500$$
$$= 324 \text{ times per year}$$

Receivables collection period:

$$= \text{receivables} \div (\text{sales} \div 365)$$
$$= \$500 \div (\$162{,}000 \div 365)$$
$$= 1.1 \text{ days}$$

(c)   Inventory turnover ratio:

$$= \text{sales} \div \text{inventory}$$
$$= \$162{,}000 \div \$1{,}500$$
$$= 108 \text{ times per year}$$

Inventory holding period:

$$= \text{inventory} \div (\text{sales} \div 365)$$
$$= \$1{,}500 \div (\$162{,}000 \div 365)$$
$$= 3.4 \text{ days}$$

(d)   Total asset turnover ratio:

$$= \text{sales} \div \text{total assets}$$
$$= \$162{,}000 \div \$103{,}000$$
$$= 1.6 \text{ times per year}$$

Discussion Questions and Problems

Discussion Questions

1. Financial statements are prepared annually. Why is one year chosen as the reporting period, as opposed to any other period?
2. Inventory and equipment, which comes first in the balance sheet, and why?
3. How are long-term assets valued for inclusion in the balance sheet?
4. How are short-term assets valued for inclusion in the balance sheet?
5. Give some examples of assets that are important to the company, but that are not included in the balance sheet.
6. To whom is the balance sheet more important: investors or creditors?
7. Give one example of the conservatism principle being used in the balance sheet.
8. In what way is the constant value of the dollar in conflict with the historical cost principle in the balance sheet?
9. One of your customers has been buying goods from you regularly for the past six months. He has always paid cash with order, as that is what your company normally does. Today you have received a call from your sales department. This customer wants to buy twice as much as he normally does in a month, but wants 30 days credit. Do you say yes or no?
10. Your company manufactures plastic mouldings. A management consultant suggested that you could be more efficient by moving to "just-in-time" ordering of raw materials. One of your plant managers has objected, saying that without that inventory, the balance sheet would have fewer assets, and they would all be worse off. Who is right?
11. Why do companies value inventory at the lower of cost and market price?
12. What would be the advantages and disadvantages of including human resource assets (the value of employees) on the balance sheet?

Problems

1. Explain how the following would be included in the balance sheet of the Radical Theatre Company, which produces its financial reports to December 31 each year. In each case identify the basis of valuation, the dollar value, and the accounting concept(s) that apply:

    (a) The Radical Theatre Company bought a new ticketing system recently, at a cost of $15,000. A competitor has just announced a better system that could be bought for $10,000. Both systems would normally be expected to be used for 10 years and then replaced. The company uses the straight-line method of amortization.

    (b) The Radical Theatre Company bought a new ticketing system two years ago, at a cost of $15,000. Due to changes in technology, tickets are now issued by Ticketmaster, and the in-house ticketing system is no longer used. The ticketing system would normally be expected to be used for 10 years and then replaced. The company uses the straight-line method of amortization.

(c) The Radical Theatre Company operates out of a disused church (which they own) in downtown Hamilton. The church cost $100,000 five years ago. The current resale value is closer to $250,000.

(d) The Radical Theatre Company spent $25,000 to buy sets and costumes for its latest production. Everyone agrees that the play will run past the end of December and into next year, and that it is likely to be revived on a regular basis in the next few years.

(e) The Radical Theatre Company spent $10,000 on commissioning a new Canadian opera. They had hoped that it would be a long-run success and be shown for two theatre seasons. However, the critics have panned it, and it will probably close by the end of September.

(f) The Radical Theatre Company has just signed a contract with a major TV star. The company expects that his $100,000 salary will be reflected in huge attendances at their comedy nights, and that profits this year will reach $500,000, and next year, $750,000.

2. As at December 31, 2005, Mmbelwa Inc. had a total of $585,000 recorded as owed by credit sale customers. Of this, $85,000 was owed by customers who are never going to pay for one reason or another. In respect of the balance, Mmbelwa Inc. has decided to introduce (for the first time) an allowance for doubtful debts of 1% of the amount owed.

Required
(a) What is the bad debt expense for year 2005?
(b) How would the accounts receivable appear on the balance sheet as at December 31, 2005?
(c) If sales revenue for 2005 was $5,940,000, calculate the receivables turnover ratio.
(d) If sales revenue for 2005 was $5,940,000, calculate the receivables collection period.

3. Chitenge Co. had accounts receivable as at December 31, 2005, of $283,400 and had an allowance for doubtful debts of $30,000. During January 2006, it was discovered that one credit customer had gone bankrupt, owing $10,000, and one credit customer had run away without paying the $2,000 she owed, both of which were amounts owed from 2005. During January 2006 a total of $190,000 was collected from the accounts receivable, but no additional credit sales were made.

Required
(a) Show how the accounts receivable would appear in the balance sheet as at December 31, 2005.

(b) Show how the accounts receivable would appear in the balance sheet as at January 31, 2006, after writing off the two bad debts, but before recording the collection of cash during January.

(c) Show how the accounts receivable would appear in the balance sheet as at January 31, 2006, after writing off the two bad debts and after recording the collection of cash during January.

(d) What accounting concepts apply to the creation of the allowance for doubtful debts?

4. Mulanje Ltd. had the following raw material and finished goods inventory on hand as at December 31, 2005:

- 10,000 litres of Xylon @ $25 per litre. As at December 31, 2005, the replacement price was $30 per litre.
- 200 kg of Ylanti @ $500 per kg. As at December 31, the replacement price was $400 per kg.
- 1,000 ten-gallon Z-type packing cartons @ $5 each. These were no longer useful as the product had been changed to metric sizes.
- 200 boxes of Alpha, which had a manufactured cost of $100 per box, and which would be sold for $175 per box.
- 100 boxes of Beta, which has a manufactured cost of $200 per box, and which would be sold for $150 per box.
- 50 boxes of Gamma, which had a manufactured cost of $50 per box, but which was past its "sell by" date, and which would have to be thrown out.

Required
Show how the inventory would appear in the balance sheet as at December 31, 2005.

5. You have just bought $250,000 of building materials from Home Depot, which is quite willing to give you one month's credit, but, alternatively, would give you a 5% discount if you paid cash now. You can pay in cash, but only by borrowing the money from your bank at 15% per year interest, or by putting it on your credit card at 25% per year interest.

Required
Work out the best payment plan for this situation.

6. List the order in which the following assets would appear in the balance sheet:

- Plant & equipment
- Amortization on plant & equipment
- Accounts payable
- Accounts receivable
- Cash
- Inventory
- Prepayments
- Deposits

- Bank chequing account
- Patents & trademarks
- Investment in a subsidiary company

7. Steamboat Brewery started business in Oakville in 1980. The company invested in beer-brewing equipment at a cost of $750,000. This was amortized over its expected useful life of 20 years. As of 2004 it was still in use, and because it has been well maintained, it was still fully functional. The company had no plans to discontinue its use anytime soon.

    (a) In which section of the balance sheet would this asset appear?
    (b) What would be the basis of valuation (i.e., what accounting concepts apply)?
    (c) Show how the asset would appear on the balance sheet on the first day it was owned.
    (d) Show how the asset would appear on the balance sheet after 10 years of use.
    (e) Show how the asset would appear on the balance sheet as at December 31, 2004.
    (f) If the company disposed of this equipment on January 1, 2005, for $80,000, what would be reported in the income statement and in the balance sheet?

8. Sealicity Co. has the following as at December 31, 2005:

Cash balances in the tills at retail outlets	$ 28,000
Accounts receivable (net of doubtful debts)	$458,000
Petty cash balances in head office	$ 5,000
Chequing account at the Bank of Toyland	$ 58,000
Accounts payable	$234,000
Inventory of goods for resale	
(at the lower of cost or market value)	$625,000
Term deposits with Investor's Trust	$500,000
Land & building (at cost)	$300,000
Accumulated amortization on building	$ 50,000
Mortgage owed to Property Trust Inc.	$125,000
Bank loan (repayable on demand)	$245,000
Utility deposit with Seal City Hydro	$ 1,000
Utility expense owed to Seal City Hydro	$ 2,000
Rent paid in advance	$ 3,000
Shares in Union Carbide Inc. (at market value)	$100,000
Plant & equipment (at cost)	$900,000
Accumulated amortization on plant	$400,000
Intangible assets (at cost)	$235,000

    Required
    (a) Show how these would be reported in the current assets section of the balance sheet.
    (b) Show how these would be reported in the long-term assets section of the balance sheet.
    (c) What is the total asset value on the balance sheet?

9. Markham Pharma Inc. has paid the following amounts in 2005. In each case show the dollar value that would be included in the balance sheet as at December 31, 2005, and list the accounting principle(s) that apply.

    (a) $500,000 for basic research into the elusive cure for the common cold
    (b) $250,000 for advertising the company's new on-line prescription drug service
    (c) $300,000 for the design of a new company logo
    (d) $400,000 for a two-year contract (2006 & 2007) for the rights to manufacture a well-established and successful slimming pill
    (e) $800,000 for testing a new depression medication: the trials were successful and the drug will be put on the market in 2006

10. The balance sheet of Icme Iron Inc. as at December 31, 2005, is as follows:

Current assets			Current liabilities		
Cash	$ 10,000		Trade payables	$ 65,000	
Receivables	50,000		Bank loan	15,000	
Inventory	65,000		Income tax due	20,000	
Total	$125,000		Total		$100,000
Long-term assets	225,000		Long-term liabilities		75,000
			Total liabilities		$175,000
			Shareholders' equity		
			Share capital	$ 50,000	
			Retained earnings	125,000	
			Total equity		175,000
Total assets	$350,000		Total liabilities & equity		$350,000

You are told that the sales revenue for 2005 was $1,200,000 and that the company made a net income of $120,000 in 2005.

Required
Calculate the following ratios:
• Receivables turnover ratio
• Receivables collection period
• Inventory turnover ratio
• Inventory holding period

11. Constable Co. had sales revenue of $4,000,000 in 2004 and $5,000,000 in 2005. The accounts receivable as at January 1, 2005, were $800,000. As at December 31, 2005, the accounts receivable had increased to $1,000,000.

    Required
    (a) Calculate the accounts receivable turnover ratio for 2004 and 2005.
    (b) Has the management of accounts receivable improved or worsened between 2004 and 2005?

(c) How much cash did Constable Co. collect from its sales in 2005?

(d) If sales for 2006 were expected to be $10,000,000, how much would you expect the accounts receivable to be at the end of 2006?

(e) Does the increase in sales create any issues for cash management?

5

The Balance Sheet (2):

Liabilities and Equity

Learning
Objectives

After studying this chapter you should be able to list and explain the following components of the balance sheet:
→ Current liabilities
→ Long-term liabilities
→ Equity share capital

And you should be able to analyze and critically comment on the following through the use of appropriate accounting ratios:
→ Liquidity
→ Risk associated with debt

5.1 Liabilities

According to the accounting equation, the assets are funded by a combination of equity and liabilities:

ASSETS = LIABILITIES + OWNERS' EQUITY

Liabilities are all the amounts the company owes to outsiders and do not include the owners' investment in the business (owners are not outsiders). Liabilities are included whether they are due immediately or are due at some time in the future. When the liabilities are listed in the balance sheet, the order of liquidity is used to show those that are more current from those that are less current. This is similar to the presentation of the assets in the balance sheet.

5.1.1 Current Liabilities

Current assets are defined as those likely to be realized within one year. Current liabilities are defined as those that are due within one year, and many are due even sooner. Current liabilities are one of the biggest threats to a company's existence. Failing to pay the current liabilities when they are due is the easiest way to get into bankruptcy. Therefore, however good the longer-term prospects are, the company has to manage the current liabilities to ensure that there is always enough liquidity to deal with them. (See Focus Box 5.1.) Comparing the current liabilities with the current assets gives some idea of whether the company is about to face a liquidity crisis. The main types of current liability are:

• trade payables;
• accrued expenses;
• deferred revenue;
• taxes due; and
• short-term loans.

Focus Box 5.1:   Automated Payments

The costs of maintaining the trade credit records are substantial. It is necessary to keep a record of every occasion when something is bought on credit. The delivery of the goods or receipt of the services has to be recorded. The goods have to be counted and checked for quality and conformance with specifications. The prices on the invoice have to be checked against the contract. The calculations on the invoice have to be checked. All the invoices for a month have to be added, and the total agreed with the supplier's monthly statement of account. Only when all this paperwork is complete and in order is the buyer in a position to write a cheque for the amount owing.

In the modern management environment, organizations have taken steps to deal with the costs and uncertainties of trade credit. Major Japanese motor manufacturers have arrangements with their suppliers whereby the supply of parts is governed by long-term contracts and just-in-time scheduling of deliveries. The delivery automatically triggers a direct transfer of the cost of the goods from the buyer's bank account to the seller's without the need for invoices, goods received notes, or cheques.

5.1.2   *Trade Payables*

The largest current liability is generally the amount the company owes to its various suppliers for goods and services received. In the same way that the company sells goods on credit (and creates the asset Accounts Receivable), it will also buy on credit. Any unpaid accounts at the end of the year will become a liability (called *Trade Payables* or *Accounts Payable*).

In the case of accounts receivable, it was necessary to make an allowance for bad or doubtful debts. There is no need to make any such reduction in the trade payables; they will be stated on the balance sheet at their full face value, as that is what the company will be paying.

Trade credit is generally offered on a 30-day basis, so it is reasonable to assume that the total amount shown as trade payables is due within a month. Some industries, though, have traditionally operated on shorter or longer periods of trade credit. If there are enough current assets available in the form of cash (and short-term investments) to pay the trade payables, the company probably has enough liquidity. If the company has to collect its receivables before it can pay the trade payables, the company is a little riskier. And if the company has to sell its inventory before it can pay its trade payables, then the risk position may be even greater.

There is no interest payable on trade credit as long as it is paid by the due date. The implication is that it is free money. If that is the case, a business would be foolish to ignore this opportunity for free financing. As the amounts involved can be very large, this is a serious issue.

If the buyer has the cash available, she or he may be able to negotiate a lower price (a cash discount) for paying "cash with order" or "cash on delivery". If that happens, the trade credit is not free. Its cost is just disguised in the invoice price.

Some sellers offer a combination of trade credit and a cash discount for prompt settlement. Terms "2/10, net 30" on an invoice mean that the buyer may deduct a 2% discount from the face value of the invoice by making payment within 10 days; failing that, the full (net) amount of the invoice is due at the end of 30 days. All other things being equal, this means that the 2% discount is given for the 20-day difference between payment at day 10 and payment at day 30. The effective annual interest rate on this is 43%! (There are 18.25 20-day periods in a year. The effective annual interest rate is 1.02 to the power of 18.25, minus 1, which is 43%.) This is so high a rate that any company in its right mind would take the opportunity.

In practice, buyers often stretch the payment terms beyond the 30 days they are allowed. If that is the case, the benefit of the 2% prompt payment discount becomes significantly less.

To combat late payers, many sellers are now writing into sales contracts a clause that charges interest on accounts not paid on time.

Look at your latest utilities bill. It will show one amount due for payment by the due date and another, higher amount for payment after the due date. This is effectively charging you interest for late payment.

Look at your latest phone bill. It will state that accounts not paid by their due date are liable to have interest added on.

5.1.3 Accrued Expenses

In addition to trade credit, companies may owe money to suppliers of other goods and services. For some of these transactions, the process is very similar to trade credit: goods or services are supplied, an invoice is issued, and if unpaid, represents a liability. Occasions also arise where the amount owing has to be estimated, because the invoice is not yet available.

Suppose it is the end of the fiscal year, December 31. A company may have an unpaid bill for electricity usage for the month up to December 20 (which was the last time the meters were read). The company would record the unpaid bill as a liability. It would also estimate the electricity usage for the 11 days from December 21 to 31 (based on past usage patterns). This would be an accrued expense in the balance sheet.

Accrued expenses are typically small in total, by comparison with trade creditors.

Companies must pay income tax on their profits. The taxes are assessed annually and are paid in a lump sum. At the end of the fiscal year, the taxes owing on the profit of that year will be unpaid. Because they will be due soon after the year-end, they will also be a current liability.

5.1.4 Short-term Debt

Trade credit, accrued expenses, and taxes due all arise, almost automatically, out of the normal operation of a business. None of them has an explicit cost. By contrast, both short- and long-term loans are the result of a definite decision to borrow, and interest is payable on the amount borrowed.

If the company has borrowed money on a short-term basis, the amount due will be shown as short-term debt. This would include a short-term loan from a bank, a trust company, or other lending institution.

A short-term loan might be due at a specific date (e.g., a 90-day loan), or it might be potentially payable within a short period of time (e.g., a loan that is "callable" on seven days notice, meaning one on which the bank can insist on repayment after seven days), even though the intention of both parties is for the loan period to be longer.

Companies should use short-term borrowing to meet short-term financing needs. Thus, if the cash budget shows that there is a liquidity crunch in the months of June and July, they will try to match the time of their borrowing to the period where cash is in need: i.e., by borrowing short-term for June and July. It would be foolish to borrow money for the entire year if the money would be sitting idle in a chequing account for 10 months.

If there is a long-term loan that is payable in instalments, that part that is due for repayment within a year is included in the short-term debt section, not as long-term debt.

5.1.5 Assessing Risk Through Liquidity Ratios

Short-term debt is a significant source of risk for the company. Failure to pay liabilities as and when they fall due is the immediate cause of bankruptcy (though its origins may go back to unprofitable business operations). To assess the likelihood of the company's getting into a liquidity crisis, it is common to calculate liquidity ratios. These set the short-term liabilities against the funds available to pay them.

The current ratio compares all the current assets against the current liabilities. (See Focus Box 5.2.)

Focus Box 5.2: Liquidity Ratios

Mike's Motors' balance sheet shows current assets of $99,000, current liabilities of $34,000, and inventory of $48,000:

Current ratio:

= current assets ÷ current liabilities
= $99,000 ÷ $34,000
= 2.9 : 1

Quick ratio:

= (current assets – inventory) ÷ current liabilities
= ($99,000 – $48,000) ÷ $34,000
= 1.5 : 1

In general, creditors will look for a current ratio of 2 : 1 or higher, or a quick ratio of 1 : 1 or higher to be sure that there is adequate liquidity. Mike's Motors, with a current ratio of 2.9 : 1, and a quick ratio of 1.5 : 1, comfortably exceeds these levels.

One of the criticisms of the current ratio is that it assumes all current assets are available to pay current liabilities. In fact, some are more liquid than others. In particular, inventory tends to be a rather slow-moving asset. A more stringent test is the quick ratio (acid-test ratio). This ratio compares current assets, excluding inventory, to current liabilities.

In general, the current ratio is expected to be 2 : 1 or higher, and the quick ratio 1 : 1 or higher.

5.1.6   Long-term Debt

Amounts owed for which the term is longer than one year are shown as long-term debt. It is important that these obligations be listed, as they will have to be repaid eventually. It is also desirable to separate them from the short-term debt, on the one hand (which has to be repaid very soon), and the equity, on the other hand (which does not have to be repaid, ever). The company has the use of long-term debt, but not forever. The two most frequently encountered types of long-term debt are mortgage loans and debentures and notes.

5.1.6.1   Mortgage Loans

When anyone (companies included) buys real estate (land and buildings), the cost is often more than they have available to spend. A mortgage loan is money advanced to assist in the purchase of such an asset, for which the real estate itself is used as security. A legal agreement is signed in which the borrower undertakes to repay the loan with interest. The repayment is either in regular instalments or in a lump sum at the end of a specific period. The interest is at a specified rate (e.g., 9% per annum). If the terms of the agreement are kept up, eventually the purchaser will have repaid the debt and the interest, and will own the real estate unencum bered. If the purchaser fails to make any of the payments due under the agreement, the asset may be sold and the proceeds used to repay the debt and any outstanding interest. The lender thus has very good security for the loan.

Mortgaging any asset means using it as the collateral security for a loan. When that happens, the asset is no longer available to any other creditors. Until the mortgage loan is repaid, the asset's value is legally tied up, and the fact that the asset is mortgaged must clearly be shown in the financial statements.

5.1.6.2   Debentures and Notes

Debentures and notes are written acknowledgements of a debt. They are used so that the company can borrow money under stated terms of interest and repayment. The lenders may be members of the general public, banks, or other financial institutions. Sometimes debentures have specific assets pledged as security, in which case they may be called mortgage debentures, but mostly they do not. The lender is relying on the reputation and past history of the company for getting paid.

A debenture is a contract and contains numerous terms. Some of the more important ones cover:

- the amount of the loan;
- the date when the loan is issued;
- the date when the loan is repayable (or a schedule of repayment dates if repaid in instalments);
- the interest rate payable;
- the dates on which interest payments will be made;
- any assets specifically pledged as security.

Debt instruments of both companies and governments are traded in a part of the stock market known as the bond market. The market for interest rates on these borrowed funds is very precise. The return on a given debenture will rise or fall as the market rises or falls. It will also change because of factors specific to the issuer. If lenders lose trust in a company's ability to fulfill the terms of a debenture, the lenders will react by selling that company's debentures, and/or by requiring a higher return. This does not affect the company directly, but there are important implications to its cost of borrowing from new sources.

5.1.7   Total Liabilities

The total of all liabilities, long-term and short-term, will be shown on the balance sheet. This total is a useful number to know: it shows how much of the company's assets have been financed by borrowed funds, as opposed to the equity funds provided by the owners. This relationship (debt vs. equity) is referred to as the leverage of the company, and is one measure of company risk. The greater the percentage of the assets financed through debt, the riskier the company.

5.1.8   Assessing Risk Through Debt Analysis

One way to measure a company's level of risk is to compare the amount of debt it has compared to its equity. A company that is financed mostly from equity capital is low risk because the shareholders have no right either to the return of their capital, or to any dividends from the company. Debt, however, implies an obligation to pay interest on a regular basis and an obligation to repay the loan at the end of its term.

If a company has a loss-making year (or even a series of loss-making years), the company financed by equity will have some unhappy shareholders but may be able to struggle through. The company with a higher level of debt will find that its obligations give rise to a higher probability of bankruptcy.

To assess the level of this risk it is common to calculate either debt as a percentage of equity, or debt as a percentage of total assets.

Debt is the sum of all short-term and long-term liabilities. As total assets is defined through the accounting equation as being equal to debt plus equity, the two debt ratios give identical economic information — they just express it in different ways. (See Focus Box 5.3.)

Focus Box 5.3:   Assessing Risk Through Debt Ratios

The balance sheet for Mike's Motors shows a total debt of $54,000, equity of $65,000, and total assets of $119,000.

Debt-to-equity ratio (%):
= ($54,000 ÷ $65,000) × 100%
= 83.1%

Debt-to-assets ratio (%):
= ($54,000 ÷ $119,000) × 100%
= 45.4%

Both of these ratios are within the usual range for acceptable levels of risk (100% and 50%, respectively).

In Canada and the United States, it is common for the debt-to-equity ratio to be kept below 100%. That is also equivalent to keeping the debt-to-assets ratio below 50%. At levels higher than these, creditors and investors start to worry about excessive risk.

5.2   Equity

Equity is the accounting way of describing the owners' interest in the business. Technically, it is a residual: what is left over after liabilities are deducted from assets. That is more than a trite rearrangement of the accounting equation (remember: assets = liabilities + owners' equity). What it means is that we use valuations to arrive at our totals for assets and liabilities: the dollar value of each element is individually determined when it is included in the balance sheet. We do not do the same thing for equity. We merely recognize it as what is left over when all the other things have been valued.

There are a number of ways that the value of equity can be changed. Initially, of course, the company has no equity, but one of the first transactions a company is likely to be involved in is when the initial investors put some of their funds into the business to get it going. Putting their money in increases the company's assets. Double-entry recording requires that some balancing entry in the records be made to recognize where that increase in assets came from, and equity is the title given to it. So, equity starts off as zero and then increases because of the owners' investment.

Owners' investment can happen later in the company's life, as well as at the start. If more money is pumped into an ongoing business by investors, that also is recognized as equity. That investment typically happens when a company wants to expand, and it needs more capital to do so.

5.2.1 **Shares**

Investment in a company is in the form of "shares". We all have an understanding of the word *share* from common English usage: it means that two or more people have equal rights to part of something. The share of the company means exactly the same thing. Each shareholder has an equal right with each other shareholder to enjoy the benefits of ownership of the company. It is perhaps a more formalized relationship, and it is evidenced by a piece of paper called a share certificate, but it is fundamentally a recognition of this equality between a number of individuals in their ownership of the company.

In theory, as owners, the shareholders have the last word in company decisions. In practice, it is not as simple as that. It would be impractical for the large modern corporation to have every shareholder actively involved in the running of the day-to-day business. Just imagine the number of shareholders in a company such as General Motors or Bell Canada, and you will get a sense of how difficult that would be. Instead, professional managers (called directors) run the company on behalf of the shareholders. This is referred to as the divorce of ownership and control. It is this separation that makes it so necessary to have financial reports prepared and sent to shareholders to keep them informed of how well the company is being run on their behalf.

The rights of the shareholders may be summarized as follows:

- attending the annual general meeting;
- voting on issues such as accepting the financial statements, the payment of dividends as proposed by the directors, appointing the auditor, and election of the directors at the annual general meeting;
- being kept informed by receiving financial statements annually.

Ultimately, if shareholders don't like the way the company is being run, or its performance, they have the right to sell their shares on the open market to anyone who will buy them.

This last right, selling shares, is actually more powerful than it looks. If one small shareholder sells his or her shares, the effect is probably insignificant. If an institutional shareholder with a large holding sells out, or a number of smaller shareholders all sell at the same time, then there may be a dramatic effect on the share price. Selling pressure can lower the share price quite sharply.

Conversely, if there are many potential buyers trying to purchase shares of the company, market forces will push the share price up. Company directors constantly monitor the share price and use it as a measure of how well the company is perceived by investors.

The shareholder gets two potential benefits from owning the shares: dividends and capital appreciation.

In the past, the initial investment in common shares would have had a "par" or "nominal" value. For example, a company might have issued one million shares of $1 each to raise $1 million of share capital. Current practice, however, is to issue shares "of no par value": i.e., they do not have a nominal value, they are just recognition of a proportional share in the company, on an equal footing with all other common shares.

If a company has shares with a par value, then complications can arise when subsequent issues of shares are made at prices in excess of par value. The excess over par has to be recorded as a separate category of the owners' equity, called contributed surplus. With no-par shares, this situation does not arise.

5.2.2   *Dividends and Capital Growth*

If the directors choose to do so, they can propose a dividend. This is a periodical payment (typically once a year) made to shareholders as a way of distributing some or all of the profit to them. It is, in effect, a repayment of part of the shareholders' investment in the company. From an accounting perspective, assets are reduced and owners' equity is reduced. Legally, dividends can be paid only to the extent that there are retained earnings. (This is supposed to protect creditors by keeping the share capital intact.) In practical terms, of course, dividends can be paid only out of cash.

If investors recognize a company as a good investment they will exert buying pressure on the shares, and that will make the price rise. As share prices increase, so, too, will the value of existing shareholders' investments. What forces make investors think a share is a good buy? Essentially, it is a forecast of the company's future prospects. That forecast will be heavily influenced by how well the company has done in the past, along with other factors, such as an assessment of its market possibilities. Dividend payment is part of the information used to judge a company: it sends signals to investors about how well the company has done, and what it expects to do in the future. So, while the initial effect of paying a dividend is to lower the assets of the company (and hence, logically, the value of each share), in the medium term, it can encourage investors and have a positive effect on share price.

When the company makes a profit, the directors and the shareholders may agree to pay a dividend. For a dividend to be paid, it must be proposed by the directors and voted for by the shareholders. Thus, either party has the power to prevent a dividend being paid. Legally, it must also come out of retained earnings. The directors have to strike a balance between their wish to send positive messages to the shareholders by paying high dividends, and their need to plough back earnings into the company to finance expansion. Realistically, if the company is growing, every dollar paid out as dividend has to be replaced with a dollar of new equity raised, or a dollar of new borrowing.

5.2.3   *Retained Earnings*

When no dividend is paid, or the dividend is less than the full amount of earnings, a fund of undistributed earnings builds up. To record this on the balance sheet, a category of equity is established called retained earnings. It is increased by net income, and decreased by net loss and/or dividends paid each year. Movements of this fund are reported in the financial statement called the Statement of Retained Earnings.

In well-established companies, the balance of retained earnings may be substantial. It may be far higher than the balance in the common share capital account. The fact that many shares are worth more on the market than their initial issue price is reflected in the large size of these companies' retained earnings. Companies that distribute all their earnings as dividends tend to stay the same size: companies that reinvest earnings tend to grow.

It should be noted that increases in the share price are a direct benefit to the shareholders. They can sell their shares at a price greater than what they paid for them. The company gets no direct benefit from a rise in the share price; however, the company does get an indirect benefit. If the company were to make a new issue of shares, they could be sold at the new, higher market price. In this way, the company can get more cash for issuing the same number of shares. That is another reason that directors monitor the share price for their companies on a regular basis.

5.2.4   *Preferred Shares*

In addition to common shares, some (but not all) companies issue preferred shares. Preferred shares are a special class of shares that have some sort of preferential right attached to them. Typically, this is a right to receive a dividend before the common shareholders receive theirs. This can mean that the preferred shareholders get a dividend, while the common shareholders do not. To offset the advantage of the dividend preference, it is usual for the preferred dividend to be restricted in some way.

Other forms of preference exist, but they are less common and far less important. The preference may, for example, extend to preference in repayment of capital if the company is wound up. Some preferred shares have preferential voting privileges, too. An 8% cumulative preferred share, for example, may get nothing if the company has had a really bad year. It may get a dividend of 8%. If it does, the common shareholders may also get a dividend. The term *cumulative* in the name means that the 8% dividend accumulates if it is not paid and must be made good before common shareholders are entitled to anything.

A preferred share has a lower risk than a common share, and we would expect this to be reflected in a lower share price, as risk and return are positively correlated. For some investors, a lower-risk, lower-return investment is more suitable than a higher-risk common share, even in the same company.

There are other elements that may appear in the equity section of the balance sheet, but the ones referred to above (retained earnings, common shares, and preferred shares) are the important ones. The main thing to remember is that owners' equity represents the owners' residual interest in the net assets of the company. (See Exhibit 5.1.)

Legally, this would mean that if the company were to be liquidated, preferred shareholders would get anything left after the creditors had been paid off. In practice, this seldom happens. Instead, shareholders realize their investment by selling their shares through a stock market.

Exhibit 5.1:   Changes in Owners' Equity

The following reasons exist for changes in owners' equity:

A. INCREASES

1. Initial investment in the company:
    • assets increase, owners' equity (common shares) increases.
2. New share issue in an established company:
    • assets increase, owners' equity (common shares) increases.
3. Issue of preferred shares:
    • assets increase, owners' equity (preferred shares) increases.
4. The company makes a profit (net income):
    • assets increase, owners' equity (retained earnings) increases.
5. The assets are revalued:
    • assets increase; owners' equity (undistributable reserve) increases.

B. DECREASES

1. The company suffers a loss:
    • assets decrease, owners' equity (retained earnings) decreases.
2. A dividend is paid:
    • assets decrease, owners' equity (retained earnings) decreases.
3. Shares are repurchased and retired:
    • assets decrease, owners' equity (common shares or preferred shares and retained earnings) decreases.
4. The company is discontinued:
    • all assets are realized;
    • all liabilities are paid;
    • if there is anything left over, it is distributed to the shareholders:
       • first to preferred shareholders;
       • then, the remainder to common shareholders.

5.2.5   *Limited Liability*

One of the most important features of shares is that they give the owner a limited exposure to risk. In the case of an individual trading on his/her own, or in the case of a partnership, the owners are exposed to a high level of risk. If the business fails, not only can the business assets be used to pay the business debts, but also the personal property of the owners can be seized to pay business debts. If the business is incorporated as a limited liability company, then shareholders cannot be held personally responsible for company debts.

This is only realistic: if a shareholder in a major corporation were to be personally liable for all corporate debts then no one would ever risk investing and the capital market could not function. The concept of limited liability is essential to the functioning of a society where the management of major corporations is separate from their ownership.

This does not imply that shareholders cannot lose money: they most certainly can, but their maximum loss is measurable, so that they can make intelligent investing decisions.

If a shareholder invests money directly into a company by buying its shares, that investment is always "at risk". If I invest $100,000 in a start-up company and that company fails, I will lose my $100,000. If an investor buys shares through the stock market (from an existing shareholder) for $100,000 and the company fails he will lose his $100,000. In both cases, however, the maximum loss will be the $100,000 invested: no one can ask the shareholder for any additional contribution, no matter how badly the company fails and no matter how big its debts were when it failed.

The limited liability concept applies to all classes of shares: common (ordinary) shares, preferred shares, and others.

The limited liability of shareholders is probably the main reason why a company would decide to incorporate, rather than trade as a partnership or as an individual.

5.3   Summary

According to the accounting equation (assets = liabilities + equity) the assets of the business are funded either from borrowings (liabilities) or by owners' equity. Liabilities are listed on the balance sheet under the general headings of current liabilities (to be paid within a year) and long-term liabilities (to be paid beyond a year). Liabilities are valued at the amounts for which they are going to be settled. The difference between the total value of assets on the balance sheet and the total value of liabilities on the balance sheet is the equity, which is owned by the shareholders. The equity may include sub-classifications for different types of shares (e.g., preferred shares, common shares) and will also include the balance of retained earnings, or undistributed profits.

Appendix 5.1
Sarbanes-Oxley Act and Bill 198

As a direct response to corporate accounting scandals that had occurred in companies such as Enron, WorldCom, and Xerox, in 2002 a piece of U.S. legislation called the *Sarbanes-Oxley Act* was passed. Canadian companies that have U.S. operations and report to U.S. authorities are directly affected by Sarbanes-Oxley.

Canada followed the Sarbanes-Oxley lead by passing Bill 198 shortly afterward. This affects all Canadian public companies. Although they are not identical, the effect of both pieces of legislation is similar.

A greater responsibility for the financial statements and the control systems that underlie them has been placed on the chief executive officer and the chief financial officer of public companies. They will both have to sign explicit statements that they have satisfied themselves that the control systems are adequate and the financial statements are accurate. These declarations may be used as evidence if it is subsequently discovered that controls had been inadequate and/or the financial statements were inaccurate.

Auditors will be required to be more independent of their clients than they were previously: for example, they will not be allowed to act as both auditor of, and management consultant to, any client.

In separate Canadian legislation a Canadian Public Accountability Board has been established to provide independent oversight of the audit process.

The objective throughout all these changes is to increase investor confidence in the information that companies publish about their financial activities.

Appendix 5.2
The Mechanics of Accounting:
The Balance Sheet

This appendix continues our introduction to the debits and credits of accounting. It will, however, be briefer than the last one. As we saw in Appendix 3.5 of Chapter 3, every revenue and expense transaction has a direct effect on the balance sheet: for example, every revenue transaction has a debit to Cash or to Accounts Receivable as well as a credit to Revenue; the measurement of Cost of Goods Sold also revalues the Inventory account. In short, we cannot separate income measurement from balance sheet changes — it is the nature of double-entry accounting. The following table lists the balance sheet account transactions we have already seen when we studied the corresponding income statement transactions in Appendix 3.5 of Chapter 3.

Income statement account transaction (Chapter 3, Appendix 3.5)	Balance sheet account affected
Revenue	Cash
	Accounts Receivable
	Other Liabilities
	— Liability for Book Returns
	— Deferred Revenue
Bad Debt Expense	Accounts Receivable (including Allowance for Doubtful Debts)
Cost of Goods Sold	Inventory
	Accounts Payable
	Cash
Overhead Expenses — accruals	Accounts Payable
— deferrals	Prepaid Expense
Amortization	Buildings, Plant, and Equipment (including accumulated amortization)

As we can see, the basic accounting for transactions involving a number of balance sheet accounts, including most of the important asset and current liability accounts, have already been covered in Appendix 3.5 of Chapter 3. In this appendix, we will complete our coverage of the mechanics of accounting for the balance sheet and income statement with the following three topics: intangible assets, borrowing money, and share issue.

Although the presentation in this appendix for each of these topics is complete in itself and can be read on its own, it may be helpful to refer to the general discussion in this and the next chapter:

- intangible assets — Chapter 4, section 4.2.2.4
- borrowing money — Chapter 5, sections 5.1.4 and 5.1.6
- share issue — Chapter 5, section 5.2.1

Other Long-term Assets

We have studied the accounting for tangible long-term assets such as property, plant, and equipment. In all cases the cost of these assets is *capitalized* (shown as an asset on the balance sheet), and, with the exception of land, the cost (less any estimated salvage value) is then amortized over its expected useful life on one basis or another (see Focus Box 5A4.1). Only land, which has an indefinite useful life, is not amortized. Natural resources is another tangible long-term asset, commonly seen on the balance sheets of industries involved in primary resource exploitation. The accounting is very similar to plant and equipment — the asset is written off over its expected useful life. The difference is that the expense is called *depletion* rather than amortization. The credit is made to a contra-asset account called *accumulated depletion* or directly against the asset account.

Accounting for long-term *intangible assets* is in some respects the same as for tangible long-term assets, but under new provisions of GAAP there is an additional distinction to be made and, then, for one class of these assets, a different accounting treatment.

Just as for tangible long-term assets, only those intangible assets acquired at a cost are accounted for. It is important to emphasize this in discussing intangible assets because many of them have a value far beyond their cost. The example of Coca-Cola's trademark is cited in the text. The value of this trademark is estimated at $83 billion. Although it is difficult to identify the carrying cost of the Coca-Cola trademark itself carried on the company's balance sheet at the end of 2004 (all the company's trademarks are aggregated on the balance sheet, along with other intangibles), it cannot be much more than $2 billion and is probably less. Although trademark costs have been written off over the years (see below), it is most unlikely that the total costs capitalized over the years have been much above the current carrying cost.

There are two categories of intangible assets: finite-life and indefinite-life intangible assets. *Finite-life* intangible assets are those that can be said to have a limited life. Examples are patents, copyrights, and leasehold improvements. Once this life has been established, these assets are subject to amortization like tangible long-term assets. The differences are that typically there is no residual value and the credit side of the amortization entry is made directly against the asset, rather than to a contra "accumulated amortization" account. There is also one proviso (which is also true for tangible long-term assets): if there is reason to think the carrying value (unamortized cost) of the intangible has been *impaired*, the asset must be written down to its realizable value. This is discussed in the next paragraph.

Indefinite-life intangible assets have an unlimited life. Indefinite-life intangible assets include trademarks and goodwill. These assets are not subject to amortization. On the other hand, they are subject to an annual impairment test. If it is deemed that the carrying value of the intangible

Focus Box 5A4.1

You will often see the terms *expense* and *capitalize* used as verbs. This use arises when something is purchased (for cash or on account) and a decision must be made as to whether the *cost* is to be debited to an expense account or to an asset account.

Let's consider an example. You own a small restaurant. Nearby is a delivery pizza outlet whose owner, John Tucci, wants to retire. The pizzeria has a well-recognized name in the neighbourhood with the name serving also as the phone number, PIZZA99. You can easily continue his business and integrate it with your current operations at relatively low additional cost beyond staff and ingredients. It will be a profitable addition. You know the name is valuable and the owner is ready to sell it, but he wants to sell everything related to the business. His premises, including kitchen equipment, is rented but he has a large, relatively new outside sign and a six-month supply of pizza boxes and advertising flyers, all with the name and phone number prominently displayed. After some negotiations, you agree to pay him $50,000 for the trademarked name, the phone number, the sign, and the flyers. It is all of value to you. You would need a sign and it would cost you $10,000. His has a 10-year useful life, no residual value. The boxes and advertising material, always necessary, would cost $3,000 and $1,000, respectively. The terms are $5,000 cash and the balance in one year at 5% simple interest. How do you account for the transaction? (It is now June 1, the middle of your financial year.) The boxes and advertising material are consumables, so you must *expense* these. The rest is *capitalized*, the sign as equipment and the balance as an indefinite-life intangible, trademark or goodwill. The entry will look like this:

Date	Accounts/Description	Dr	Cr
June 1/0X	Supplies {SE — expense}	3,000	
	Advertising {SE — expense}	1,000	
	Equipment {asset}	10,000	
	Trademark {asset}	36,000	
	Cash {asset}		5,000
	Note Payable {liability}		45,000

Purchase of assets of pizzeria, for cash and one year note @ 5%

Starting at year-end, the equipment will be amortized (see Chapter 3, Appendix 3.5). We will discuss the treatment of the trademark and the note payable below.

has been *impaired*, i.e., that it will not be realized in the normal course of business, the impairment loss must be recognized; in other words, the asset must be written down to its realizable value. Assume that purchased goodwill was being carried on the balance sheet at $500,000. If, after the annual impairment test, its fair value was deemed to be $200,000, the difference would have to written off against the year's operations as follows:

Date	Accounts/Description	Dr	Cr
year-end 0X	Impairment Charge {SE — expense}	300,000	
	Goodwill {asset}		300,000

Recognition of the loss of goodwill after impairment test.

Borrowing Money

A liability or a debt is a promise to transfer an asset — usually, but not always, cash — to the creditor in the future. It typically arises out of a transaction undertaken before the balance sheet date, with the settlement, the transfer of the asset, to take place in the future. The asset transfer, when it occurs, extinguishes the liability.

One liability we have studied is deferred revenue, which arises out of an incomplete revenue transaction that will be settled when the goods or services contracted for are delivered to the customer. Actually, deferred revenue is somewhat exceptional as liabilities go, since it will be settled with goods or services, not cash. Most liabilities are settled by the company's paying cash. Such liabilities are what we usually think of as debts — an obligation to pay money in the future. A common characteristic of a debt is that it usually accrues an interest charge from when it is contracted until it is repaid. Accounts payable and accrued liabilities, which arise out of the company's purchase of goods and services on credit, comprise one common type of liability. We have seen examples of the accounting treatment of accounts payables and accrued liabilities. Loans are the other important type of liability, and when companies take advantage of such debt financing, the liability on the company's balance sheet can be quite significant. Although interest may or may not be charged by trade creditors on accounts payable, interest will always be charged by lenders on loans, and the resulting expense on the income statement is usually material.

Bank Loans. For most companies, even those that are just marginally profitable, day-to-day operations are largely self-financing. Cash is required to pay employees, suppliers, and other trade creditors; the cash comes from cash sales and collection of receivables. There is typically an annual cycle, however, and even if over the whole year operating cash flow is positive, there is variation from month to month. In some months the cash flow is positive but in others it is negative. Providing cash to bridge these cycles is the role of banks and other short-term lenders (see section 5.1.4.). Once a bank agrees to lend a company money, "demand loan" financing is relatively flexible. Within the terms of the loan, the amount borrowed can be increased when necessary, and is reduced whenever possible.

Consider the following situation. A company has an agreement with its bank that it can borrow in units of $5,000 and can repay it on the same basis. Interest is charged at the end of each month on the average daily balance of the loan in the month and deducted from the company's chequing account. The company must provide the bank with annual financial statements through the period of this agreement, and monthly statements at any time that there is loan balance outstanding — in this example covering the first quarter of 2005. Fashion Fabrics Distributing Ltd. borrows $40,000 on January 1, 2005, increases the loan by $20,000 on February 1, reduces the loan by $50,000 on March 15, and pays off the entire balance on March 31, 2005. The current interest rate is 6% per annum. The relevant journal entries and T-accounts, January through March 2005, are shown as well as the relevant sections of the financial statements at the end of the quarter. The only evidence of the loan on the statements is the interest expense on the income statement. Since the loan was completely paid off by the end of March, no liability remains on that date. If a balance sheet had been drawn up while money was owing, Bank Loan would be the first item under current liabilities.

Date	Accounts/Description	Dr	Cr
Jan. 1/05	Cash {asset}	40,000	
	Bank Loan {liability}		40,000
	Demand loan advance		
Jan. 31/05	Interest Expense {SE — expense}	204	
	Cash {asset}		204
	Interest on demand loan, Jan.: {31/365 × 40,000} @ 6%.		
Feb. 1/05	Cash {asset}	20,000	
	Bank Loan {liability}		20,000
	Demand loan advance		
Feb. 28/05	Interest Expense {SE — expense}	276	
	Cash {asset}		276
	Interest on demand loan, Feb.: {28/365 × 60,000} @ 6%		
Mar. 15/05	Bank Loan {liability}	50,000	
	Cash {asset}		50,000
	Demand loan repayment		
Mar. 31/05	Bank Loan {liability}	10,000	
	Interest Expense {SE — expense}	174	
	Cash {asset}		10,174
	Demand loan repayment & interest, Mar.: {(15/365 × 60,000) + (16/365 × 10,000)} @ 6%		

		Cash			Bank Loan	
2005		X	X	**2005**		
Jan. 1 loan advance		40,000		Jan. 1 loan advance		40,000
Jan. 31 interest			204	Jan. 31 balance		40,000
		X	X			
Feb. 1 loan advance		20,000		Feb. 1 loan advance		20,000
Feb. 28 interest			276	Feb. 28 balance		60,000
		X	X			
Mar. 15 loan repayment			50,000	Mar. 15 loan repayment	50,000	
Mar. 31 loan repayment			10,000	Mar. 31 loan repayment	10,000	
Mar. 31 interest			174	Mar. 31 balance	0	
		X	X			

	Interest Expense
2005	
Jan. 31	204
Feb. 28	276
Mar. 31	174
bal., 1st Q.	654

Interest accrues and is payable monthly. At any time the balance in the Bank Loan account shows the amount owing. If financial statements were drawn up at the end of the quarter, we would see interest expense on the income statement:

Fashion Fabrics Distributing Ltd.
Partial Income Statement
for first quarter 2005

....

Expenses

....

Interest on bank loan $654

....

Long-term debt. Long-term debt is usually incurred for reasons other than normal operations, such as the purchase of property plant and equipment, repayment of long-term debt coming due, or the development of a new line of business or general expansion (either of which could include the purchase of another company). As a rule, such loans are large relative to the size of the company; moreover, by definition, the principal repayments are far in the future. To protect the lenders against all the risks this entails, the terms of such loans tend to be quite complex (see section 5.1.6), with the consequences of default clearly spelt out. One standard feature of long-term debt contracts is a fixed schedule of repayment of interest and principal. We will follow through such an example.

No Down Time Ltd. is a successful web hosting company. Using internally generated funds, the company has financed its growth from an operation with one refurbished server in the owner's basement to a state-of-the-art installation, generating revenues of $500,000. The company has a reputation for uninterrupted service thanks to the hard work of the owner, Joya Dutt, but she is now in the unenviable position of having to turn away business because of the capacity limitations of her equipment. She has accumulated $50,000 in investable funds but the next logical stage of expansion requires an investment in equipment of approximately $250,000.

It is now early January 2005. On the strength of her reputation and prospects, a hardware supplier is prepared to sell her $225,000 worth of equipment (including tax, delivery, and set-up) for $25,000 cash, taking back the balance of $200,000 as a term loan secured on the computer assets. Ms Dutt has accepted the offer and the transaction is to go through on February 1, 2005. The loan interest rate is 4.63%, payable semi-annually. The principal is to be repaid in $50,000 instalments at the end of years 2, 3, 4, and 5 (i.e., February 1, 2007, 2008, 2009, 2010). The company's year-end is December 31.

The supplier is essentially lending its customer $200,000 for the purpose of purchasing this equipment. In that sense it is as if No Down Time is buying goods on credit with an extended-term account payable. The difference is that interest is now an explicit feature of the debt. As a result, pre-determined payments of both interest and principal as well as year-end accruals must be made on specified dates. The accounting is, accordingly, more involved. The journal entries are as follows.

Date	Accounts/Description	Dr	Cr
Feb. 1/05	Computer Equipment {asset}	225,000	
	Cash {asset}		25,000
	Term Loan {liability}		200,000
	Purchase of computer equipment for cash and term loan		
Aug. 1/05	Interest Expense {SE — expense}	4,630	
	Cash {asset}		4,630
	Term loan interest payment, 6 months to Aug. 1, 2005 $200,000 @ 4.63% × 6/12		
Dec. 31/05	Interest Expense {SE — expense}	3,858	
	Accrued Interest Payable {liability}		3,858
	Accrued term loan interest to Dec. 31, 2005 $200,000 @ 4.63% × 5/12		
Feb. 1/06	Accrued Interest Payable {liability}	3,858	
	Interest Expense {SE — expense}	772	
	Cash {asset}		4,630
	Term loan interest payment, 6 months to Feb. 1, 2006 $200,000 @ 4.63% × 6/12		

[On August 1, 2006 and Dec. 31, 2006, entries identical to the August 1, 2005 interest payment and the Dec. 31, 2005 accrual will be made.]

Date	Accounts/Description	Dr	Cr
Feb. 1/07	Accrued Interest Payable {liability}	3,858	
	Interest Expense {SE — expense}	772	
	Cash {asset}		4,630
	Term loan interest payment, 6 months to Feb. 1, 2007 $200,000 @ 4.63% × 6/12		
Feb. 1/07	Term Loan Payable {liability}	50,000	
	Cash {asset}		50,000
	First instalment of term loan repayment		

[The cycle of entries — interest and repayment — continues until the loan is fully repaid on February 1, 2010. Each year's interest cycle — August 1 payment, December 31 accrual and following February 1 payment will be smaller as the principal is reduced at the beginning of the cycle. For example, the six-month interest payments on August 1, 2007, and February 1, 2008, will each be $3,473. The related accrual on December 31, 2007, will be correspondingly smaller as well.]

Shareholders' Equity

In Appendix 2.1 to Chapter 2, on page 64, shares were issued for Example Co. Ltd. However, we had not introduced the journal entry form at that point, so we will take this opportunity to review this transaction as a standard journal entry.

We know that the shares were issued for $25,000. These will be common shares because there must always be a residual class of shares outstanding — usually called *common shares* — and thus the first shares issued must be common shares. The number of shares issued was not indicated. In a sense, the number of shares in the first issue is arbitrary. All the same, the number would have to be specified at this point. If there is only one shareholder, there need be only one share, worth 100% of the company. (Crown corporations owned 100% by the government may issue one share, but this is exceptional.) Typically, the number of shares is big enough to allow for the division of ownership envisaged for the company. It is convenient for this to be multiples of 100 shares or more. (Of course, if there are subsequent share issues, the number of shares outstanding will increase.) In this case, let us assume that the initial share issue is 1,000 shares. That means that on the date of issue, a share is worth $25. We will assume that these are not par value shares, which is normally the case for common shares. What this means is that the full amount of the proceeds is credited to share capital.

Date	Accounts/Description	Dr	Cr
Dec. 31/05	Cash {asset}	25,000	
	Common shares {SE}		25,000
	Issue of 1,000 shares @ $25		

Note that the actual account within the share capital (or capital stock) section of shareholders' equity to which the common shares are credited is called *Common Shares* (or, less commonly in Canada, *Common Stock*).

Self-Study Problem

1. As at December 31, 2005, Charley Farley had owner's equity of $46,000. He owed $5,000 to his suppliers and there was a long-term bank loan of $51,000. Accrued utilities amounted to $1,000.

    [Note: This is a continuation of Self-Study Problem 4.1 on page 160. You may need to refer back to that problem to help in doing this one.]

    Required
    (a) Show how these would appear in the Liabilities and Equity part of his balance sheet.
    (b) What was the current ratio?
    (c) What was the quick ratio?
    (d) What were the debt-to-equity and debt-to-assets ratios?

2. As at January 31, 2001, Bombardier Inc. had a balance of retained earnings of $2,660 million. During the year ended January 31, 2002, the company made net income of $391 million. Dividends (and other minor adjustments) were $266 million.

    The share capital as at January 31, 2001, was $1,170 million: $300 million of preferred shares and $870 million of common shares. New common shares were issued under employee share option plans in the amount of $26 million.

    Required
    (a) Prepare a statement of retained earnings for the year ended January 31, 2002.
    (b) What was the maximum dividend legally payable as at January 31, 2002?
    (c) Calculate the balance of preferred shares, common shares, and total share capital.

3. Bombardier Inc. had 12 million preferred shares, each of $25, for a total of $300 million of preferred shares in issue as at January 31, 2002. These paid a quarterly dividend on $0.34375 ($1.375 per share per year). As at February 18, 2003, they were trading at $17.25 per share. The preferred shares were cumulative and redeemable.

    Required
    (a) How much was the total annual dividend on the preferred shares?
    (b) If the dividend on the preferred shares was passed up in 2003, what would happen in 2004?
    (c) What return on equity did the dividend represent for someone buying a Bombardier preferred share as at February 18, 2003?

Solution

1. (a) **Liabilities and Equity**
        Current liabilities:

Trade payables	$ 5,000
Accrued utilities	1,000
	$ 6,000
Long-term liabilities (bank loan)	51,000
Total liabilities	$ 57,000
Owners' equity:	46,000
Total liabilities & owners' equity	$103,000

  (b) Current ratio:

$$= \text{current assets} \div \text{current liabilities}$$
$$= \$13,000 \div \$6,000$$
$$= 2.2 : 1$$

  (c) Quick ratio:

$$= (\text{current assets} - \text{inventory}) \div \text{current liabilities}$$
$$= (\$13,000 - \$1,500) \div \$6,000$$
$$= 1.9 : 1$$

  (d) Debt-to-equity ratio:

$$= \text{total debt} \div \text{owners' equity}$$
$$= (\$57,000 \div \$46,000) \times 100\%$$
$$= 124\%$$

  Debt-to-assets ratio:

$$= \text{total debt} \div \text{total assets}$$
$$= (\$57,000 \div \$103,000) \times 100\%$$
$$= 55\%$$

2. (a)
Bombardier Inc.
Statement of Retained Earnings
For the Year Ended January 31, 2002 ($ million)

Retained earnings as at January 31, 2001	2,660
Add: Net income for year ended January 31, 2002	391
Available:	3,051
Less: Dividends paid	266
Retained earnings as at January 31, 2002	2,785

  (b) The maximum dividend legally payable would have been $3,051.

  (c)
Bombardier Inc.
Share Capital
As at January 31, 2002 ($ million)

Preferred shares (same as opening balance)		300
Common Shares		
Opening balance	870	
Issued during the year	26	
Balance of common shares		896
Total share capital		1,196

3. (a) Total annual preferred share dividend:

$$= 12 \text{ million} \times \$1.375$$
$$= \$16.5 \text{ million}$$

(b) Because the share is cumulative, if the preferred share dividend is passed up in any year it is carried forward, and it must be made good before the common shares can receive a dividend.

(c) Return on equity (based on dividends):

$$= \text{dividend} \div \text{share price}$$
$$= (\$1.375 \div \$17.25) \times 100\%$$
$$= 7.97\%$$

Discussion Questions and Problems

Discussion Questions

1. What is the definition of a *liability*?
2. What is the definition of *equity*?
3. How are liabilities valued for inclusion in the balance sheet?
4. Which accounting principle(s) apply to valuing liabilities?
5. In what order do liabilities appear in the balance sheet?
6. What are the distinguishing features of a preferred share?
7. Why is retained earnings shown separately from common equity?
8. Is retained earnings cash, or is it some other type of asset? Who owns it?
9. How is common equity valued for inclusion in the balance sheet?
10. Which would you rather have: $10,000 owed to you by a company or $10,000 invested in the company's equity?

Problems

1. Byzantium Co. has $500,000 of retained earnings and $200,000 of common shares. The company owes $50,000 income tax, which is due next month. The company has borrowed $160,000 from the bank as a demand loan (payable whenever the bank calls it). There is a five-year mortgage on the property of $700,000. Trade payables are $325,000, and trade receivables are $485,000. Unpaid wages are $25,000. There is a debenture loan of $300,000, payable in 10 years. Accrued expenses are $40,000. Preferred shares are $100,000. The dividend paid was $100,000, and interest expense for the year was $255,000.

   Required
   Show how these would be shown in the liabilities and equity section of the balance sheet.

2. Turko Inc. has the following assets and liabilities:

Cash	$ 15,000
Inventory	$ 60,000
Trade receivables	$225,000
Long-term assets (net of amortization)	$900,000
Trade payables	$250,000
Bank overdraft (short-term)	$ 50,000
Debenture loan	$300,000

   Required
   (a) Calculate the current ratio.
   (b) Calculate the quick ratio.
   (c) Is the company adequately liquid?
   (d) What would happen to the liquidity ratios if they issued $300,000 of new common shares for cash?
   (e) What would happen to the liquidity ratios if they borrowed $300,000 of long-term debt?

(f)   What would happen to the liquidity ratios if they borrowed $300,000 of short-term debt?

3.   Constant Co. has the following assets and liabilities:

Cash	$ 45,000
Inventory	$ 180,000
Trade receivables	$ 675,000
Long-term assets (net of amortization)	$2,700,000
Trade payables	$ 750,000
Bank overdraft (short-term)	$ 150,000
Debenture loan	$ 900,000

Required
(a)   Calculate the debt-to-equity ratio.
(b)   Calculate the debt-to-assets ratio.
(c)   Comment on the leverage of the company.

4.   Isthmus Inc. has common shares of $500,000 and retained earnings of $500,000. Show how each of the following independent transactions would affect the common shares and retained earnings:

(a)   Paid a dividend of $100,000 in cash.
(b)   Issued additional common shares for $500,000 in cash.
(c)   Issued additional common shares to acquire a competitor's business; the acquired business had a fair market value of $250,000.
(d)   The company made a net loss for the year of $200,000.
(e)   Half the common shares were repurchased by the company for $250,000 cash.

5.   AM Co. has the following balance sheet:

Current assets		
Cash	$ 15,000	
Trade receivables	225,000	
Inventory	60,000	$ 300,000
Long-term assets		900,000
Total assets		$1,200,000
Current liabilities		
Trade payables	$250,000	
Bank loan	50,000	$ 300,000
Long-term liabilities		300,000
Total liabilities		$ 600,000
Equity		
Common shares	$400,000	
Retained earnings	200,000	600,000
Total liabilities & equity		$1,200,000

AM Co. has just gone bankrupt. The following amounts were collected from the realization of the assets:

Cash	$ 15,000
Trade receivables	$ 5,000
Inventory	$ 50,000
Long-term assets	$500,000

Required
(a) Show how much total cash the shareholders would get.
(b) Would it have made any difference to answer (a) if the long-term liabilities were secured against the long-term assets?

Appendix 5.2

6. Wilkins Ltd. has an arrangement with the bank to borrow money on a demand loan basis to finance large inventory purchases from late summer through mid-fall. The loan is repaid over the winter. Interest is charged at the end of each month to Wilkins's chequing account on the average daily balance of the loan outstanding that month. In 2006, Wilkins borrowed $75,000 on September 1 and another $50,000 on October 15. It made a $40,000 repayment on December 15 and paid off the balance at the end of February 2007. The interest rate was 5.5% in September 2006; on October 1, it fell to 5.25% and remained there until June 2007. Wilkins's year-end is December 31.

Required
(a) Prepare journal entries for the transactions related to the demand loan in 2006 and post them to T-accounts.
(b) Assuming that these are the only loan transactions, show how they would appear on the balance sheet and income statement in the December 31, 2006, financial statements.

7. On March 1, 2007, Dorricks Ltd. borrowed $500,000, issuing a five-year mortgage bond. No principal payments are due until the end of the five-year loan period, but interest, at a nominal annual rate of 4%, is to be paid every six months beginning September 1, 2007. The company's year-end is December 31.

Required
(a) Using T-accounts, record the 2007 transactions related to the mortgage bond.
(b) Show the relevant sections of the balance sheet and income statement in the December 31, 2007, financial statements.

6
Statement of
Cash Flows

Learning
Objectives

After studying this chapter you should be able to describe and explain:
→ The statement of cash flows (statement of changes in financial position)

6.1 Introduction

In the previous chapters we have dealt with three of the required financial statements: the income statement, the balance sheet, and the statement of retained earnings. In this chapter we shall deal with the statement of cash flows.

One of the crucial aspects of running a business is to ensure that it does not run out of cash. If there is insufficient cash available to pay the creditors, the company is in danger of being declared bankrupt and closed down. This is a serious external threat, and it happens to large numbers of companies every year. Avoiding bankruptcy may be impossible in some circumstances, but short-term cash management can help in avoiding unnecessary bankruptcy.

Within the company, the chief financial officer (CFO) will engage in cash forecasting and cash budgeting. Based on existing cash, accounts receivable, inventory, sales forecasts, trade credits, other payables, production plans, capital expenditure plans, etc., the CFO will prepare a detailed prediction of cash flows for the immediate future. This cash budget should alert management to any impending problems coming up in the next one to six months. If the company receives adequate notice, it may be able to avoid a potential problem. The company can arrange perhaps to take a short-term loan from the bank, or delay payment on its trade payables, or defer purchase of some plant and equipment. Cash budgets are discussed more fully in Chapter 7.

All well-managed companies carry out cash budgeting. When applying for a bank loan, one of the most important questions the bank lending officer will ask is to see the company's cash budget to ensure the loan is planned and its repayment is a realistic probability. Cash budgets are, however, rather confidential documents, and apart from sharing them with a potential lender, they are not publicly available.

What *is* publicly available is one of the financial reports called the Statement of Cash Flows or Statement of Changes in Financial Position. This reports on the past (like all the financial statements) rather than predicting the future (as a budget would). It deals exclusively in cash flows, not in the accrual-based revenues and expenses of the income statement.

The cash flow statement is presented in four parts:

(i) cash from operations;
(ii) cash from financing activities;

(iii) cash from investing activities; and
(iv) change in cash.

We will discuss each part in detail using Canadian Tire's 2004 and 2005 financial statements. (See Exhibit 6.1.)

6.2 Cash from Operations

In this section the cash generated from the normal business of the company is reported. The starting point is operating income. From operating income, interest and taxes are deducted: these are related to ongoing operations, and they have to be paid in cash. In the simplest of businesses, run entirely on a cash basis, net income is the same as cash inflow. In more complex businesses, the operating income has to be adjusted in several ways to get cash flow.

First, there may be expenses included in the annual income statement that are not represented by cash outflows at this time. Principal among these is the amortization expense. Amortization, you will remember, refers to a situation where a long-term asset has been bought, and its cost is gradually allocated to the income statement over its useful life. The cash outflow in respect of that asset took place when it was bought. The amortization expense is a non-cash-flow expense. All amortization expenses and the like are added back to the operating income. If there were any non-cash revenues (these are much rarer), they would be deducted from operating income.

With the exception of amortization, the rest of the revenues and expenses in the income statement are more closely (though not perfectly) represented by cash receipts and cash payments. There may be differences, and if there are, they are reflected in changes in working capital. An expense that is not identical to its related cash flow results in an increase or decrease in payables and accruals. If the cash payment is less than the expense, the payables will rise; if the cash payment is more than the expense, the payables will fall. Revenue that is more than cash received results in receivables increasing. Revenue that is less than cash received results in receivables falling. Inventory that is constant does not affect cash flows; inventory that is increasing causes a cash outflow; inventory that is decreasing results in a cash inflow.

We can address all these changes by looking at the working capital (current assets less current liabilities). In practice, because the fourth part of our cash flow statement will deal in the changes in cash itself, cash would be eliminated from the working capital. Operating income, then, is to be increased by any net fall in non-cash working capital, and decreased by any net increase in non-cash working capital.

' In some circumstances, the result can be a negative figure: if, for example, instead of having an operating income, there is an operating loss; or, if the decrease in non-cash working capital is larger than the net income plus amortization. In those circumstances there would be a net amount of cash *used* in operations.

Exhibit 6.1: Financial Statements — Canadian Tire

The 2004 and 2005 financial statements of Canadian Tire are summarized as follows:

Canadian Tire
Consolidated Statement of Earnings and Retained Earnings ($ million)

	2005		2004	
Gross operating revenue		$7,774		$7,154
Less: Cost of goods sold and operating expenses				
Various (paid in cash)	$6,985		$6,452	
Depreciation	185	7,170	171	6,623
Operating income		$ 604		$ 531
Less: Interest	$ 84		$ 78	
Income taxes	190	274	162	240
Net income		$ 330		$ 291
Add: Retained earnings at start of year		1,547		1,318
		$1,877		$1,609
Less: Cost of repurchase of shares	$ 17		$ 22	
Dividends paid	47	64	40	62
Retained earnings at end of year		$1,813		$1,547

Canadian Tire
Balance Sheet ($ million)

	As at end of			
	2005		2004	
Cash	$ 838		$ 802	
Accounts receivable	1,425		987	
Inventory	676		621	
Prepaid expenses	42		24	
Total current assets		$2,981		$2,434
Long-term assets		2,975		2,809
Total assets		$5,956		$5,243
Current liabilities	$1,821		$1,487	
Long-term liabilities	1,324		1,205	
Total liabilities		$3,145		$2,692
Minority interest		300		300
Shareholders' equity				
Share capital	$ 704		$ 710	
Retained earnings	1,813		1,547	
Foreign exchange adjustment	(6)	2,511	(6)	2,251
Total liabilities and equity		$5,956		$5,243

A positive flow of cash from operations is a sign of corporate health. Without it the company has to borrow to even stay alive. A company that shows cash used in operations is in a precarious situation.

6.3   Cash from Financing Activities

The second section of the cash flow statement is cash from (or used in) financing activities. (See Exhibit 6.2.) Financing activities are those connected with the issuance or redemption of shares and the borrowing or repaying of long-term loans. Items, such as interest and dividends that relate to financing, may also be reported here.

Canadian Tire engaged in a number of financing activities in 2005. If you look at the balance sheets for the two years you will notice that the company has increased the amount of its long-term loans. These went up

---

Exhibit 6.2:   Cash from or Cash Used in Operations — Canadian Tire

Cash from operations is calculated as:

		Net income
	+	depreciation and any other non-cash operating expenses
	+	net decrease in non-cash working capital
OR	–	net increase in non-cash working capital
	=	cash from operations

	2005	
Net income (after tax and interest)	$ 330	
Add: Non-cash expense — depreciation	185	
Less: Increase in non-cash working capital	(177)	(see calculation below)
Cash from operations	$ 338	

As a result of its normal business operations, Canadian Tire's cash increased by $338 million.

Calculation of change in non-cash working capital

	2005	2004
Non-cash working capital:		
Receivables	$1,425	$ 987
Inventory	676	621
Other	42	24
	$2,143	$1,632
Less: Current liabilities	1,821	1,487
Net non-cash working capital, end of year	$ 322	$ 145
	145	
Increase of non-cash working capital	$ 177	

Between 2004 and 2005, the net non-cash working capital has risen from $145 to $322. This is an increase of $177. Increased working capital is a use of cash.

Exhibit 6.3:   Cash from and Cash Used in Financing Activities — Canadian Tire

Cash from increased long-term debt	$119 million
Cash used in redeeming shares	(23)
Cash used for dividends	(47)
Cash from financing activities	$ 49 million

In total, $71 million of cash was generated from financing activities.

from $1,205 million in 2004 to $1,324 million in 2005 — an increase of $119 million. An increase in borrowings is a source of funds to the company.

Canadian Tire got an additional $119 million by acquiring new debt. While the share capital account has fallen from $710 million to $704 million — a decrease of $6 million, the statement of retained earnings also shows that an expense of $17 million was charged there to the repayment of shares. The net result of these two transactions is that $23 million was used in share redemptions. Dividends of $47 million are also reported here, as part of the cash flow associated with financing.

The net effect is that Canadian Tire got $49 million from financing activities. (See Exhibit 6.3.)

6.4   Cash from and Cash Used in Investing Activities

The third category in the report is the cash used to buy long-term assets (or, conceivably, the cash generated by selling long-term assets). The balance sheet for 2004 shows long-term assets as $2,809 million. In the income statement, $185 million of amortization was shown as depreciation expense. All other things being equal, this would have resulted in long-term assets declining to $2,624 million in 2005, after the amortization had been deducted. However, the long-term assets are reported as $2,975 million in 2005, so $351 million of additional long-term assets must have been added. This is a use of cash. (See Exhibit 6.4.)

6.5   Change in Cash Balance

The last category in the cash flow statement is the change in cash itself, which can be obtained by comparing the cash level in the current year's balance sheet with the one in the previous year's. In the Canadian

---

**Exhibit 6.4: Cash from or Cash Used in Investing Activities
— Canadian Tire**

Long-term assets at start of year	$2,809 million
Less: Amortization expense	185
	$2,624
Less: Long-term assets at end of year	2,975
Cash used in investing activities	$ (351) million

**Exhibit 6.5: Statement of Cash Flows (Simplified)
— Canadian Tire**

	2005
Cash from operations	$ 338
Cash from financing activities	49
Cash used in investing activities	(351)
Changes in cash balance (increase)	$ 36

Tire example, the cash level in 2004 was $802 million but $838 million in 2005, indicating an increase of $36 million. The result can be reached by adding (or subtracting) the three other items in the statement of cash flows: cash from (or used in) operations, financing activities, and investing activities. (See Exhibit 6.5.)

6.6   Interpreting the Statement of Cash Flows

From the statement of cash flows in Exhibit 6.5, we observe an increase of $36 million in cash in Canadian Tire from 2004 to 2005. This can be interpreted as follows:

Canadian Tire is in an aggressive expansion mode. They have invested a net $351 million in additional long-term assets. They financed this expansion partly from operating cash flows ($338 million) and partly from financing activities ($49 million).

If Canadian Tire wishes to continue investing in new long-term assets, it will need to raise additional financing (either by long-term debt or new share issues).

6.7 Summary

Cash flow analysis is one of the important parts of analyzing a company's past activities and future prospects. A stable, profitable company is internally self-sufficient in cash flow, and this is likely to be seen in a positive flow of cash from operations. The company's financing and investing activities are clearly revealed by referring to the cash flow effects of the actions they have taken. Cash from (or used in) operations, financing activities, and investing activities are reported in the statement of cash flows (also known as the statement of changes in financial positions).

Appendix 6.1
Example of a Cash Flow Statement

The cash flow statement reproduced below was prepared from information on page 28 of Wendy's International Inc.'s "10-K" report, which has to be filed under U.S. law. The complete report is available on the Wendy's International Web site: **www.wendys.com**

Wendy's International, Inc. and Subsidiaries
Consolidated Cash Flow Statements ($ million)

	Years Ended	
	January 1 2006	January 2 2005
Operating activities:		
Net income	$ 224	$ 52
Add: Amortization	204	372
Add: Decrease (deduct increase) in non-cash working capital	31	72
Other adjustments	18	6
Net cash from operations	$ 477	$ 502
Investing activities:		
Investing in long-term assets	$ 400	$ 416
Sale of long-term assets	(213)	(93)
Net cash used in investing	$ 187	$ 323
Financing activities:		
Issuance of notes payable	$ 3	$ 40
Issuance of shares (employee stock options)	216	31
Repurchase of shares	(100)	(138)
Repayment of debt	(131)	(62)
Dividends paid	(66)	(55)
Net cash from (used in) financing	$ (78)	$ (184)
Increase (decrease) in cash	$ 212	$ (5)
Cash at start of period	167	172
Cash at end of period	$ 379	$ 167

Appendix 6.2
The Mechanics of Accounting: Cash Flows

The *statement of cash flows*, **SCF**, (also called the cash flow statement or the statement of changes in financial position) *explains the change in cash over the accounting period in terms of the changes of the other balance sheet accounts*. This is illustrated in Exhibit 6A2.1. If cash has changed by some amount from the end of year 0 to the end of year 1 (illustrated here as a decrease), the double-entry nature of accounting means that there must be an equal decrease in all the other balance sheet accounts taken together. We can state this more formally in algebraic terms:

From the accounting equation:

$$A = L + S/E$$

Break each side down into its components, using the acronyms in Exhibit 6A2.1:

$$C + NCA + LTA = NCL + LTL + CS + RE$$

Date the components using subscripts, C_0, NCA_0, etc., for the balances at the end of year 0, and C_1, NCA_1, etc., for the balances at the end of year 1.

Hence there is one accounting equation at the beginning of the year and another at the end

$$C_0 + NCA_0 + LTA_0 = NCL_0 + LTL_0 + CS_0 + RE_0 \tag{1}$$

$$C_1 + NCA_1 + LTA_1 = NCL_1 + LTL_1 + CS_1 + RE_1 \tag{2}$$

Subtract equation (1) from equation (2) to get the change in each component over the year, $C_1 - C_0$, $NCA_1 - NCA_0$, etc. Writing these as ΔC, ΔNCA, etc. we have

$$\Delta C + \Delta NCA + \Delta LTA = \Delta NCL + \Delta LTL + \Delta CS + \Delta RE \tag{3}$$

Rearrange to isolate the change in cash on the left-hand side

$$\Delta C = \Delta NCA + \Delta LTA + \Delta NCL + \Delta LTL + \Delta CS + \Delta RE \tag{4}$$

Thus the change in cash is equal to the change in all the other balance sheet accounts.

In order to convey information, form is also important. The statement of cash flows arranges these balance sheet changes in a particular way, grouping separately balance sheet changes that are the result of *operating activities*, *investing activities*, and *financing activities*.

Exhibit 6A2.1: Statement of Cash Flows

The statement of cash flows explains the change in cash over the reporting period *in terms of changes in the other balance sheet accounts*

Operating activities are summarized by *net income* and *dividends*, in other words, ΔRE, as well as changes in the *non-cash working capital accounts*, $\Delta NCA + \Delta NCL$. Investing activities are changes in the *long-term asset accounts* (both purchases and sales), ΔLTA. Financing activities are changes in the *long-term liabilities and capital stock*, $\Delta LTL + \Delta CS$ (again, both increases and decreases). Rearranging equation (4), we have the statement of cash flows in algebraic form:

change in cash	=	operating activities
ΔC		$\Delta RE + \Delta NCA + \Delta NCL$
	+	investing activities
		ΔLTA
	+	financing activities
		$\Delta LTL + \Delta CS$

There are some variations in practice. Many companies include dividends with financing activities rather than operating activities, while others put dividends in a separate category of its own. Still, the general principle holds: *the statement of cash flows explains the change in cash in terms of the changes in the other balance sheet accounts organized by type of activity.*

Unlike the three statements we have seen up to now, we cannot "read" the SCF directly from the ledger balances. The books are not set up to do that. We could go through the cash account and use the other side of each entry to build up the statement, but, apart from companies with a few, simple transactions, this would be quite onerous. (There were only 10 transactions in Example Co. Ltd., which was used to illustrate debits and credits in Appendix 2.1, so analyzing these cash transactions is feasible. As an exercise, you might try to see how the information in the journal entries that affect the cash account — use the last version of the spreadsheet — are regrouped to form the statement of cash flows at the end of that section.)

The cash flow statement does not contain new information. It is a reorganization of information that already exists on the opening and closing balance sheets, supplemented by information on the income statement and statement of retained earnings for the period. You have seen this as you worked through sections 6.2 to 6.5 in Chapter 6. The T-account method presented in this appendix simply formalizes the comparison of balance sheets used in Chapter 6. The method shown here makes use of our knowledge of debits, credits, and T-accounts to provide a systematic way of constructing an SCF.

There are four steps to constructing an SCF using the T-account method:

1. Calculate the *change in each balance sheet account* between the beginning and end of the period.

2. Transfer these changes to a set of T-accounts.

3. Using information from the income statement and the statement of retained earnings, reconstruct, in summary form, the transactions that affected cash in the period.

4. When all the changes have been explained, use the summary information to prepare the SCF.

The method will be illustrated using the data for Canadian Tire over the 2005 reporting period (the period that began at the end of 2004 and ended at the end of 2005).

Step 1: Calculate the change in each balance sheet account between the beginning and end of the period.

The closing and opening balance sheets for Canadian Tire can be found in Exhibit 6.1 on page 200 of the text. In calculating the changes we must recall whether a particular balance is a debit balance or a credit balance. In general, asset accounts have debit balances while liability and shareholder equity accounts have credit balances — that is the case here. However, you should be aware that this is not always true. If accumulated amortization is shown separately, it must be included as a balance sheet change, but you must remember that the opening and closing balances are *credits*, not debit balances. Similarly, if there is an *unamortized discount* in the long-term liabilities section, those will be *debit* balances, as would be the balances in the *deficit* account (negative retained earnings).

If an account that has *debit* balances *increases* from the beginning of the year to the end, we conclude that there must have been more debits to the account than credits; we say that there were *net debits* to that account. If such an account *decreases* from the beginning of the year to the end, then there were *net credits* to that account. The opposite is true for accounts with credit balances. If an account that has *credit* balances *increases* from the beginning of the year to the end, we say that there were *net credits* to that account. If such an account *decreases* from the beginning of the year to the end, we say that there were *net debits* to that account. (You can easily work out what has happened in the rare case that an account switches sign: if it goes from a debit balance to a credit balance, there must have been net credits, and vice versa.)

Here is a list of all the balance sheet account changes for Canadian Tire over the 2005 financial year, organized as net *debit* and net *credit* balance changes. It is a good idea to check that the columns balance.

Canadian Tire
Balance Sheet Changes
for the year 2005
($ million)

	Dr	Cr
Cash	36	
Accounts receivable	438	
Inventory	55	
Prepaid expense	18	
Long-term assets	166	
Current liabilities		334
Long-term liabilities		119
Share capital	6	
Retained earnings		266
	719	719

Exhibit 6A2.2

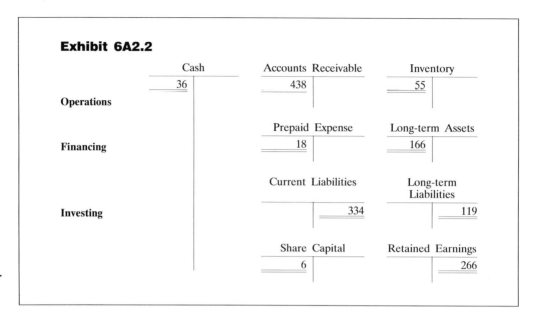

	Cash		Accounts Receivable		Inventory	
	36		438		55	
Operations						
			Prepaid Expense		Long-term Assets	
Financing			18		166	
			Current Liabilities		Long-term Liabilities	
Investing				334		119
			Share Capital		Retained Earnings	
				6		266

Step 2: Transfer these changes to a set of T-accounts.

Set up a set of T-accounts, one for each of the accounts in your list of accounts. Allow considerably more space, vertically and horizontally, for the cash account and divide this T-account into three sections: operations; financing; investing. This is where you will be organizing the information for the SCF. Enter each change at top of the appropriate T-account and double-underline it. This is the figure in each account that you have to explain. (All figures in this illustration are in millions of dollars.) See Exhibit 6A2.2.

Step 3: Using information from the income statement and the statement of retained earnings, reconstruct, in summary form, the transactions that affected cash in the period.

We will begin with cash from operations. It is convenient to do this in two steps: transaction (a) uses net income to get a first approximation to cash from operations; transaction (b) takes into account changes in non-cash working capital accounts to get the final value of cash from operations. (See Exhibit 6A2.3 for all transactions discussed in Step 3.)

(a) Looking at all the revenue and expense transactions in the year in an aggregated way, if we were to record them in one entry, treating all revenues and expenses except amortization, *as if they were cash transactions*, it would be as follows:

Entry	Accounts/Description	Dr	Cr
a	Cash {asset}	515	
	Long-term Assets {asset}		185
	Retained Earnings {SE}		330

First approximation of cash from operations in 2005

Where does this entry come from? It is in fact a consolidation of the following three entries. The first aggregates all the regular revenue entries that have this form:

(1)	debit a current asset or current liability	A	
(2)	credit revenue		A

The second aggregates all the regular expense entries (excluding depreciation) that look like this:

(3)	debit expense	B	
(4)	credit a current asset or current liability		B

The third is depreciation, the one expense entry that does not involve a credit to a current asset or current liability:

(5)	debit depreciation expense	185	
(6)	credit long-term assets (accumulated depreciation)		185

Return to Entry *a* earlier. The last line, the credit to Retained Earnings, is the net income of $330. This is the combination of lines (2), (3), & (5) of the three entries above. The credit to Long-term assets (accumulated depreciation), is line (6) above. The debit to cash is our first approximation to cash from operations. This is lines (1) & (4) above (since $A - (B + 185) = \$330$, the debit to cash, $A - B$, is $515).

(b) Since we took net income (excluding depreciation) as the first approximation to cash from operations, we adjust for the changes in all the non-cash working capital accounts to arrive at the actual cash from operations. For example, entry (a) effectively treats all revenue as an increase in cash. However, to the extent that credit sales are not collected at year-end (Accounts Receivable has increased), that revenue is not a cash inflow in 2005. As we see, the net effect of these changes is a reduction in our first approximation of cash from operations by $177.

Entry	Accounts/Description	Dr	Cr
b	Accounts Receivable {asset}	438	
	Long-term Assets {asset}	55	
	Prepaid Expense {asset}	18	
	Cash {asset}		177
	Current Liabilities {liability}		334

Non-cash working capital accounts and cash from operations

The non-cash working capital accounts are now cleared.

211

(c) The information about the dividends appears on the Statement of Retained Earnings (Exhibit 6.1). Like net income, since the Dividends account has been closed to Retained Earnings, the entry is to that account:

Entry	Accounts/Description	Dr	Cr
c	Retained Earnings {SE}	47	
	Cash {asset}		47
	Dividend payment in 2005		

(Note that Canadian Tire classifies a dividend payment as a financing transaction.) This entry completes the explanation for the changes to the Retained Earnings account, so we can clear this account.

(d) Shares have been redeemed in the year. We can see this because there are net debits of $6 to the share capital account and there is also a charge of $17 to retained earnings in connection with share repurchase (Exhibit 6.1). In principle, a net debit to the share capital account could include the issue of shares as well (shares repurchased exceeded shares issued by $6), but since there is no information about share issue, we assume there was none. The simplest transaction consistent with the information we have is a share repurchase with the excess over the original issue cost charged to Retained Earnings:

Entry	Accounts/Description	Dr	Cr
d	Share Capital {asset}	6	
	Retained Earnings {SE}	17	
	Cash {asset}		23
	Effect on cash of share redemption in 2005		

This use of cash is classified as financing and is entered in that section of the cash T-account. The share capital account is cleared.

(e) There was a net increase in long-term assets (Long-term Assets at cost less Accumulated Amortization) of $166. We know that there were credits of $185 to this pair of accounts (Accumulated Amortization specifically) and the depreciation (amortization) expense. We can thus conclude that the company must have purchased new long-term assets of $351 (= $166 + $185). Long-term assets is cleared. This is a use of cash in investing activity.

Entry	Accounts/Description	Dr	Cr
e	Long-term Assets {asset}	351	
	Cash {asset}		351

(f) We have no other information about long-term liabilities, so we can assume that the increase (net credits) in this account represents cash from financing activities. Long-term liabilities is now cleared.

Entry	Accounts/Description	Dr	Cr
f	Cash {asset}	119	
	Long-term Liabilities {liability}		119

Exhibit 6A2.3

	Cash			Accounts Receivable			Inventory	
	36			438			55	
Operations			d	438		d	55	
a	515			✓			✓	
d		177						
	338							

				Prepaid Expenses			Long-term Assets	
				18			166	
Financing			d	18		a		185
b		23		✓		e	351	
c		47					166	
f	119						✓	
	49							

				Current Liabilities			Long-term Liabilities	
					334			119
Investing			d		334	f		119
e		351			✓			✓
		351						
net	36							
	✓			Share Capital			Retained Earnings	
					6			266
			b		6	a		330
					✓	d	17	
						c	47	
								266
								✓

At this point we have cleared (explained) all the changes. When we check all the net changes in the cash account, we see that there is a final net debit of $36 — a net increase of cash of $36 — just as the comparison of balance sheets showed us. We now have all the ingredients for the SCF.

Step 4. When all the changes have been explained, use the summary information to prepare the SCF.

The information needed for the statement is in the Cash T-account. The finished statement can be seen in Exhibit 6A2.4. Notice that the organization of the statement reflects its objective: it explains the change in cash over the accounting period in terms of the changes of the other balance sheet accounts. The balance sheet changes are grouped by the

Exhibit 6A2.4

Canadian Tire
Statement of Cash Flows
for 2005
($ million)

Cash from and cash used in operating activities		
Net income	$330	
Add: non-cash expense — depreciation	185	
Less: increase in non-cash working capital	(177)	
Cash from operations		$338
Cash from and cash used in financing activities		
Cash from increased long-term debt	$119	
Cash used for redeeming shares	(23)	
Cash used for dividends	(47)	
Cash from financing activities		49
Cash used in investing activities		
Cash used for purchase of long-term assets		(351)
Increase in cash		$ 36
Cash at the beginning of the year		802
Cash at the end of the year		$ 838

nature of the activity that generated them — operations, finance, and investment. Finally, at the foot of the statement, the change in cash is reconciled to the opening and closing balance of the cash account.

Self-Study Problem

1. You are given the balance sheet as at December 31 for Charley Farley, who went into business on October 1, 2005.

Charley Farley
Balance Sheet as at December 31, 2005

Assets
Current assets:

Cash		$ 3,000
Receivables		500
Inventory		1,500
Prepaid rent		5,000
Prepaid insurance		3,000
		$ 13,000
Long-term assets:		
At cost	$99,000	
Less: Accumulated amortization	(9,000)	90,000
		$103,000

Liabilities and Equity
Current liabilities:

Trade payables		$ 5,000
Accrued utilities		1,000
		$ 6,000
Long-term debt		51,000
Total debt		$ 57,000
Owners' equity:		
Cash invested	$50,000	
Add: Net income	11,000	
Less: Withdrawals	(15,000)	46,000
		$103,000

[Note: This is a continuation of Self-Study Problem 4.1 on page 160. You may need to refer back to that problem to help in doing this one.]

Required
Prepare a statement of cash flows for the three months to December 31, 2005.

Solution

1.

Charley Farley
Statement of Cash Flows
for the three months to December 31, 2005

Cash from Operations

Net income	$ 11,000	
Add: Amortization (non-cash expense)	9,000	
	$ 20,000	
Less: Increase in net non-cash working capital ($13,000 – $3,000 – $6,000)	4,000	$16,000

Cash from financing activities

Cash introduced by owner	$ 50,000	
Add: Bank loan	55,000	
Less: Bank loan repaid	(4,000)	
Less: Owners' withdrawals	(15,000)	86,000

Cash used in investing activities

Purchase of long-term assets	(99,000)

Increase in cash balance	$ 3,000

Discussion Questions and Problems

Discussion Questions

1. What is the purpose of the statement of cash flows?
2. According to economist Milton Friedman, when a company makes a profit it has a duty to pay the whole profit to shareholders as a cash dividend. Discuss the effect of this on the company and on the shareholders.
3. What is the effect of amortization expense on cash flow?
4. What is the effect on cash flow of increasing inventory?
5. Your business allows customers to pay in 30 days: what is the effect on cash flow of allowing customers to pay in 60 days?
6. Why is reporting on cash flows so very important?
7. What are the four main headings in a cash flow statement?
8. Should the Cash from Operations be positive or negative?
9. If a firm has positive Cash from Investing Activities, what would you infer?
10. If a company is expanding, would you expect Cash from Financing Activities to be positive or negative?

Appendix 6.2

11. Why does the change in cash over a year equal the change in all the other balance sheet accounts?

12. Define each of the following terms as they relate to the statement of cash flows:
    (a) Operating activities
    (b) Investing activities
    (c) Financing activities

13. Why do we distinguish among the three types of activities listed in Question #12?

Problems

1. Gallagher has the following cash flow statement for 2002:

Cash from operations	$ 250,000
Cash used in financing activities	(200,000)
Cash used in investing activities	(100,000)
Decrease in cash	$ 50,000

Discuss this statement and its implications for the management of the company.

2. Wilson Co. had sales revenue of $9.54 million in 2001 and $8.756 million in 2002. Accounts receivable balance was $105,500 on January 1, 2001, $120,000 on December 31, 2001, and $158,000 on December 31, 2002.

Required
Calculate the cash received from sales for 2002.

3. What would be the effect of the following events on Wilson Co.'s cash flow during the month of January?
   (a) Increasing its inventory from $200,000 to $250,000.
   (b) Decreasing accounts receivable by $160,000.
   (c) Decreasing accounts payable by $60,000.
   (d) Buying a new truck for $100,000, in cash.
   (e) Buying a new truck for $100,000, $20,000 down, and using a bank loan for the remainder.
   (f) Getting a new $100,000 truck on a five-year lease at $30,000 per year.
   (g) Repaying a loan of $100,000.
   (h) Converting a loan of $100,000 into common shares.
   (i) Borrowing $500,000.
   (j) Issuing 500 new common shares @ $100 each, for cash.
   (k) Repaying $100,000 of redeemable preferred shares.
   (l) Paying a cash dividend of $50,000.

4. Healey Inc. had the following operating data for 2002.

Income Statement

	2002
Sales revenue	$ 5,750,000
Operating expenses	3,540,000
Operating income	$2,210,000
Add: Opening retained earnings	510,000
Less: Dividend paid	(1,000,000)
Closing retained earnings	$ 1,720,000

Balance Sheet

	December 31, 2002	January 1, 2002
Cash	$1,500,000	$ 100,000
Accounts receivable	1,600,000	1,500,000
Inventories	1,630,000	750,000
Total current assets	$4,730,000	$2,350,000
Long-term assets (net)	1,500,000	2,050,000
Total assets	$6,230,000	$4,400,000
Current liabilities	$ 760,000	$ 890,000
Long-term liabilities	2,500,000	2,000,000
Total liabilities	$3,260,000	$2,890,000
Common shares	$1,250,000	$1,000,000
Retained earnings	1,720,000	510,000
Total equity	$2,970,000	$1,510,000
Total liabilities and equity	$6,230,000	$4,400,000

You are told that operating expenses include $550,000 amortization.

Required
(a) Calculate the increase or decrease in net working capital (current assets – current liabilities).
(b) Calculate the increase or decrease in non-cash net working capital [(current assets – cash) – current liabilities].

(c) What was the cash from/used in operations?
(d) What was the cash from/used in financing activities?
(e) What was the cash from/used in investing activities?
(f) What was the change in cash over the year?
(g) Prepare a statement of cash flows for 2002.
(h) Draft a short report that identifies the main features of this company's cash flows.

5. Consider each of the following independent events that occurred in Goya Inc. in August 2005. In each case state whether it would increase cash flow, decrease cash flow, or leave cash flow unchanged.

(a) They paid accounts payable of $500,000.
(b) They paid wages of $200,000.
(c) They bought inventory for $240,000, in cash.
(d) They bought inventory for $160,000, on 30 days credit.
(e) They sold goods for cash for $600,000.
(f) They sold goods on credit for $900,000.
(g) They allowed their payables to increase by $90,000.
(h) They decreased their inventory by $160,000.
(i) They decreased their accounts payable by $30,000.
(j) They took out a bank loan of $400,000.
(k) They repaid $250,000 owed to credit card companies.
(l) They bought new machinery for $100,000 cash.
(m) They bought a new truck for $120,000, trading in an old truck for $40,000.
(n) They leased a new bottling machine for $20,000 per month.
(o) They paid interest for the month on a 12% convertible debenture of $100,000.
(p) A 12% convertible debenture of $100,000 was converted into $100,000 of common shares.
(q) 1,000 new common shares were issued, the new shareholders paying $10,000 into the company.
(r) Senior managers were issued $100,000 new common shares as part of their remuneration.

6. (a) Seargent Co. had operating income for 2005 of $500,000. Included in the expenses was a total of $100,000 of amortization. Net non-cash working capital had increased by $50,000. Interest expense was $25,000, and income taxes were $100,000.

   Required: Calculate the cash from operations for 2005.

   (b) Seargent Co. had 100,000 common shares in issue at the start of 2005. During the year the company issued an additional 50,000 shares that were given to managers as bonuses, and bought 10,000 shares from existing shareholders for $50,000 and retired them. The company paid a total of $100,000 in dividends in 2005, and also borrowed $200,000 as a long-term loan from a bank.

   Required: Calculate the cash from financing activities for 2005.

(c) Seargent Co. had long-term plant assets of $400,000 at the start of 2005. During the year the company charged $100,000 amortization on these assets. The company bought new assets for $250,000, and sold existing assets for $75,000.

Required: Calculate the cash used in investing activities for 2005.

(d) Seargent had cash balances totalling $25,000 at the start of 2005. By the end of 2005 the cash balances had increased to $325,000.

Required: Calculate the increase in cash for 2005.

(e) Based on (a) through (d) above, prepare the statement of changes in financial position for Seargent Co. for 2005.

7. Van Ympen Co. had the following cash flow statement for 2005:

Van Ympen Co.
Statement of Cash Flows: Year Ended December 31, 2005

Operations:	
Net income	$250,000
Add: amortization	80,000
Add: decrease in non-cash working capital	60,000
Total cash from operations	$390,000
Financing activities:	
Cash from borrowing	$200,000
Investing activities:	
Purchase of plant assets	($750,000)
Total change (decrease) in cash	$160,000

Required
Comment on the sustainability of the company's activities.

8. You are given the combined income statement and statement of retained earnings for O'Keefe Inc. for the year ended December 31, 2005, and the balance sheets as at December 31, 2004 and 2005:

O'Keefe Inc.
Income Statement for the Year Ended December 31, 2005

Sales revenue		$9,500,000
Operating expenses*		4,000,000
Operating income		$5,500,000
Interest expense	$ 300,000	
Income taxes	2,400,000	2,700,000
Net income		$2,800,000
Add: retained earnings as at 1/1/2005		5,300,000
		$8,100,000
Dividends paid		2,100,000
Retained earnings as at 31/12/2005		$6,000,000

* This includes $750,000 amortization.

O'Keefe Inc.
Balance Sheet as at December 31

	2004	2005
Assets		
Cash	$ 500,000	$ 600,000
Accounts receivable	13,200,000	11,800,000
Inventories	22,500,000	22,100,000
Total current assets	$36,200,000	$34,500,000
Long-term assets (net)	20,000,000	22,500,000
Total assets	$56,200,000	$57,000,000
Liabilities & Equity		
Current liabilities	$15,900,000	$16,000,000
Long-term liabilities	20,000,000	18,000,000
Total liabilities	$35,900,000	$34,000,000
Common shares	$15,000,000	$17,000,000
Retained earnings	5,300,000	6,000,000
Total equity	$20,300,000	$23,000,000
Total liabilities & equity	$56,200,000	$57,000,000

Required

(a) Calculate the increase or decrease in net working capital (current assets – current liabilities).

(b) Calculate the increase or decrease in non-cash working capital [(current assets – cash) – current liabilities].

(c) Calculate the cash from or cash used in operations.

(d) Calculate the cash from or cash used in financing activities.

(e) Calculate the cash from or cash used in investing activities.

(f) Calculate the increase or decrease in cash.

(g) Prepare the Statement of Cash Flows for 2005.

(h) Comment on the Statement of Cash Flows you have prepared.

Appendix 6.2

9. Refer to Problem #4 in this chapter (Healy Inc.). Use the T-account method to construct a Statement of Cash Flows for 2002 for Healey Inc.

10. Refer to Problem #8 in this chapter (O'Keefe Inc.). Use the T-account method to construct a Statement of Cash Flows for 2005 for O'Keefe Inc.

2

Budgeting for Planning & Control

Management Accounting:

"...the process of identification, measurement accumulation, analysis, preparation, interpretation and communication of information that assists managers in making decisions."

C.T. Horngren, G.L. Sundem, W.O. Stratton & H.D. Teall
Management Accounting, 4th Canadian Edition
Toronto, Prentice Hall, 2002

Budgeting 7

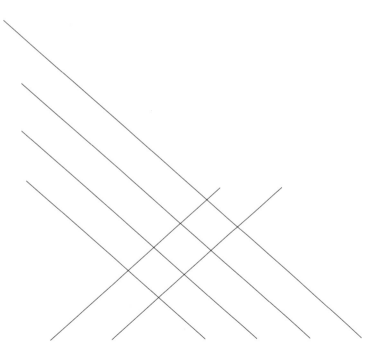

Learning
Objectives

After studying this chapter you should be able to:
→ Identify planning and control as the main objectives of budgeting
→ Identify a number of different approaches to budget preparation
   → Prepare an operating budget for a service department of an organization
   → Prepare an operating budget for a production department of an organization
   → Prepare an operating budget for a simple organization
   → Prepare a cash budget for a simple organization
→ Understand the role of participation in budget setting

7.1   Introduction

Planning is one of the five "functions of management" identified by Fayol (the others are: organizing, commanding, co-ordinating, and controlling). Any competently run organization will make plans about its future. The source of planning information is generally the managers and other senior staff who run the organization: each manager will contribute information from his or her own area of expertise, which together will become the organizational plan.

When the organizational plan is expressed in financial terms, it is called a budget. The operating budget is the budget for all the activities that get reported in the income statement, and it is presented in the same format as the income statement. The main difference is the income statement summarizes past events, while the budget forecasts future events. The cash budget is a list of forecast receipts and payments and their effect on cash balances. In this chapter we shall consider how both these budgets can be prepared, and in the following chapter we shall consider how they may be used for control (another of Fayol's five management functions). In the control exercise, actual results are compared to budgeted results to see if the organization is on track or not. Without the budget that judgment would be more difficult or even impossible to make.

While planning and control are the most common uses to which budgeting will be put, it is also true that both perform valuable service in communicating information to managers (e.g., by implication, they map out the organizational structure, and they also communicate profit expectations) and that they may be used as motivational devices to encourage managers to strive for organizational goals.

Because the budget has so many purposes, it is a very important part of the management process. Also, because budgets can be prepared with several different uses in mind, it is sometimes unclear as to how they should best be executed.

If the primary purpose of the budget is to support the planning process, then its most important characteristics should be, first, that it is integrated with the organizational objectives and strategy, and, second, that it should be accurate. Use of the budget for planning is probably of greatest interest to top management, such as the board of directors, or the chief executive officer and his immediate area managers.

If the primary purpose of the budget is to enable control, then its most important characteristics should be, first, that it is linked to the responsibility areas over which functional managers have control, and, second, that it represent a fair basis for the control process. Fairness can be achieved by both the parties (the manager exercising control and the manager being controlled) agreeing to the budget before it is put into use. Control of activities is normally exercised by (and on) functional managers, such as plant managers, marketing managers, and human resource managers.

Although communication and co-ordination are unlikely to be primary purposes of any budget, they should be borne in mind when considering the accuracy of the picture they give of the organization. The structure of the budget should not mislead the observer as to the reality of the organizational structure.

In sales and marketing situations (and occasionally in production and service units) the budget may have a major motivational objective. In that case, the budget should represent some challenging, but achievable, level of performance.

As a further gloss on this situation, the degree to which budgets are regarded as important varies among organizations. In some, the budget is regarded with almost religious fervour, and achieving or not achieving the budget is strongly linked to rewards and punishments. Those who exceed budget expectations are likely to receive bonus payments and promotions, while those who fail to meet their budgets will be denied such rewards. In other organizations the budget is treated more lightheartedly: it is a source of valuable information, but rewards and punishments are unlikely to follow as a result of achieving or not achieving the budget.

7.2 Preparing the Budget for a Service Department

Sarah Smith has recently been promoted from salaries and benefits manager to being in charge of the whole human resource management department at Tizer Foods Inc. The previous manager was given a $20,000 severance package in September, and told to go away. Sarah has the most recent departmental cost report on her desk (see Exhibit 7.1), which is for the month of September. It is now mid-October, and she has received a request from the management accounting department for her departmental budget for next year. How should she proceed?

Where is Sarah going to start in setting her proposed budget for next year? Her choices could include the following:

Exhibit 7.1: Tizer Foods Inc.
— Human Resource Management Department
Monthly Cost Report: September

Details	September Actual	Budget	Year to date Actual	Budget
Manager's salary	$ 28,000	$ 8,000	$ 92,000	$ 72,000
Other salaries	75,000	72,000	675,000	658,000
	$103,000	$ 80,000	$ 767,000	$ 730,000
Employee benefits (5%)	5,150	4,000	38,350	36,500
Total staff costs	$108,150	$ 84,000	$ 805,350	$ 766,500
Travelling expense	5,300	15,000	104,500	135,000
Advertising expense	10,700	17,500	173,200	157,500
Amortization expense	2,000	2,000	18,000	18,000
Occupancy expense (5,000 metres^2 @$2,000)	10,000	10,000	90,000	90,000
Total	$136,150	$128,500	$1,191,050	$1,167,000

1. Previous Year's Budget

Take the current year's budget ($128,500 per month) and say that it can be used again next year.

There are a number of issues with approach #1. First, the world does not stand still, and prices tend to rise through time, so with inflation in Canada running at around 3% per year, last year's budget will not be enough for next year. Sarah would be unwise to commit herself and her co-workers to meet an unrealistic budget, based on out-of-date data.

2. Previous Year's Budget + Inflation Adjustment

Take the current year's budget ($128,500 per month) and add 3% for general inflation, to make it $132,355 per month.

Although that is a little more realistic, there are still some issues with approach #2. The 3% inflation rate will not necessarily be relevant to all expense items. Some (salaries is a good example) may rise at rates higher than inflation. Others (amortization, for example) may not rise at all.

We can also see that the actual expenses (both for the month of September and for the year to date) are greater than the budgeted expenses. Why was this? Was the budget inadequate, or was control lax? At this point Sarah does not know. It would be reckless to commit to a budget without full information.

3. Previous Year Actual + Inflation Adjustment

Take the current month's actual expenses ($136,150) and add 3% for inflation, to make the budget $140,234.50 per month.

In approach #3 we institutionalize whatever was going on in September and immortalize it in our budget. Any inefficiencies that happened now become part of next year's budget request. In addition to any uncontrolled overspending in the month, closer examination of the cost report shows that the $20,000 severance payment for the previous HR manager is included, for example, and that the travelling expenses were underspent by $10,000. It would be incorrect for Sarah to base next year's budget on the expenses that were incurred in September as September was not typical. Probably any given month is atypical in some respect.

4. Zero-Based Budget

If Sarah were to go back to basics she would go through each line of the budget, and try to justify the $ amount. So, her salary as manager would be line 1, and the budget would be based on her expected actual salary for next year: likewise for the remaining employees, the employees' benefits, travelling, advertising, etc. Her monthly budget might appear as follows:

Details	Monthly Budget
Manager's salary	$ 7,500
Other salaries	72,000
	$ 79,500
Employee benefits (5%)	3,975
Total staff costs	$ 83,475
Travelling expense	12,000
Advertising expense	17,500
Amortization expense	2,000
Occupancy expense (5,000 metres^2 @ $2,000)	10,000
Total	$124,975

Approach #4 is often referred to as "zero-based budgeting", as it assumes a starting point of zero, and every expense item has to be justified before being included. President Jimmy Carter introduced zero-based budgeting to the U.S. government because he was appalled by the waste in government offices. Sadly its two big problems soon became apparent: first, it takes an unreasonable amount of time to prepare budgets this way, and second, managers who are preparing budgets soon become adept at sneaking unjustified expenses into the list to pad the budget, thus frustrating its main objective. Although it may be unmanageable to do zero-based budgeting every year, as an occasional exercise in cost control it has much to recommend it.

5. The Padded Budget

While talking to other department managers, Sarah might have heard that whatever budgets were put forward, the management accounting department routinely cut them back by 10%, to get rid of the fat. That being the case, whatever budget she wants to finish up with (say, for example, the budget of $124,975 per month in #4 above), she would add 10% to each of the line items, so that the total budget she puts in for will be $137,472.50.

What started off as a rational process has now become a political football. The only reason the management accounting department should have to cut back a budget by an arbitrary amount is if it expects managers to pad the budget in the first place, so the remedy is giving rise to the disease here.

6. The Compromise Budget

A compromise solution, which many organizations are comfortable with, is to base the budget of one year on that of the previous year but to make appropriate adjustments in respect of routine changes, such as inflation, and also challenge some of the major assumptions that underlie the budget. In this department, for example, salaries are the largest line item: there would be a periodic review of what the employees do and how that contributed to the goals and strategy of the organization.

7. Activity-Based Costing

Taken to its logical conclusion, both zero-based budgeting and challenging major assumptions lead to the identification of the activities the unit is carrying out and why it is doing so, and the related cost that should be incurred to carry out the activities. This is currently referred to as the idea of "activity-based" costing and management (ABC/ABM). The underlying theme of ABC/ABM is that there is a chain of activities that add value to the product or service the organization is selling. All activities that the organization executes should be part of the value chain, otherwise they should be eliminated. ABC/ABM is discussed more fully in Chapter 8.

8. Benchmarking

Some organizations are lucky enough to be able to compare the cost of their activities with those of competitors. Car makers, for example, routinely share cost and efficiency information at various car plants worldwide. If that information is available, then budgets may "benchmarked" against the best standards in the industry. Sarah probably does not have this information to help her.

9. Kaizen System

The Japanese "Kaizen" approach to budgeting regards standing still as unacceptable. Each period's costs must be lower than those of the previous period, so a continuous series of efficiency-based improvements is required. By itself, any single improvement may be trivial, but cumulatively, they may add up and keep efficiency on a steady upward path. The Kaizen system is widely used in manufacturing situations, but in theory at least, it could be applied to any activity.

Whatever budget amounts Sarah submits, we must recognize that it will then become part of a negotiation process. Whoever is co-ordinating the budget for the whole organization has the right to ask Sarah to reconsider her submission. If the overall operating budget is not able to meet the organization's profit expectations, then everyone will have to rethink how their contribution affects that overall picture. Only when all parties agree that the budget is possible and that it will achieve organizational objectives should it be approved and implemented.

7.3 Preparing the Budget for a Production Department

In the example above Sarah Smith was preparing the budget for a department that provided a service to the rest of the organization (human resources management). The managers of any service department, including HR, accounting, marketing, research and development, and maintenance, would face a similar task. In the case of service departments, the budgeting issue is somewhat (but not totally) separated from the issue of how much work they are expected to do.

Production departments face a different situation. In the case of a department that makes a product or that renders a service for sale to customers, there are some costs that behave like service department costs (essentially fixed costs) and others that would be expected to rise or fall with the number of products made, or the number or services sold: these are called variable costs, as they vary in direct proportion to activity.

Barbara Byng is the production manager of the Coated Nut Division of Tizer Foods Inc. Her monthly operating budget for the current year is shown in Exhibit 7.2.

When Barbara Byng prepares her operating budget for the following year, not only will she have to think about all the issues that Sarah Smith had to consider (such as changing prices), but she will also have to think about how many kg of coated nuts are planned for production.

If the output of coated nuts is going to rise by 10% (from 600,000 kg to 660,000 kg), then even if the rate per kg stays the same (variable cost is currently $1.50 per kg), the budgeted cost would rise by 10% (from $900,000 to $990,000). Likewise if the budgeted output of coated nuts were to be 20% lower (480,000 kg) then the budgeted total variable cost would fall by 20% (from $900,000 to $720,000).

The fixed costs have a current budget of $450,000. Price changes and increased efficiency may make the following year's budget for fixed costs different, but the level of activity should not change the budget for fixed costs. It would not matter if the output was the same (600,000 kg), was lower (e.g., 480,000 kg) or was higher (660,000 kg), these would still be expected to be $450,000 (plus or minus any price or efficiency changes).

Suppose Barbara Byng is preparing her budget for the next year. She has been given the following information to help her:

1. The sales department plans on selling an average of 750,000 kg of coated nuts per month (an increase of 25%).
2. The purchasing department expects the following price changes:
    * the cost of nuts will increase to $0.60 per kg
    * the cost of coatings will increase to $3.00 per kg

Exhibit 7.2: Tizer Foods Inc. — Coated Nut Division
Monthly Operating Budget: Current Year

Activity: Budgeted monthly output of coated nuts		**600,000 kg**
Variable operating costs:		
Raw materials and packaging		
Nuts	500,000 kg @ $0.500	$ 250,000
Coating	100,000 kg @ $2.750	275,000
Packing materials	600,000 kg @ $0.050	30,000
Labels and inserts	600,000 kg @ $0.075	45,000
Total		$ 600,000
Labour	8,000 hours @ $25	200,000
Other variable operating costs	8,000 hours @ $12.50	100,000
Total variable costs ($1.50 per kg of output)		$ 900,000
Fixed operating costs:		
Supervisory salaries (5 @ $5,000 each)		$ 25,000
Rent & taxes		100,000
Utilities		50,000
Maintenance		75,000
Amortization of plant & equipment		200,000
Total fixed operating costs ($0.75 per kg of output)		$ 450,000
Total operating costs ($2.25 per kg of output)		$1,350,000

- the cost of packing materials will decrease to $0.04 per kg
- the cost of labels and inserts is not expected to change
3. The human resources department will agree to a new collective bargaining agreement that will increase wage rates by $5 per hour.
4. Automation of the nut-roasting process will reduce the required labour hours to 0.01 labour hours per kg of output.
5. The variable operating cost rate will increase to $15 per labour hour.
6. One supervisor will be let go, at a cost saving of $5,000 per month.
7. The remaining four supervisors will be paid $6,000 each per month.
8. Amortization will increase by $50,000 per month.

In Exhibit 7.3 we show how Barbara Byng would prepare the monthly operating budget for next year for her division.

Note that 750,000 kg is a 25% increase in activity over the current year, so the quantities of all the variable cost inputs will have to increase by 25%, before considering any price changes.

The budget in Exhibit 7.3 shows the following:

- Variable costs have risen from $1.50 per kg to $1.565 per kg: mostly this is due to rising raw material costs.
- Fixed costs have risen in total (from $450,000 to $499,000) but have actually decreased on a $ per kg output basis (from $0.75 per kg to

Exhibit 7.3   Tizer Foods Inc. — Coated Nut Division Monthly Operating Budget: Next Year

Activity: Budgeted monthly output of coated nuts   **750,000 kg**

Variable operating costs:

Raw materials and packaging

Nuts	(500,000 kg + 25%) @ $0.600	$ 375,000
Coating	(100,000 kg + 25%) @ $3.000	375,000
Packing materials	(600,000 kg + 25%) @ $0.040	30,000
Labels and inserts	(600,000 kg + 25%) @ $0.075	56,250
Total		$ 836,250
Labour	(750,000 × 0.01) hours @ $30	225,000
Other variable operating costs	(750,000 × 0.01) hours @ $15	112,500
Total variable costs ($1.565 per kg of output)		$1,173,750

Fixed operating costs:

Supervisory salaries (4 @ $6,000 each)	$ 24,000
Rent & taxes: no change	100,000
Utilities: no change	50,000
Maintenance: no change	75,000
Amortization of plant & equipment ($200,000 + $50,000)	250,000
Total fixed operating costs ($0.6653 per kg of output)	$ 499,000
Total operating costs ($2.2303 per kg of output)	$1,672,750

$0.6653 per kg) because of the increased production activity: the fixed cost is spread over a greater quantity of production.
- Total cost has decreased from $2.25 per kg to $2.2303 per kg: considering the substantial raw materials cost increases, this is a remarkable achievement.

7.4   The Master Budget

In addition to the various production and service departments creating budgets for their individual responsibility areas, there will be an operating budget for the whole organization. It will look like an income statement, listing the budgeted sales revenues and the budgeted costs and expenses incurred. It will also show the budgeted operating income and the budgeted net income.

In addition to the operating budget, most organizations will prepare budgets for a range of other items, such as a capital budget (for major investment expenditures), a cash budget (for movements in the cash balances), and a budgeted balance sheet. We shall discuss the cash budget later in this chapter because it is so important for organizational survival that all managers need to be aware of the effect their actions have on cash flow, but the rest of the master budget can safely be left to accounting experts, and will not be discussed here.

In Exhibit 7.4 we show the relationship between the various elements of the master budget.

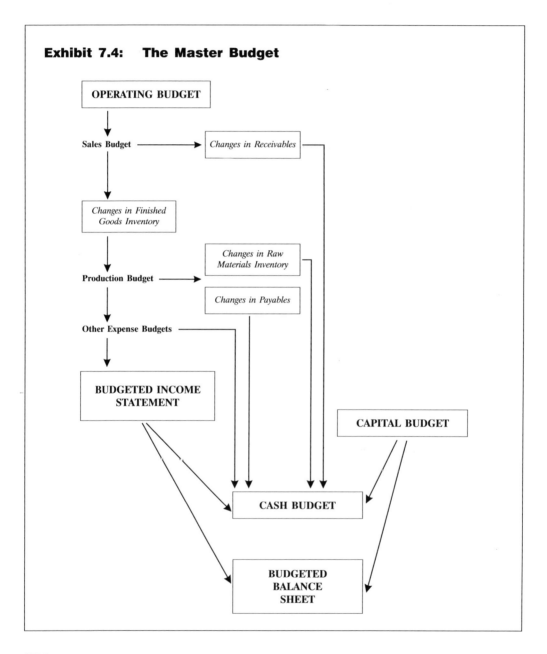

Exhibit 7.4: The Master Budget

7.5 The Operating Budget

The process starts with a forecast of sales. All organizations are subject to some limiting factor that determines the highest level of activity at which they could operate. Because we live in a vibrant modern market economy, sales level is almost always the limiting factor. If potential sales exist, most organizations can somehow find the resources to deal with the additional customers.

Sales forecasts can come from various sources: extrapolations of past trends, the considered opinion of sales and marketing personnel, analysis of market and competitor activity, or any combination of these sources. They will consist of a schedule of products, prices, and volumes that are expected to occur.

In these days of "just-in-time inventory management" it is highly probable that the sales forecast will be virtually identical with the planned production. If, however, it is planned to build up inventory over the budget period, then planned production will exceed planned sales. Conversely, if it is planned to run inventories down, then production will be less than sales. Planned production levels, then, will be sales levels adjusted up or down for changes in finished goods inventories.

Production levels drive manufacturing costs. The raw material purchases necessary for the production plan will have to be bought and paid for. As with sales, if there is little or no inventory, raw materials and bought-in parts will be driven precisely by the production plan. Only if there is a build-up or run-down of raw materials inventory will purchase requirements differ from production. Production levels also drive wage costs and manufacturing overhead. (See Focus Box 7.1.)

As a separate exercise, expense budgets will also be prepared for service departments, such as sales and distribution, human resource management, accounting and administration, research and development, and any other areas of the organization that are separately managed.

Focus Box 7.1: Morgan Cars

Morgan Car Co. has been making cars since the 1930s. By the look of the cars, it seems as though the design may not have changed much in the past 70 years. The traditional appearance, however, masks a thoroughly modern car in many respects. What has not changed is the "craft" mentality used in their construction. Morgan has studiously avoided moving up to large-scale production so that the company can maintain its reputation for quality manufacturing. As a result, demand has consistently outstripped supply in recent years. If you want a Morgan, you can order one, any time, but as of the late 1990s the waiting list was an incredible eight years.

Clearly, Morgan cannot use "sales demand" as the starting point for preparing its budget, but it can use "production capacity" as a starting point, as that is its binding constraint.

Fortunately, as an area manager, it will never be your role to put together the master operating budget. That consolidation is done by the accounting staff. The accountants, however, rely on managers for their inputs. As a functional area manager, it is important to understand that your input into the budgeting process is not an empty exercise in number shuffling, but is one of the ingredients that make the whole thing reasonable and accurate. It is, therefore, essential that the process be taken seriously.

As a manager, you will be expected to budget for your area of control. You can expect some base data to be given to you by the budgeting department. The data would consist of expected rates of inflation, wage settlement prospects, activity levels, etc. Translating that into a reasonable budget is your job.

7.5.1   *Sales Forecasting*

If sales activity is the driving force for other parts of the budget, we should start by considering the sales forecasting process. (See Focus Box 7.2 for an example of poor sales forecasting.)

The past is not a perfect predictor of the future, but it is a very good starting point. Suppose that sales revenue has been growing steadily over the past few years. The most likely projection would be that it would continue to grow, as long as the underlying factors have not changed. We might even expect the rate of growth to remain the same.

Shelburne Heating reports that its gross sales revenues have increased every year from 2001 to 2005:

	$ million
2001	5.7
2002	6.1
2003	6.5
2004	7.2
2005	7.9

Focus Box 7.2:   Rogers@Home

With considerable fanfare, Rogers announced its @Home Internet service. Because it was piped into your house through the TV cable, it was much faster than the phone line connections, which had been the main source of home Internet access up to that point. Rogers was successful: too successful, in fact. The number of customers increased beyond all expectations, including Rogers' own. The sales level was so high that Rogers' systems could no longer handle it effectively. Although the hookup was wickedly fast, it became increasingly unreliable. Customers defected to other services, or retreated to old, slow modems. Eventually, in 2001, a class action suit was brought against Rogers for failing to live up to its promises.

You could say that Rogers had two failures from a budgeting perspective: it had been inaccurate in its sales forecast, and it had taken on additional customers without having the service capacity to provide effective services.

**Exhibit 7.5:   Shelburne Heating
— Sales Revenue (2001 to 2005)**

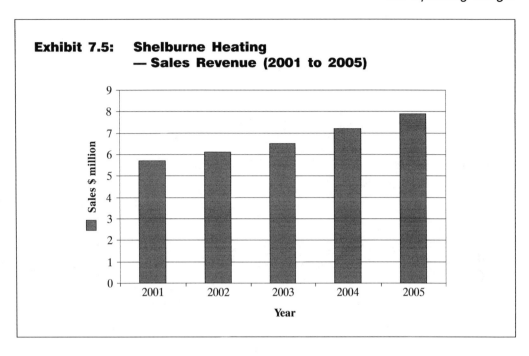

Plotting the sales on a graph (see Exhibit 7.5) shows that the increase is roughly the same each year. Alternatively, year-on-year growth rates could be calculated: sales in 2002 were 7.0% higher than in 2001, for example.

Year	Sales ($ million)	Growth	% Growth
2001	5.7		
2002	6.1	0.4	7.0 (0.4 ÷ 5.7)
2003	6.5	0.4	6.6 (0.4 ÷ 6.1)
2004	7.2	0.7	10.8 (0.7 ÷ 6.5)
2005	7.9	0.7	9.7 (0.7 ÷ 7.2)
Average growth rate			8.5

On average, sales have grown by 8.5% per annum over the four years since 2001. A reasonable forecast for 2006, on that basis, would be for sales of $7.9 million plus 8.5%, which would be $8.6 million.

A more sophisticated analysis of this data might draw a trend line through the data points, either by eye on the graph, or by a calculation, such as a regression analysis. We do not need to go into the mechanics of regression analysis, but the best estimate of sales for 2006 would also be $8.6 million.

Analyzing the trend is quite legitimate if the underlying circumstances are unchanged. If there have been any disturbances in the pattern, however, that might make the trend less reliable. Suppose that you are the manager of a Shelburne Heating in Shelburne, Ontario. Superior Propane has just opened a store 500 metres away. It is inevitable that this will affect your sales, as Superior Propane is such an effective competitor, and the store is so close to yours. A change such as that would have to be built into the sales forecast.

7.5.2   *Production Forecasting*

Once the sales level has been estimated, we have to consider the implications for the rest of the business.

Ontario Brewery has forecast sales of 12 million hectolitres of beer in 2005. Clearly, the brewery will need manufacturing capacity for 12 million hectolitres. If the brewing process takes a month, the plant capacity will have to be rated at 1 million hectolitres, assuming that a steady production of 1 million hectolitres a month is sufficient to meet the annual demand. This would certainly be true if demand were constant, but demand for beer is very seasonal. It goes up in the summer and at holiday times, and is generally lower in colder weather. Suppose the demand was forecast with a seasonal pattern, as shown in Exhibit 7.6.

If sales demand can only be met with current production, then a plant rated at maximum demand (1.7 million hectolitres a month) will be necessary. Apart from the three months of maximum demand, there will be unused capacity for the rest of the year, when demand is less than 1.7 million hectolitres.

With this pattern of demand, it will be possible to meet demand with a plant rated at 1 million hectolitres per month if the product can be carried in inventory. Storing inventory enables production and demand to be "uncoupled" and their capacities do not have to be precisely

---

Exhibit 7.6:   Ontario Brewery 2005 Demand Forecast

Forecast demand in 2005	Millions of hectolitres
January	0.5
February	0.5
March	0.7
April	0.7
May	0.9
June	1.0
July	1.7
August	1.7
September	1.0
October	0.8
November	0.8
December	1.7
Total	12.0

Exhibit 7.7:   Ontario Brewery — Production Plan 2005

Hectolitres (in million)

	Opening inventory	Production	Available	Demand	Closing inventory
January	0.0	1	1.0	0.5	0.5
February	0.5	1	1.5	0.5	1.0
March	1.0	1	2.0	0.7	1.3
April	1.3	1	2.3	0.7	1.6
May	1.6	1	2.6	0.9	1.7
June	1.7	1	2.7	1.0	1.7
July	1.7	1	2.7	1.7	1.0
August	1.0	1	2.0	1.7	0.3
September	0.3	1	1.3	1.0	0.3
October	0.3	1	1.3	0.8	0.5
November	0.5	1	1.5	0.8	0.7
December	0.7	1	1.7	1.7	0.0
Total		12		12.0	

matched. Demand can be effectively met by the production plan shown in Exhibit 7.7.

The brewery is able to build inventory levels up gradually over the light months so that it can effectively meet demand in the heaviest months. Of course, there is a price to pay: the inventory has to be stored. This production plan calls for storage with a peak level of 1.7 million hectolitres. If the company has a plant that could meet the maximum monthly demand every month, then this storage would be unnecessary.

The decision to add 700,000 hectolitres of production capacity, or 1.7 million hectolitres of storage capacity, is one that would have to be made on its own merits.

Although the main focus of the production forecasting exercise was to budget the production activity, there was a spinoff effect: changing inventory levels were planned. In other words, the financial budget is being constructed in parallel with the operating budget.

7.5.3   *Labour Planning*

Once production activity levels have been budgeted, it is possible to schedule the labour force necessary to carry out the production plan. Suppose Ontario Brewery now has a production plan that calls for 1 million hectolitres of beer to be produced each month. A constant level of labour would be appropriate to operate the production plant. Sales, however, are very seasonal, from a low of 500,000 hectolitres to a seasonal peak of 1.7 million hectolitres per month. Planning for the labour requirements in bottling and distribution will have to match that seasonal trend. Either

Exhibit 7.8:   Ontario Brewery — Labour Cost Budget 2005

Month	Millions of hectolitres produced	Production	Millions of hectolitres sold	Bottling and distribution
		10 × $25 × 40 hrs		Sales × 10 × $15 × 40 hrs
January	1.0	$ 10,000	0.5	$ 3,000
February	1.0	10,000	0.5	3,000
March	1.0	10,000	0.7	4,200
April	1.0	10,000	0.7	4,200
May	1.0	10,000	0.9	5,400
June	1.0	10,000	1.0	6,000
July	1.0	10,000	1.7	10,200
August	1.0	10,000	1.7	10,200
September	1.0	10,000	1.0	6,000
October	1.0	10,000	0.8	4,800
November	1.0	10,000	0.8	4,800
December	1.0	10,000	1.7	10,200
		$120,000		$ 72,000
Supervisors		40,000		40,000
		$160,000		$112,000
10% fringe benefits, etc.		16,000		11,200
Total		$176,000		$123,200

casual workers will have to be added at the busy times, or overtime will have to be scheduled, or some combination of the two.

When budgeting labour costs, do not forget that there are several labour-related costs incurred by the company in addition to the wages paid to staff, including unemployment insurance and workers compensation premiums, the employer's contribution to pension schemes, holiday pay, and so on. Typically, for budgeting, a constant percentage is added to raw labour costs for these fringe benefits.

We have the production and sales budget for Ontario Brewery (see Exhibit 7.8). The production activity requires a workforce of 10 all year round. Production workers' are paid $25 per hour, and work a 40-hour week. Bottling and distribution workers are needed at the rate of 10 people for every million hectolitres sold. Bottling and distribution workers are paid on average $15 per hour and they, too, work a 40-hour week. There are two supervisors (one for production and one for bottling and distribution), each earning $40,000 per year. Fringe benefits are expected to cost an additional 10% of wage costs. The labour budget would be as shown in Exhibit 7.8.

7.5.4   Preparing the Operating Budget

The operating budget for Ontario Brewery for 2005 is shown in Exhibit 7.9.

Exhibit 7.9: Ontario Brewery — Operating Budget 2005

Sales: millions of hectolitres   12

    $ millions

Sales revenue: Gross	$4,800	
Brewing excise & sales taxes	1,200	
Net sales revenue		$3,600
Variable costs:		
Raw material & packaging	$1,800	
Variable distribution & marketing	240	
Total variable costs		2,040
Contribution margin		$1,560
Fixed costs:		
Fixed distribution & marketing	$ 180	
Fixed general & administrative	300	
Total fixed costs		480
Operating income		$1,080
Interest expense		80
Taxable income		$1,000
Taxes: 40%		400
Net income		$ 600

The brewery plans on selling a total of 12 million hectolitres of beer in 2005, with the demand showing a seasonal peak in the summer, with another, smaller peak in December, with lower demand in the rest of the year. Beer is retailed in the beer stores for $5 per litre. The beer stores take a 20% margin ($1), leaving $4 per litre as gross revenue for the brewer. The government takes $1.00 for duties and taxes, leaving $3.00 per litre net of tax revenue for the brewer. Total budgeted sales of 12 million hectolitres will result in budgeted revenue of $3,600 million.

Raw material costs and packaging costs are $1.50 per litre. For 12 million hectolitres, this will be a budgeted cost of $1,800 million.

Variable distribution and marketing costs are $0.20 per litre. For 12 million hectolitres this will be a budgeted cost of $240 million.

Fixed distribution and marketing costs are budgeted to cost $180 million for the year.

Fixed general and administrative costs are budgeted to cost $300 million for the year.

Interest expense is budgeted to cost $80 million for the year.

Income taxes expense is budgeted to be 40% of the pre-tax profit.

If this business were to be evenly spread over the year, then the monthly budget would be calculated by dividing the annual total by 12. However, we know that it is a very seasonal business, so the budget for each month would have to be separately calculated to include its own level of production and the associated costs.

7.6 Cash Budgeting

One of the most important aspects of budgeting is to make sure that there is enough cash and liquid assets to keep the organization going. If there is not enough cash, the organization will be unable to pay its liabilities when they become due, and the threat of bankruptcy looms.

Most organizations will prepare a very detailed budget for cash flows, to ensure that if there is a cash flow problem, they will have adequate warning to be able to deal with the problem effectively.

7.6.1 Cash Receipts

Sales revenues are the main source of cash receipts. In a pure cash business (many retail outlets deal only in cash) the sales revenue will be received immediately, and receipts and revenue will be identical. A business that sells on credit, however, will have to wait to receive its cash until the debtor pays. So, in the same way that inventory uncouples production and demand, allowing them each to happen at different rates, making credit sales uncouples the act of making a sale and the collection of the related cash.

Tizer Foods Inc. makes credit sales to some of its customers. The budgeted sales for the first quarter of the year are:

January:	$6.8 million
February:	$7.6 million
March:	$8.2 million

The company's expectation is that:

- 25% of all sales will be cash sales, received immediately.
- 75% of all sales will be on 30 days credit terms.
- 50% of all sales (that is, two-thirds of the credit sales) will be collected by the end of the month following the sale.
- 25% of all sales (that is, the remaining one-third of credit sales) will be collected during the second month after the sale.

During the month of March the company would budget to collect the following:

25% of the March sales, received in cash:	
$8,200,000 × 25%	$2,050,000
50% of the February sales, collected in March:	
$7,600,000 × 50%	$3,800,000
25% of the January sales, collected in March	
$6,800,000 × 25%	$1,700,000
Total cash collections in March from sales	$7,550,000

There may be other receipts of cash, from the sale of assets, the sale of shares, and from borrowing. Each of these would be carefully estimated as to its expected amount and its timing.

Together with whatever beginning balance of cash existed at the start of the period, these provide a pool of available cash out of which cash payments can be made.

7.6.2   Cash Payments

Most of the regularly recurring payments will arise because of some activity that is shown as expense in the operating budget. Some expenses represent payments that are made immediately: wages, for example, are paid as earned. For other payments there may be a delay between incurring the expense and paying for it (such as the purchase of raw materials on credit), or the payment may be made in advance of the expense being incurred (e.g., rent may be paid one month in advance). Some expenses (amortization of plant, for example) may not involve any payment at all.

Additionally, there will be occasional payments that arise because of reasons separate from the operating budget. These might include the payment of dividends, the payment of loan interest or repayments, and the purchase of new equipment.

The objective for cash budgeting is to list the expected payments, month by month, so that the adequacy of the cash resources can be assured.

7.6.3   Preparing the Cash Budget

Tizer Foods Inc. is preparing its cash budget for the first quarter of the year. Budgeted sales, as stated before, are:

January: $6.8 million
February: $7.6 million
March: $8.2 million

Also, November sales were budgeted to be $10.4 million, and December sales were budgeted to be $12.5 million. We need to know this information as collection of November and December sales happens in January and February.

The sales collection pattern has already been looked at above:

- 25% is collected immediately as cash sales
- 50% is collected the month after the sale
- 25% is collected in the second month after sale

In February the company plans to take out a loan of $4 million to help buy some new equipment. There are no other receipts expected.

All raw materials are bought on one month's credit, and amount to 50% of the sales $ each month.

All wages are paid in the month they are earned, and amount to 10% of the sales for the month.

Fixed production costs are $2 million per month and fixed selling and administrative expenses are $3 million per month. Included in these fixed

**Exhibit 7.10 Tizer Foods Inc.
— Cash Budget, First Quarter ($ thousands)**

	November	December	January	February	March
Sales Revenue	$10,400	$12,500	$ 6,800	$ 7,600	$ 8,200
Receipts:					
Cash sales: 25%	$2,600	$3,125	$ 1,700	$ 1,900	$ 2,050
Previous month: 50%	?	5,200	6,250	3,400	3,800
2 months back: 25%	?	?	2,600	3,125	1,700
Total cash from sales			$10,550	$ 8,425	$ 7,550
Other receipts: loan			nil	4,000	nil
Total receipts			$10,550	$12,425	$ 7,550
Payments:					
Raw materials (50% × previous month's sales)			$ 6,250	$ 3,400	$ 3,800
Wages (10% × current month's sales)			680	760	820
Fixed production costs			2,000	2,000	2,000
Selling & administrative expenses			3,000	3,000	3,000
Less: amortization expenses (not paid in cash)			(1,000)	(1,000)	(1,000)
Total operating payments			$10,930	$ 8,160	$ 8,620
Other payments:					
Interest			$ 100	$ 100	$ 100
Dividend			nil	nil	4,000
Equipment purchase			nil	5,000	nil
Total			$ 100	$ 5,100	$ 4,100
Total payments			$11,030	$13,260	$12,720
Net cash increase / (decrease) in month			$ (480)	$ (835)	$(5,170)
Beginning cash balance			200	(280)	(1,115)
Ending cash balance			$ (280)	$(1,115)	$(6,285)

costs is a total of $1 million per month of amortization expense, which has no cash flow effect.

The company must pay $0.1 million of loan interest each month, and the company plans to buy new equipment for $5 million in February. A dividend payment of $4 million is due to be paid in March.

The cash balance at the beginning of January is expected to be $200,000.

The first pass at the cash budget is shown in Exhibit 7.10.

The following points are worthy of mention:

• It was necessary to have the budgeted sales amounts for November and December so that cash collections in January and February could be calculated.
• Even though January is the month with the lowest budgeted sales, it has the highest budgeted cash receipts from sales as it is picking up

the cash from December and November, which were very good months for sales.

Although the company is profitable, each month the payments exceed the receipts. As a result, there is a cash deficiency at the end of January, February and March. By the end of March, the company is short by $6,285,000.

However, forewarned is forearmed, and now that Tizer knows about the problem, the company can take steps to deal with it. These steps could include the following:

• delaying or cancelling the dividend payment
• delaying or cancelling the equipment purchase in the previous month
• taking out a short-term loan
• selling off any short-term assets that are available

Cash budgeting is an essential step in the good management of any organization. While most managers will not have to deal with cash budgeting directly (it is definitely a job for the accounting staff), they should be aware of the effect of decisions, such as a large increase in output, the building up of inventory balances, or the purchase of major pieces of plant, which will have negative effects on cash flows and cash balances.

The cash budget is essentially an internal management report. It is seldom shared with shareholders or outside parties. It measures the same things (cash flows) as are reported in the statement of changes in financial position, but it does so in a different format.

7.7   Participation in Budgeting

In some organizations the budget is handed down from above, as something the unit is expected to achieve, but without giving the unit any say in the budget's contents. This is called an imposed budget. In general we can expect the manager of the unit to be suspicious and resentful of an imposed budget, and to have a low level of commitment to it. The organization may find that it has to set up a system of strong sanctions against managers who do not reach their budgets in order that they become realized.

By contrast some other organizations will treat the budget-setting process as a dialogue, with managers sharing information and expectations to agree on a budget. The budget does not become formally adopted until both the manager and her superiors have signed off (a) that they regard it as a reasonable task to undertake and (b) that it meets organizational expectations. This is referred to as a participatory budget. In general we can expect that the manager of a unit who has participated in the budget-setting process will be more highly personally committed to achieving the budgeted results. She will need fewer "sticks and carrots" to persuade her to work enthusiastically toward organizational success. Behaviourally, participatory budgets are superior to imposed ones.

7.8   **Summary**

The management activity of planning is realized through the preparation of budgets, which give the financial dimension of organizational plans. Budgeting consists of estimating operating revenues and expenses and, hence, operating income, as well as planning cash receipts and payments. Budget preparation (covered in this chapter) paves the way for budgetary control, which is covered in the next chapter.

Appendix 7.1
Budgeting Is Dead:
Long Live Budgeting!

A claim made in recent years is that budgeting is a wasteful and divisive activity that consumes more resources than the value it creates; that it should be got rid of; and that it has been successfully discontinued in a number of major organizations.

Here is the description from the Beyond Budgeting Round Table Web site:

Beyond Budgeting is the first great management idea
of the twenty-first century[1]

A radical proposition?
Budgeting, as most corporations practice it, should be abolished. That may sound like a radical proposition, but it is merely the final (and decisive) action in a long running battle to change organizations from centralized hierarchies to devolved networks. Most of the other building blocks are in place. Firms have invested huge sums in quality programs, IT networks, process reengineering, and a range of management tools including EVA, balanced scorecards, and activity accounting. But they are unable to establish the new order because the budget, and the command and control culture it supports, remains predominant.

Gap between rhetoric and reality
The [gap] between the rhetoric and the reality of devolved decision-making is huge. But to succeed in the global market, it must be bridged. Much is at stake. Responding effectively to change, finding and keeping talented people, producing imaginative strategies, reducing fixed costs, building closer relationships with customers, and improving ethical behaviour and reporting — all these key success factors depend, to some degree or another, on winning the battle for the devolved organization together with its culture of personal responsibility. The central planning and budgeting process perpetuates a culture of dependency. It supports the belief that decisions improve the higher in the organization they are taken. This is a ridiculous idea to most employees.

Budgeting has few admirers
Gaming the numbers is pervasive. One large survey of U.S. companies concluded that managers either did not accept the budgetary targets and opted to beat the system, or they felt pressured to achieve the targets at any cost. This pressure is squeezing the life and spirit out of many organizations and their people. It's the

---

[1] Source: **www.beyondbudgeting.plus.com/BBRTweb4/beybud.htm** from the Beyond Budgeting Round Table (BBRT) Web site at **www.bbrt.org/** [Accessed 2006-07-22]. Copyright by BBRT. All rights reserved. For further discussion, see J. Hope and R. Fraser, *Beyond Budgeting: How managers can break free from the annual performance trap* (Boston: Harvard Business School Press, 2003).

mentality that says, "Do what I say or your future is at risk." It is driven by greed and a need for instant gratification and immediate results. This was evident at both Enron and WorldCom. The WorldCom culture, say those who worked there, was all about living up to [CEO] Bernard Ebbers's demands. "You would have a budget, and he would mandate that you had to be 2 percent under budget. Nothing else was acceptable."

Beyond Budgeting, a more adaptive and devolved alternative
Replacing the budgeting model with a more adaptive and devolved alternative is the solution that [organizations] need to achieve their goals of becoming devolved networks. Criticizing budgets is not new. But defining a set of principles that guides leaders toward a new lean, adaptive and ethical management model is a new idea — perhaps the first great new idea of the twenty-first century.

If you read more deeply about the companies that have adopted this approach (Volvo, for example), you will find that the major thing that has changed is the use to which budgets are put. No longer is the budget seen as a fixed target, with severe sanctions for not being met. The companies still prepare forecasts (i.e., budgets) but they are used as guidelines, not straitjackets. Budgets, however, in the sense of plans for the future, are still prepared and widely used.

Self-Study Problems

1. Sales revenue for the Bombardier Inc. group of companies was:

Year to January 31	$ billion
1998	8.3
1999	11.3
2000	13.4
2001	15.9
2002	21.6

   Required
   (a) Calculate the year-on-year increase in sales revenue in both $ and %.
   (b) What is your best estimate of the sales revenue for the year to January 31, 2003?

2. One of the products made by Bombardier is the Ski-Doo snow-mobile. Assume that in 2006 Bombardier plans to sell 80,000 snow-mobiles at a price of $7,500 each. At the start of the year, the company will have 5,000 snowmobiles in inventory. The company would like to have an inventory of 3,000 snowmobiles at the end of the year.

   Required
   (a) What is the budgeted sales revenue for snowmobiles for the year?
   (b) How many snowmobiles should Bombardier plan on manufac-turing in the year?
   (c) What monthly manufacturing capacity should Bombardier plan to have for the Ski-Doo snowmobile plant?

3. You are the manager of Excellent Trading Inc. On November 1, 2006, you will have the following balances of current assets:

cash on hand	$ 10,000
accounts receivable	120,000 (25% of October's sales)
inventory	175,000

   and you will owe $240,000 to trade creditors (50% of October's sales). Actual sales revenues were as follows:

September 2006	$360,000
October 2006	480,000

   Budgeted sales revenues were:

November 2006	$600,000
December 2006	720,000
January 2007	240,000

Experience has shown that 75% of the sales will be collected within the month of purchase, and the other 25% will be collected within the month following the purchase.

Goods for resale are marked up by 100% on cost to get selling price: i.e., a product that had cost $5 would be sold for $10. The goods purchased are paid for the month after they are sold (goods sold in October will be paid for in November).

Selling and marketing expenses are 10% of the sales revenue each month and are paid during that same month.

General and administrative expenses are $100,000 per month, including $20,000 per month of amortization expense.

Required
(a) Prepare a cash budget for the months of November and December 2006.
(b) Is there a cash flow problem for November and December (and if so, what should you do about it)?

4. Carlton Co. makes luxury travel bags. They are sold to retailers for $250 each. Material costs are $40 per bag; labour costs are $60 per bag; overhead is a fixed amount of $100,000 per month. The company expects to sell 1,000 bags per month.

Required
Prepare budgets for production and sale of 800, 1,000, and 1,200 bags.

Solution

1. (a) **$ billion**

Sales revenue	Sales revenue	Increase	Increase %
1998: $ 8.3	1999: $11.3	$3.0	($3.0 ÷ $ 8.3) × 100% = 36.1%
1999: $11.3	2000: $13.4	$2.1	($2.1 ÷ $11.3) × 100% = 18.6%
2000: $13.4	2001: $15.9	$2.5	($2.5 ÷ $13.4) × 100% = 18.7%
2001: $15.9	2002: $21.6	$5.7	($5.7 ÷ $15.9) × 100% = 35.8%

(b) Average sales growth rate over past four years:

$$= (36.1\% + 18.6\% + 18.7\% + 35.8\%) \div 4$$
$$= 27.3\%$$

Estimated sales revenue in 2003:

$$= \$21.6 \text{ billion} + 27.3\%$$
$$= \$27.5 \text{ billion}$$

2. (a) Budgeted sales revenue:

$$= 80,000 \times \$7,500$$
$$= \$600,000,000$$

(b)
Budgeted sales units	80,000
Less: Opening inventory	5,000
	75,000
Add: Budgeted closing inventory	3,000
Budgeted production	78,000

(c) If Ski-Doo snowmobile production is carried out continuously during the year, then the required manufacturing capacity is:

$$78,000 \div 12 = 6,500 \text{ per month}$$

If production is seasonal, then a larger capacity would be required. Suppose the plant makes Ski-Doo snowmobiles for only four months, and then changes to making Sea-Doo watercrafts. The required capacity is:

$$78,000 \div 4 = 19,500 \text{ per month}$$

3. (a)

Cash on hand November 1, 2006		$ 10,000
Budgeted receipts: November		
Collection of 25% of October's sales	$120,000	
Collection of 75% of November's sales ($600,000 × 75%)	450,000	570,000
Cash available		$580,000
Budgeted payments: November		
Suppliers: (beginning accounts payable)	$240,000	
Sales and marketing expense (10% × $600,000)	60,000	
General and administrative expense ($100,000 – $20,000 amortization)	80,000	380,000
Cash balance as at November 30, 2006		$200,000
Budgeted receipts: December		
Collection of 25% of November's sales (= accounts receivable at December 1)	$150,000	
Collection of 75% of December's sales* ($720,000 × 75%)	540,000	690,000
Cash available		$890,000
Budgeted payments: December		
Suppliers ($600,000 × 50%)	$300,000	
Sales and marketing expense (10% × $720,000)	72,000	
General and administrative expense ($100,000 – $20,000 amortization)	80,000	452,000
Cash balance as at December 31, 2006		$438,000

* $720,000 × 25% receivable in January 2007

(b) Yes, there is a problem: the company has too much cash. The company should investigate useful ways to deploy the surplus funds, such as the following:
• loan repayments
• purchase of new equipment
• dividends to shareholders
• temporary investments.

4.

Number of bags (= n)	800	1,000	1,200	
Sales revenue	$200,000	$250,000	$300,000	(n × $250)
Materials	$ 32,000	$ 40,000	$ 48,000	(n × $40)
Labour	48,000	60,000	72,000	(n × $60)
Overhead	100,000	100,000	100,000	
Total expense	$180,000	$200,000	$220,000	
Operating profit	$ 20,000	$ 50,000	$ 80,000	

Discussion Questions and Problems

Discussion Questions

1. What are the objectives of budgeting?
2. Compare and contrast a budget based on the previous period with a zero-based budget: which is more appropriate?
3. Why does budget preparation start with a forecast of sales?
4. How are sales and production linked in the planning process?
5. Why is it important to distinguish between variable costs and fixed costs in preparing a budget for a production division?
6. Describe the difference between a participative budget and an imposed budget.
7. Why is cash budgeting important?
8. Who, in the organization, is responsible for forecasting sales quantities and selling prices?
9. Who, in the organization, is responsible for preparing the master budget?
10. What are the advantages and disadvantages of selling goods on credit?

Problems

1. You are given last year's budget and actual financial report for the internal audit department at Woodhouse Warehouse:

Details	Budget	Actual
Staff salaries	$600,000	$575,000
Salary-related expense	60,000	57,500
Travel & lodging	200,000	150,000
Equipment-related expense	50,000	50,000
Training	25,000	nil
Total	$935,000	$832,500

The salaries were below budget because of a vacancy in the last quarter of the year; a new audit employee will be starting work on January 1. Audit staff earned a salary of $100,000 each in the current year. Next year the salary rate will be $110,000 (that includes the new employee). Salary-related expenses (health, pension, etc.) are 10% of salary expenses.

Travel and lodging expenses were down because site visits (at 15) were fewer than planned (the department had planned 20 visits). Next year 25 visits are planned. Travel and lodging expense is expected to cost 5% more next year. Training was not carried out as expected this year, but next year a $75,000 training expense is expected.

Required
(a) Prepare a budget for next year.
(b) If you expected that the budget committee would "automatically" cut your proposed budget by 5%, what should you do?

253

2. AM Inc. makes breakfast cereals at its plant in London, Ontario. Sales of Wheat Squares for the current year were as follows:

1st quarter	300,000 tonnes
2nd quarter	200,000 tonnes
3rd quarter	240,000 tonnes
4th quarter	360,000 tonnes

Required

(a) Wheat Squares have a short shelf life because some of the ingredients are perishable, so they cannot be kept more than one month. How much should the company produce each month? What capacity plant is necessary?

(b) The food lab has developed a recipe based on genetically modified ingredients so that the shelf life is increased to six months. Now how much should the company produce each month? What capacity plant is necessary?

3. AM Inc. makes the Oaties breakfast cereal at its plant in London, Ontario. The actual results for the current year were as follows:

Production	40,000 tonnes	
Raw materials		
Oats	35,000 tonnes @ $100/tonne	$3,500,000
Sugar	10,000 tonnes @ $200/tonne	2,000,000
Flavourings	500 tonnes @ $800/tonne	400,000
		$5,900,000
Direct labour	5,000 hours @ $20	100,000
Variable production overhead	5,000 hours @ $250	1,250,000
Fixed production overhead		1,250,000
Total production cost		$8,500,000

Next year the plant is expected to produce 50,000 tonnes of Oaties, due to increased demand from health-conscious customers. Oats are in good supply, so the price will remain at $100/tonne. Sugar price is expected to fall to $150/tonne. Flavourings will probably cost $1,000/tonne.

Direct labour hours will increase in proportion to production, but the rate will increase to $25 per hour.

Variable production overhead will be charged to the Oaties line on the basis of the number of labour hours, but the rate will remain constant at $250 per hour.

Fixed production overhead is expected to fall to $1,200,000 due to increased automation in the inspection system.

Required

Prepare an operating budget for the Oaties line for next year.

4. A Co. sold $1,000,000 of self-help books in 2005. The Canada-wide market for self-help books was $25,000,000. Next year, due to the entry of a new competitor, the total market is expected to double in size, but A Co.'s market share will fall by 20%.

Required

Estimate the sales revenue for A Co. for next year.

5. You are given the sales figures for BC Co. for the past five years:

Year	Sales Revenue
1	$10,000,000
2	10,700,000
3	11,500,000
4	12,300,000
5	13,200,000

Required

(a) Calculate the % year-on-year increase in sales.
(b) Use the average % increase to estimate sales for year 6.
(c) What weaknesses are there to basing estimates purely on past data?

6. Calcide Co. manufactures auto batteries. Its two main models are the regular, which is sold to wholesalers for $50, and the heavy-duty, which is sold to wholesalers for $75. There were 4,000 regular and 2,500 heavy-duty batteries in inventory at the start of the period. Sales demand in units is estimated to be as follows:

	Regular	Heavy-duty
1st month	8,000	5,000
2nd month	6,000	2,000
3rd month	5,000	2,000
4th month	9,000	4,000

The production plan is to produce enough batteries that the inventory at the end of each month is half of the following month's expected sales.

Sales are all on credit terms. In the company's experience, half the customers pay in the month following sale, 40% pay the month after that, and the remaining 10% pay in the third month. The company does not expect any bad debts.

Required

(a) Prepare a production budget for the first three months.
(b) Prepare a sales budget for the first three months.
(c) Prepare a cash receipts budget for the fourth month.

7. Argenti Inc. has accumulated the following information for preparing its annual budget:

Sales	54,000 units @ $200
Unit cost of goods sold includes	
Materials	2 kg @ $5 per kg
Direct labour	4 hours @ $20
Production overhead	4 hours @ $10 per direct labour hour
Beginning inventory	10,000 units
Ending inventory	6,000 units
Selling and administrative expense	$2,500,000

Required
(a) Prepare a production budget in units.
(b) Calculate the cost of goods manufactured.
(c) Calculate the cost of goods sold.
(d) Calculate the budgeted sales.
(e) Prepare a budgeted income statement for the year.

8. Tryon Co. has a cash balance of $150,000 on January 1. Relevant budgeted information includes the following:

	January	February
Cash collected from customers	$950,000	$900,000
Payments to suppliers	200,000	300,000
Direct labour expense	300,000	350,000
Production overhead expense	250,000	250,000
Selling and administrative expense	150,000	150,000

All expenses are paid in the month incurred. The production overhead expense includes $50,000 of amortization of plant.

Required
(a) Prepare a cash budget for January and February.
(b) Is there a problem? If there is, suggest ways of dealing with it.

9. Harrington Co. sells food products. The following is the budgeted sales for the first half of the year:

January	$200,000
February	$250,000
March	$300,000
April	$350,000
May	$400,000
June	$450,000

Half of the sales are collected during the month of sale;
40% are collected in the month after sale;
8% are collected two months after the sale; and
2% are bad debts, and never get collected.

Required
(a) Calculate the cash received from sales in May.
(b) What steps could Harrington take to eliminate the bad debts?

10. Tennant Co. manufactures cleaning materials that are sold to industrial cleaning companies. It operates five autonomous divisions, each of which operates a separate plant. Material purchases are managed centrally to get the benefit of bulk purchase, and labour rates are governed by a centrally negotiated collective agreement. In November each year Head Office tells each division its budgeted sales and budgeted costs for the following year. Regular monthly reports are circulated showing performance against budget, and managers who fail to meet budget targets are called to Head Office to explain.

Required
(a) Is this a participative budget situation?
(b) Is this budgeting system appropriate for Tennant Co.?

Budgetary 8
Control

Learning
Objectives

After studying this chapter you should:
→ Be aware of the way budgets are used in controlling companies
→ Be able to explain the difference between an imposed budget and a participatory budget
→ Be able to explain how responsibility can only be exercised where there is a high level of control
→ Be able to execute budgetary control in revenue centres, cost centres, and profit centres
→ Be able to interpret a simple balanced scorecard
→ Be aware of the behavioural aspects of budgeting

8.1 Control

As was described in the previous chapter, a primary objective of a budget is planning: the budget represents the financial dimension of the organizational plan.

Another objective of a budget is that it enables budgetary control. The budget is used as an objective or standard. It represents an acceptable level of performance. From the perspective of the senior management, achieving the budget is evidence of having achieved the organization's objectives, and failing to achieve the budget indicates that the objectives have not been met.

If the budget in question is a budget for the whole organization, the bottom line will be a budgeted profit, and achieving the budget means bringing in an actual profit at least as big as the budgeted profit. If the budget is for a smaller part of the organization (e.g., a human resources management department), achieving the budget may be a question of keeping actual costs below budgeted costs.

Budgetary control of this type is extremely important, but there are also many other aspects to the control process that are non-financial in nature. Maintaining good customer relations and preserving the organization's reputation for quality products or services, for example, are both control issues, but largely fall outside the strict limits of budgetary control. As we shall see later in this chapter, the balanced scorecard can bring these non-financial controls into a routine control report.

The essence of budgetary control can be found in the idea of "management by exception". This idea proposes that once organizational objectives have been set and communicated to organizational members, then a routine process of comparison of actual outcomes with the objectives will reveal one of two states. Either the objectives will have been achieved, in which case no action is required, or the objectives will not have been achieved (this is regarded as an "exception"), and management will have

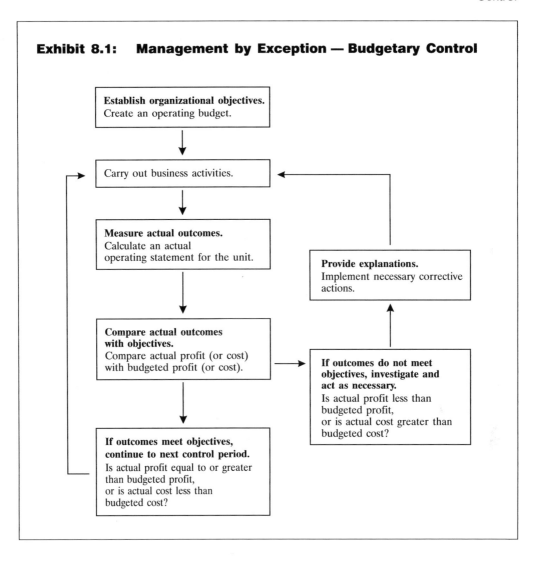

Exhibit 8.1: Management by Exception — Budgetary Control

an obligation to investigate the situation so that an explanation of the exception can be found, and appropriate corrective action can be implemented. This can also be described as a feedback loop, and it is illustrated in Exhibit 8.1.

So, a company may have budgeted for a profit of $500,000 for the month of August. If the actual profit were to be $520,000, the company would probably consider it (a) close enough and (b) erring on the plus side rather than the negative. The idea of management by exception would imply that the organizational objectives had been achieved, and they could carry on with business as usual.

If, on the other hand, the actual profit were to be $370,000, management by exception would call for an investigation because the variance (minus $130,000) is both large and unfavourable. If the investigation then revealed that there had been production problems and that these had resulted in customers' orders not being fulfilled, then the production manager would be expected to show what changes had been made to prevent it happening again. Because there was an exception (missing the profit target by $130,000), management action was required (reports and corrections).

A human resources department may have had an operating budget that authorized it to spend $200,000 in August. If the actual expense were to be $190,000, it would probably be treated as "in control". If the actual expense were to be $250,000, then the department manager would have to explain what happened (perhaps she had to deal with an unusually high level of production employee turnover) and show what she had done to prevent the overspending recurring.

8.2   Imposed and Participative Budgets

In order for the budget to be an effective control it has to have validity: that is, all the people involved have to accept it. There are two broad approaches to achieving acceptability: imposed budgets and participative budgets.

An imposed budget is one that is dictated by the higher levels of management, without the people responsible for carrying it out having any say in what it comprises. The roots of imposed budgets are in a hierarchical approach to management, such as would be found in a military unit. The superiors are recognized as having authority to impose the budget by virtue of their position in the organization. The inferiors are required to accept the budget because they have been ordered to do so, and the order comes from a source with legitimate authority.

There are a number of situations where this is an appropriate way to plan and to exercise control, considering the context in which the organization operates. For example, if there are factors that are known to senior management, but not known to lower levels, then an imposed budget may be the only way that information can be recognized in the organizational plan. More commonly, though, an imposed budget reflects an organizational style of tight control that is caused by the personalities of the senior managers.

One danger of imposed budgets is that they may be set at an unreasonable level of performance. If people know that the budget is impossible to meet, they may become careless and cease trying because they know they are going to fail anyway.

A participative budget, by contrast, is one where the people who have to actually carry out the work engage in an interchange of information with their managers, such that both sides can eventually agree on a budget that is mutually acceptable. This budget represents performance that is acceptable to the senior managers because it meets the organization's objectives, and to the operating staff because they regard it as a reasonable task that is within their capabilities.

As with imposed budgets, a participative budget can be the result of situational factors (such as the operatives having detailed knowledge of things senior managers do not know) and can also be caused by the psychology of the senior managers of the organization, who are more open to discussion and compromise.

There is a high level of agreement that a participative budget is likely to have a higher degree of "buy-in" than an imposed one. The people controlled by a participative budget will be more motivated to achieve it, and they are likely to have a more positive attitude toward their work situation. The downside is that the budget-setting process sometimes allows people to set unreasonably low standards: budgets that have a lot of budgetary slack or padding built in, and that are relatively easy to meet.

Pseudo-participation can be observed where an organization wants to be seen to have adopted a participatory approach, so it introduces superficial participation and seeks the formality of approval by lower level employees, without giving them the reality of being able to say no. Pseudo-participation is most unlikely to result in an appropriate budget or in superior motivation.

Few organizations are likely to run things at either the totally imposed or the totally participative extreme, and most exhibit some budget behaviours of each type. Smart organizations will choose the budget style that matches the underlying factors of each budget situation, rather than insisting on a universal approach throughout.

8.3 Responsibility and Control

Underlying the control process is another management theory: that of responsibility and control. It is a reasonable assumption that you can hold someone responsible for the things they can control, but you should not hold them responsible for things over which they have no control. What is meant by this is that each manager has a responsibility area within which his or her decisions affect the outcomes. They can be held accountable for those outcomes through the control process.

A production manager, for example, has control over the production process, and his or her decisions will affect the quantity and quality of production output. If production is at acceptable levels of quantity and quality, everything is OK. If there is a shortfall of quantity or an unacceptable deterioration of quality that is going to have serious negative consequences for the organization, the control system should be identifying the production area as the problem and, probably, the production manager as being the person responsible.

Further investigation may lead to the conclusion that the problem had been caused by the purchasing department buying below-standard raw materials. If the production manager was not in control of the purchasing decision, he cannot be held responsible for the effects of a purchasing decision. The responsibility then shifts to the purchasing manager.

Like many management theories, this is obviously correct at the extremes but tends to become highly problematical in real cases due to blurred lines of responsibility.

Missing the sales budget, for example, might be caused by:

- marketing decisions, leading to an inappropriate product specification
- design decisions, leading to a poor design
- production decisions, leading to poor quality
- sales decisions, leading to a low level of sales effort
- marketing decisions, leading to advertising in the wrong media
- logistics decisions, leading to late deliveries
- after-sales decisions, leading to poor warranty work

An unacceptably high production cost could be impossible to control if several products are made in common facilities, and the company loses track of what costs are caused by which product-related decisions.

Often the costs of common facilities are allocated to departments or products through an overhead recovery system. Although this makes sense in establishing the full cost of operating the department or making the product, it is not a situation where the manager has any control over the cost, so it becomes problematical to hold him or her responsible for these allocated central costs.

8.4   Control in Organizational Sub-Units

We can consider responsibility and control by relating it to the organizational sub-units that have been chosen. Sub-units can be classified as either revenue centres, cost centres, or profit centres. Cost centres can be further divided into those responsible for delivering a service and production cost centres. Profit centres can be further divided into those that have no control over investment in assets and those with investment control. The budgetary control reports should match the realities of what is controlled.

8.4.1   Control in Revenue Centres

A sales department is an example of a revenue centre. It is responsible for making sales. Its success or failure may be judged by the difference between budgeted and actual sales. This can be measured in units, or in sales revenue dollars, or even in terms of the contribution margin the sales have earned. (Contribution margin is the sales revenue, less the variable cost of sales.)

> **Example:** Northgate Supplies has budgeted to sell 2,000 widgets in the month of September, creating $50,000 of sales revenue (before taxes). Actual sales were 2,100 widgets, and actual sales revenue was $54,600. Northgate has exceeded its budget in both units (widgets sold) and revenues, so the company has more than met its budget.

Further investigation shows that the budgeted price was $25 per widget ($50,000 ÷ 2,000 widgets = $25), whereas the actual price per widget was higher ($54,600 ÷ 2,100 widgets = $26 each). This is another cause for satisfaction.

8.4.2 *Control in a Cost Centre 1: Service Departments*

A department of human resources management is an example of a cost centre that delivers a service. Its role and objective would be to provide HRM services and expertise to the rest of the organization. It has (i.e., its manager has) control over how much HRM to provide. In doing so the HR manager will be strongly influenced by the resources he or she is allowed to consume by virtue of his or her budget. When the budget is established it would be the HR manager's role to argue the case for an adequate budget to carry out the task at hand (hence the importance of a participative budget). During the execution phase, the manager will allocate resources appropriately to carry out the work. Two linked but separate control questions can then be addressed. First, did the required HR services and expertise get delivered? Second, did the HR department operate within the budget? Clearly, budgetary control as such can only address the second question.

> **Example:** The Southgate Co. has a human resources department with an operating budget of $500,000 in 2006. This is comprised of salaries for the employees, travel and entertainment expenses, supplies, and the costs of operating a computer system for the payroll. The actual expense for 2006 has come out to $565,000, as follows:

Southgate Co.
Budgetary Control Report for Year 2006

	Budget	Actual	Variance
Salaries	$250,000	$300,000	$50,000 U
Travel & entertainment	50,000	70,000	20,000 U
Supplies	10,000	10,000	nil
Computer system costs	190,000	185,000	5,000 F
Total	$500,000	$565,000	$65,000 U

The salaries and travel and entertainment lines are both overspent, while the supplies are exactly on target and the computer system costs are underspent. If asked, the HR manager may have a rational and logical explanation. For example if the organization had been required to deal with some unexpected hiring and firings or adapt to new HR legislation, then the overspending could be treated as a legitimate response to a situation that has changed since the budget was set. Conversely, if no such changes from the original business plan could be identified, the HR manager should be in serious trouble for the overspending and should provide a detailed description of the actions that have been taken to avoid overspending in future.

Note that, by convention, any difference between a budget and an actual is called a variance, and variances that decrease profits are called unfavourable (U), while variances that increase profits are called favourable (F). This easier to deal with than calling them plus or minus.

8.4.3 *Control in a Cost Centre 2: Production Departments*

A production department is responsible for producing a good or a service for sale. Because there is some measurable production or service activity, the work done can be expressed not only as a total, but also on a "per unit" basis. This enhances the control process as the effect of changes in the volume of activity can be separated from the effect of changes or efficiency changes.

Example: Eastgate Co. manufactures ethical pharmaceuticals (i.e., prescription medicines). The budget for the production of Patent Pain Pills for October and the actual results are as follows:

Eastgate Co.
Production Budget for Patent Pain Pills — October

	Budget	Actual	Variance
Volume	**500,000**	**600,000**	**100,000**
Raw material	$ 5,000	$ 6,300	$1,300 U
Direct labour	2,000	2,400	400 U
Allocated overhead			
Variable	4,000	4,800	800 U
Fixed	6,000	7,200	1,200 U
Total	$17,000	$20,700	$3,700 U

The original budget (called a static budget) is for total expense of $17,000 — that is, the materials, the direct labour costs, and the overhead required for producing 500,000 Patent Pain Pills. The overhead is an allocation based on 200% of the budgeted labour cost in respect of variable overhead and 300% of the budgeted labour cost in respect of fixed overhead. Both overhead amounts represent the use of facilities shared by all products made by the company.

The actual cost is made up of the actual raw materials and direct labour, plus allocated variable overhead (200% of the actual labour cost) and allocated fixed overhead (300% of the actual labour cost).

The first thing we would probably notice is that the budget has been overspent — a budget of $17,000 has become an actual reported cost of $20,700 — and that the unfavourable variances total $3,700. However, it is important to note that the budget was for the production of 500,000 units, while the actual was the cost of producing 600,000. Clearly this comparison of totals is unfair, because the amount of work done has increased by 20%.

This work increase can be seen, however, if the cost is expressed on a per unit basis. The budget was for 500,000 pills to cost $17,000, which is $34 per thousand units. The actual cost of $20,700 made 600,000 pills, at a cost of $34.5 per thousand units. Although there has still been overspending, it is not as extreme as the crude totals would indicate.

In order to separate the effect of volume changes from the effect of price and efficiency changes, a calculation can be done with the budget that would have been set if the actual volume had been known in advance: this is called a flexible budget (to contrast it with the static, or original budget).

Eastgate Co.
Production Budget for Patent Pain Pills — October

Volume	Rate $ per unit	Static Budget 500,000	Flexible Budget 600,000	Actual 600,000
Raw material	$0.010	$ 5,000	$ 6,000	$ 6,300
Direct labour	0.004	2,000	2,400	2,400
Allocated overhead				
Variable	0.008	4,000	4,800	4,800
Fixed	0.012	6,000	7,200*	7,200
Total	$0.034	$17,000	$20,400	$20,700

* Fixed costs are not normally "flexed" in a flexible budget.

The effect of the volume change (increase of production from 500,000 to 600,000) is that we would expect the expense to increase from $17,000 to $20,400. The $3,400 change does not represent an "out-of-control" situation, it represents a reasonable additional expense of making the additional 100,000 units.

The difference between the flexible budget ($20,400) and the actual expense ($20,700) is a relatively minor amount of $300 overspent. In this case it is all overspending on materials. As a percentage of the raw materials budget, this is only 5% and may be regarded as relatively unimportant ($300 ÷ $6,000 × 100% = 5%).

We can be clear that materials are overspent by $300. It is not clear at this stage whether that was due to a price increase, a reduction in efficiency, or a combination of the two.

Despite the apparent overspending, this production department is reasonably in control.

This concept of flexing the budget for changes in activity should be applied in all circumstances where there is a relevant measure of the volume of activity. Generally, that means it should be applied for control of all production cost centres.

8.4.4   *Control in a Profit Centre*

A profit centre is an organizational sub-unit that has control over both revenues and costs and, therefore, over the operating profit. The same techniques that are available for controlling revenue centres and cost centres are available for controlling profit centres. Additionally, control in a profit centre is exercised by comparing the actual profit to the budgeted profit. In the same way that a production department has a physical measure of its activity (the number of units produced), a profit centre also has a physical measure of activity (the number of units sold). This also enables "flexing" of the budget to enable changes in the level of activity to be separated from other spending changes.

Example: The appliance division of Westgate Inc. had budgeted to make an operating profit of $10,000 in September, but its actual operating profit was $15,400.

Westgate Inc.
Appliance Division — Budget Report for September

Units	Budget per Unit	Static Budget 1,000	Actual 1,200	Variance 200 F	
Sales revenue	$50	$50,000	$62,400	$12,400	F
Less: Cost of goods sold	30	30,000	35,000	5,000	U
Contribution margin	$20	$20,000	$27,400	$ 7,400	F
Less: Fixed costs	10	10,000	12,000	2,000	U
Operating profit	$10	$10,000	$15,400	$ 5,400	F

The operating profit has increased from $10,000 to $15,400. The first thing that can be said is that the profit objectives have been comfortably exceeded. Clearly the increase in sales from 1,000 in the budget to 1,200 actual is a part of the change in profit. Further analysis calls for creating a flexible budget: the expected profit for selling 1,200 units.

Westgate Inc.
Appliance Division — Budget Report for September

Units	Budget per Unit	Static Budget 1,000	Flexible Budget 1,200	Actual 1,200
Sales revenue	$50	$50,000	$60,000	$62,400
Less: Cost of goods sold	30	30,000	36,000	35,000
Contribution margin	$20	$20,000	$24,000	$27,400
Less: Fixed costs	10	10,000	10,000	12,000
Operating profit	$10	$10,000	$14,000	$15,400

With the flexible budget column added, the volume effect can be separated from any other effects. The original budget called for sales of 1,000 units of product and an operating profit of $10,000. The flexible budget shows that sales of 1,200 units should have resulted in an operating profit of $14,000. The $4,000 increase is due to the additional sales of 200 units, each one of which makes a contribution margin of $20.

The difference between the flexible budget operating profit ($14,000) and the actual operating profit ($15,400) is $1,400. We can explain this line by line from the statement.

Sales revenue was $62,400, compared to the flexible budget's $60,000. We got a $2,400 favourable variance by selling products at prices higher than the budgeted prices.

The cost of goods sold was actually $35,000, compared to the flexible budget of $36,000. Either because we paid less for inputs, such as raw materials and labour (a price effect), or because we used fewer raw materials and less labour (an efficiency effect), we spent less overall that was expected, and created a $1,000 favourable variance.

The budgeted spending on fixed overhead was $10,000. Note that this item does not get flexed in the flexible budget. Whereas revenues and the cost of goods sold are expected to rise or fall when the volume of activity rises or falls, fixed costs are not expected to be affected by volume changes. The actual expense was $12,000, so an overspending or unfavourable variance of $2,000 has occurred.

Summarizing these variances we get the following:

Sales price variance	$2,400 F
Cost of goods sold variance	1,000 F
Fixed cost variance	2,000 U
Net flexible budget variance	$1,400 F

and

Sales volume variance	4,000 F
Total change	$5,400 F

This profit centre has done very well overall. It has generated an additional $4,000 of profit from increasing sales volume and has generated an increased profit of $2,400 by increasing selling prices, and a further $1,000 by reducing the direct cost of goods sold. The profit centre reduced its profit by $2,000 by overspending on fixed costs.

Whoever was in responsible for the increased sales and the reduced cost of goods sold is likely to be praised and maybe rewarded. Whoever was responsible for the overspending on fixed costs will have to explain exactly what happened, why it happened, and what corrective actions have been implemented.

8.4.5   *Control in an Investment Centre*

An investment centre is a profit centre with one addition: in addition to having control over its profit-making activities, it also has control over the investment in assets. An investment centre can be controlled using all the methods available for controlling revenue centres, cost centres, and profit centres. Additionally, an investment centre can be controlled through the ratio of profit-to-assets employed.

Example: Compass Inc. is a multi-divisional organization for which the budgeted and actual results for 2005 were as follows:

Compass Inc.
Budgetary Control Report for 2005
($ millions)

	Budget	Actual
Sales revenues	$200	$240
Cost of goods sold	150	180
Gross margin	$ 50	$ 60
Operating expense	20	24
Operating income	$ 30	$ 36
÷ Total assets	$300	$450
Return on assets	10%	8%

Exhibit 8.2: A Budgetary Control Report

Compass Inc.
Budgetary Control Report for 2005 ($ millions)

	Aircraft		Motor Vehicles		Consulting		Total	
	Budget	Actual	Budget	Actual	Budget	Actual	Budget	Actual
Sales revenues	$ 50	$ 40	$100	$135	$ 50	$ 65	$200	$240
COGS	25	24	89	109	36	47	150	180
Gross margin	$ 25	$ 16	$ 11	$ 26	$ 14	$ 18	$ 50	$ 60
Operating expense	10	10	5	9	5	5	20	24
Operating income	$ 15	$ 6	$ 6	$ 17	$ 9	$ 13	$ 30	$ 36
÷ Total assets	$150	$150	$120	$170	$30	$130	$300	$450
ROA%	10%	4%	5%	10%	30%	10%	10%	8%

Although sales and profits have increased, so have assets. The budgeted return on assets was 10%, but the actual return is only 8%. Compass Inc. is not performing as well as was expected.

All organizations can be controlled in total as investment centres, as they are all capable of exercising control over both profits and investment. Most large organizations will extend the idea down through the company. They do this by splitting the company up into sub-units that have control over both profits and investment in assets. This creates a decentralized organizational structure and it makes each autonomous sub-unit controllable through the return on assets ratio.

Suppose Compass Inc. had structured itself into three autonomous sub-units: aircraft, motor vehicles, and consulting services. Its budgetary control report might look like Exhibit 8.2. (All amounts follow are in millions.)

Compass Inc. started off with the expectation of earning $30 of operating income, which is a 10% return on $300 of invested assets. The actual results come out as a higher profit ($36), but also a higher asset total ($450). This is a return of only 8%, so the company has not met its profitability objective of a 10% return on assets. Fundamentally, the $6 of additional earnings do not justify the $150 of additional investment. Because the company controls its three sub-units as investment centres, the location of the discrepancy can be located quite precisely.

The aircraft division expected to make $15 of income on $150 of assets, which is a 10% return. The actual result is a smaller profit ($6) on the same level of assets, for a 4% return. The division contributed to the problem by making insufficient operating profit, while the assets are the same as were budgeted.

The motor vehicles division budgeted to make a profit of $6 on $120 of assets, which is a 5% return on assets. The actual result shows a higher operating profit ($17) on a greater amount of assets ($170), and an actual return that has gone up to 10%. Clearly this division is not the problem!

The consulting division planned to make a $9 profit on $30 of assets, which is a 30% return. Actually the division made a larger profit ($13), but had a massive increase in assets, which rose from $30 to $130, and the return on assets fell to 10%. The division made more profit, but it was not enough to justify the additional investment.

The aircraft division and the consulting division were the culprits in the drop in return on assets from 10% to 8%.

Further ratio analysis can also be carried out on these data. For example, the ratio of gross margin to sales could be looked at, and its budgeted rate could be compared to its actual rate. In the aircraft division, for example, the gross margin was budgeted to be 50% (gross margin: $25 divided by sales revenue of $50 = 50%). The actual gross margin was 40% (= $16 ÷ $40). This goes a long way to explaining why the division did so badly.

Note that as with most budgetary control analyses, the accountant can accurately calculate the effect of a deviation from the budget and measure how much it damages the organization, but the accountant has no idea what the underlying causes are. That part of the management process has to come from the managers who are in control of the sub-units or departments.

8.5　The Balanced Scorecard

One of the criticisms of the budgetary control approach is that it dwells only on financial measures and deals only with what has already happened. Business has wider objectives than can be described purely financially, and management should be about the future, not the past. The balanced scorecard has been developed to change this emphasis. It is a report that considers the past, the present, and the future, and it considers both financial and non-financial information. In this way the control process can be explicitly linked to the organizational strategy.

Step one is to make an explicit list of the company strategy and the plans that have been put in place to achieve that strategy. For each of the identifiable initiatives a measure of its success or failure should be identified, and a target set. Actual results are then reported against that target to see whether or not it was achieved.

A typical balanced scorecard contains four sections (see Exhibit 8.3):

1. *Financial perspective:* Financial measures such as profitability rates are reported here. Financial measures are not ignored in the balanced scorecard, but their dominance is mitigated by the presence of other measures.

2. *Customer perspective:* The customer's perspective is considered through primary measurement, such as getting customers to fill in questionnaires about service levels and satisfaction, and through indirect measures, such as the number of complaints and the number of sales returns. The customer perspective, unlike the financial perspective, is about the present, not the past.

Exhibit 8.3: The Balanced Scorecard

Carberry Hotels
Balanced Scorecard for September 2002

Objective	Measure	Target	Actual
Financial perspective:			
Shareholder value	Return on equity	15.0%	15.6%
	Share price growth	5.0%	6.0%
Customer perspective:			
Quantity	Occupancy rates	90.0%	93.2%
Quality	Room rack-rate growth	4.0%	5.0%
	Customer satisfaction	9/10	9.3/10
	Written complaints	0	0
Internal business perspective:			
Cleanliness	Random checks	10/10	10/10
Restaurant	Menu changes	5	6
Accessibility	Wheelchair access	98.0%	98.0%
Learning and growth perspective:			
Staff training	Training hours	100	75
Market segments	New segments targeted	2	1
Product development	New facilities	1	0

Assessment: Carberry Hotels has done very well in three areas, meeting or exceeding its targets on each criterion for financial, customer, and internal business perspective. However, it has failed to meet its targets for learning and growth. It is probable that learning and growth, which are about developing the future, have been compromised in their efforts to achieve current success.

3. *Internal business perspective:* The ways in which the business has changed its internal operations to better achieve its objectives are considered through such measures as process restructuring, technology, and logistics improvements.

4. *Learning and growth:* The organization will have a successful future only if it learns and grows over time. This section is future oriented. It lists the activities that have been engaged in that create that rosy future. Here it would report training initiatives, employee motivation, new product development, and basic research.

A good balanced scorecard has the following characteristics:

• It articulates between strategy and operations.
• It helps to communicate strategy to employees.
• It creates a balanced perspective between financial and non-financial measures for employees.

- It creates a balanced perspective between the past, the present, and the future in the management process.
- It restricts itself to a few key measures.
- It identifies the effect of trade-offs between competing objectives.
- It is integrated with the motivation and reward system.

8.6   The Behavioural Aspect of Budgeting

Budget preparation and budgetary control may seem like mechanical processes: they may be described by a series of rules about how the budgets are prepared, how actual results are compared with budgets, and how management actions arise from the comparison. In reality a substantial degree of influence over how the process is carried out is exerted by the people involved. This is referred to as the behavioural aspect of budgeting.

A unit manager who is responsible for preparing a budget may be motivated to reduce her forecast of sales, or increase her forecast of expense, for example. Either of these actions results in a budget that is easier to achieve. A manager who approve unit managers' budgets, on the other hand, would only accept their budgets if the budgets have an optimistic estimate of profit, which is an incentive for the units to strive for superior performance. In general, this conflicting situation arises because both the organization and its employees have goals and objectives that are not the same, and the organization's goals can only be met through the actions of the employees.

The ideal situation is where the organization's goals can be met by the employees pursuing their own goals. This is called "goal congruence". One example of how to create goal congruence is through the use of incentive rewards.

Basing part of remuneration on whether or not goals have been achieved is called an incentive-based reward system. It makes the link between doing what the organization wants and the presumed economic objectives of employees immediate and tangible. The typical incentive scheme gives a monetary reward (a bonus) for achieving some small, but clearly defined step that is part of the organization's plan. The rewards are frequently monetary but can also be non-monetary (such as being recognized as "employee of the month"). Threat of punishment for not achieving goals can also be used but tends to set up a negative and confrontational work atmosphere.

Examples of incentives include the following:

- A salesperson might be given a $1,000 bonus for every 1% increase in sales volume.
- A shift of production workers might be given a $250 bonus for every week when no product defects were identified.
- An employee might have his or her picture displayed in the lobby for helping customers beyond the call of duty.
- A manager might be dismissed for failing to meet profit objectives.

Creating a climate of goal congruence should be a carefully thought out process rather than a lucky accident. Ideally, goal congruence fits in with other ideas mentioned earlier in this chapter, such as the creation of realistic budgets, the linkage between responsibility and control, the participative budget-setting process, and feedback loops (which should be frequent, and which should clearly and frequently indicate what are going well and what are going badly).

Failure to create a system of goal congruence may lead to dysfunctional behaviours, such as the creating of budgetary slack (such as padding the budget with unnecessary expense), and employees making decisions that benefit them but that frustrate the achievement of the organizational goals.

8.7 Summary

The management activities of planning and control are realized through the preparation and use of budgets. Budgeting consists of estimating operating income, expense, and cash flow, and using the budget to keep the organization on track to meet its objectives. Recently, budgeting as a financial activity has been supplemented with the balanced scorecard, which brings non-financial data into the equation, and tries to deal with the present and the future as well as the past.

Self-Study Problems

1. The maintenance and cleaning department at Concordia Hospital had the following budget for July:

Wages	$ 500,000
Supplies	300,000
Vehicle expenses	250,000
Office expenses	100,000
Total	$1,150,000

The actual expense totalled $1,250,000, as follows:

Wages	$ 475,000
Supplies	430,000
Vehicle expenses	250,000
Office expenses	95,000
Total	$1,250,000

Required
(a) Should this unit be controlled as a revenue, cost, profit, or investment centre?
(b) Was the department in control or out of control?

2. Carlton Co. makes luxury travel bags that are to be sold to retailers for $250 each. Material costs are $40 per bag; labour costs are $60 per bag; overhead is a fixed amount of $100,000 per month. The company expects to sell 1,000 bags per month.

Required
(a) Should Carlton Co. be controlled as a cost centre, a profit centre, or an investment centre?
(b) What is the budgeted monthly profit?
(c) The actual results for August were as follows:

Sales revenue	900 bags @ $260	$234,000
Materials	$ 35,000	
Labour	50,000	
Overhead	102,000	187,000
Operating profit		$ 47,000

Was the company in control or out of control?

3. As part of an exercise in preparing a balanced scorecard, identify three customer satisfaction measures and say how you would assess them for (a) Tim Horton's (a fast food franchise) and (b) Air Canada (an airline).

Solution

1. (a) This unit should be controlled as a cost centre, specifically a "service" cost centre. The department has a responsibility to clean and maintain and the right to spend $1,150,000 per

month to do so, but the department does not produce a sale-able product, and it has no revenue.

There is an overspending of $100,000 in the month, which represents a little under 10% of the budget of $1,150,000. This would probably be regarded as a significant amount. The department would have to (at the very least) explain why the overspending happened. Yes, on the face of it, the department is out of control.

(b)   On a "line-by-line" examination of the budget we can see that the department actually underspent on each expense area except supplies, so spending on supplies (overspent by $130,000) is the only problem. There may be a good explana-tion (for example, an unexpected major repair to a piece of equipment or a building), but it is up to the unit manager to justify the overspending.

2.   (a)   Like most autonomous organizations, Carlton Co. has control over its revenues and its costs and, hence, over its profit, and would also have control over its investment in assets. Therefore, in theory, it should be controlled as an investment centre. In this example the information presented includes revenues and expenses but does not include investment, so we would have to treat it as a profit centre for control purposes.

(b)   The budgeted monthly profit is:

Sales revenue	(1,000 bags @ $250)		$250,000
Materials	(1,000 bags @ $40)	$ 40,000	
Labour	(1,000 bags @ $60)	60,000	
Overhead		100,000	200,000
Operating profit			$ 50,000

(c)   The original (or static) budget was that Carlton Co. would make an operating profit of $50,000. The actual operating profit was only $47,000, so the company missed its target. The $3,000 gap can be further analyzed as follows. The actual results and the static budget results are the bookends in the following chart. In the middle is the flexible budget. The flexi-ble budget shows that at a sales level of 900 units, we would expect Carlton Co. to make a profit of $35,000.

	Actual 900 bags	Flexible Budget (900 bags)	Static Budget (1,000 bags)
Sales revenue	$234,000	$225,000	$250,000
Materials	$ 35,000	$ 36,000	$ 40,000
Labour	50,000	54,000	60,000
Overhead	102,000	100,000	100,000
Total expense	$187,000	$190,000	$200,000
Operating profit	$ 47,000	$ 35,000	$ 50,000

Sales volume effect: The company planned to sell 1,000 bags, but actually sold only 900 bags. Each bag not sold could be expected to earn a "contribution margin" of $150. (The contribution margin is the difference between the selling price [$250] and the variable cost [$40 + $60] and is $150 for this product: see next chapter for a fuller discussion of contribution margin.)

Variance = 100 bags @ $150 = $15,000 (unfavourable).

This $15,000 U variance explains the difference between the static budget profit of $50,000 and the flexible budget profit of $35,000.

Selling price effect: The company planned to sell its bags for $250: the actual price was $260. Each of the 900 bags brought in an additional $10 of sales revenue, due to the price increase.

Variance = 900 @ $10 = 9,000 (favourable).

Materials cost effect: The company planned to spend $40 per bag on materials; for 900 bags, that would be $36,000. The actual cost was $35,000, so the company saved $1,000.

Variance = $1,000 (favourable).

Labour cost effect: The company planned to spend $60 per bag on labour; for 900 bags, that would be $54,000. The actual cost was $50,000, so the company saved $4,000.

Variance = $4,000 (favourable).

Overhead cost effect: The company planned to spend $100,000 (total) on overhead; the actual cost was $102,000, so the company overspent by $2,000.

Variance = $2,000 (unfavourable).

Summary:

Original budgeted profit (static budget)	$50,000
Actual profit	47,000
Difference	$ 3,000 (unfavourable)

Which is explained by the variances:

Sales volume variance	$15,000 U
Sales price variance	9,000 F
Material cost variance	1,000 F
Labour cost variance	4,000 F
Overhead cost variance	2,000 U
Total	$ 3,000 U

Was the company out of control? It is a judgment call as to whether the gap of $3,000 is a serious issue or a relatively trivial one. That $3,000 net unfavourable variance conceals an unfavourable sales variance of $15,000, which is almost certainly a cause for concern.

3. (a) Tim Horton's:
   - percentage of customers responding "very satisfied" to a customer satisfaction survey
   - number of written or email complaints in the complaints log
   - speed of customer service, as measured by observation

   (b) Air Canada:
   - percentage of customers responding "very satisfied" to a customer satisfaction survey
   - number of written or email complaints in the complaints log
   - number of flights arriving on time as measured by observation

Discussion Questions and Problems

Discussion Questions

1. What is the purpose of feedback in budgetary control?
2. Who should set a budget: the upper management of the organization or the employees who have to carry out the actual work?
3. How should a service department (such as a human resource management department) be controlled?
4. How should a production department (such as a bottle filling station in a food factory) be controlled?
5. How should a revenue centre (such as a sales team) be controlled?
6. How should a retail store that is a branch of a national chain be controlled?
7. What is the link between responsibility and control?
8. If a product is sold at a higher price than the budgeted price, is it "out of control"?
9. Is spending less than the budget always a good idea?
10. How can the organization create "goal congruence"?
11. What are the four sections usually found on a balanced scorecard?
12. How does a balanced scorecard improve the budgetary control process?

Problems

1. For the following examples, what type of control centre should be used?

   (a) The downtown Winnipeg ticketing office of Air Canada
   (b) Air Canada's Calgary airport aircraft maintenance unit
   (c) Air Canada's domestic flight division
   (d) Air Canada as a whole

2. Between a participative system of budget control and an imposed one, which is better and why?

3. You are given last year's budget and actual financial report for the internal audit department at Woodhouse Warehouse:

Details	Budget	Actual
Staff salaries	$600,000	$575,000
Salary-related expense	60,000	57,500
Travel & lodging	200,000	150,000
Equipment-related expense	50,000	50,000
Training	25,000	nil
Total	$935,000	$832,500

   The salaries were below budget because of a vacancy in the last quarter of the year; a new audit employee will be starting work on January 1. Audit staff earned a salary of $100,000 each in the current year. Next year the salary will be $110,000 (that includes the new employee). Salary-related expenses (health, pension, etc.) are 10% of salary expense.

Travel and lodging expenses were down because site visits (at 15) were fewer than planned (they had planned 20 visits). Next year 25 visits are planned. Travel and lodging expense is expected to cost 5% more next year. Training was not carried out as expected this year, but next year a $75,000 training expense is expected.

Required
(a) Is the internal audit department financially in control or out of control?
(b) Do you think it is likely that the internal audit department was effective?
(c) What type of control centre should the internal audit department be treated as?

4. The balanced scorecard has been introduced into a number of organizations in recent years. Comment on its suitability for controlling the following types of organization:

(a) a service unit, such as a human resources department
(b) a production unit, such as an ice cream manufacturing plant
(c) a sales organization, such as Ticketmaster
(d) a retail outlet, such as an appliance sales store
(e) a hospital

5. Hardy Industries has estimated that it will get a 10% share of a total market of 250,000 for the locks it produces. On average each lock unit sells for $20, so the company's sales revenue is estimated to be $500,000. The standard production cost of a lock is $10 per unit. Fixed costs are budgeted to be $100,000. At the end of 2005 the company discovers that the total market was 300,000 locks, and the following financial report is presented:

Sales	27,500 locks @ $21	$577,500
Actual cost of goods sold	27,500 locks @ $11	302,500
Gross profit		$275,000
Fixed costs		120,000
Operating profit		$155,000

Required
(a) Is the company in control or out of control?
(b) Identify and quantify the deviations from the budget.

6. Oliver & Co. makes pasta. The budget for 2005 was to produce and sell 50 tonnes of pasta. All the company's sales are to small delicatessens, all of whom pay cash on the nail at the end of each month for the pasta deliveries in that month. Oliver & Co. is profitable, but the business runs on a shoestring, with barely enough cash to stay afloat.

Oliver & Co. has just signed an agreement to supply Trawlmart, a major retailer. The terms are that Oliver & Co. will supply 10 tonnes per month to the Trawlmart stores. The contract promises to turn Oliver & Co. into a very profitable business.

Trawlmart has agreed to pay for pasta supplied on the last day of the month following delivery, but rumour in the business has it that Trawlmart often pays late.

What is the likely effect of the new contract on the cash flow of the business?

7. The cash budget for Northern Inc. for the first three months of 2005 is as follows:

$ millions	January	February	March
Opening cash balance	$ 2.5	$ 0.0	$(3.2)
Cash collected from sales	10.0	15.0	8.5
New long-term loan			10.0
Total available	$12.5	$15.0	$15.3
Payments			
Trade suppliers	$ 3.5	$10.2	$5.4
Wages	5.0	5.0	5.0
New equipment	1.0	2.0	
Loan repayment	3.0		
Dividend		1.0	
Total payments	$12.5	$18.2	$10.4
Closing cash balance	$ 0.0	$(3.2)	$ 4.9

Required
(a) Is there a problem?
(b) If there is a problem, how could it be fixed?

8. Western Co. expects to earn a return of 25% on sales. The management accountant at Western Co. has issued the following budget and actual data for the company's two main divisions:

	Division A		Division B	
	Budget	Actual	Budget	Actual
Sales revenue	$2,000,000	$2,200,000	$5,000,000	$5,000,000
Cost of goods sold	800,000	850,000	2,000,000	2,400,000
Gross profit	$1,200,000	$1,350,000	$3,000,000	$2,600,000
Expenses	500,000	520,000	2,000,000	2,300,000
Operating income	$ 700,000	$ 830,000	$1,000,000	$ 300,000

Required
(a) Is there a problem?
(b) If there is a problem, where should the solution be found?

9. Sirocco Co. has produced a budget and actual data for the year as follows:

$ millions	Budget	Actual
Sales revenue	$100.0	$92.0
Cost of goods sold	40.0	36.8
Gross profit	$ 60.0	$55.2
Expenses (all fixed)	40.0	40.0
Operating profit	$ 20.0	$15.2

It is clear that the company has missed its profit target by a substantial margin. Further investigation shows that the main problem was that sales in the month of December were less than the budgeted amount. Identify the possible causes of the decline and what corrective action would be appropriate.

10. The Activo Co. franchises fitness centres in various locations. The company has produced the following balanced scorecard:

Objective	Measure	Target	Actual
Financial perspective			
Add shareholder value	share price	$10.00	$9.50
Add franchisee's value	franchisee's income	+10%	static
Customer perspective			
Add market share	% new members	+25%	+20%
Customer satisfaction	survey	9/10	8/10
	complaints	0	50
Internal business perspective			
Training	training hours	10 per unit	6 per unit
New equipment	equipment age	2 years	2.7 years
Cleanliness	survey	10/10	8/10
Learning & growth perspective			
New equipment	# new products	4 per unit	2 per unit
Customer awareness	advertising $	$250,000	$250,000

Required
(a) Does the balanced scorecard capture the main issues for this business?
(b) How well is the business doing?
(c) Does the balanced scorecard indicate how the business could improve?

9

Cost Behaviour, Break-Even, and Product Costing

Learning
Objectives

After studying this chapter you should be able to describe and explain:
→ How variable costs behave
→ How fixed costs behave
→ How fixed and variable costs are used in the break-even model
→ How overhead is allocated using traditional methods
→ How overhead is allocated using activity-based costing

9.1 Introduction

In using the budget for planning and control, it is essential to have a good understanding of how costs behave. In this chapter, we shall start by making some simple assumptions: classifying all costs as either variable or fixed. This will enable us to examine the break-even model for decision analysis. Later in the chapter, we shall relax this simple approach to cost behaviour. The costs will be treated as being caused by activities, which is a more complex behaviour pattern but far more realistic.

9.2 Cost Behaviour

Cost behaviour describes the relationship between cost and different activity levels. There are many cost behaviour patterns, but they can usually be categorized as variable, fixed, and mixed.

9.2.1 Variable Costs

When goods are sold, the cost of inventory used becomes an expense. The more you sell, the bigger the expense. When goods are produced, the cost of raw materials used is directly related to the number made. The more you make, the more raw materials are used. Raw materials are an example of variable cost. A variable cost is one that is positively correlated with activity.

The goods sold in a retail outlet, the raw materials used in a manufacturing plant, the wages of production workers and some of the production overhead (e.g., utilities used to run production machinery) are all variable costs.

For planning and control purposes, it is necessary to understand this variable cost relationship: the more activity that is planned, the greater the amount of variable costs planned. The cost per unit is constant, but as the number of units increases, so does total cost.

Holiday Computer uses three circuit boards per computer, and each circuit board costs $15, so the cost of circuit boards is $45 per computer.

Number of computers built	Cost of circuit boards @ $45
0	0
1	45
2	90
10	450
100	4,500
1,000	45,000
10,000	450,000
100,000	4,500,000

9.2.2   Fixed Costs

Fixed costs are the opposite of variable costs. Changing the level of activity does not change the fixed costs: they are constant at all pre-determined activity levels.

Examples of fixed costs would be rent, heating, property taxes, and management salaries.

The description *fixed costs* is, perhaps, slightly misleading. Fixed costs will change as a function of time, for example, or as the result of a management decision to spend more. The key to understanding fixed costs is that they are fixed in relation to production activity.

Fixed costs are sometimes referred to as capacity costs, as they endow the company with the ability to carry out its business, up to a certain level. If the fixed cost resources are unused, however, unlike variable costs (which would be avoided), fixed costs are still incurred as expense. Unused capacity has no value.

Holiday Computer employs a staff of eight production managers, each of whom is paid $75,000 per year. This enables up to 100,000 computers to be manufactured each year.

Number of computers built	Total cost of eight production managers	Cost per computer
0	$600,000	N/A
1	600,000	$600,000
2	600,000	300,000
10	600,000	60,000
100	600,000	6,000
1,000	600,000	600
10,000	600,000	60
100,000	600,000	6

As can be seen from the table, because the total cost for the eight production managers is constant, even though the volume increases the cost per unit falls. At maximum volume, the cost per unit is a mere $6.

The fixed cost would be a different amount if more than 100,000 computers were to be manufactured. The eight managers provide a production capacity of 100,000. If Holiday Computer wants to go over that limit, it would have to hire an additional production manager. By spending an additional $75,000 to hire one more production manager, the company might be able to increase production to 112,500 units per year. Fixed costs that increase by large increments such as this are sometimes referred to as "step-fixed" costs.

Fixed cost might increase because of a management decision. Suppose Holiday Computer agreed to increase production managers' salaries from $75,000 to $80,000. That is a $40,000 increase in the total fixed cost ($5,000 × 8 managers). Thus, fixed costs are not static; they are just fixed in relation to activity level (or output volume).

9.2.3 Mixed Costs

Some costs do not fall neatly into either category because they are made up of a fixed element and a variable element. Electricity expense, for example, is almost always a combination of a fixed charge and a metered charge for units consumed. The cost of operating a car is a combination of fixed (insurance, registration, garaging) and variable (gas, repairs, servicing) expenses. For planning and control, a mixed cost should be separated into its fixed and variable components.

9.3 The Break-Even Model

The variable or fixed cost behaviour pattern can be used in the break-even model. It is a simple way of looking at the relationship between costs and revenues to determine the operating income at any level of activity. It is a useful planning and decision support tool.

9.3.1 Contribution Margin

When goods are sold, revenue is generated. At the same time, variable costs are incurred. The difference between the selling price and the variable cost is called the unit contribution margin. It measures how much better off the company is as a result of the sale of one additional unit. Likewise, the contribution margin measures how much worse off the company is from reducing sales by one unit.

Tony's Drinks sells coffee, tea, and soft drinks. Each drink is priced at $0.80 and has a variable cost of $0.50. The contribution margin is $0.30 per drink. In other words, for every drink sold, Tony's Drinks will have an additional $0.30. If 1,000 drinks are sold in a day, the total contribution margin will be $300. If 1,001 drinks are sold, the total contribution margin will be $300.30.

9.3.2 Break-Even Point

Once variable costs are subtracted from sales revenue, the amount left behind is the contribution margin. The contribution is used to pay for the business's fixed costs. When that has been achieved, the business has reached its break-even point. It is useful to know how much business activity is necessary to reach break-even. If this level of activity is unlikely

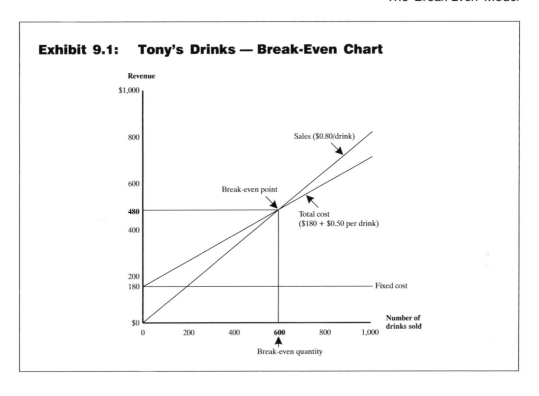

Exhibit 9.1: Tony's Drinks — Break-Even Chart

to be reached, there is no reason for the business to exist. If the break-even level is likely to be exceeded, the company will be profitable. Knowing the break-even enables a sensible decision to be taken as to whether or not to go ahead with a business venture.

To calculate the break-even point, the fixed cost for a given period of time is divided by the contribution margin per unit. The answer indicates how many units need to be sold in that period to reach the break-even point.

Tony's Drinks has fixed costs of $180 per day. Selling price is $0.80 per drink and variable cost is $0.50 per drink. Contribution margin is $0.30 per unit. Break-even is 600 drinks per day ($180 ÷ $0.30). If Tony's can sell 600 drinks in a day the company will break even. (See Exhibit 9.1.) If Tony's sells fewer than 600 there will be fixed costs not covered by contribution, and a loss will occur.

9.3.3 Activity Above the Break-Even Point

At activity levels above the break-even point, the company will be making a profit. For every unit sold above the break-even point, the contribution margin is pure profit. The greater the number sold, the higher the profit becomes.

Earlier, we calculated that Tony's Drinks will break even if it sells 600 drinks per day ($180 ÷ $0.30). Tony, the manager, estimated that his average sales will be 850 drinks per day. His estimated average profit, therefore, will be $75. This may be calculated by totalling the $0.30 contribution margin on every drink sold in excess of the break-even point: $0.30 × (850 – 600) = $75.

Tony's Drinks
Budgeted Daily Income Statement

Sales (850 × $0.80)	$680
Variable cost (850 × $0.50)	425
Contribution margin (850 × $0.30)	$255
Fixed costs	180
Operating profit	$ 75

In addition to paying the fixed costs, an organization may have an expectation or hope about the profit level. This can only come out of the contribution margin earned from sales. Expected profit may be treated in the same way as fixed cost for calculation of the sales level required. The total of the fixed costs and the required profit is divided by the contribution margin to determine the required sales level.

Tony has decided that unless he can make a profit of $120 per day, it's just not worth getting out of bed. To make $120 profit, he has to make enough of the $0.30 contribution margins to pay the fixed costs ($180) plus $120: that is, a total of $300. To make this level of profit he will need to sell 1,000 drinks ($300 ÷ $0.30).

Based on Tony's profit expectation, if he cannot sell 1,000 drinks a day, it is not worth his while being in business. If he estimates that he can sell more than 1,000 drinks a day, then he has a potentially viable business. If his prediction is that he can sell exactly 1,000 drinks a day he has reached a point of indifference: he does not mind whether he is in business or not.

If, as above, his prediction is that he can sell 850 units per day, then his profit objectives will not be met. He will fall short by $45 ($120 – $75).

9.3.4 Using the Break-Even Model to Analyze Changes

The break-even model lends itself to simple (but sometimes very effective) "what if" type analysis. In a "what if" analysis, the numbers, assumptions, and so on are changed to study the effect of the change. You might want to consider the effect of increasing the selling price, for example. This would increase the contribution margin, but (unless the product is perfectly inelastic) would also reduce the sales volume. Or you might want to decrease the selling price, which would increase the volume but decrease the contribution margin. It is almost always the case that changing one variable will also result in change in one of the other variables. Sometimes the effects are extremely complex, with several variables changing at once.

Tony's break-even calculation informs him that he will need to sell 1,000 drinks to pay his fixed costs and get the $120 profit he is hoping for. His best estimate is that he can sell 850 drinks per day at a price of $0.80, which is not enough volume to give him his required profit. Tony is considering two alternatives: he could raise the price of drinks from $0.80

to $1.00, in which case his volume will decrease to 600 units; alternatively, he could decrease the price of drinks from $0.80 to $0.70, in which case volume will increase to 1,600 units.

Selling price	Variable cost	Contribution margin/unit	Volume	Total contribution	Objective
$1.00	$0.50	$0.50	600	$300	Met
$0.70	$0.50	$0.20	1,600	$320	Exceeded

Both actions result in achieving his stated profit objective. Raising the price meets his requirements exactly. Reducing the price gives him his required profit, and another $20 per day. Tony would now have a good basis for making a decision. Which route he chooses would be a matter of personal preference, but both are feasible.

Another calculation to reach the same conclusion would be as follows:

Existing situation
850 units, $0.30 contribution margin per unit; $300 required; shortfall $45.

Option 1: Increase Price
Effect of decreasing volume: $(600 - 850) \times \$0.30$	=	($ 75)
Effect of increasing price: $600 \times (\$1.00 - \$0.80)$	=	120
Net increase in contribution margin		$ 45

Forty-five dollars is exactly enough to meet the $45 shortfall, so the objective has been met.

Option 2: Decrease Price
Effect of increasing volume: $(1,600 - 850) \times \$0.30$	=	$225
Effect of decreasing price: $1,600 \times (\$0.80 - \$0.70)$	=	(160)
Net increase in contribution margin		$ 65

A net increase of $45 would have been enough to meet the shortfall, so the objective has been met and superseded by $20.

The break-even model can be used to evaluate a wide range of decisions, such as using better raw materials to increase quality, using advertising to boost sales, expanding the product range, and so on.

Tony is considering the effect of advertising on his outlet. At a cost of a mere $60 per day, he can have posters put on all the transit stop benches within one kilometre of his place of business. If he does that he estimates that sales will increase by 250 units per day. His current fixed cost is $180 per day, and his contribution margin is $0.30 per drink sold.

Additional contribution margin: $250 \times \$0.30$	$75
Additional fixed cost	60
Additional net income	$15

Advertising increases his net income, so it is a sound business idea. We should also recognize that it makes his business a little riskier. His fixed cost has now increased from $180 per day to $240 per day. His break-even point has increased from 600 units a day ($180 ÷ $0.30) to 800 units a day ($240 ÷ $0.30). Although he is likely to do better, his exposure to risk is higher, as measured by the increased break-even level.

Note that in this calculation, the existing situation is irrelevant, and none of the data about the existing situation enters into the decision. The only relevant facts are those that are marginal to the decision: i.e., those that change as a result of the decision. The increased advertising spending is a marginal cost. The increased contribution from additional sales is a marginal benefit. The net effect is the marginal benefit of the decision to advertise.

9.4   Product Costing

The break-even model is a simplification of the complexities of the real world. There are situations where the model is sufficiently close to reality that it is useful. Tony's Drinks, for example, is a simple enough situation for it to be a perfect description of the company activities and decisions. Many retailers, like Tony's, find that their costs can be adequately described as either variable or fixed. The more we move away from retailing and get into manufacturing where companies manufacture a huge range of products, the more the simple split between variable cost and fixed cost becomes an inadequate description of cost behaviour. That world of large, complex organizations, with a wide product and customer range, is much more realistic than its simpler counterparts.

To be sure, large and complex organizations still have some variable costs. They still buy goods for resale and use raw materials in production. These will be directly proportional to volume. In activity-based costing these are referred to as *unit-variable costs*. They change with the number of units sold or produced (activity level).

Likewise, the organizations will have some purely fixed costs. The cost of head office operations, the expenses of the board of directors, the cost of the annual audit, and similar costs are all virtually independent of other sales and/or production activities. In activity-based costing these are referred to as *business-sustaining costs*.

It is a feature of large modern corporations to have a large amount of what would be described as overhead expenses. Some of it is production overhead, some administrative overhead, some marketing overhead. Activity-based costing shows how overhead is caused by activities, and that these activities are the result of decisions, conscious or unconscious, made by management.

An example of an activity is moving finished goods from the place they were made to the finished goods warehouse. The cost rate for that activity depends on how far the goods have to move, which is, in turn, caused by the plant layout and the convenience of the warehouse. The number of times the cost is incurred depends on how often goods are moved. That depends on factors such as the number of production runs. The number of production runs is a decision made by management. At the extremes, production can be carried out in a single, large production run (when only one movement will take place), or in a series of many small production runs (when many movements will take place). So the decision as to how much cost to incur depends on how many production runs are scheduled. In traditional cost accounting systems, costs such as this are lost in a general account called production overhead. In activity-based costing, such costs are analyzed according to their cause.

If all products (and all customers) were roughly equal in the activities they used, then there would not be too serious a problem. However, where products and customers demand different levels of activities, they should bear the differential cost of those activities. Simple systems of cost behaviour and cost allocation fail to capture these differences. As a result, products may be allocated too much cost (more cost than they generate through their activities), or too little cost (less than the cost they generate through their activities). If we have an incorrect perception of the cost a product is causing, we are likely to make incorrect decisions. This would happen in decisions such as product addition or deletion, product pricing, advertising, product design, and production run size.

In activity-based costing, in addition to unit-variable costs and business-sustaining costs, at least two further classifications are introduced: batch level costs and product-sustaining costs.

Batch level costs are a function of the number of times that a batch is run. A batch may be a production run or it may also be the ordering of raw materials or the dispatch of finished goods. The features of batch-related costs are that they are fixed in relation to each batch, no matter how large or how small, and they are variable in respect of the number of batches; so the greater the number of batches, the greater the total batch costs.

In a production run, the batch costs would include scheduling the batch into the production plan, ordering and delivery of raw materials, setting up the machines to produce the product, inspection of the batch for quality control, and dispatching output. These costs will be incurred every time a new batch happens. The size of the batch may be a single product, or it may be a large batch. There are obvious implications for product cost. The larger the batch, the smaller the per unit cost for batch-related costs.

Once the dynamics of the cost of a batch are understood, there is a tendency to make each batch as large as possible. By averaging the (fixed) batch cost over the largest number of units, the cost per unit is minimized. One spinoff effect of this is that substantial inventories of partly produced and finished goods occur. This creates interesting tensions between cost minimization in the production area and cost minimization elsewhere. The plant may be operating on a just-in-time basis, which tries to avoid inventory. Juggling these competing needs becomes a difficult decision.

Activity-based costing also identifies "product-sustaining costs". These are the costs associated with having the product in existence. Product-sustaining costs would include engineering design and redesign, cataloguing, advertising, and sales education.

There is a tendency toward product proliferation in most businesses. Frequently, the costs of adding a new product or a new variant are poorly understood and not fully factored into the new product decision. Similarly, the decision of a product deletion is seldom rigorously addressed.

291

9.4.1 Product Costing Using Traditional Cost Allocation

Simple situations call for simple solutions. In a simple organization where all the output is the same product, it is acceptable to use simple cost allocation systems.

There should be no difficulty in tracing materials and labour to the products or services where they are used. In both cases, keeping a detailed record system of where these resources are used is part of the normal process of management.

It is much more problematic to allocate overhead to products and services. There is no direct measure of use. How do you measure the amount of rent or property tax a product has consumed in its manufacture, for example? We have to use a cost allocation system so that some estimate of each product's fair share of resources is measured. Without such an allocation, we would not know how much to charge for the goods or services we sell.

Traditional cost allocation consists of the following steps:

1. The total budgeted overhead is estimated.
   - For Madoc Co., the budgeted overhead for 2005 is $640,000.

2. An overhead recovery base is selected. This should be some measurable activity that is highly correlated with the incurred costs.
   - Madoc Co. has selected machine hours as its cost recovery base. The company it thinks that the more machine hours a product uses, the more overhead costs it causes and, therefore, the more of the overhead costs the product should bear. Other possible cost recovery bases include labour hours, material cost, etc.

3. The amount of the overhead recovery base is estimated.
   - Madoc Co. has estimated that 16,000 machine hours will be worked in 2005.

4. The overhead recovery rate is calculated.
   - For Madoc Co., $640,000 of overhead is to be recovered through 16,000 machine hours, so the overhead recovery rate is $40 per machine hour ($640,000 ÷ 16,000 = $40).

5. The overhead recovery rate can be used in selling price estimation.
   - If the Madoc Co. is asked to quote for a job that will incur $20,000 of material cost, $10,000 of labour cost, and use 300 machine hours, the company should base its price quotation on the budgeted cost of $42,000:

Estimated material cost	$20,000
Estimated labour cost	10,000
Estimated overhead cost	12,000 (300 machine hours @ 40 per hour)
Estimated total cost	$42,000

   After adding a suitable profit markup, the estimated selling price can be calculated.

6. The overhead recovery rate can be used to allocate overhead to product lines so that product profitability can be calculated.
   - In Madoc Co., hole punches have used 10,000 machine hours, so they have been allocated $400,000 of overhead cost; staplers have used 6,000 machine hours, so they have been allocated

Exhibit 9.2: Madoc Inc. — Income Statements as of 2005

	Hole punches	Staplers	Total
Sales units	500,000	200,000	700,000
Selling price	$1.64	$2.50	
Sales revenue	$820,000	$500,000	$1,320,000
Direct costs			
Raw materials	$180,000	$ 80,000	$ 260,000
Labour	90,000	40,000	130,000
	$270,000	$120,000	$ 390,000
Overhead*	400,000	240,000	640,000
Total cost	$670,000	$360,000	$1,030,000
Operating profit	$150,000	$140,000	$ 290,000
Operating profit as % of sales	18.3%	28.0%	22.0%
Machine hours	10,000	6,000	16,000

* Allocated in proportion to machine hours

$240,000 of overhead cost. The entire $640,000 of estimated overhead has been shared between these two products on the basis of machine used.

A single overhead recovery rate works really well in situations where the company's products are all approximately equal in their demands on the system, and the recovery base makes a fair allocation of overhead. The more differences there are in resource usages between products, the less well the single overhead recovery rate system works.

Madoc Inc. produces office equipment (hole punches and staplers). Management is quite happy with the 2005 results as both products are seen to be profitable. (See the income statements in Exhibit 9.2.) However, management has been putting pressure on the manager in charge of hole punches, as their rate of return on sales (18.3%) is lower than that of staplers (28.0%). The hole punch manager is puzzled by this as he knows he runs an efficient operation.

9.4.2 Product Costing Using Activity-Based Costs

Further analysis of the costs reveals that the allocation of overhead on the basis of machine hours is problematic. Machine hours only captures the activity once a production run has started. Hole punches are made in four production runs a year, each of 12,500 units. Staplers, by contrast, are made in a lot of short runs of about 2,000 units each. This means that staplers should be allocated a greater amount of batch-related costs. Additionally, product level support for hole punches is inexpensive as the

Exhibit 9.3: Madoc Inc. — Revised Product Cost Report

	Hole punches	Staplers	Total
Sales units	500,000	200,000	700,000
Selling price	$1.64	$2.5	
Sales revenue	$820,000	$500,000	$1,320,000
Direct costs			
Raw materials	$180,000	$ 80,000	$ 260,000
Labour	90,000	40,000	130,000
	$270,000	$120,000	$ 390,000
Overhead:			
Unit-related costs	$ 50,000	$ 20,000	$ 70,000
Batch-sustaining costs	100,000	250,000	350,000
Product-sustaining costs	10,000	50,000	60,000
	$160,000	$320,000	$ 480,000
Total product cost	$430,000	$440,000	$ 870,000
Product profitability	$390,000	$ 60,000	$ 450,000
Net profit as % of sales	47.6%	12.0%	
Business-sustaining costs (not allocated to products)			160,000
Net profit			$ 290,000

design has not changed in years, while the stapler line is regularly re-engineered to meet changing tastes in the office. Some overhead is unit-related and can be traced to the two production lines. Some overhead is purely fixed (business sustaining).

A revised product cost report has now been prepared, reflecting this activity-based costing information in Exhibit 9.3.

As we can see, if activity-based costing is used to allocate costs, those allocated to the stapler line are substantially higher. This reflects the fact that the staplers are the users of activities that result in more costs. The hole punches are a cheaper product to produce. The perception that hole punches were not pulling their weight was altogether incorrect. In fact, their return on sales is far higher than that of the staplers.

Hole punches and staplers may seem trivial, but they are being used to illustrate a more complex reality. A company that manufactures 1,000 products will almost always have some that are more expensive to produce and maintain than others. In particular, the effect of mass production versus small batch production generally means that the small-scale products are more expensive to produce. This is always disguised by simple overhead allocation bases (such as the machine hour allocation used for Madoc Co., or allocation according to labour hours, which is also common). Only activity-based costing can capture the relation between activities and costs.

9.4.3 Using Activity-based Costing for Customer Profitability

In the same way that products are not all equal causes, or users of cost, not all customers are equal. Activity-based costing can be used to analyze customer profitability.

Tryfan Inc. sells building materials to five major hardware retailers. Activated Hardware is the biggest customer, taking half of all output. In 2005, Tryfan's total sales were $10 million at full selling price. Contribution margin was 25% of this, or $2.5 million. Selling expenses total $1 million. Activated Hardware is seen as the most important customer because of the high proportion of sales made on its account.

Because Activated Hardware's volume is so high, the company is allowed a 5% volume discount of $250,000. Sixty percent of all sales-personnel time is spent dealing with the Activated account ($150,000), while the other 40% is spent dealing with the other customers ($100,000). Deliveries have to be made to each of Activated's retail outlets (at a cost of $375,000), whereas the other customers have their purchases delivered to their central warehouses (at a total cost of $125,000). An activity-based costing analysis of customer profitability shows that Activated is not Tryfan's best customer, by any means, as shown in Exhibit 9.4.

Although Activated Hardware is a good customer, the high costs of servicing it makes it less profitable than the other four, smaller customers.

Once again, like the production situation, it is the differential demands placed on the system by different customers (or products) that make simplistic cost allocations problematic, and make activity-based costing the only sensible way to allocate costs.

Exhibit 9.4: Tryfan Inc. — Activity-based Cost Analysis

	Activated Hardware	Four smaller customers	Total
Sales	$5,000,000	$5,000,000	$10,000,000
Contribution margin	$1,250,000	$1,250,000	$ 2,500,000
Customer specific costs			
5% discount	250,000		
Sales staff	150,000	100,000	
Delivery costs	375,000	125,000	
	$ 775,000	$ 225,000	$ 1,000,000
Profit	$ 475,000	$1,025,000	$ 1,500,000
Profit as % of sales	9.5%	20.5%	15%

9.5 Over- and Under-Recovered Overhead

An overhead recovery rate is used to allocate overhead to products. This is true whether the company is using a traditional recovery rate based on labour hours, or a more precise system such as activity-based costing. It is important to remember that overhead recovery rates are based on estimates, and the estimates may not tie in exactly with the actual data.

The overhead recovery rate is calculated by dividing the budgeted overhead (an estimate) by the budgeted recovery base, such as labour hours (another estimate). If either of these is materially different from the actual value, then the recovery rate will have been set at too high a level or too low a level.

If the recovery rate is too high, then the overhead allocated to products will be too much. This could be a problem because it might have made the company charge too high a price for the product. The logical effect of too high a price is that sales will be lost. Lost sales result in lost profitability.

Over-recovery of overhead would be the result of either underspending on overhead or more than expected overhead recovery base (e.g., labour hours).

If the overhead recovery rate is set too low, then the overhead allocated to products will be too little. This could be a problem because at the end of the year there will be overhead incurred that has not been carried by any of the products. Product prices may have been set too low for the products to be truly profitable.

Under-recovery of overhead would be the result of overspending on overhead compared to the budget, or the overhead recovery base is set too high (e.g., working fewer labour hours than were planned).

In Exhibit 9.5 the Sebastian Co. has budgeted its production overhead to be $500,000 for the year. The company anticipated working 20,000 labour hours, so the overhead recovery rate throughout the year was $25 per labour hour. Every time a product used a labour hour it would be charged with $25 of overhead. The expectation was that by the end of the year the total overhead charged to all products would be exactly $500,000.

In Exhibit 9.5, (1), a combination of $20,000 of underspending on overhead plus an additional 2,000 labour hours charged to production at $25 per hour has resulted in a $70,000 over-recovery. Over-recovery may not be seen as a huge problem.

In Exhibit 9.5, (2), a combination of $25,000 of overspending on overhead combined with not working 5,000 of the planned labour hours charged to production at $25 per hour has resulted in a $150,000 under-recovery. Under-recovery of a significant amount is a major problem, as it results in losses. It is also important, though less so, if overhead is over-recovered by a significant amount, as it erodes competitiveness.

9.6 Summary

Understanding cost behaviour is an important skill in budget preparation, budgetary control, and decision analysis. Simple situations may be adequately represented by treating costs as either variable or fixed. The

**Exhibit 9.5:   The Sebastian Co. —
                 Over- and Under-Recovery of Overhead**

Budgeted production overhead	$500,000	
Budgeted labour hours	20,000	
Overhead recovery rate ($500,000 ÷ 20,000 hours)	$25	

(1) Over-Recovery

Number of labour hours worked	22,000	
Total overhead charged to products (22,000 hrs. × $25)		$550,000
Actual overhead incurred		480,000
Over-recovered overhead		$ 70,000

(2) Under-Recovery

Number of labour hours worked	15,000	
Total overhead charged to products (15,000 hrs. × $25)		$375,000
Actual overhead incurred		525,000
Under-recovered overhead		($150,000)

classification of costs as fixed or variable enables break-even analysis to be carried out. In the more complex situations found in reality, break-even is an inadequate description of cost behaviour. Activity-based costing relates costs to the activities carried out, as used by products, processes, or customers. In doing so, activity-based costing provides a more precise measure of costs and profitability.

Self-Study Problems

1. Michael Manufacturing has budgeted overhead of $5 million. The company has chosen to allocate overhead to products on the basis of direct labour hours. Budgeted labour hours in 2005 were 100,000.

   Actual results for 2005 showed that the company spent $5.4 million on overhead, and incurred 110,000 direct labour hours. Product X93 incurred $700,000 of direct material cost, and $400,000 of direct labour cost (10,000 direct labour hours).

   Required
   (a) What is Michael Manufacturing's overhead recovery rate for year 2005?
   (b) How much overhead would be charged to product X93?
   (c) How much is the overhead over- or under-recovered for the company as a whole?

2. Daniel's Dress Shop sells fashions in the Mississauga Mall. The shop buys from manufacturers in Toronto and Singapore. A typical dress costs $12 and is sold for $40. Sales staff get no wages, but receive 20% commission on all goods sold. Insurance, storage, and handling cost $5 per garment. The store pays a rental of $1,000 per month, plus 12.5% of turnover. The manager receives a salary of $5,000 per month. There are incidental operating costs of $2,500 per month.

   Required
   (a) What is the variable cost per dress sold?
   (b) What is the fixed cost per month?
   (c) What is the contribution margin per dress?
   (d) What is the gross profit to sales ratio?
   (e) How many dresses must the shop sell each month to break even?
   (f) In a month when the shop sells 1,000 dresses, how much operating profit will it make?
   (g) The manager is thinking about advertising Daniel's Dress Shop by mailing a flyer to all the households within five kilometres of the mall, This would cost $2,000. How many additional dresses must be sold to make it worthwhile?

3. The human resources department at Treblanc Inc. has estimated its costs for 2005 as $500,000. This is based on a careful activity-based costing exercise that establishes the following cost drivers and expected levels of activity:

Hiring for new positions	20 @ $5,000	$100,000
Replacing existing positions	50 @ $2,000	100,000
Maintaining existing positions	1,000 @ $ 100	100,000
Fixed costs (allocated 1/5 to each of 5 departments)		200,000
Total budgeted costs		$500,000

Required

(a) Using the traditional cost allocation method, calculate an overhead recovery rate for the human resources department, based on charging overhead to user departments on the basis of the existing workforce of 1,000 employees.

(b) Using the overhead allocation rate calculated in (a), how much would be the budgeted expense charged to the production department, which has 200 employees?

(c) How much expense would be charged to the production department using the activity-based costing information if you are told that the shop has 200 employees, and it is proposing to hire no new positions but replace two existing positions?

(d) Which is fairer, (b) or (c) above?

Solution

1. (a) Overhead recovery rate:

$$= \text{budgeted overhead} \div \text{budgeted direct labour hour}$$
$$= \$5,000,000 \div 100,000$$
$$= \$50 \text{ per direct labour hour}$$

(b) Overhead for product X93 would be:

$$= 10,000 \times \$50$$
$$= \$500,000$$

(c) Overhead charged to production

($50 × 110,000 direct labour hours)	$5,500,000
Actual overhead incurred	5,400,000
Over-recovered overhead	$ 100,000

2. (a) Variable cost per dress:

Cost of dress	$12	
Sales commission	8	($40 × 20%)
Insurance, handling, etc.	5	
Part of rent	5	($40 × 12.5%)
Total variable cost per dress	$30	

(b) Fixed cost per month:

Rent	$1,000
Manager's salary	5,000
Incidental expenses	2,500
Total fixed cost per month	$8,500

(c) Contribution margin per dress:

$$= \text{selling price} - \text{variable cost}$$
$$= \$40 - \$30$$
$$= \$10$$

(d)   Gross profit to sales %

= [(selling price – cost of goods sold) ÷ selling price] × 100%
= [($40 – $12) ÷ $40] × 100%
= 70%

(e)   Break-even point (unit):

= fixed cost ÷ contribution margin
= $8,500 ÷ $10
= 850

The shop must sell 850 dresses per month to break even.

(f)   In a month when the shop sells 1,000 dresses, it will make an operating profit of $1,500:

Income Statement

Sales revenue	1,000 × $40		$40,000
Cost of goods sold	1,000 × $12		12,000
Gross margin			$28,000
Less Expenses:			
Sales commission	$40,000 × 20%	$8,000	
Insurance, handling, etc.	1,000 × $5	5,000	
Rent	$1,000 + ($40,000 × 12.5%)	6,000	
Manager's salary		5,000	
Incidental expenses		2,500	26,500
Operating profit			$ 1,500

OR

Actual sales	1,000 dresses
– Break-even point	850
Sales in excess of break-even point	150
× Contribution margin/unit	$10
= operating profit	$1,500

(g)

Additional cost of flyer	$2,000
Contribution margin/unit	$10

The shop must sell $2,000 ÷ $10 = 200 additional dresses to make the flyer pay for itself.

3.   (a)   Traditional cost allocation: single overhead cost pool and charge-out rate:

= $500,000 ÷ 1,000 employees
= $500 per employee

(b)   Overhead expense charged to the production department:

= 200 employees × $500
= $100,000

(c) Activity-based costing overhead allocation for the production department:

Hire new employees	0 × $5,000	$ 0
Replace existing employees	2 × $2,000	4,000
Maintains existing employees	200 × $100	20,000
Share of fixed costs	$200,000 × 1/5	40,000
Total overhead allocated		$64,000

(d) The activity-based costing allocation is fairer: it charges the human resource department costs to users based on the causes of those costs. Because the production department is very stable (low turnover of staff), it causes less cost. This is reflected in the lower cost allocation ($64,000 compared to $100,000).

Discussion Questions and Problems

Discussion Questions

1. Describe how fixed costs and variable costs behave with respect to activity.
2. How is the contribution margin useful in decision making?
3. Is the break-even model a realistic description of real world organizations?
4. Is it possible to change one variable in a break-even calculation without affecting any of the others?
5. Give two examples of batch-related costs and describe what causes them to behave the way they do.
6. Give two examples of product-sustaining costs and describe what causes them to behave the way they do.
7. Do unit-variable costs occur in activity-based costing?
8. How would you treat research and development costs in an activity-based costing analysis of a company?
9. What are the main features of a situation where activity-based costing will give a better understanding of product cost than traditional cost allocation?
10. Which is more precise, break-even or activity-based costing?

Problems

1. The following is a list of expenses incurred by the Muskoka Manufacturing Co. Label each one as variable, fixed, or mixed.

   (a) plastic stock used as raw material
   (b) consumable stores, such as glue and screws
   (c) lubricating and cleaning materials for the production machinery
   (d) cleaning materials for the administrative offices
   (e) production workers' wages
   (f) insurance (fire and theft of property)
   (g) insurance (product and public liability)
   (h) rent of production facility
   (i) rent of administrative building
   (j) property taxes
   (k) amortization of production equipment
   (l) amortization of marketing department's computer system
   (m) amortization of delivery vehicles
   (n) amortization of salespeople's vehicles
   (o) amortization of computer system used in human resource management department
   (p) research & development costs
   (q) quality control department costs
   (r) heating expense

2. The utility bill for Muskoka Manufacturing Co. was $5,000 in January, when the plant was closed for its annual winter break. In the

months of February through April the utility bills were $9,000 per month on average, and production was 160,000 units per month.

Required
(a) Describe situations where the utility bill for a company is likely to be a fixed cost, a variable cost, and a mixed cost.
(b) Assuming the utility bill for Muskoka Manufacturing Co. to be a mixed cost, estimate the fixed element and the variable cost per unit produced.

3. You are told that the cost for public liability insurance at Snowden Financial Advisors Inc. is a base amount of $10,000 per month, plus 2.5% of gross billings. In a year where gross billings were $5,000,000, estimate the public liability insurance expense.

4. Harry Houdini has a number of hot sausage stands in downtown Orillia. He pays $0.50 for each sausage, and $0.10 for each bun. Each sausage uses an average of $0.05 of condiments. Wrappings are $0.10 per sausage. Sausages sell for $2.25 each. He rents his cart for $50 per day, which includes gas for cooking. He pays the sausage cart operator $25 per day, plus $0.25 per sausage sold. There is a $20 per day cost for moving each cart to its site.

Required
(a) What is the variable cost per sausage sold?
(b) What is the contribution margin per sausage sold?
(c) What is the fixed cost per cart per day?
(d) What is the break-even point per day, in units?
(e) What is the break-even point, in sales revenue?
(f) How many sausages must each cart sell to make a profit of $100?
(g) If Harry Houdini has 10 carts, and he wants to make a profit of $750 per day, how much total sales revenue must be earned?
(h) If Harry Houdini has 10 carts, and each one sells an average of 1,000 sausages per day, what is his daily profit?
(i) If Harry Houdini spent $50 on advertising, how many additional sausages would he need to sell to make it worthwhile?
(j) If Harry Houdini increased his prices from $2.25 to $2.50, and there was a 10% decrease in sales quantities, from 1,000 sausages per day to 900 sausages per day, on each of his 10 carts, by how much would his profit change?

5. Harry Houdini has a number of hot sausage stands in downtown Orillia. He pays $0.50 for each sausage, and $0.10 for each bun. Each sausage uses an average of $0.05 of condiments. Wrappings are $0.10 per sausage. Sausages sell for $2.25 each. He rents his cart for $50 per day, which includes gas for cooking. He pays the sausage cart operator $25 per day, plus $0.25 per sausage sold. There is a $20 per day cost for moving each cart to its site.

Most of Harry's 10 carts sell between 750 and 1,200 sausages per day, with an average of 1,000. Unused sausages have to be dumped at the end of each day. If a cart runs out of sausages, Harry can deliver extras at a cost of $25 per trip. All other variable cost items can be re-used the following day.

Required

Evaluate the following in terms of fixed and variable costs and profitability:

(a) sending each cart out with 750 sausages only

(b) sending each cart out with 750 sausages, and delivering extras as needed: five trips would be needed

6. The training department of Muskoka Manufacturing Co. runs courses in quality control for production staff at the company's 15 operating subsidiaries. There is a high turnover of staff, so the department has training courses every month. Each course can accommodate up to 50 trainees. The courses are charged to the subsidiary companies at a rate of $500 per trainee. The costs for a recent course with 50 participants were as follows:

Advertising	$5,000
Instructor's fees	$2,000
Refreshments	$5,000
Photocopying materials	$2,000
Room rental	$1,000
Computer hire	$5,000
($50 per workstation, plus $2,500, one time only, set-up fee)	
Software licence	$2,500
($1,000 per course, plus $30 per trainee)	

Required

(a) With respect to trainees, classify each cost as variable, fixed, or mixed.

(b) Separate mixed costs into their variable and fixed components.

(c) Calculate the total variable cost per trainee, and the total fixed cost per course.

(d) Calculate the contribution margin per trainee.

(e) Calculate the break-even point in number of trainees per course.

(f) Calculate the profit for a course with 50 trainees.

(g) Course #03.2005Z is full (50 trainees). As a favour, the training department is going to allow registration by one additional trainee, and charge that trainee the minimum amount such that the training department will not lose money: how much will this trainee be charged?

(h) Is the break-even model a good description of the training department's training course activities?

(i) An outside organization has offered to run the same training course for $20,000. Should the training department accept or decline this offer?

(j) Should the training department be making a profit on these courses?

7. Kawartha Inc. has budgeted production overhead of $600,000 per year. The company allocates overhead costs to products on the basis of machine hours. In 2005 the company budgeted to use 12,000 machine hours. Products are priced by calculating the estimated raw materials, direct labour, and production overhead, and then adding 70% to cover selling and administration and a profit margin.

Job #05.2005 X32 has had the following estimates prepared:

Raw materials	$50,000
Direct labour	200 hours @ $25
Machine time	40 hours

Required
(a) Calculate the total cost for job #05.2005 X32.
(b) Calculate the selling price for job #05.2005 X32.
(c) Is this price estimation method fair?

8. Kawartha Inc. has budgeted production overhead of $600,000 per year. The company allocates overhead costs to products on the basis of machine hours. In 2005 the company budgeted to use 12,000 machine hours. Products are priced by calculating the estimated raw materials, direct labour, and production overhead, and then adding 70% to cover selling and administration and a profit margin.

In year 2005 the actual cost of production overhead was $700,000. The actual machine hours used were 15,000. Calculate the over-recovery or under-recovery of production overhead.

9. Kawartha Inc. has budgeted production overhead of $600,000 per year. This is incurred in three departments: production, painting, and assembly, for which relevant details are as follows:

	Production	Painting	Assembly	Total
Budgeted overhead	$300,000	$200,000	$100,000	$600,000
Machine hours	10,000	1,000	1,000	12,000

The sales department is presently pricing two jobs:

Job #	06.2005 XK120	06.2005 Z80
Raw materials	$10,000	$10,000
Direct labour	$10,000	$10,000
Machine hours		
Production	200	nil
Painting	nil	75
Assembly	nil	125
Total	200	200

Selling price is targeted to be raw materials plus direct labour plus production overhead (allocated according to machine hours), plus 70% markup to cover selling and administration and a profit margin.

Required

(a) Calculate a "plant-wide" overhead recovery rate per machine hour.

(b) Calculate the target selling price for each job using the "plant-wide" overhead recovery rate per machine hour.

(c) Calculate a "departmental" overhead recovery rate per machine hour for each of the three departments.

(d) Calculate the target selling price for each job using the three "departmental" overhead recovery rates per machine hour.

(e) Which is more precise: the plant-wide or the departmental overhead recovery rates?

(f) What is likely to be the outcome of using plant-wide overhead recovery rates in price setting?

10. Kawartha Inc. has budgeted production overhead of $600,000 per year. This is incurred in three departments: production, painting, and assembly, for which relevant details are as follows:

	Production	Painting	Assembly	Total
Budgeted overhead	$300,000	$200,000	$100,000	$600,000
Machine hours	10,000	1,000	1,000	12,000
Raw material moves	100 @ $1,000			
Set-ups	25 @ $2,000			
Product designs	10 @ $7,500			
Other	$75,000			

The sales department is presently pricing up two jobs, as follows:

Job #	06.2005 XK120	06.2005 Z80
Raw materials	$10,000	$10,000
Direct labour	$10,000	$10,000
Machine hours		
Production	200	nil
Painting	nil	75
Assembly	nil	125
Total	200	200
Raw material moves	5	1
Set-ups	1	10
Product designs	1	1

Production overhead is allocated according to the identified cost drivers, with any remaining overhead allocated according to machine hours. A 70% markup is added to the total cost to cover selling and administration and a profit margin.

Required

(a) Calculate the target selling price for each job.

(b) Which is more precise: plant-wide overhead allocation rates; departmental overhead allocation rates; activity-based costing?

11. Haliburton Co. has calculated the following cost pools for production overhead:

Pool	Budgeted cost per month	Cost driver	Budgeted level
Set-ups	$500,000	# of set-ups	200
Material handling	$750,000	# of material moves	500
Material storage	$200,000	# of tonnes stored	500
Maintenance	$600,000	# of machine hours	12,000
Inspection	$200,000	# of inspection hours	4,000
Labour hours			50,000

The following data refers to two jobs that were completed in June:

Details	Job A	Job B
Direct material cost	$5,000	$7,500
Direct labour cost	$7,500	$5,000
Direct labour hours	300	100
Set-ups	5	1
Materials moves	10	3
Tonnes of material stored	2	5
Machine hours	70	30
Inspection hours	20	10

Required

(a) Using labour hours as the overhead allocation base, calculate a plant-wide overhead recovery cost rate, and calculate the cost of each job.

(b) Using activity-based costing, calculate the cost of each job.

(c) Which is more precise: the plant-wide overhead allocation or the activity-based costing allocation?

12 Killarney Wholesale Foods distributes canned goods to independently owned groceries and supermarkets in Northern Ontario. The company has gathered the following data on three types of customer:

	Supermarkets	Groceries	Corner stores
Monthly sales revenue	$800,000	$500,000	$100,000
Gross profit %	10%	12%	15%
Monthly costs			
Sales visits ($500 each)	1	1	1
Order processing ($200 each)	10	5	1
Deliveries ($1,000 each)	5	5	1
Rush deliveries ($200 each)	10	2	0
Sales promotions	$5,000	$1,000	0

Required

(a) Calculate the profitability of each type of customer as % of sales revenue.

(b) If you wanted to improve the profitability of the Groceries sector, where would you look for cost reductions?

3

Financial Decision Making

Finance:

"...the acquisition, management and financing of resources needed by firms."

A.H.R Davis & G.E Pinches
Canadian Financial Management, *4th Canadian Edition*
Toronto, Addison Wesley Longman, 2002

10

Analysis of Short-Term Decisions

Learning
Objectives

After studying this chapter you should be able to:

→ Identify differential costs and revenues
→ Describe the role of capacity
→ Explain how to decide whether to make or buy
→ Identify sunk costs and committed costs
→ Explain the difference between a short-term and a long-term decision

---

10.1 Introduction

In part one of this book we examined financial accounting, which is the use of accounting for scorekeeping; in part two, we discussed the use of accounting for attention directing, through budgets and budgetary control. In this part (part three) we deal with the ways accounting can support decision making. The topic is addressed, first, with respect to short-term decisions (Chapter 10) and, second, with respect to long-term decisions (Chapters 11 and 12).

10.2 Differential Costs and Revenues: New Orders

In Chapter 9, we looked at cost behaviour: understanding cost behaviour is essential for competent planning and control. Those same ideas of cost behaviour will now be used as the basis for making short-term decisions. The simple approach to cost behaviour splits costs into variable (those that change as production or sales activity changes) or fixed (those that do not change when production or sales go up or down). That idea is close to (but not identical to) the idea of differential costs and revenues.

Differential costs and revenues are those that change as a result of a decision. Variable costs are normally differential costs, and fixed costs are normally not differential costs. In making a decision, the only elements that are relevant are those that are differential to the decision.

Revenues are generally differential, in the sense that they behave in a variable way: as sales rise or fall, revenue from sales rises or falls in proportion. There is seldom a problem incorporating sales revenues into a decision. More revenue is virtually always better than less revenue.

Costs, on the other hand, frequently give rise to confusion, and the way they are reported may lead to incorrect decision making. The principle problem is that, typically, organizations use full cost as their way of reporting accounting information. The financial accounts tend not to split costs on the basis of behaviour (fixed vs. variable); instead, costs are

Exhibit 10.1: Standard Cost at Gery's Gelati

Gery's Gelati makes ice cream. The budget for each 100-litre batch is as follows:

		100 litres	per litre
Raw material:			
Dairy products	100 litres @ $0.50/litre	$50	$0.50
Flavouring	2 kg @ $20/kg	40	0.40
Additives	1 kg @ $10/kg	10	0.10
		$100	$1.00
Labour	1 hour @ $25	25	0.25
Overhead (2 machine hours @$25/hour)		50	0.50
Standard manufacturing cost		$175	$1.75
Selling and administrative overhead ($50/batch)		50	0.50
Standard cost of goods sold		$225	$2.25
Profit margin		75	0.75
Standard selling price		$300	$3.00

reported functionally (materials, wages, utilities, rent, etc.). Inventories are normally valued at full cost, rather than variable cost.

If full cost accounting data is used in short-term decision making, the effect of the decision will be inaccurately perceived.

For example, in the normal course of events, Gery's Gelati's product is sold to customers for $3 per litre, as shown in Exhibit 10.1. Suppose a new customer offers $2 per litre for a special order of 10,000 litres — would it be worthwhile?

The initial response may be negative. We should look at the reasoning behind the "no" decision.

First, the company may not be prepared to consider any sales at less than its "normal" selling price of $3 per litre. There are frequently good behavioural reasons for such an attitude. This is not, however, an answer that can be supported by short-term economic analysis.

Second, suppose the decision was based on the fact that the standard cost of goods sold is $2.25/litre, and the $2 offer does not cover the full cost. Is "no" still a reasonable answer? To analyze this, we have to know more about the costs included in the $2.25.

It is clear that the ingredients ($1/litre) will be incurred to make the order for the new customer. Likewise, it is probable that the order will require additional labour ($0.25/litre). As a selling price, $1.25 would cover the materials and labour.

Suppose that all the production overhead is fixed cost. As long as there is production capacity to make the additional order, there is no differential cost. The production overhead allocation is, therefore, irrelevant to the decision and should not influence the decision. It can be ignored.

Suppose the selling and administrative overhead ($0.50/litre) is half fixed and half variable. Half ($0.25) is relevant to the decision, and the other half, which is fixed cost, is irrelevant to the decision.

313

So a minimum selling price of $1.50 (materials $1.00, labour $0.25, and variable selling overhead $0.25) is required to cover the differential (or marginal) cost. Any selling price in excess of $1.50 will create additional contribution margin for the firm.

At a selling price of $2, the contribution margin is $0.50/litre. An order for 10,000 litres will add $5,000 to total contribution and to operating income.

The "full cost" reporting system (which is prevalent in organizations) does not reveal the effect of the decision; it merely confuses matters.

With the differential cost information, the decision maker is now in a position to make an informed decision. The answer may still be negative because of other qualitative factors. For example, Gery's may perceive that lowering the cost to this customer would have knock-on effects with other customers, who would also negotiate for lower prices. Or Gery's may consider that additional contribution of $5,000 not to be worth the effort of the additional production. At least Gery's now has all the relevant information to make a rational decision.

10.3 Capacity Issues

One of the keys to Gery's Gelati's decision is the existence of idle capacity. If the additional 10,000 litres cannot be made within the existing capacity, then a decision to sell the 10,000 litres at $2 each would be incorrect. If there is insufficient spare capacity, then either more capacity would have to be added (at an additional cost) or sales to "regular" customers would have to be sacrificed, with an associated loss of contribution margin.

Using unused capacity is, effectively, free. Where there is no unused capacity, then capacity has to be created and this always has a cost.

Consider Gery's Gelati again, but this time assume the company has spare capacity to make only 7,000 litres. Gery's has several choices:

(a) Accept the order for 7,000 of the 10,000 litres requested.
(b) Accept the order for the full 10,000 litres, and reduce sales to regular customers by 3,000 litres.
(c) Accept the order for 10,000 litres, and incur an additional fixed cost of $2,800 to temporarily increase capacity.

Choice (a) will result in additional contribution margin, but not as much as before. Gery's will get $0.50 contribution margin on 7,000 litres, for a total of net $3,500 benefit.

Choice (b) will result in losing the contribution margin on regular sales of 3,000 litres. The regular contribution margin is $1.50 (selling price, variable cost, $3 – $1.50 = $1.50).

3,000 × $1.50 = $4,500

This must be set against the $5,000 of additional contribution margin from the special order. The net effect is an increased contribution margin of $500.

We should also recognize the potential drawback associated with failing to supply the regular customers with the products they normally buy from Gery's. There are few things more expensive in the business world than a dissatisfied customer. Unfortunately, it is very difficult to put an accurate dollar value on dissatisfaction and, for that reason, it is frequently omitted from the calculation.

Choice (c) will result in increased contribution margin of $5,000 from the new order, less the additional capacity cost of $2,800. The net effect is a $2,200 profit increase.

All three alternatives increase profit, so there is a good economic argument for accepting the order, whichever way it is to be satisfied. Of the three, choice (a) is the best since it adds the greatest amount of profit: $3,500.

10.4 Make or Buy

The same type of analysis can be applied to situations calling for a decision to produce something internally, or to sub-contract it to a third party. Once again, the issue is to discover what costs and revenues are differential to the decision. Costs that can be eliminated by sourcing outside are differential costs, and costs that continue are not differential. Once again, the use of full costing in the accounting system is likely to provide misleading information.

Consider Cumberland Sausage Co., which produces food products. All production and service activities are subject to rigorous cost control. Among other things, use of office space in the corporate headquarters is charged out at cost, based on square metres occupied, and corporate overhead is charged to all departments at a rate of $1,000 per full-time employee.

The human resource department has the following budget for 2006:

Salaries and wages (25 employees)	$1,000,000
Fringe benefits (10% × salaries and wages)	100,000
Computer system costs	500,000
Office expense	500,000
Corporate overhead (25 × $1,000)	25,000
Total	$2,125,000

HR Solutions, a specialist human resources agency, has offered to take over the entire HR function for Cumberland Sausage at a cost of $1,800,000 per year.

The initial response might be that this is a good deal. The reported cost will decrease from $2,125,000 to $1,800,000, and savings of $325,000 will result. However, the "full cost" approach has introduced some irrelevant data. The salaries and wages will be eliminated (we assume, otherwise it's never going to be a good idea) as will the fringe benefits and the computer system costs. The office expense, however, which is an allocation of head office occupancy, will probably not change, and the corporate overhead will not change.

Outsourcing will not affect the office expense, and corporate overhead will also stay the same in total, but will now have to be allocated to other parts of the business, increasing the reported costs.

The effect of the outsourcing will be to add $1,800,000 of additional cost, and eliminate $1,600,000 of avoidable costs. The net effect is that Cumberland Sausage Co. will be $200,000 worse off.

10.5 Sunk Costs

One of the costs that is always irrelevant is a sunk cost. A sunk cost is one that has already happened or has been committed, so that it is unavoidable.

Take the computer system costs of $500,000 in the previous Cumberland example. If those are currently incurred costs, such as hardware rental, software licensing, and supplies, then they may be avoidable costs. By sub-contracting the HR department, they could be cancelled.

Alternatively, suppose the computer system was set up two years ago, at which time there was a major acquisition of hardware, and special software was custom written for the Cumberland Sausage applications. The costs are now predominantly amortization of computer hardware and software. Discontinuing the use of the computer will not make these costs go away. They are sunk costs.

Sunk costs are typical when the financial accounting model uses matching to spread a cost incurred in one period to future periods where the use is to continue. Amortization is the most frequently found sunk cost.

10.6 Committed Costs

A committed cost is one that the organization is obliged to incur, even though it has not yet been spent. An example of a committed cost is the rent payable on a lease, or the salary of an employee on a five-year employment contract.

Even though the money has not yet been spent, the obligation to spend it is unavoidable. Such costs may be treated exactly the same way as are sunk costs.

Suppose that the manager of the HR department of Cumberland Sausage Co. is on a two-year employment contract. His salary for the next two years should be added to the unavoidable costs in making the decision of whether or not to outsource the HR function.

10.7 Short-Term vs. Long-Term

The shorter the timespan of the decision, the more likely that the differential cost and revenue will be the appropriate way to make the decision. As timespans get longer, the choices available to the organization become wider, and marginal approach cost will give way to something nearer a full-cost model.

Capacity, for example, may be unused in the short term. If there is spare production capacity today, or this week, there is little or nothing that can be done about it. As time goes by, the company can reduce its spare capacity by replacing machines with smaller ones, or moving to smaller premises when the lease comes up for renewal. In the long term, very few costs are totally unchangeable, and the idea of a truly fixed cost disappears. Perhaps the company will be able to introduce new products that absorb the spare capacity. In the longer term, unused capacity should not exist.

Full costs are the current costs of providing the existing capacity. As the time horizon of the decision gets longer, these costs become more and more relevant, as they become a closer approximation of the long-term differential costs.

The short-term analysis presented earlier implies that every new decision may be made with a price that just covers the variable cost. If that approach is used for all decisions, it will rapidly lead to a disastrous situation where none of the products or services provides enough contribution to pay the fixed costs, let alone any profit.

In the longer term, fixed costs must be covered by contribution from the various activities of the company, and full costs have a role to play in establishing the fair share each product or service must generate.

10.8 Summary

Decisions in general should be based on differential factors: the costs and revenues that change as a result of the decision. Short-term decisions should reflect short-term differential factors, which are very close to being contribution margin analysis (i.e., revenues less variable costs), although other differential factors should also be considered. These would include costs such as special packaging, additional design costs, or reduction in costs resulted from deleting features that are normally part of the product. In the short term, capacity constraints and unused capacity are unalterable; but as the decision horizon becomes longer, it will be possible to raise or lower capacity to deal with capacity constraints and unused capacity. Full costs tend to give inappropriate short-term signals for decisions; but as the decision horizon gets longer, full costs become more appropriate measures of the relevant costs. In the longest term, all costs, fixed and variable, must be covered by revenues, or the organization will fail.

Self-Study Problems

1. Marcia's Millinery makes women's hats. The company has a work-shop in the Toronto garment district. The capacity of the workshop is 1,500 hats per week. Each hat uses $6 of materials and takes 40 minutes to make. The cutters and machinists earn $12 per hour. The fixed expenses total $6,000 per week. The hats are sold to retailers for $30 each, and the retailers sell them to customers for $50 each. In recent months, Marcia's has sold 1,000 hats per week.

   Canadian Tire has decided that it wants to sell women's hats as well as its existing line of hardware products. They have asked Marcia's Millinery to supply 400 hats per week every week for the next year at a price of $18.

   Required
   (a) What are the variable costs per hat, the fixed costs per week and the full cost per hat, the profit per hat, and the contribution margin per hat for Marcia's Millinery's existing trade?
   (b) Should Marcia's accept the offer from Canadian Tire?
   (c) If Canadian Tire wanted Marcia's Millinery to sell the company 1,500 hats per week, what price per hat would be necessary so that Marcia would make the same profit as before?
   (d) If the capacity of Marcia's workshop was 1,000 hats instead of 1,500 hats, how would this affect the decision to accept Canadian Tire's offer of 400 hats at $18?
   (e) What are the qualitative factors in this decision?

Solution

1. (a) Variable cost per hat

Materials	$ 6
Labour ($12 × 40 minutes)	8
Total variable cost per hat	$14
Fixed cost ($6,000 ÷ 1,000 hats)	6
Full cost per hat	$20
Profit per hat	10
Price per hat to retailers	$30
Contribution margin per hat ($30 – $14)	$16

   (b) The price offered by Canadian Tire is $18.

   If Marcia's compares this to the normal selling price of $30, the company would reject the Canadian Tire offer.

   However, the additional cost of making a hat is $14 (i.e., the variable cost), and Marcia's has enough spare capacity to make the additional hats. At a price of $18, Marcia's will make $4 contribution margin per hat.

   Increased contribution margin:

   Per week = $4 × 400 = $1,600

   Per year = $1,600 × 52 weeks
   = $83,200

As there is no increase in the fixed cost, this $83,200 will all be profit.

(c) Existing situation

1,000 hats × $16 contribution margin	$16,000 per week

$16,000 contribution margin ÷ 1,500 hats =	$10.67
Variable cost	14.00
Required price	$24.67

Note: It is not necessary to use the fixed cost in this comparison as it is the same whether the hats are sold to regular customers or to Canadian Tire; it is not a cost that is marginal to the decision.

(d) If the capacity of the workshop is only 1,000 hats, then Marcia's is currently operating at capacity. To sell 400 hats to Canadian Tire at a contribution margin of $4 each means not selling 400 hats to regular customers at a contribution margin of $16 ($30 – $14). Marcia's will be worse off by:

$$= (\$16 - \$4) \times 400 \text{ hats} \times 52 \text{ weeks}$$
$$= \$12 \times 400 \text{ hats} \times 52 \text{ weeks}$$
$$= \$249,600 \text{ per year}$$

(e) Qualitative factors in this decision:
  • Can sales of 1,000 per week to regular customers be maintained for the foreseeable future?
  • Is there any growth in sales likely?
  • What will happen to the reputation of Marcia's Millinery?

Discussion Questions and Problems

Discussion Questions

1. What are the characteristics of a cost that is relevant to a short-term decision?
2. Describe a sunk cost and give two examples.
3. Why is it important to know whether a plant is operating at or below full capacity?
4. What are the qualitative factors that affect the make-or-buy decision?
5. Are direct materials and direct labour always relevant costs for short-term decisions?
6. Why do managers rely on full costs for pricing decisions?
7. Is the cost of raw materials a fixed cost or a variable cost?
8. Is the cost of raw materials a relevant cost or an irrelevant cost?
9. Is amortization of production equipment a fixed cost or a variable cost?
10. Is amortization of production equipment a relevant cost or an irrelevant cost?

Problems

1. Xtreme Co. is planning on adding an additional shift of workers in its production facility. Production would be increased from 500 units per week to 1,000 units per week. Identify each of the following costs as:

    (i) fixed (F), variable (V), or mixed (M)
    (ii) relevant (R) or not relevant (NR) to the additional shift decision

    (a) direct materials
    (b) direct labour
    (c) production overhead
    (d) amortization (calculated on the straight-line basis)
    (e) a production-based royalty of $0.25 per unit
    (f) energy costs of $200 per machine hour to operate production machines
    (g) insurance
    (h) sales commissions, based on units sold

2. For the Xtreme Co. identify each of the following as a sunk cost (S), a committed cost (C), or neither (N):

    (a) direct materials (not yet ordered)
    (b) direct materials (ordered, but not yet delivered)
    (c) direct materials (in inventory)
    (d) next year's payments on a lease for a car
    (e) machine amortization
    (f) sales commissions where sales staff are entitled to a commission of 5% of sales
    (g) an annual bonus payable at the discretion of management
    (h) maintenance payable monthly under a contract

    (i)   maintenance payable at the discretion of management
    (j)   warranty costs on products sold

3.   Federal Financial provides financial advice to its clients on investment, retirement planning, and tax management. Federal has calculated the cost of providing retirement planning at $314 per client,
as follows:

Ho & Robinson's "Personal Financial Planning"	$ 37.00
Photocopying	5.00
Advisor's time: 2 hours @ $50	100.00
Computer simulation fee	15.00
Direct costs	$157.00
Overhead (100% of direct costs)	157.00
Total	$314.00

    The overhead is typical for this type of business and consists of
40% variable costs and 60% fixed costs. In 2004 Federal Financial
advised 250 clients on retirement planning.

    RP Inc., a specialist retirement planning company, has offered to
service all Federal Financial's retirement planning clients.

Required
    (a)   If the offer from RP Inc. is $200 per client, should the offer
be accepted?
    (b)   If the offer from RP Inc. is a $50,000 lump sum, for which
they would advise up to 300 clients, should the offer be accepted?

4.   Steeples Inc. makes office hardware, such as desks and file cabinets.
The income statement for 2004 was as follows:

Sales revenues (20,000 units)		$6,000,000
Direct materials	$1,500,000	
Direct labour	750,000	
Production overhead	1,250,000	3,500,000
Gross margin		$2,500,000
Selling & distribution	$ 900,000	
Administration	600,000	1,500,000
Operating income		$1,000,000

    Production overhead is estimated to be 50% variable and 50%
fixed. Selling & Distribution expense includes $200,000 variable
expense, and the remainder is fixed. All the administrative expense
is fixed.

Required
Calculate:
    (a)   the variable cost per unit manufactured
    (b)   the variable cost per unit sold
    (c)   the full cost per unit manufactured
    (d)   the full cost per unit sold
    (e)   the minimum price at which a unit could be sold, while cover-
ing its marginal cost

    (f)   the minimum price at which a unit can be sold, while covering its full cost

    (g)   the minimum price at which the products can be sold so that operating income is $200,000

5.   Basra Supply Inc. has asked Steeples to supply 10,000 office desks at a price of $170 each, for export to Iraq. There would be no variable selling and distribution cost incurred.

Required

Given the information provided in Problem #4:

    (a)   Should Steeples accept the order if there is adequate capacity to make the additional units?

    (b)   Should Steeples accept the order if there is no spare capacity to make any of the additional units?

    (c)   Should Steeples accept the order if there is adequate capacity to make 9,000 of the additional units, but the remaining 1,000 units would have to come from reductions in sales to regular customers?

6.   The Famous Fish Farm breeds salmon and trout for sale to supermarkets across Canada. The company has prepared the following product cost analysis for 2005:

	Salmon	Trout	Total
Kg shipped	100,000	150,000	250,000
Sales revenue	$200,000	$225,000	$425,000
Costs:			
Fish feed	$ 50,000	$ 75,000	$125,000
Labour	25,000	37,500	62,500
Distribution costs	30,000	45,000	75,000
Maintenance	6,000	9,000	15,000
Amortization	10,000	15,000	25,000
Administration	30,000	45,000	75,000
Total costs	$151,000	$226,500	$377,500
Operating income	$ 49,000	$ (1,500)	$ 47,500

    It has been suggested that the trout product should be discontinued, as it is making a loss.

    All costs have been allocated to the two product lines on the basis of kg of fish shipped. Fish feed, labour, and half of the distribution costs are variable costs; all the remaining costs are fixed, and none of them would be eliminated if trout were discontinued.

Required

Do you agree with the suggestion to discontinue the trout? (Calculate how much the net income would be after making that decision.)

7.   In order to improve performance, it has been suggested that Famous Fish Farm should outsource the maintenance to a local engineering company. The engineering company has quoted $12,000 as an

annual maintenance fee. If that were to be done, the existing part-time maintenance employee (salary cost: $8,000 per year) would be let go, and maintenance supplies of $2,000 would be avoided. Famous Fish Farms would still have to pay $5,000 per year on a maintenance contract for its computer system.

Required
(a)   Should the maintenance be outsourced?
(b)   What qualitative factors should be considered?

8.   The 2005 product cost analysis for the Famous Fish Farm shown in Problem #6 has been done with all costs allocated to the two product lines on the basis of kg of fish shipped. Fish feed, labour, and half of the distribution costs are variable costs, and all the remaining costs are fixed. The current set-up has the capacity to grow 500,000 kg of fish per year.

It has been suggested that the company should add a third fish, koi, to their product line. The estimates show that 150,000 kg of koi can be shipped each year, at a selling price of $1.5 per kg. Variable costs would be the same rate as for salmon or trout.

Required
(a)   Should the koi be added?
(b)   Show how the income statement would appear if the koi product line were to be added.

9.   Turner Inc. sells three products: meat, fish, and cheese. Turner has prepared the following departmental income statement for year 2005:

$ '000	Meat	Fish	Cheese	Total
Sales revenue	$700	$200	$1,800	$2,700
Cost of goods sold	350	140	1,000	1,490
Gross margin	$350	$ 60	$ 800	$1,210
Direct fixed expenses	100	70	300	470
Departmental operating income	$250	$(10)	$ 500	$ 740
Common fixed expenses				340
Operating income				$ 400

The cost of goods sold is all variable expense. The direct fixed expenses consist of the amortization of specialized refrigeration equipment used in each department. None of this equipment could be sold by itself. The common fixed expenses represent expense that cannot be traced to any one department.

It has been suggested that the fish department be closed, as it is losing money.

Required
(a)   Do you agree with the proposal to drop the fish department? (Hint: calculate the profit that would remain after dropping the fish department.)

(b) Assume that 25% of sales in the meat department would be lost if the fish department were closed. Calculate the effect of dropping the fish department.

(c) Assume that all fish sales would be transferred to meat sales if the fish department were dropped. Calculate the effect of dropping the fish department.

10. Horatio Co. makes farm machinery. The company has always manufactured the hydraulic control units itself. The standard cost of a typical two-lever hydraulic control unit is $73.00, made up as follows:

Direct material:		
Aluminum casing	$10.00	
Neoprene bushings	3.00	
	$13.00	
Direct labour	5.00	(15 minutes @ $20 per labour hour)
Variable overhead	25.00	(30 minutes @ $50 per machine hour)
Fixed overhead	30.00	(30 minutes @ $60 per machine hour)
Total	$73.00	

Horatio used 2,000 hydraulic control levers in 2005.

The Mainland Mache Co. imports hydraulic control levers from the Far East and is anxious to get a contract to supply Horatio Co. The Mainland Mache Co. has quoted a price of $50.00 per unit.

Required

Should Horatio accept the offer from Mainland Machine Co.?

Sources
of Capital

11

Learning
Objectives

After studying this chapter, you should be able to describe the role of the following in raising capital:
→ Common shares
→ Dividends and retained earnings
→ Preferred shares
→ Equity capital
→ Debt and interest
→ Assessing risk through the interest cover ratio
→ The effect of financial leverage

11.1 Introduction

A business may be thought of as two separate, but related, decision activities: raising capital and investing capital.

Investing capital in short-term assets is dealt with earlier (in Chapters 4 and 5) under working capital management (how much inventory to carry, how much credit to allow our customers, how much credit to get from our suppliers, how much cash liquidity to keep on hand, etc.). Investing capital in long-term assets is dealt with in the next chapter by capital budgeting techniques (net present value, accounting rate of return, payback, etc.).

In this chapter, we shall discuss the other part of the equation: the sources of capital, deciding how much capital to raise and from where. The sources of capital will be discussed under the following headings: common shares, retained earnings, preferred shares, equity capital, and debt. We shall also include a discussion of the cost of capital and the effect of leverage.

11.2 Common Shares

A business that is just starting up has no capital until the owners put some in. The double entry principle tells us that for every investment in an asset, there must have been a source of capital of the same value. All organizations will have some capital provided by the owners to get the company going.

In a sole proprietorship, this is *owner's equity*.

In a partnership, this is *owners' equity* (note the apostrophe has moved, indicating there are multiple owners in a partnership).

In a corporation (a limited liability company), this is *common stock* (otherwise known as common shares or ordinary shares). We shall concentrate on corporations, as they are the most important type of business structure.

In the simplest situations, this initial investment is all the share-related activity that happens, and it remains unchanged from one balance sheet to the next over the life of the company. All companies have at least one common share class in issue. Most situations, however, are more complex.

The initial investment is an exchange process: the investor gives something of value to the business (typically cash, though it could equally well be business assets); in return, the company gives the investor a share certificate.

The bookkeeping entry shows the cash received being added to the cash balance in the company, and the common shares account credited with an equal dollar amount. This preserves the balance sheet equation. Where the shares are issued in exchange for non-cash assets, the fair market value of the assets is recorded, and that same dollar amount is credited to the common shares account. Share certificates are then issued to the contributors.

The share certificate is an acknowledgement that the investor owns, literally, a share in the business. If there is only one share issued, then the owner of that share owns 100% of the company. If there are two shares, each owns 50%. With 100 shares, each owns 1%; with one million shares, each share represents a one-millionth part of the ownership in the company. The more shares there are, the less the proportion of the company each share owns.

Common shareholders are said to have a residual interest in the company. That means they own everything left over after all the other claims have been met. In the normal course of events, where a company is a continuing entity, that really does not mean a lot. However, when a company is wound up (officially terminated), that residual status may make a very big difference. If the company is wound up because it has failed, it generally means that the common shareholders will get nothing. In other situations, where assets are in excess of liabilities, closing the company may mean a large surplus that would be paid out to common shareholders.

The nature of the residual interest makes common shares a relatively high-risk investment for shareholders and, by counter argument, a relatively low-risk source of capital for the company.

11.2.1 Net Income and Dividends

The residual interest concept applies to winding up situations; it also applies to the ongoing activities during the normal operation of the company. When a company generates sales revenue, its first obligation is to pay the costs and expenses that were incurred. What is left over is net income, which is beneficially owned by the shareholders. They do not always get their hands on it, however, due to the existence of dividend policies, which are largely under the control of the board of directors.

Companies are owned by their shareholders, but they are frequently run by others. In smaller (typically family-owned) businesses, the shareholders may be the directors. In larger companies, particularly ones where the shares are publicly traded on a stock exchange, the directors are elected by the shareholders to manage the company on their behalf, but the shareholders themselves play no part in the day-to-day management of the company. This is only practical. Imagine what would happen if shareholders in Ford Motor Company of Canada, Ltd. felt that they could dabble directly in the active management of the company: it would be chaos.

When a company makes a net income, the directors of the company must make a decision about what to do with it. Their choices are to pay the net income to the shareholders as a dividend; to retain the net income in the company for reinvestment; or to pay some as dividend, and retain the rest for reinvestment.

Many shareholders (though not all) will want to maximize the amount of their dividend from the company whose shares they hold. The quicker they get their money, the sooner they are able to spend it, or reinvest it in another company. Most company directors (and some shareholders), by contrast, will want to minimize the amount of the dividend. The smaller the dividend, the more there is to reinvest in the company, and the larger the company will grow. There is thus a conflict of interest between the two. The result is often the payment of a compromise dividend that is part of the net income, but not all of it.

The process is that both directors and shareholders have to be in agreement that a dividend should be paid. The shareholders cannot initiate a dividend payment; the proposal can only come from the directors. Thus, if the directors feel that there is not enough liquidity to pay a dividend (or for any other reason), merely by not acting, they can ensure that there will be no dividend. If, and only if, the directors propose a dividend, the shareholders still have to approve the proposal before the dividend becomes legally payable. If the shareholders vote the proposal down, the directors cannot force it, and no dividend is paid.

How much dividend is being paid out can be measured through the dividend cover ratio:

$$\text{Dividend cover ratio} = \text{net income} \div \text{dividend}$$

A company that makes $5 million in net income and pays a total dividend of $1 million has a dividend cover ratio of 5.

In theory, the amount of the dividend should not matter. One dollar earned as net income makes the common shareholders $1 richer. If it is paid out as dividend, they have the $1 in their hands and they can use their increase in wealth in whatever way they wish. One dollar earned as net income that is then ploughed back into the company means that their share certificates now represent a share of a company that has $1 more assets than it had before. In a just and proper world, the market price of the shares should rise by exactly $1 to reflect this. Sadly, we live in a naughty world, and it does not always work out exactly as the theory tells us it should. In general, though, the theory is fairly robust, and reduced dividends are largely reflected in increased share prices. Share price increases are frequently referred to as "capital growth".

11.2.2 *Stock Splits and Stock Dividends*

A company that does well, making substantial profits, will find its share price increase over time. The lower the dividend payout, the greater this growth is likely to be. While this is a benefit to the shareholder, it may result in an unmanageably high share price. If the price of an individual share gets to be too high, buying the shares may be beyond the resources of some small investors. Stock splits alleviate this problem. (See Exhibit 11.1.)

In a stock split, the total value of the company remains unchanged, as does the balance sheet value of the common shares. The number of common shares, however, is increased.

The value of each individual share should fall in proportion to the rate of the split.

A company that wishes to pay a dividend, but has insufficient liquidity to pay the dividend in cash, may pay a stock dividend.

In a stock dividend, additional shares are allocated to existing shareholders. If the shareholders so wish, they can sell these in the stock market, turning their stock dividend into a cash dividend.

From the company perspective, this is very similar to a stock split. The one difference is that in a stock dividend, the market value of the new shares issued is deducted from retained earnings and added to common stock. Because both accounts are part of equity, there is no effect on the rest of the balance sheet, but now some of the retained

---

Exhibit 11.1: Stock Splits and Stock Dividends

P. Bunyan Inc.
Balance Sheet as at December 31, 2005

Assets		Equity	
Various assets	$100,000	100 common shares of $500 each	$ 50,000
		Retained earnings	50,000
	$100,000		$100,000

(a) After a 5-for-1 stock split, the balance sheet would be:

Assets		Equity	
Various assets	$100,000	500 common shares of $100 each	$ 50,000
		Retained earnings	50,000
	$100,000		$100,000

(b) After a 20% stock dividend, the balance sheet would be:

Assets		Equity	
Various Assets	$100,000	120 common shares of $500 each	$ 60,000
		Retained earnings	40,000
	$100,000		$100,000

earnings (which is a distributable reserve) has been reclassified as (non-distributable) common shares. Neither stock splits nor stock dividends change the amount or types of assets.

11.2.3 *Rights of Common Shareholders*

Common shareholders have the following rights:

- To be informed about the company financial performance by being given copies of the annual financial statements.
- To attend annual general meetings and to vote on important issues, including the appointment of the auditor, the approval of dividends proposed by the directors, and the acceptance of the financial statements.
- To receive dividends, when approved, on an equal footing with all other common shareholders.
- To receive the net proceeds of winding up the company, on an equal footing with other common shareholders.
- Limited liability: if the company goes into bankruptcy, the shareholders are not required to contribute to the shortfall, except to the extent of their investment in the company's shares.

11.3 Retained Earnings

The payment, or non-payment, of dividends needs to be reflected in the financial records and reports.

The company that always pays out 100% of its net income as dividend will maintain its common equity at the same level (as long as there are no increases or decreases in the number of shares themselves). All other things being equal, the company will stay the same size.

The company that pays out less than 100% of its net income as dividend will grow. The amount ploughed back will be invested in new assets, and total company assets will increase. This is reflected in the financial statements by the creation of a new heading called retained earnings in the equity section of the balance sheet. Retained earnings are profits made by the company, but not distributed as dividends to shareholders.

Over time, the retained earnings can become a very large amount. They often exceed the recorded amounts of the common equity. Canadian Tire, for example, had, at the end of December 2005, $704 million in share capital and $1,813 million in retained earnings.

Where retained earnings are significant, the market value of the common shares is likely to be much higher than the amount originally contributed to the company for the shares.

11.4 Preferred Shares

A preferred share is a share that has some preferential right attached to it. Typically, this is a right to receive a dividend before the common shareholders. A $1, 8% preferred share, for example, is entitled to receive

8% of its nominal value ($1) in dividend (i.e., eight cents). Only when this preferred dividend has been paid can common shareholders receive any dividend.

Preferred shares are a way of reducing the risk for investors. If, however, the risk is a finite amount, by reducing the risk for preferred shareholders, the risk level of the common shares is increased.

From a legal perspective, preferred shareholders are still part owners of the company. In the same way that common shareholders cannot force the directors to pay them a dividend, preferred shareholders cannot force their dividend to be paid to them. Like common shares, then, preferred shares represent a low-risk way of financing the company.

There are many variations on the theme of preferred shares. The more important ones are listed below:

- *Redeemable:* a redeemable preferred share is required or allowed to be repaid at some future time. To be redeemable, a preferred share has to have a nominal value: a stated cash amount at which it will be redeemed. Common shares, by contrast, are never redeemable.
- *Convertible:* a convertible preferred share is one that is allowed or required to be exchanged for common shares at some future time, and at a stated rate of conversion.
- *Cumulative:* a cumulative preferred share is one that allows unpaid preferred dividends to accumulate, and only after all arrears of preferred dividends are paid can common shareholders get any dividend.
- *Participating:* a participating preferred share is one that enjoys the regular dividend preference at a set rate, and is also entitled to a further dividend on a par with the dividend paid out to common shareholders.
- *Capital preference:* in the event of the winding up of the company, a preferred share may carry the right to repayment of its nominal amount before the common shareholders get anything.
- *Voting preference:* some preferred shares carry a right to outvote common shares in company meetings, though this feature is rare and is frowned on by most stock exchanges.

Preferred share capital has its own heading within the equity section of the balance sheet.

11.5 Equity Capital

The three categories discussed so far (common shares, retained earnings, and preferred shares) are the main items found in the equity section of the balance sheet. In order, preferred shares will generally be listed first, followed by common shares, followed by retained earnings.

Other categories that may be encountered, but that are less important, include the following:

- *Contributed surplus:* this is the excess amount received for shares over their nominal value. Current practice is to issue common shares without a nominal value (no par value shares), so this heading is not very important, except to accountants.

- *Foreign exchange adjustments:* some of the wilder results of translating numbers originally expressed in foreign currencies are recorded in this heading.

In general, equity represents a pool of capital with two important features:

- First, it does not have to be repaid (with the exception of redeemable preferred shares). This means that it is low risk for the company. There is never a threat to the liquidity situation from having to repay the capital.
- Second, it is rewarded through the payment of dividends, and dividends do not have to be paid if the directors are against them. Again, this is a low risk for the company.

Both features are in stark contrast with the nature of debt, which is discussed later.

11.5.1 *Cost of Equity*

Equity has a cost to the company, though it is sometimes difficult to see.

Investors have expectations about investing in the company. If they do not receive a reward of some type, then they will not want to continue as investors and they will sell their shares.

The company's profits are the source of investors rewards: they can be paid to the investor as they are earned in the form of a dividend, or the earnings can be ploughed back into the company as retained earnings. If some or all of the profits are retained by the company, we expect the share price to increase, as it has more assets than it had previously.

The return to the shareholders is, therefore, a combination of dividends received and growth in share price. (See example in Exhibit 11.2.)

Exhibit 11.2: Dividend and Cost of Equity

Market value of shares at start of 2008	$100,000
Net income for 2008	$ 20,000
Shareholders expected return on equity	20%

1. If a dividend of $20,000 is paid, the shareholders will get a return of 20% ($20,000 ÷ $100,000 = 20%).
2. If the profit is ploughed back into the company, then assets are greater by $20,000, so market value should increase from $100,000 to $120,000.

    The shareholder has gained $20,000, but this is because the market value of the has increased. ($20,000 ÷ $100,000 = 20% return on equity)
3. The company could also pay a dividend that is less than $20,000. The result would be a smaller rise in the market value of the shares, but the shareholders' return would still total 20%.

The shareholders' expected return and the cost of equity to the company are mirror images of each other.

11.6 Debt

A company that wants to invest in assets can choose to raise money through selling shares, and/or by ploughing back retained earnings. It can also choose to borrow (i.e., debt). Shares represent an ownership relationship between the shareholder and the company. Debt is a creditor relationship, which is very different. Debt has an interest obligation and a repayment obligation, and so it is much riskier for the company.

There are several features of debt that need to be described, and we shall do that under these headings: Level, Interest, Repayment, and Security.

11.6.1 Level

The level of debt is commonly expressed as a ratio. (See Exhibit 11.3.) This may be the ratio of debt to equity, or the ratio of debt to total assets:

Debt-to-equity ratio: $\dfrac{\text{total debt}}{\text{total equity}} \times 100\%$

Debt-to-assets ratio: $\dfrac{\text{total debt}}{\text{total assets}} \times 100\%$

From the accounting equation we know that the total debt and the total equity add up to the total assets, so these two are not really differ-

---

Exhibit 11.3: Debt Ratios

Creative Consultants Inc. has total assets of $900,000. Current liabilities are $100,000; long-term liabilities are $200,000; equity consists of common shares of $50,000 and retained earnings of $550,000.

Debt-to-equity ratio: $\dfrac{(\$100,000 + \$200,000)}{(\$550,000 + \$50,000)} \times 100\% = 50\%$

Debt-to-assets ratio: $\dfrac{(\$100,000 + \$200,000)}{(\$900,000)} \times 100\% = 33.33\%$

These could also be expressed as there being $0.50 of debt for every $1 of equity (debt-to-equity ratio of 50%), or there being $0.33 of debt for every $1 of assets (debt-to-assets ratio of 33.33%).

---

ent ratios, just a different way of expressing the same idea. The debt-to-equity ratio is potentially infinitely large; the debt-to-assets ratio cannot exceed 100% (apart from very unusual circumstances where the equity is negative).

The higher the level of debt, the greater the risk of default. Generally speaking, debt-to-equity ratios of more than 100% are regarded as excessive. Likewise, debt-to-asset ratios of more than 50% are regarded as excessive.

11.6.2 *Interest*

When a company borrows, there is a contractual relationship that provides for, among other things, interest payments. The interest is normally expressed as an annual percentage rate on the amount outstanding. Thus, a 10% bank loan carries interest at 10% of whatever the loan balance is.

The company is required to pay this interest, whether or not it has sufficient profit, and whether or not it has sufficient liquidity. The company is, therefore, exposed. This makes debt a high-risk source of capital for the company, but a low-risk investment for the lender.

The company's ability to service its debt interest is measured by the interest cover ratio (also known as times interest earned ratio):

$$\frac{\text{operating income (income before taxes and interest)}}{\text{interest expense}}$$

A company with an operating income of $11 million, interest of $2 million, and taxes of $5 million will have net income after tax and interest of $4 million. The interest cover ratio will be 5.5:

$$\frac{\$11,000,000}{\$2,000,000} = 5.5$$

The smaller this ratio, the higher the risk that interest cannot be paid.

An additional feature of debt interest is that it is a tax-allowable expense, unlike a dividend. When $1 of interest is paid, the taxable net income falls by $1, too. The effect is that the after-tax interest rate is less than the nominal rate, by the amount of the tax rate.

After-tax interest rate = nominal interest rate × (1 – tax rate)

If the nominal interest rate is 10%, and the marginal tax rate is 40%, then the after-tax interest rate is 6% — the after-tax cost of debt.

11.6.3 *Repayment*

All debt has to be repaid eventually. The terms of the contract will show whether it has to be repaid sooner, or repaid later. Debt that is to be repaid within one year is recorded in the current liabilities section of the balance sheet. Debt that is to be repaid after one year is classified as long-term debt and is shown as a long-term liability.

Repayment may be at a fixed future date (e.g., debt borrowed in 2005, repayable in 2015). Repayment may be over an extended period (e.g., debt borrowed in 2005, repayable in equal annual instalments from 2015 to 2020).

Whatever the date of repayment, it may come at an inconvenient time, when corporate liquidity is low. Repayment obligations are a risk to the company.

11.6.4 Security

The good name of the borrowing company is always important in lending situations. Having a good reputation for paying interest on time and repaying debt when due improves access to further borrowing. A poor reputation for meeting loan obligations can make borrowing virtually impossible. In some situations the lender will reduce risk exposure by taking a legal charge against some assets of the company.

This is common in the case of families or individuals buying a house. The house itself is the security for the loan. In fact, mortgagors limit their risk further by lending (typically) 75% or less of the house's value. If the mortgagee defaults, the house may be seized and sold to pay off the debt.

Companies may be subject to similar terms. A loan may be advanced, secured on specific assets (e.g., the inventory). If there is default, the pledged assets may be seized and sold to pay the debt. This reduces the risk for the lender.

11.6.5 Reporting

When the debt is recorded in the balance sheet, it is required that the interest rate, the repayment terms, and any security be disclosed, too. Frequently there are so many different debt issues with different terms that the disclosure has to take place in the "notes to the accounts", rather than in the balance sheet itself.

11.7 Debt, Risk, and Financial Leverage

From the perspective of the providers of capital:

1. Equity capital earns a return, which is in the form of dividends or growth in the market value of shares.
2. Debt has a return, which is in the form of interest received.

From the perspective of the company we see the mirror image of these costs:

1. Equity capital has a cost to the company represented by shareholder's expectations of a return.
2. Debt has a cost to the company represented by interest paid. Because interest is a "tax allowable" expense, its net cost is the gross amount of interest less the tax savings it causes.

Taken together the cost of equity and the cost of debt are the cost of capital of the company.

If the company is financed wholly by equity, the cost equity is the company's cost of capital.

If the company is financed wholly by debt, the cost of interest (net of tax) is the company's cost of capital.

If the company is financed partly by equity and partly by debt, then its cost of capital will be a weighted average of the cost of equity and the cost of debt, weighted according to their relative proportions on the balance sheet. This is called the *weighted average cost of capital*.

Because of the terms relating to interest, repayment, and security, debt is low risk for the lender. However, it is for the same reasons that debt is a relatively high-risk source of capital for the company.

Because it is low risk, lenders will have modest expectations about return. They will charge a relatively low interest rate. Thus, it should be cheaper for companies to borrow money than to get additional investors to buy shares. Additionally, as interest expense is tax allowable, the net cost of debt is again lower.

If a company uses a judicious amount of debt to finance its investments, it can engage in financial leverage. Financial leverage is a way of reducing a company's overall cost of capital and making it more profitable.

A company that is financed entirely by common stock has the cost of common stock as its cost of capital, which is normally a relatively high cost. However, when a company borrows money, as long as the cost of debt is lower than the cost of equity, its cost of capital overall will fall.

> **Example:** Assume that the return required by investors for ABC Co.'s shares is 15%, and interest has a nominal rate of 10%. The marginal tax rate is 40%.

For ABC Co. to be financed entirely by equity, its cost of capital will be 15%. If ABC Co. finances half its assets by borrowing and half from equity, it will have a cost of capital of 10.5%. (See Exhibit 11.4.)

Exhibit 11.4: Weighted Average Cost of Capital (WACC)

Weighted average cost of capital is an average expected return on all of a company's capital. It is calculated by weighting each source of capital proportionately. The WACC for ABC Co. is as follows:

Source	Rate with tax effect	After-tax rate		Proportion		Weighted average
Debt	$10\% \times (1 - 0.4) =$	6%	×	50%	=	3.0%
Equity	15%	15%	×	50%	=	7.5%
Total				100%		10.5%

Also, a company that can reduce its cost of capital will increase its earnings per share and thereby increase the share price.

Suppose ABC Co.'s operating income is $50, and the company is financed entirely from equity. Its shares, therefore, will be worth $200:

Operating income	$ 50
Interest	0
Taxes (40%)	(20)
Net income	$ 30
Required return on equity	15%
Value of equity ($30 ÷ 15%)	$200

If ABC Co. were to borrow $100 at an interest cost of 10% and use it to repay $100 of its equity, its return on equity would increase:

Operating income	$ 50
Interest ($100 × 10%)	10
Taxable income	$ 40
Taxes (40%)	(16)
Net income	$ 24
Value of equity: less repaid ($200 – $100)	$100
Return on equity [($24 ÷ $100) × 100%]	24%

By moving from 100% equity to 50% debt and 50% equity, ABC Co.'s weighted average cost of capital reduces from 15% to 10.5%. Its common shareholders are also better off because their returns increase (from 15% to 24%).

It appears that it would be beneficial for ABC Co. to move even further along the same path. The company would perhaps like to finance itself entirely by debt, at a net cost of 6%.

Unfortunately, that reasoning is flawed. By the time 100% of the company is financed by debt, all the risk of the company would have been transferred from the shareholders to the debt holders. Beyond a certain point of "reasonable" levels of debt, the 10% rate of interest will no longer apply. Realizing how risky their situation has become, lenders will demand higher interest rates, which erodes the benefit of extreme leverage.

What is a reasonable level of debt is a judgment call, and it varies from one industry to another. Measurement of the situation is done through the debt ratio, or the debt-to-equity ratio. Typically, debt ratios greater than 50% (which is equivalent to a debt-to-equity ratio of 100%) are regarded as the limit for prudent investors.

Borrowing, instead of using all equity to finance a company, increases the earnings for the common shareholders, but also increases their volatility. Exhibit 11.5 shows what happens to retained earnings when operating earnings fluctuate.

Take operating earnings of $50 as a base case, and increase them by 10% or decrease them by 10%, for a company entirely financed by equity. The results would be what appear in Exhibit 11.5, (1).

Exhibit 11.5: Impact on Retained Earnings Using Borrowing to Finance

(1) Through Equity Alone

| | | Change in Operating Earnings | |
| | | Good | Bad |
Results	Base	(+10%)	(−10%)
Operation earnings	$ 50	$ 55	$ 45
Interest	nil	nil	nil
Taxes (40%)	(20)	(22)	(18)
Net income	$ 30	$ 33	$ 27
Shareholders' equity	$200	$200	$200
Return on equity (ROE)	15.0%	16.5%	13.5%
Increase/Decrease of ROE from Base		+10%	−10%

(2) Using Borrowing and Equity to Finance

| | | Change in Operating Earnings | |
| | | Good | Bad |
	Base	(+10%)	(−10%)
Operation earnings	$ 50	$ 55	$ 45
Interest	(10)	(10)	(10)
Taxable income	$ 40	$ 45	$ 35
Taxes (40%)	(16)	(18)	(14)
Net income	$ 24	$ 27	$ 21
Shareholders' equity	$100	$100	$100
Return on equity (ROE)	24%	27%	21%
Increase/Decrease of ROE from Base		+12.5%	−12.5%

A 10% change, up or down, in operating income results in the same 10% change in the return on equity. If the required return on equity is 15%, then the $200 value of the shares would increase or decrease to reflect this. The market price of the shares increases from $200 to $220 ($33 ÷ 0.15), or decreases from $200 to $180 ($27 ÷ 0.15), thus restoring the 15% return for shareholders.

Now look at what happens if the company is financed half from equity and half from debt. Interest of $10 (10% of $100) has to be paid in each case as is shown in Exhibit 11.5, (2).

A same 10% change in operating income has been translated into a much larger gain or loss in return on equity. A 10% increase results in a 12.5% increase in the return on equity (from 24% to 27%), while a 10% decrease brings a 12.5% loss to the return on equity (from 24% to 21%). The debt has levered the return, making not only net income higher, but also the ROE more variable.

11.8 Summary

In capital structure, there is a fundamental choice between debt and equity financing. Equity is lower risk, but higher cost; debt is higher risk, but lower cost. A reasonable level of debt will minimize the cost of capital, as this will make the company more profitable for the equity shareholders. At extremely high levels of debt, there is a risk of bankruptcy, so high levels of debt are to be avoided. Minimizing the cost of capital is important, as we shall see in the next chapter: it is a constraint on what projects the company can invest in.

Appendix 11.1
Risk and Return

Students coming to this subject for the first time often find that the question of where the rates of return on shares and debt come from is problematic. Earlier in this chapter, in order to make the topic relatively straightforward, the source of these rates is deliberately glossed over. Statements are made such as "the debt pays 6% interest" or "the required return on equity (shares) is 15%". In this appendix, we discuss the market model. The market model tells us that risk and return have a positively correlated straight-line relationship. Basically, the market sets interest rates.

The market model starts with the idea that return (the benefit an investor gets from holding an investment) is a good thing: all other things being equal, an investor will prefer more return to less return.

Return comes partly in the form of dividends from profit and partly in the form of change in the share price. Where the directors pay only a fraction of the profit as dividends and plough the rest back into the business, it is logical to expect the share price to increase because the reinvestment of profits would make the company bigger. Most investors would also expect share prices to rise because of other factors such as the company's ability to make not just investment decisions but good investment decisions, and the general upward trend of the economy.

When the return is expressed as a percentage of the share price, we get a measure of return on equity. (Note that this is similar to, though not identical with, the return on equity calculated in Chapters 2 and 13, where it is done entirely on the basis of the company's financial statements and does not include any reference to the share price.)

Shareholders' return:

= (dividend received + change in share price)
    ÷ beginning share price

Example: Common shares of the Energen Co. had a market price of $10 each on January 1, 2005. During 2005, the shares paid a dividend of $1. At the end of the year the share price had risen to $10.50.

Shareholders' return:

= ([$1 + ($10.50 – $10.00)] ÷ $10.00) × 100%
= 15%

As the calculation above indicates, the return is independent of the dividend decision. The company profit is either paid now, as dividend, or is reflected in share price increases (which can be rationalized as the expectation of future dividends).

The holder of a common share in Energen Co. has achieved a return of 15% per annum. This would be compared with other available returns to see how well the share had performed relative to the alternative investments available. It would also be used to estimate future returns, on the basis that shares that have performed well in the past are likely to continue to perform well in the future.

If shareholders find or expect this return to be lower than other available returns they will sell their shares in Energen Co. and buy those other investments. The effect of selling pressure will be that the share price of Energen Co. starts to fall. As the share price falls, the expected future return increases. Eventually the expected future return will become the same as that of any comparable alternative investment, and there will no longer be any need to sell the shares. At that point selling pressure will cease and the share price will stabilize at the new, lower level.

On the other hand, if investors see that Energen's share is expected to yield a higher return than other investments, they will try to buy its shares. This will put upward pressure on the share price, and it will rise. As the share price rises, Energen's expected future return will fall. Eventually the price will stabilize where the expected future return is the same as that of any comparable investment.

Thus, the market rules in both situations. It is theoretically impossible for two shares that are alike in every respect to have different share prices. The effect of buying and selling causes share prices to stabilize at a point where equivalent investments produce equivalent returns, all other things being equal.

However elegant this theory is, there are a number of ways in which its practical application makes it somewhat less tidy.

In the first place, we are talking about expected future returns. Predicting the future is an uncertain process. The greater the uncertainty, the more divergent individual investors' expectations will be. Different expectations lead to different buying and selling decisions.

Second, it is not easy to find shares that are exact equivalents of each other. Two different companies will always have some features that are unique. To make the market model work effectively, we would, at the very least, need a way of reflecting the most basic of these differences: the level of risk of each company.

Third, not all investors are created equal. Some are tax-exempt on their earnings (charities, for example). Most individual investors pay different rates of tax on the return that is received as dividend and the return that is received due to an increase in the share price. Investors are, therefore, not indifferent to whether they receive their return as dividends, or as capital growth. Also, different investors have different attitudes toward risk. While most investors are risk averse, some are "risk prone": they actually like to gamble.

Because of these (and other) differences, there is a lot of uncertainty about the whole investing process, particularly in investing in the shares of companies. As we shall see, there are some investments that are less uncertain, but they tend to give a lower return.

One of the underlying ideas of finance is that the market is efficient. Efficiency in respect of shares implies that the share price at any given point in time accurately represents the available information about that share. If this is true, then it is impossible to beat the market. However, investors constantly strive to beat the market, so they buy and sell shares in pursuit of improved returns. Logically, investors can only be doing so because they believe the market is inefficient. Ironically, it is this investor buying and selling pressure that makes the market efficient. The market is, therefore, efficient because investors do not believe that selfsame efficiency.

An important feature of company shares is that they are risky. The common usage of the term *risk* is entirely negative. We would talk about the risk of losing our job, or the risk of becoming ill. We would not, normally, talk about the risk of winning Lotto 6/49.

In finance, risk generally includes upside risk as well as downside risk. Risk is perceived as something to be avoided. All other things being equal, investors would prefer less risk to more risk. Once again, the actions of investors in the marketplace, buying and selling shares, reflect this preference.

If, as is suggested, investors are risk averse (and most are), then faced with two investment opportunities with equal returns but different levels of risk, investors will sell the one with the higher risk and use the proceeds to buy the investment with the lower risk. In doing so, they will drive the price of the high-risk share down (increasing its expected future return) and drive the price of the low-risk share up (decreasing its expected future return). Eventually the prices will stabilize at a point where the difference in risk levels is adequately compensated for by the difference in prices, and hence the differences in expected future returns.

At the lowest end of the risk scale, there are some investments that carry virtually no risk. The Government of Canada, for example, is a regular borrower from the financial system. It does so by selling treasury bills (T-bills) to banks and other financial institutions. These are sold by an auction process, with the potential buyers putting in bids for the T-bills. The highest bidders get them. Because they paid the highest prices, the return they get is the lowest return. Once again, the market has determined the return to the investor and the rate of interest that the government has to pay. As of mid-2007, the return on Government of Canada 91-day T-bills is about 4.52%. An average of bonds maturing within the next two years is about 4%, so we could say that the risk-free return is 4%.

At the normal level of risk, there is the market. In the case of Canada, this could be taken as a well-diversified portfolio of the shares listed on the Toronto Stock Exchange. Suppose, for illustration, that this market return is 15%.

We can plot the risk and return of both the risk-free investment and the normal risk investment on a graph with the horizontal axis representing risk and the vertical axis representing return (see Exhibit 11A.1).

Having plotted these two points (the risk-free rate and the return on a normal-risk portfolio), we can join them up with a straight line that represents any combination of risk and return. As long as we assume that the relationship is linear (and that is no more than an assumption), we now have a market line that enables us to rationally price any investment, as long as we know its expected risk level.

Exhibit 11A.1: The Market Model

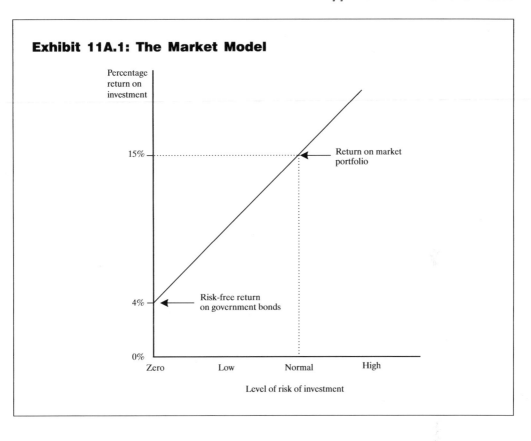

This market line is where we get the returns that are used so blithely in ideas such as the weighted average cost of capital.

The return on a common share that is equally risky as the rest of the market will be the same as the market earns on average. If that return is out of line, investor buying and selling pressure will push it back into line.

The return on a common share that is riskier than the market should earn a higher return, through the same process. The amount of the additional return should depend on the amount of the additional risk.

The return on a common share that is less risky than the market should earn a lower return, through the same process. The amount of the reduction in return should depend on the extent of the reduced risk.

The return on a preferred share, being inherently lower risk to the investor than a common share, should be lower than the return on a similar common share.

The return on borrowed money, being inherently lower risk (for the lender) than that of an equity investment, should always be lower than a return on an equity investment.

The return on a secured investment, such as a mortgage loan, should be lower than the return on an unsecured loan, because it is lower risk.

The government should be able to borrow at the lowest rates as it offers a no-risk investment.

Some rates of return as at mid-2007:

What you can earn:

Government of Canada: 91-day T-bill	4.52%
TD Bank term deposits	3–4%

What you must pay:

TD Bank prime rate	6.25%
Mortgage interest rates (best bank rate for a 5-year fixed mortgage)	5.84%
TD Visa interest rate	19.75%
TD Bank interest on unsecured loan	8.75%
Store-specific credit card	25% to 28%

Self-Study Problems

1. As at January 31, 2002, Bombardier Inc. had assets of $27,753 million. These were represented by the following sources of finance:

	$ million	
Short-term and other borrowings	$15,684	
Long-term debt	7,979	
Total liabilities		$23,663
Shareholders' equity		
Preferred shares (12 million × $25)	$ 300	
Ordinary shares (1,371 million)	896	
Retained earnings	2,894	4,090
Total liabilities and equity		$27,753

Required
(a) What were the ratios of debt to equity and debt to assets?
(b) What is your opinion of the leverage (debt) situation at Bombardier?
(c) The preferred dividend is stated as being a quarterly amount of $0.34375 per share. Calculate the total amount of the preferred dividend for the year.
(d) The total dividend on the common shares was $248 million. How much was the dividend per share?
(e) What was the (total) dividend cover ratio if earnings were $390.9 million?
(f) Total earnings for the year were $390.9 million. What was the earnings per share figure for the common shares? (First deduct the preferred dividend from the earnings, then divide it by the number of common shares.)
(g) Total interest expense was $477 million for the year. Calculate the rate of interest per the dollar amount of the debt and the interest cover ratio. (Operating income was $1,700 million.)

2. The Gearing Co. is financed 30% by debt, carrying an interest rate of 8%, and 70% by equity, which has a cost of 12%. The marginal tax rate is 50%.

Required
What is the weighted average cost of capital?

3. The Bonzer Corporation and the Dinkum Company are the same size: each has $100,000 of assets. They both make $25,000 operating profit and pay income taxes at a rate of 30%. Bonzer is financed entirely by $100,000 of equity. Dinkum is financed 40% by debt, which requires 10% interest, and 60% by equity (i.e., equity = $60,000).

Required
(a) Calculate the return on equity for the two companies.
(b) Suppose earnings in Year 2 fall from $25,000 per year, by 40%, to $15,000 per year. Calculate the return on equity for the two companies in Year 2.

Solution

1. (a) Debt-to-equity ratio:

    $$= (\$23,663 \div \$4,090) \times 100\%$$
    $$= 579\%$$

    Debt-to-assets ratio:

    $$= (\$23,663 \div \$27,753) \times 100\%$$
    $$= 85\%$$

   (b) There is too much debt here. (Debt to equity exceeds 100%; debt to assets exceeds 50%.)

   (c) Total preferred dividend for the year:

    $$= \text{preferred dividend per share} \times \# \text{ of preferred shares}$$
    $$= (\$0.34375 \times 4) \times 12 \text{ million shares}$$
    $$= \$1.375 \text{ per share} \times 12 \text{ million shares}$$
    $$= \$16.5 \text{ million}$$

   (d) Dividend per share:

    $$= \$248 \text{ million} \div 1,371 \text{ million shares}$$
    $$= \$0.18 \text{ per share}$$

   (e) Dividend cover ratio:

    $$= \text{earnings} \div \text{dividend}$$
    $$= \$390.9 \text{ million} \div (\$16.5 \text{ million} + \$248 \text{ million})$$
    $$= 1.48$$

    (That is a low but reasonable cover ratio.)

   (f) Earnings available for common shares:

    $$= (\$390.9 \text{ million} - \$16.5 \text{ million preferred dividend})$$
    $$\div 1,371 \text{ million common shares}$$
    $$= \$374.4 \text{ million} \div 1,371 \text{ million common shares}$$
    $$= \$0.27$$

   (g) Interest rate:

    $$= (\text{interest paid} \div \text{amount of debt}) \times 100\%$$
    $$= (\$477 \text{ million} \div \$23,663 \text{ million}) \times 100\%$$
    $$= 2.02\%$$

    Interest cover ratio:

    $$= \text{operating income} \div \text{interest}$$
    $$= \$1,700 \text{ million} \div \$477 \text{ million}$$
    $$= 3.56$$

2. After-tax cost of debt [$8\% \times (1 - 0.50)$]   4.0%
   Cost of equity   12.0%
   Weighted average cost of capital
       [$(4\% \times 0.3) + (12\% \times 0.7)$]   9.6%

3. (a) **Year 1**

	Bonzer	Dinkum
Operating income	$ 25,000	$25,000
Interest on debt	0	4,000 ($40,000 × 10%)
Taxable income	$ 25,000	$21,000
Taxes @ 30%	7,500	6,300
Net income	$ 17,500	$14,700
Equity capital	$100,000	$60,000
Return on equity	17.5%	24.5%

(b) **Year 2**

	Bonzer	Dinkum
Operating income	$ 15,000	$15,000
Interest on debt	0	4,000 ($40,000 × 10%)
Taxable income	$ 15,000	$11,000
Taxes: @ 30%	(4,500)	(3,300)
Net income	$ 10,500	$ 7,700
Equity capital	$100,000	$60,000
Return on equity	10.5%	12.8%

A 40% decline in operating income causes a 40% decline in the return on equity in Bonzer Corporation.

A 40% decline in operating income causes a 47.76% decline in the return on equity in Dinkum Company because of leverage.

Dinkum shareholders get a higher return, but it is also a riskier investment.

Discussion Questions and Problems

Discussion Questions

1. What are the rights and benefits of owning common shares?
2. What are the features that distinguish preferred shares from common shares?
3. How is debt different from equity? (Answer the question from the perspective of both the borrower and the lender.)
4. Who has control over dividend policy?
5. Explain why retained earnings appear on the balance sheet of most companies.
6. What is the meaning of the interest cover ratio?
7. What is the meaning of the debt-to-equity ratio?
8. What is the leverage effect?
9. How can a lender reduce the risk of default on debt?
10. What are the features of a good leverage policy for a company?

Problems

1. Show the balance sheet of Excalibur Inc. after each of the following transactions:
   (a) K. Arthur invests $500,000 in cash to get the company going: he is issued 100 common shares.
   (b) K. Arthur deeds a shopping mall to Excalibur Inc. The shopping mall has an appraised value of $500,000. K. Arthur is issued 100 common shares.
   (c) 100,000 cumulative, redeemable, convertible 5% preferred shares with a nominal value of $1 each are issued to Mr. L.A. Lot, who pays $100,000 to the company.
   (d) The common shares are split: 1,000 for 1.
   (e) There is a public offering of shares: 100,000 common shares are sold for $6 each.
   (f) Excalibur Inc. buys a commercial property in the Camelot region for $2,000,000: $500,000 is paid in cash and the balance is financed by a mortgage loan from the Merlin Bank. The loan carries an interest rate of 5%, and is for a five-year fixed term.
   (g) The company made a net profit for the year of $250,000.
   (h) The company paid the preferred share dividend.
   (i) The company paid a dividend of $0.50 per share on the common shares.
   (j) The 100,000 preferred shares were converted into 25,000 common shares.

2. Piri Inc. was started up in 2000: it has 100,000 common shares of no par value and 5,000 cumulative 10% preferred shares of $100 each. The company made a net profit of $300,000 per year each year from 2000 through 2004, but did not pay any dividend so far; as a result, prior to paying the 2004 dividend the company had retained earnings of $1,500,000.

In 2004 the company wanted to pay a dividend of $10 per common share. Show the statement of retained earnings for 2004, including all dividend payments.

3. There are 12,800 common shares of Angel Ltd. in issue. Angel Ltd. had net income (after tax and interest) of $320,000 in 2005. Interest expense for 2005 was $128,000, and tax expense was $200,000. A common share dividend of $256,000 was paid.

   Required
   Calculate:
   (a) the interest cover ratio
   (b) the dividend cover ratio
   (c) the earnings per share
   (d) the dividend per share

4. Angel Ltd. had total assets of $4,680,000. These were financed by the following: current liabilities of $1,340,000; long-term debt of $1,000,000; common shares of $256,000; retained earnings of $2,084,000.

   Required
   Calculate:
   (a) the debt-to-assets ratio
   (b) the debt-to-equity ratio
   (c) the risk level of the company

5. Spike Co. has $5 million of secured debt, which carries interest at 7%, and $10 million in common shares, which have a required rate of return of 12%. The company tax rate is 40%.

   Required
   (a) Calculate:
        (i)   the after-tax cost of debt
        (ii)   the debt-to-assets ratio
        (iii) the weighted average cost of capital
   (b) What would be the effect on the weighted average cost of capital of taking out additional borrowings of the following amounts, each at 10% interest?
        (i) $1 million
        (ii) $5 million
        (iii) $10 million
        (iv) $25 million

6. Milton Inc. has made a net income of $500,000. How much dividend should the company pay to the common shareholders?

7. Bill Inc. and Ben Ltd. are both wholesalers of electrical fittings. Each has an operating income of $500,000 in year 2004. Bill Inc., which is financed entirely from common shares, has a total market value of $5,000,000. Ben Ltd. is also worth $5,000,000, but it is financed 40% by common shares, and 60% by long-term debt that

349

carries an interest rate of 5%. The tax rate for both companies is 30%.

Required
(a) Calculate the return on equity for each company.
(b) If, in 2005, the operating income increases by 15%, by what percentage will the return on equity change for each company?
(c) If, in 2005, the operating income falls to $400,000, by what percentage will the return on equity change for each company?

8. Garden Gnomes Inc. has the following financial statements:

Garden Gnomes Inc.
Balance Sheet as at December 31, 2005 ($ millions)

Current assets			Current liabilities		
Cash		$ 60	Trade creditors		$400
Receivables		300	Bank loans		50
Inventory		200			$450
Prepaid		40	Long-term debt		150
		$600			$600
			Equity		
			Common shares	$ 50	
Long-term assets (net)		300	Retained earnings	250	300
Total assets		$900	Total liabilities & equity		$900

Garden Gnomes Inc.
Statement of Retained Earnings
Year to December 31, 2005 ($ millions)

Retained earnings as at January 1, 2005	$150
Net income for 2005	300
	$450
Dividend paid	200
Retained earnings as at December 31, 2005	$250

Required
(a) If there were one million common shares in issue, what was the dividend per share?
(b) What were the dividend payout ratio and the dividend cover ratio for 2005?
(c) What is the maximum dividend that Garden Gnomes Inc. could have legally paid out in 2005?
(d) What is the maximum dividend that Garden Gnomes Inc. could have paid out in 2005 without recourse to additional borrowing?
(e) If Garden Gnomes Inc. wants to invest $100 million in a new plot of agricultural land, how would the company finance it?
(f) Would you, as a bank lending officer, lend Garden Gnomes Inc. $5 million to buy a new office building? If so, under what terms?

(g) Would you, as a bank lending officer, lend Garden Gnomes Inc. $5 million to launch a new weed-killer product the company has developed? If so, under what terms?

9. Given the financial statements shown in Problem #8, answer the following:

   (a) If the common shares of Garden Gnomes Inc. were split six for one, how would the balance sheet change?

   (b) If Garden Gnomes Inc. declared a stock dividend of $250 million, how would the balance sheet change?

   (c) Between a stock split and a stock dividend, which is better?

10. Planters Co. made a net income of $500,000 in 2005. The equity consists of $2,000,000 in common shares and $1,000,000 in 10% preferred shares. The directors recognize that they have to pay the preferred dividend first, but they want to pay a dividend totalling $100,000 to the directors who own half the common shares, and a dividend totalling $50,000 to the outside shareholders who own the other half of the common shares. Can they legally do so? If not, how can they legally achieve their planned distribution?

11. Westbourne Plumbing Supplies has a capital structure that consists of 25% long-term debt, paying 10% interest before tax. The effective corporate tax rate is 20%. The other 75% of the capital are common shares, and their expected return is 24%.

    Required
    Calculate the weighted average cost of capital.

12

Long-Term Decision Making

Learning
Objectives

After studying this chapter you should be able to explain:
→ Why capital budgeting is important to corporate strategy
→ The payback technique
→ The return on investment technique
→ The net present value technique
→ The weighted average cost of capital
→ The role of uncertainty

12.1 Introduction

Long-term decisions are those such as buying new equipment, moving to new premises, and launching new products. These decisions are critically important as they commit the organization to a particular way of doing things over a number of years. Additionally, the long-term decisions tend to involve large amounts of money. Because of these two factors (size of investment and time period), there is a special class of decision-analysis techniques that deal with the assessment of long-term decisions. By making such decisions in a more structured and thoughtful way, we try to avoid committing significant amounts of money to a direction that will not help the organization achieve its long-term objectives.

We can contrast long-term decisions with short-term operating decisions such as hiring a worker or buying raw materials. If a short-term decision is made in error, there is a way of escaping from it. We could sell the unwanted raw materials, or we could terminate the unwanted employee. There would be a cost, but not an unbearably high cost. Those "get out" options are not so easily available for long-term decisions, or are only available at a very high cost. Suppose that, after buying a new plant, the chosen location proved to be grossly inefficient. There may be no alternative use for a specially constructed building and its specialized equipment. If no buyer can be found, its value is worthless.

Long-term decision making is sometimes referred to as the "capital budgeting" decision as it monitors the process through which the capital of the company is budgeted to be spent. There are three main decision-analysis techniques: payback, the return on investment, present value. Each technique has a role to play, but the third (present value) is theoretically rigorous. Ideally, no long-term decision should go ahead without having successfully passed the screen of present value analysis.

The capital investment proposals that a company examines may come from various sources: proposals to replace machinery may come from the production manager; proposals to increase efficiency may come from engineering; new product ideas may come from the marketing department; a proposal to invest in a training facility may come from the human resources department; strategic analysis may result in a proposal to relocate operations to a more favourable site.

It is important that, no matter where the proposal originates, the same standard of care is exercised over the decision, and the same criteria are used to judge whether the proposal is acceptable or not. If not, that same proposal might get a "yes" from one source, and a "no" from another. This would be illogical. So we shall try to develop decision rules that we can apply across the whole organization in an even-handed way.

All proposals must provide the same quality and quantity of information, including, at a minimum, the following:

- a strategic analysis;
- the amount of the investment;
- the effect on revenues, costs, and, hence, profits;
- the effect on cash flows; and
- a consideration of the risk.

12.2 Strategic Analysis

Organizations are purposive: they have objectives, and they act in pursuit of those objectives. Once objectives have been identified, it is necessary to have a strategy to achieve them. Subsequent to setting the strategy, operational activities are initiated to give effect to it. Long-term decisions should be ways of moving that strategy forward. A proposal that does so is worthy of further consideration, and a proposal that militates against the strategy should be rejected.

Consider ExxonMobil Corporation. Suppose it identified "functional and geographic diversity" as a core strength upon which its strategy is based. ExxonMobil is considering a proposal to increase the range of chemical manufacturing in its Australian subsidiary. By doing so it would increase its functional and geographic diversity. The proposal is therefore appropriate to the strategy. It would pass this strategic screening.

Strategy could include ideas such as being a "least cost" manufacturer. For that, strategy proposals that increase production efficiency are appropriate. Strategy could equally well be based on consumer satisfaction through product differentiation. In that case, a proposal that increases the range of products, or their suitability to meeting the needs of customers, would be ideal.

As an aspect of strategic analysis, most companies will assess the ethical dimension of a proposal. Having an ethical position is inevitable, and with increased publicity and scrutiny of their ethics, companies are likely to wish to appear more responsible. Capital projects frequently have strong ethical implications. Assessing whether or not a proposal contravenes ethical standards is part of deciding whether or not to proceed with the analysis.

Let's return to the ExxonMobil example. Thirty-five of the shareholders of ExxonMobil corporation proposed a motion at the 2001 AGM to shift away from fossil fuels and into ecologically friendly fuels. For a variety of reasons, the directors of ExxonMobil urged shareholders to vote against this motion. They can only have made that recommendation after considering the ethics of capitalism, the ethics of the ecological lobby, and the ethical position of the company. In the view of the dissenting shareholders, ExxonMobil may be perceived as having allowed the economic aspects to take precedence over the ethical dimension.

(Of course, an organization that has not clearly identified its strategy and/or its ethics is at a disadvantage when doing any form of strategic analysis. If you don't know where you are going, it really does not matter which bus you catch: they all go there.)

Having passed the strategic analysis, a project should then be judged on its economic consequences for the company. Most proposals (or projects, as they are often called) will call for an investment of a substantial amount of cash at the beginning, and they will generate cash and earnings over a period of years. The key to any decision-analysis technique is that it should measure whether the future returns justify the investment.

In comparing the three main capital budgeting decision-analysis techniques — payback, the return on investment, and present value — we shall see how they would treat a proposal to acquire a patent:

> The investment consists of the cost to the company: $300,000. The patent has six years to run, and the best estimate of the outcome is an increase in revenues of $500,000 per year. Costs will increase by $475,000 per year. These estimated costs consist of materials, wages, and other cash costs totalling $425,000 per year, and amortization of $50,000 per year. At the end of six years, the patent will expire, and it will have no residual value.

For ease of analysis, we shall ignore the fact that there will be some increases in the receivables, the payables, and the inventory, although such changes are likely in reality.

12.3 Payback

The first technique we shall look at is called payback. Payback considers the cash invested in a project and the cash generated by that project. When the cash generated is sufficient to repay the investment, then payback is said to have occurred.

Consider our initial investment of $300,000. Each year, the project's sales revenues are $500,000, and each year the cash expenses total $425,000. Each year the project generates $75,000 in cash. Note that the amortization expense is not relevant to a payback calculation, as it is not represented by a cash flow.

At the end of the first year, $75,000 is generated to pay off the $300,000 investment, so the cumulative cash flow becomes –$225,000. At the end of year two, another $75,000 is paid back, so the cumulative cash flow becomes –$150,000. At the end of year three, another $75,000 is paid back, so the cumulative cash flow becomes –$75,000. At the end of year four, another $75,000 is paid back, so the cumulative cash flow becomes

Exhibit 12.1: Payback

	Year						
	0	**1**	**2**	**3**	**4**	**5**	**6**
Cash flow ('000)	$(300)	$ 75	$ 75	$ 75	$75	$75	$75
Cumulative cash flow	$(300)	$(225)	$(150)	$(75)	nil		

↑
Payback point
(end of Year 4)

nil. At the end of year four the initial investment has been completely recovered and payback is said to have occurred. (See Exhibit 12.1.)

It is a quick and easy calculation, and it has some merit. A project that never achieves payback, for example, is never going to be acceptable. Also, if you are comparing two very similar projects it is probable that the one with the shorter payback is less risky than the one with the longer payback. However, this technique has at least two serious drawbacks.

The first deficiency is that it considers only part of the project's life. Everything that happens after the payback date is ignored. That cannot be right. Suppose you were offered an investment opportunity that cost $300,000 now, and with the following choices of future cash inflows:

- $75,000 per year for years one to four
- $75,000 per year for years one through six
- $75,000 per year forever

Comparison of these alternatives is made easier by deducting years one through four, which are common to all three. After eliminating the first four years, the following cash flows remain:

- nothing
- $75,000 in year five and $75,000 in year six
- $75,000 per year from year five onward, forever

It does not take much imagination to recognize that the third option is preferable to the other two. Yet each of these three situations would be described as having a four-year payback period. Only if we have no preference among them is it logical to have our screening technique regard them all equally, but we do have a preference. (See Exhibit 12.2.)

The second deficiency is that payback ignores the pattern of cash flows. Suppose there are two projects, each with a payback period of two years. The initial investment is $100,000, and the two projects have the following cash inflows:

357

**Exhibit 12.2: Cash Flow
— Which One Would You Rather Have?**

Year

Choice	0	1	2	3	4	5	6	7 to Infinity
1	($300,00)	$75,000	$75,000	$75,000	$75,000			
2	($300,00)	$75,000	$75,000	$75,000	$75,000	$75,000	$75,000	
3	($300,00)	$75,000	$75,000	$75,000	$75,000	$75,000	$75,000	$75,000

↑
Payback point
(end of Year 4)

Payback fails to consider what happens after the investment is repaid!

- Project A: year one, $99,000; year two, $1,000
- Project B: year one, $1,000; year two, $99,000

Most investors would prefer to get their money sooner, rather than later. Project A would be preferred according to that criterion. However, the payback period regards both projects as equally good as each has a two-year payback.

Despite its shortcomings, payback has some popularity among managers, and it is used in a number of organizations. We stress again, though, that it is an imperfect appraisal technique, and it is insufficient, by itself, to judge whether a project is acceptable or not.

12.4 Return on Investment

The second technique we shall examine is return on investment. This is a ratio that should already be familiar to you. It was introduced earlier in this book to show how ratios can be used to assess the overall performance of a company. In that context, the ratio was defined as:

$$ROI = (\text{operating income} \div \text{total assets}) \times 100\%$$

If that is how we are going to judge the company as a whole, then it makes some good sense to apply the same criterion to assessing an individual investment project. After all, what is a company, but a portfolio of interconnected investment projects? If each of them is justified according to return on investment, then the company as a whole will achieve an acceptable return on investment.

Exhibit 12.3: Return on Investment

($ '000)	0	1	2	3	4	5	6
				Year			
Cash flow	(300)	75	75	75	75	75	75
Amortization		50	50	50	50	50	50
Operating income		25	25	25	25	25	25

$$\text{ROI} = \frac{\$25,000}{\$300,000} \times 100\% = 8.33\%$$

The return on investment for this project is 8.33%.

In assessing the project we will want to compare the income that the project creates with the investment for the project.

ROI = (operating income from the investment ÷ investment) × 100%

The operating income from the investment in the patent we looked at earlier is $25,000 per year for six years. (See Exhibit 12.3.) We had previously calculated cash flow as $75,000 per year. To get from cash flow to net income, the major difference is that we have to deduct amortization. Using a straight-line amortization approach, the entire $300,000 investment will be written off in six annual amounts of $50,000 each. Cash flow of $75,000, less $50,000 of amortization expense, leaves operating income of $25,000 per year.

The return on investment for this project is 8.33%.

This is actually the return on the initial investment of $300,000. Another version of ROI expresses the operating income as a percentage of the average investment. Because the average investment is assumed to be half of the initial investment, the return on average investment is always exactly two times the return on initial investment. The return on average investment for this project would be 16.67%:

Return on average investment (ROAvI)

$$= \frac{\$25,000}{(\$300,000 \div 2)} \times 100\%$$

$$= 16.67\%$$

In general, either ROI or ROAvI ratio will be compared with some sort of standard or expectation. So, an investment might be considered acceptable if it had an ROI of 12%. When using the ROAvI, the expectation would be twice as much: the investment would need to show an ROAvI of 24% to be regarded as acceptable.

ROI, whether based on initial investment or on average investment, is superior to payback as it uses the estimated income from all six years of

---

Exhibit 12.4: Cash Flow
— Which One Would You Rather Have?

	Year			
	0	**1**	**2**	**3**
Project X	($600,000)	$340,000	$220,000	$220,000
Project Y	($600,000)	$220,000	$220,000	$340,000

Both X and Y produce the same total cash flow and the same total profit; they have the same return on investment.

X produces its cash flow sooner and is, therefore, preferable to Y.

This is not captured by the return on investment calculation, which averages profits out over the project's life.

---

the project's life. However, it is still a deficient technique because it does not consider the pattern of cash flows over the life of the project any more than the payback does.

Suppose there are two projects, each with a cost of $600,000, and with the following cash inflows (see Exhibit 12.4):

- Project X: year one, $340,000; year two, $220,000; year three, $220,000
- Project Y: year one, $220,000; year two, $220,000; year three, $340,000

Straight-line amortization will reduce each year's profit by $200,000, leaving the following operating income:

- Project X: year one, $140,000; year two, $20,000; year three, $20,000
- Project Y: year one, $20,000; year two, $20,000; year three, $140,000

The total profit for each project is $180,000 over the three years, which is $60,000 per year on average. With an initial investment of $600,000, both projects have a 10% return:

$$\frac{(\$180,000 \div 3)}{\$600,000} \times 100\% = 10\%$$

Although the total income and ROI are the same, the pattern of earning income over time is different, and that causes the pattern of receiving cash inflows to be different also. If we compare the two projects, we can see what that different pattern of cash flows is. Once again, the deduction of one series of cash flows from the other highlights the effect. In each year the $200,000 amortization charge has been added to the income to show the cash flow:

- Project X: year one, $340,000; year two, $220,000; year three, $220,000
- Project Y: year one, $220,000; year two, $220,000; year three, $340,000

Difference (X – Y):

- year one: $120,000
- year two: nil
- year three: ($120,000)

With the similar deficiency as the payback period, it is only logical to regard these two projects as equally worthwhile if investors are indifferent about getting their money back sooner or later. But we know they want it sooner, because only with the cash in their hand are they able to spend it or reinvest it. The ROI method is faulty because it fails to discern the cash flows between the two projects. Note that return on investment ratios can be used to assess both new investments (as discussed here) and also ongoing situations (as shown in Chapter 2, page 26).

12.5 Present Value

The third technique is called present value. What we are faced with is a theoretical approach along the following lines:

- The assessment of a project should be based on its cash flows.
- Cash flows arising at different times are not directly comparable to one another.
- It is possible to discount a future cash flow back to the present time by allowing for the interest effect: this calculates its present value.
- Present values can be meaningfully added to one another.
- When the present values of all the cash flows from a project are added, a project with a positive net present value will increase the value of the firm, while a project with a negative net present value will decrease the value of the firm.

The present-value approach is the underpinning of techniques with the following names:

- present value
- net present value
- discounted cash flow
- discounting
- internal rate of return

To understand present value, we will have to begin with a small discussion of interest.

12.5.1 Simple and Compound Interest

A dollar today is not worth the same as a dollar tomorrow. There are at least two good reasons for this phenomenon: interest and risk. We shall look at risk later in this chapter. For now, let us consider only the interest effect.

The reason $1 today is not worth the same as $1 tomorrow is that between today and tomorrow there is the opportunity of earning interest. One day's interest is, of course, trivial (unless you are a bank or a financial institution, in which case the amounts are so enormous that even one day's interest is significant). To make the issue sensible, we shall consider not one day, but one year: a period when the interest effect becomes meaningfully large.

The accounting equation treats assets as if they were equivalent and interchangeable. For example, the asset Cash on the balance sheet is treated in almost the same way as the asset Accounts Receivable. From a present value perspective, however, they are not equivalent.

If you have $100 cash on hand, you can invest it to earn interest. If, instead of cash, you have $100 in the form of an account receivable, you do not have that investment opportunity. You cannot invest expectations, and an account receivable is an expectation. How much that opportunity is worth depends on two factors: how long you have to wait before the cash is received and how high the rate of interest is. The longer you have to wait, the more interest opportunities are passed up. The higher the rate of interest, the greater the interest opportunity that is passed up.

Assume you are trying to compare $100 cash in hand against $100 that might be received in one year. Assume that the rate of interest is 5%, 10%, 15%, 20% per year. The $100 invested at these rates would grow in one year to the following:

Interest Rate:		5%	10%	15%	20%
Present value	$100				
Future value in 1 year		$105	$110	$115	$120

Clearly, the higher the rate of interest, the greater the interest opportunity. In 2006, interest rates in Canada were at a very low level. You could get a medium-term mortgage to buy a house for about 6%, for example. Because of this, the interest effect was substantially less than it would have been be in times of higher interest rates. However, it is still important.

The calculation above is called simple interest. The interest rate per year is multiplied by the principal ($100) and added to the principal to get its future amount at the end of the year. If more than one year elapses, then the interest-earning process is repeated.

In compound interest it is assumed that the principal and the first year's interest are available to earn interest in the second year. The future amount at the end of the second year is available to earn interest in the third year, and so on.

A $100 investment with an interest rate of 10% per annum will grow to $161.05 in five years:

$110.00 in one year:	$100.00 + ($100.00 \times 0.10) = $110.00
$121.00 in two years:	$110.00 + ($110.00 \times 0.10) = $121.00
$133.10 in three years:	$121.00 + ($121.00 \times 0.10) = $133.10
$146.41 in four years:	$133.10 + ($133.10 \times 0.10) = $146.41
$161.05 in five years:	$146.41 + ($146.41 \times 0.10) = $161.05

If the interest rate were higher, the growth would be greater. For example, $100 invested at 20% per annum would grow to $248.83 in five years:

$120.00 in one year:	$100.00 + ($100.00 × 0.20) = $120.00
$144.00 in two years:	$120.00 + ($120.00 × 0.20) = $144.00
$172.80 in three years:	$144.00 + ($144.00 × 0.20) = $172.80
$207.36 in four years:	$172.80 + ($172.80 × 0.20) = $207.36
$248.83 in five years:	$207.36 + ($207.36 × 0.20) = $248.83

The effect of compound interest can be seen by looking at the way $100 will grow if invested at different interest rates and for different periods of time:

Interest rate:		5%	10%	15%
Present value	$100			
Future value in:				
one year		$105.00	$110.00	$ 115.00
two years		110.25	121.00	132.25
three years		115.76	133.10	152.09
four years		121.55	146.41	174.90
five years		127.63	161.05	201.14
10 years		162.89	259.37	404.56
20 years		265.33	672.75	1,636.65

The formula to calculate future value is as follows:

$$FV = PV (1 + i)^n$$

where:

FV is the future value (the amount to which the investment will grow).
PV is the present value (the amount originally invested).
i is the interest rate.
n is the number of years the amount is invested for.

This formula makes it possible to calculate the future value for any combination of amount, interest rates, or number of years. To make life easier, the formula is built into the functions of all business calculators. Check your calculator's instruction book to see how to enter the data and get the result. That will not be possible with really simple calculators or those designed mainly for other applications. The formula is also built into many computer programs and applications (Excel spreadsheets, for example).

Future values are very useful for some calculations: for example, they will be handy in finding out how much your RRSPs increase over your working life, so that you will be able to estimate your wealth at retirement. They are not so useful for project appraisal, however, and the main reason they are being described is so that we can turn the interest concept (which people largely understand) into its corollary: discounting. By inverting the interest process, we get discounting.

12.5.2 *Discounting*

If a present amount can grow to a larger future amount through the process of compound interest, then a future amount can be expressed as its present equivalent by eliminating the interest opportunity.

If $100 would grow to $110 in a year when invested at 10%, then a future amount of $110 receivable in one year's time is equivalent to $100 now.

In other words, discounting $110 at 10% for one year gives it a present value of $100.

The compound interest factor in the FV formula is

$$(1 + i)^n$$

Discounting uses the inverse of the compound interest factor, and its formula is as follows:

$$PV = FV \times \frac{1}{(1+i)^n}$$

Or, if you prefer:

$$PV = \frac{FV}{(1+i)^n}$$

The extent of the discounting process varies with the interest rate and the number of years. High interest rates and long time periods make future values far higher than the initial investment. In the same way, high interest rates and long time delays before receiving a cash flow mean that its present value may be far less than the dollar amount eventually received.

So, if the interest rate is 10% and you have to wait two years for your money, it is the same as having $82.64 now. The 10% interest would grow the $82.64 into $100 over two years. (See Exhibit 12.5.)

$82.64 \times 1.1 = $90.91 at the end of year one
$90.91 \times 1.1 = $100.00 at the end of year two

If the interest rate is 15% and you have to wait 20 years for your money, it is worth only $6.11 in present value. That is because $6.11 invested now at 15% interest would grow into $100 in 20 years:

$$FV = PV (1 + i)^n$$
$$FV = \$6.11 (1 + 0.15)^{20}$$
$$= \$100$$

With very high interest rates, and/or with long time periods, the present values of future cash flows approach (but never quite reach) zero.

As with future value, the discounting formula is readily available as a function of calculators, computers, and software. As a leftover from the days when calculators and computers were less readily available, there are also tables that show the value of $1 \div (1 + i)^n$ for a range of values

Exhibit 12.5: The Effect of Discounting

Interest rate:		5%	10%	15%
Future value	$100			
Present value if time period is:				
one year		95.24	90.91	86.96
two years		90.70	82.64	75.61
three years		86.38	75.13	65.75
four years		82.27	68.30	57.18
five years		78.35	62.09	49.72
10 years		61.39	38.55	24.72
20 years		37.69	14.86	6.11

of i and n. These are called discount tables or present value tables, as they enable calculating the amount by which a future value must be discounted to get its present value. (A present value table is included in Exhibit 12.6.)

To use the table for a particular combination of i and n, look up the number at the intersection of the i (interest rate) column and n (number of years) row. Multiply the future cash flow by that discount factor to get its present value.

Suppose a contract entitles you to receive $1,000 in two years, and 10% is the relevant interest rate. The discount factor (Exhibit 12.6) for a 10% interest rate and a two-year time period is 0.8264 (all discount factors are less than 1), the contract's value, therefore, is $826.40. You should see no difference between receiving $826.40 now and receiving $1,000 in two years.

The discounting process enables all future cash flows to be restated at their present equivalents. These present values can be added or subtracted, as they are at a common point in time, unlike the future values, which could not be meaningfully added as they were stated at different times. When present values of all future cash flows are added, we get "net present value".

12.5.3 *Net Present Value*

The cash flows that were estimated to arise from an investment in the patent proposal are:

Initial investment now	$300,000
Years one through six	
Revenues	$500,000
Cash expenses	425,000
Annual cash inflow	$ 75,000

Exhibit 12.6: Present Value of $1

Interest rate	3%	5%	8%	10%	12%	14%	16%	18%	20%	25%
Number of years										
1	0.9709	0.9524	0.9259	0.9091	0.8929	0.8772	0.8621	0.8475	0.8333	0.8000
2	0.9426	0.9070	0.8573	0.8264	0.7972	0.7695	0.7432	0.7182	0.6944	0.6400
3	0.9151	0.8638	0.7938	0.7513	0.7118	0.6750	0.6407	0.6086	0.5787	0.5120
4	0.8885	0.8227	0.7629	0.6830	0.6355	0.5921	0.5523	0.5158	0.4823	0.4096
5	0.8626	0.7835	0.6806	0.6209	0.5674	0.5194	0.4761	0.4371	0.4019	0.3277
6	0.8375	0.7462	0.6302	0.5645	0.5066	0.4556	0.4104	0.3714	0.3349	0.2621
7	0.8131	0.7107	0.5835	0.5132	0.4524	0.3996	0.3538	0.3139	0.2791	0.2097
8	0.7894	0.6768	0.5403	0.4665	0.4039	0.3506	0.3050	0.2660	0.2326	0.1678
9	0.7664	0.6446	0.5002	0.4241	0.3606	0.3075	0.2630	0.2255	0.1938	0.1342
10	0.7441	0.6139	0.4632	0.3855	0.3220	0.2697	0.2267	0.1911	0.1615	0.1074
15	0.6419	0.4810	0.3152	0.2394	0.1827	0.1401	0.1079	0.0835	0.0649	0.0352
20	0.5537	0.3769	0.2146	0.1486	0.1037	0.0728	0.0514	0.0365	0.0261	0.0115

Exhibit 12.7: Calculating Net Present Value

Year	Cash flow	12% Discount factor*	Present value
0 (now)	($300,000)	1.0000	($300,000.0)
1	$75,000	0.8929	66,967.5
2	75,000	0.7972	59,790.0
3	75,000	0.7118	53,385.0
4	75,000	0.6355	47,662.5
5	75,000	0.5674	42,555.0
6	75,000	0.5066	37,995.0
Present value of cash inflows			$308,355.0
Net present value of the project			$ 8,355.0

* Taken from Exhibit 12.6.

To restate these cash flows at their present values we would multiply each one by an appropriate discount factor. If 12% is the relevant interest rate, we can read the discount factors from the 12% column of Exhibit 12.6.

Note that the initial investment is not discounted. It occurs now and, therefore, its present value is equal to its cash value.

Each of the $75,000 annual cash flows is multiplied by the applicable discount factor to reduce it from a cash amount of $75,000 to some lower present value. As the time period increases, so the effect of discounting becomes more. Thus the $75,000 we are to receive in year six is only worth $37,995 today ($75,000 × 0.5066).

The discounted cash inflows can be added. They total $308,355 (see Exhibit 12.7). That is the total present value of the inflows from this patent project, and it is a good measure of how worthwhile the project is. If these cash flows had cost more than $308,355 to "buy", it would not be worthwhile.

By deducting the investment from the total of the inflows, we get the "net present value". If the net present value of a project is positive, it is acceptable. If the net present value is negative, the project is not acceptable. And if the net present value is zero, we should be indifferent between investing and not investing. (See Exhibit 12.8 for steps in a net present value calculation.)

Here, the patent project costs $300,000 to invest; the present value of its cash inflows ($308,355) is greater than the present value of its cash outflows ($300,000). With a positive net present value of $8,355, the project is worthwhile.

Exhibit 12.8: Steps in a Net Present Value Calculation

1. Estimate the amount of the cash investment.
2. Estimate the amount and timing of the cash flows that the investment will cause.
3. Decide on an appropriate discount rate (i.e., interest rate).
4. Discount each future cash flow to its preset value.
5. Add the present values of all the inflows.
6. Deduct the investment, leaving the net present value.
7. If the net present value is a positive number, the investment is acceptable; if the net present value is a negative number, the investment is unacceptable.

12.5.4 Annuities

A series of cash flows that is the same each year for a period of time is called an annuity. As such, the cash flow of the patent proposal is an annuity since its cash inflows are the same each year — it will give cash flows of $75,000 per year for six years. There are some shortcuts to doing the calculations for annuities.

First, your business calculator or computer will have annuity routines, much like the present value routines. Second, there are the tables.

Exhibit 12.6 shows the discount factors for any combination of i and n so that a cash flow arising at a known future date can be discounted. Exhibit 12.9 shows discount factors for annuities. As with Exhibit 12.6, it is an array, with columns for i and rows for n. The big difference is that n in Exhibit 12.9 means every year for that number of years, rather than arising at year n, as it would in Exhibit 12.6.

Technically, Exhibit 12.9 is a cumulative version of the numbers in Exhibit 12.6. Compare the two tables. The first row in each table is identical. That is because an annuity for one year is the same as receiving a single payment one year from now. The second row in Exhibit 12.9 is the total of the first and second rows in Exhibit 12.6. The third row in Exhibit 12.9 is the total of the first three rows in Exhibit 12.6, and so on.

Exhibit 12.9 is used in much the same way as Exhibit 12.6. A known or estimated annual cash flow is multiplied by the annuity factor from Exhibit 12.9 to get its present value.

For i of 12% and n of six years, the annuity factor is 4.1114.

A six-year annuity of $75,000 is worth: $75,000 × 4.1114 = $308,355.

If the initial investment was $300,000, the net present value would be $8,355.

This is the same answer that we get from the calculation in Exhibit 12.7. There should be no surprise to that, as they are just different presen-

Exhibit 12.9: Present Value of an Annuity of $1 per Year

Interest rate	3%	5%	8%	10%	12%	14%	16%	18%	20%	25%
Number of years										
1	0.9709	0.9524	0.9259	0.9091	0.8929	0.8772	0.8621	0.8475	0.8333	0.8000
2	1.9135	1.8594	1.7832	1.7356	1.6901	1.6467	1.6053	1.5657	1.5277	1.4400
3	2.8286	2.7232	2.5770	2.4869	2.4019	2.3217	2.2460	2.1743	2.1064	1.9520
4	3.7171	3.5459	3.3399	3.1699	3.0374	2.9138	2.7983	2.6901	2.5887	2.3616
5	4.5797	4.3294	4.0205	3.7908	3.6048	3.4332	3.2744	3.1272	2.9906	2.6893
6	5.4172	5.0756	4.6507	4.3553	4.1114	3.8888	3.6848	3.4986	3.3255	2.9514
7	6.2303	5.7863	5.2342	4.8685	4.5638	4.2884	4.0386	3.8125	3.6046	3.1611
8	7.0197	6.4631	5.7745	5.3350	4.9677	4.6390	4.3436	4.0785	3.8372	3.3289
9	7.7861	7.1077	6.2747	5.7591	5.3283	4.9465	4.6066	4.3040	4.0310	3.4631
10	8.5302	7.7216	6.7379	6.1446	5.6503	5.2162	4.8333	4.4951	4.1925	3.5705
15	11.9379	10.3797	8.5595	7.6061	6.8109	6.1422	5.5755	5.0916	4.6755	3.8593
20	14.8775	12.4622	9.8181	8.5136	7.4694	6.6231	5.9288	5.3257	4.8696	3.9539

tations of the same mathematical process. However, using annuity tables makes for a much shorter calculation.

PV of an annuity = annual amount × discount factor

12.5.5 *Weighted Average Cost of Capital*

One of the deliberate omissions in all the previous calculations is any indication of where the discount rate, or relevant interest rate, comes from. There are a number of possibilities, but we are going to restrict ourselves to one of them — the weighted average cost of capital (WACC), which was introduced in the previous chapter. WACC is the appropriate discount rate because it represents the cost of all financing (debt and/ or equity) a company can use to invest in projects. And by using WACC, the proposal will only be accepted if its return is sufficient to maintain the company's share price and keeps its shareholders and creditors happy.

12.6 Uncertainty

It cannot be stressed too strongly that assessment of long-term projects is an inaccurate science. The assessment is based on future cash flows, and the future is always uncertain. At best, we have estimates of what the cash flows will be. At worst, we have wild guesses. Clearly, we will be better at estimating some things than at estimating others.

A proposal that consists of a relatively minor change in existing operations would tend to be low risk. To sell a 10-tonne truck and replace it with a 15-tonne truck, for example, would be subject to very little uncertainty.

A proposal that involves a more radical change would likely be less well understood and more uncertain. For example, the introduction of a performance-related bonus scheme may represent a completely new way of rewarding employees, and its outcomes may be highly uncertain.

Proposals that involve brave new ventures (introduction of new products, excursions into new markets) offer the least reliability and the greatest levels of uncertainty. Such proposals are often the most lucrative, as well as being the riskiest.

It is not good management practice to ignore risk, though that is clearly the behaviour we see exhibited on occasion. We should, as a first step, try to understand where risk comes from (changing technology, developments in markets, etc.), and we must try to measure the risk associated with major long-term decisions. Once the risk has been measured, however crudely, we must incorporate it into the decision process.

One way of doing this is through the discount rate. If the WACC is the appropriate rate at which to discount a cash flow of "normal" risk, then it can be argued that a higher discount rate should be used for a riskier cash flow. Several companies adopt this approach. They will use different rates to discount different projects, perhaps adding two percentage points to the rate where the project is perceived as risky.

Another method is to use what is called "sensitivity analysis". If all the data in respect of a project are entered into a spreadsheet, then it is a relatively simple process to vary the input factors one by one to see what effect a change would have on the outcome. This is called sensitivity analysis.

In the first edition of this book, the following example of risk was given:

> A project might critically depend on there being crude oil available as an input at a price of $25 or less per barrel. If the price is $25 or less, the net present value would be positive. If the price rises to $27, then the net present value would become negative.

As of this writing (mid-2007), the price of crude oil is hovering at around $77 a barrel, a price that was unimaginable five years ago. The decision to go ahead with the project would then become an exercise in estimating the future price of crude oil, as that is what the project is sensitive to.

Risk analysis is a very complex art, and sophisticated modelling techniques may be necessary to incorporate it into the long-term decision process. Just because it is difficult, however, is no reason to ignore it.

12.7 Summary

Long-term decisions have to be carefully vetted to make sure they move the company forward toward its objectives. Such decisions may be assessed using payback, return on investment, and present value. Of these, present value is far more rigorous than the others. Because these projects are about the future, there is risk involved, and that is another dimension to be considered in making the decision.

Self-Study Problems

1. A project has a required investment of $100,000. It will result in cash inflows as follows:

Year	$
1	10,000
2	20,000
3	35,000
4	35,000
5	55,000

Required
(a) Calculate the payback period.
(b) Calculate the return on initial investment and the return on average investment.
(c) Calculate the net present value using a cost of capital of 16%.
(d) Is this investment acceptable?

2. A project has an initial investment of $1.2 million. It will result in cash flows of $600,000 per year for each of the next six years.

Required
(a) Calculate the payback period.
(b) Calculate the return on initial investment.
(c) Calculate the net present value, using a cost of capital of 12%.
(d) Would you recommend this investment?

Solutions

1. (a)

Year	$ Cash inflow	$ Cumulative cash inflow
0	($100,000)	$100,000
1	10,000	90,000
2	20,000	70,000
3	35,000	35,000
4	35,000	nil

Payback is at the end of year 4.

(b) Amortization: $100,000 ÷ 5 years = $20,000 per year

Year	$ Cash inflow	Amortization	Operating income
1	$ 10,000	$ 20,000	($10,000)
2	20,000	20,000	nil
3	35,000	20,000	15,000
4	35,000	20,000	15,000
5	55,000	20,000	35,000
Total	$155,000	$100,000	$55,000

Average annual operating income:

$$= \$55,000 \div 5 \text{ years}$$
$$= \$11,000$$

Return on initial investment:

$$= (\text{average annual operating income} \div \text{initial investment})$$
$$\times 100\%$$
$$= (\$11,000 \div \$100,000) \times 100\%$$
$$= 11\%$$

Return on average investment:

$$= (\text{average annual operating profit} \div \text{average investment})$$
$$\times 100\%$$
$$= [\$11,000 \div (\$100,000 \div 2)] \times 100\%$$
$$= 22\%$$

(c)

Year	Cash flow	16% Discount factor	Present value
1	$10,000	0.8621	$ 8,621
2	20,000	0.7432	14,864
3	35,000	0.6407	22,425
4	35,000	0.5523	19,331
5	55,000	0.4761	26,186
Present value of cash inflows			$ 91,427
Initial investment			100,000
Net present value			($ 8,573)

(d) No, this investment does not pass the financial hurdle, as it has a negative net present value. It is not acceptable.

2. (a) Payback:

$$= \text{investment} \div \text{annual cash flow}$$
$$= \$1,200,000 \div \$600,000$$
$$= 2 \text{ years}$$

(b) Annual amortization expense, using the straight-line method:

$$= \$1,200,000 \div 6 \text{ years}$$
$$= \$200,000 \text{ per year}$$

Annual operating income:

$$= \text{cash flow} - \text{amortization}$$
$$= \$600,000 - \$200,000$$
$$= \$400,000$$

Return on initial investment:

$$= (\text{annual operating income} \div \text{initial investment}) \times 100\%$$
$$= (\$400,000 \div 1,200,000) \times 100\%$$
$$= 33.33\%$$

Return on average investment would be twice that: 66.67%

(c)   Net present value of project:

Net present value of cash flows:
Annual cash flow × (12%, 6-year annuity discount factor)
= $600,000 × 4.1114* $2,466,840

Investment:	1,200,000
Net present value	$1,266,840

* From Exhibit 12.9

(d)   Yes, the project has a positive net present value, so it is acceptable on financial grounds.

Discussion Questions and Problems

Discussion Questions

1. Why is long-term decision making so much more important than short-term decision making?
2. What are the likely sources of proposals for long-term investments?
3. Name the three appraisal techniques used for long-term investment analysis, and describe how each one is applied.
4. What are the main weaknesses of the payback method?
5. What are the main weaknesses of the return on investment method?
6. Should return on investment be calculated on the basis of the original investment or the average investment?
7. In the net present value method, what interest rate should be used to discount future cash flows?
8. Why is amortization "added back" to net income to get cash flow?
9. What is risk, and how can it be accommodated in project appraisal?
10. Describe the relationship between strategic planning and capital project appraisal.

Problems

1. The Software Solutions Corporation is a software development company based in Southern Ontario. The company has decided that its strategy is to be based on offering state-of-the-art, differentiated, high-end software solutions to organizations that are prepared to pay for the best products available. Software Solutions is considering a number of long-term investment decisions. For each one describe how well it fits with the corporation's strategy, and decide whether or not you would proceed to evaluate the proposal's economic merits.

   (a) Acquisition of a new software management program that would integrate existing software development activities and enable products to be more functional when they were introduced to the market: cost — $2 million
   (b) Acquisition of an existing software development company that had unique expertise in an area Software Solutions wanted to develop: cost — $55 million
   (c) Relocation of company offices from downtown Toronto to Richmond Hill, which would save substantial operating costs: cost — $1 million
   (d) Hiring Jennifer Wong, who is currently the software manager of a rival company: proposed salary — $250,000 per year
   (e) Spending on an advertising campaign in trade magazines to attract new customers: cost — $750,000
   (f) Outsourcing programming activities to a specialist organization in Southeast Asia: expected savings — $500,000 per year

2. A project has an initial investment of $500,000 and estimated future cash flows of $125,000 per year for six years.

Required
(a) Calculate the payback period.
(b) Calculate the return on initial investment.
(c) Calculate the return on average investment.
(d) Is the investment worthwhile?

3. For each of the following alternatives, state which is preferable:
   (a) $100 per month at the end of every month for a year, or $1,200 now
   (b) $100 per month at the end of every month for a year, or $1,200 at the end of the year
   (c) $1,000 now, or $1,150 at the end of one year

4. If the relevant rate of interest is 5%, calculate the present value of the following:
   (a) $1,000 now
   (b) $1,000 at the end of one year
   (c) $1,000 at the end of five years
   (d) $1,000 at the end of each of the next five years
   (e) $1,000 at the end of each year forever

5. Xtron Co. has a cost of capital of 20%. The company is considering a project that has the following cash flows:

Investment (now)	($500,000)
Cash inflow: year one	300,000
Cash inflow: year two	250,000
Cash inflow: year three	200,000
Cash inflow: year four	150,000

   Required
   (a) Calculate the payback period.
   (b) Calculate the return on initial investment.
   (c) Calculate the return on average investment.
   (d) Calculate the present value of the cash inflows.
   (e) Calculate the net present value of the project.

6. Xtron Co. is considering a new project that will yield an operating profit of $625,000 per year for each of the next four years. The operating profit is calculated after amortizing the initial investment of $2,000,000 on the straight-line basis. The company has a cost of capital of 20%.

   Required
   (a) Calculate the payback period.
   (b) Calculate the return on original investment.
   (c) Calculate the return on average investment.
   (d) Calculate the annual cash inflow.
   (e) Calculate the net present value.

7. Westbourne Plumbing Supplies has a number of wholesale outlets in Ontario. The company is considering opening at a new location in Mississauga. The investment required is $5 million, which will buy and equip a new "state-of-the–art" store. The entire $5 million would be amortized over a 10-year period. Sales are expected to be $8 million per year each year for the next 10 years. The gross margin percentage is 25%. Other cash operating expenses are budgeted to be $700,000 per year. The company's cost of capital is 10%.

Required

(a) Calculate the annual operating income.
(b) Calculate the annual cash inflow.
(c) Calculate the payback period.
(d) Calculate the return on initial investment.
(e) Calculate the return on average investment.
(f) Calculate the net present value.
(g) Would you advise the company to go ahead or not?

8. Westbourne Plumbing Supplies has a number of wholesale outlets in Southern Ontario. Westbourne has identified a number of projects that are in line with company strategy, all of which have positive net present values and acceptable payback periods. For each one consider how reliable the underlying estimates are likely to be, and state whether you think the project is "normal risk", "low risk", or "high risk".

(a) Purchasing a forklift truck for the Barrie warehouse
(b) Refitting all forklift trucks with environmentally friendly natural gas motors
(c) Outsourcing all forklift truck operations
(d) Redesigning one of the warehouses so that fewer forklift trucks are required
(e) Opening a new plumbing supplies outlet in Mississauga
(f) Opening a new plumbing supplies outlet in California
(g) Introducing a new line of electrical supplies
(h) Diversifying into building a new sub-division
(i) Diversifying into computer software development in Australia

9. Westbourne Plumbing Supplies is considering investing in a new warehouse management system. This is budgeted to cost $1,637,200, which will be amortized on the straight-line basis over the project's expected five-year life. The project is expected to increase cash inflows by $500,000 per year. The company's cost of capital is 20%. Because this investment is perceived as being "low risk", it has been suggested that it be evaluated using a "risk adjusted" cost of capital of 14%.

(a) What is the net present value of the project when the cash inflows are discounted at 20%?
(b) What is the net present value of the project when the cash inflows are discounted at 14%?

(c)   Is the investment justified?

(d)   What would happen if the cash inflows were to be discounted at 16%?

13

Financial Statement Analysis

Learning
Objectives

After studying this chapter you should be able to calculate and interpret financial accounting ratios that deal with:

→ Liquidity
→ Profitability
→ Debt
→ Efficiency
→ Market-related measures

13.1 Introduction

Accounting ratios are used to better understand the numbers in financial statements. When an accounting number is compared to another accounting number, the ratio is sometimes very informative: more informative than the numbers would be by themselves. Thus, the dollar value of inventory from the balance sheet, by itself, tells us little. The value of inventory compared to the sales revenue gives us a valuable clue to assess the efficiency of the company's inventory control; it expresses the information as the number of times per year the inventory is turned over. The value of the inventory turnover ratio for one year when compared with the same ratio for a subsequent year tells us whether inventory management is improving or getting worse.

Within the various chapters of this text we have introduced a number of financial accounting ratios. In order to understand these ratios better and understand their interrelationships, in this chapter we carry out a financial ratio analysis on the results of the Canadian Tire Corporation.

We start off with the financial statements themselves. To make the task more straightforward, the financial statements have been summarized to some extent (see Exhibit 13.1). Their principal characteristics, however, remain intact. You are encouraged to compare these with the published financial statements, which are available on the Canadian Tire Web site, **www.canadiantire.ca**. (Once at the Web site, click on "Company Information", and then click on "Investor Relations" under "Investor & News Room".)

The analysis will concentrate on the following:

• *Liquidity:* whether or not the company is likely to run out of cash.
• *Profitability:* how well the company has performed.
• *Debt:* the extent to which debt increases company risk.
• *Efficiency:* how well the company used its assets.
• *Market-related measures:* information about share values.

This is not an exhaustive list of financial ratios, but it is sufficient to give a reasonable assessment of the company's performance and prospects.

Exhibit 13.1: Summarized Financial Statements — Canadian Tire

Canadian Tire
Consolidated Statement of Earnings and Retained Earnings ($ million)

		2005		2004
Gross operating revenue			$7,774		$7,154
Less: Cost of goods sold and operating expenses:				
Various (paid in cash)	$6,985		$6,452	
Depreciation	185	7,170	171	6,623
Operating income		$ 604		$ 531
Less: Interest	$ 84		$ 78	
Income taxes	190	274	162	240
Net income		$ 330		$ 291
Add: Retained earnings at start of year		1,547		1,318
		$1,877		$1,609
Less: Cost of repurchase of shares	$ 17		$ 22	
Dividends paid	47	64	40	62
Retained earnings at end of year		$1,813		$1,547

Canadian Tire
Balance Sheet ($ million)

		As at end of		
	2005		2004	
Cash	$ 838		$ 802	
Accounts receivable	1,425		987	
Inventory	676		621	
Prepaid expenses	42		24	
Total current assets		$2,981		$2,434
Long-term assets		2,975		2,809
Total assets		$5,956		$5,243
Current liabilities	$1,821		$1,487	
Long-term liabilities	1,324		1,205	
Total liabilities		$3,145		$2,692
Minority interest		300		300
Shareholders' equity				
Share capital	$ 704		$ 710	
Retained earnings	1,813		1,547	
Foreign exchange adjustment	(6)	2,511	(6)	2,251
Total liabilities and equity		$5,956		$5,243

13.2 Liquidity

A major concern to any organization is its ability to survive. Short-term survival is critically dependent on the relationship between immediate obligations and the liquid assets that are available to pay them. Cash will be needed to pay these short-term debts, but cash is not the only available resource: other short-term assets may also be turned into cash and used to pay liabilities. Thus, liquidity analysis is concerned primarily with the current assets and the current liabilities. The greater the ratio of current assets to current liabilities, the more liquid the company is, and the lower the threat of running out of cash. Two ratios are used for liquidity analysis: the current ratio and the quick ratio.

13.2.1 Current Ratio

Definition: current assets ÷ current liabilities

2005

$$\frac{\$2,981}{\$1,821} = 1.64:1$$

2004

$$\frac{\$2,434}{\$1,487} = 1.64:1$$

Analysis: The company does not look to be highly liquid: its current ratio is considerably less than the norm of $2:1$ in both 2004 and 2005.

13.2.2 Quick Ratio

Definition: (current assets – inventories) ÷ current liabilities

The quick ratio recognizes that inventory, though a current asset, is less liquid than other current assets, and its availability to pay off obligations is questionable. Hence, inventory is removed, and the more liquid current assets are compared to current liabilities.

2005

$$\frac{(\$2,981-\$676)}{\$1,821} = 1.27:1$$

2004

$$\frac{(\$2,434-\$621)}{\$1,487} = 1.22:1$$

Analysis: The ratio is almost unchanged at about 1.2 to 1, which indicates normal liquidity.

13.3 Profitability

Once it has survived extinction in the short term, a company has an objective of profitability to meet. Profitability ratios express some measure of profits against the resources used to create them. In this way the results are scaled. This means that the results of different-sized companies can be compared. You would not expect the same dollar amount of profit from IBM and a corner grocery store, but you might expect the same percentage return on their respective assets. The profitability ratios we shall calculate are return on sales (%), return on assets (%), and return on shareholders' equity (%).

13.3.1 Gross Profit on Sales (%)

Definition: (gross profit ÷ sales) × 100%

This ratio measures what is left over out of sales after the direct cost of sales is deducted. In a retail organization such as Canadian Tire the direct cost is the replacement of the inventory that has been sold. It is a very useful control measure that monitors whether the company is controlling its merchandising activities effectively. If sales revenue or inventory are being misappropriated, this ratio will be lower than what would be expected from the official profit markups.

Canadian company law does not require disclosure of the direct costs as a separate category, so we cannot calculate this ratio for Canadian Tire. It is always, however, calculated internally for control purposes.

13.3.2 Return on Sales (%)

Definition: (operating income ÷ sales) × 100%

This ratio measures what is left over out of each dollar of sales after all the operating expenses have been paid. It measures many things that are under the control of the management (such as the total number of employees and their remuneration) and also a number of things that are outside management's control (such as the purchase price of raw material inputs). The more carefully management controls the costs under their influence, the higher this ratio will be.

2005

$$\frac{\$604}{\$7,774} \times 100\% = 7.8\%$$

2004

$$\frac{\$531}{\$7,154} \times 100\% = 7.4\%$$

Analysis: The ratio has risen by a small amount between 2004 and 2005. Because mass-market retailing is a low-margin business, the return is in general not high.

13.3.3 Return on Assets (%)

Definition: (operating income ÷ total assets) × 100%

The return on assets measures how well the company has used its assets in carrying out its business mission. (Here, it is retailing.)

2005

$$\frac{\$604}{\$5,956} \times 100\% = 10.1\%$$

2004

$$\frac{\$531}{\$5,243} \times 100\% = 10.1\%$$

Analysis: This is a modest return on assets and has not changed between the two years.

There is a connection between the return on sales, the total asset turnover ratio (see later) and the return on assets.

2005

Return on sales × Total asset turnover = Return on assets
    7.8%   ×   1.30   =   10.1%

To achieve a higher return on assets, Canadian Tire could either increase its return on sales or increase its total asset turnover (or both).

13.3.4 *Return on Equity (%)*

Definition: (net income ÷ shareholders' equity) × 100%

This is similar to the return on assets, in that it attempts to measure overall economic performance; however, it does so from the perspective of the shareholder, rather than the business unit. There are two differences between these two ratios.

First, the return on equity is measured on the basis of income after interest, which is then compared to the assets, net of liabilities (in other words, the owners' equity). This means, effectively, that the finance provided by borrowings and the interest cost of borrowings have both been excluded. Thus, a smaller definition of income is being compared with a smaller definition of investment. Return on equity compares the income to which the shareholders are entitled to the finances they have supplied. All other things being equal, this should result in the return on equity being the same as, or being higher than, the return on assets. This is because interest costs on debt (low-risk) should be lower than the required return on equity.

Second, the return on equity is measured on an after-tax basis. This is because investors are really interested in what is left over for them after taxes have been paid. All other things being equal, this should cause the return on equity to be lower than the return on assets.

Because these two effects (leverage, taxes) work in opposite directions (leverage increases the return on equity; taxes decreases the return on equity), it is not always clear what the net effect will be.

2005

$$\frac{\$330}{\$2,811} \times 100\% = 11.7\%$$

2004

$$\frac{\$291}{\$2,551} \times 100\% = 11.4\%$$

Analysis: The ratio has risen slightly between 2004 and 2005. However, it is still not high for a normal business investment. An investor would compare this return with returns that are available from investing in other shares, and they may find a higher return elsewhere. (Note that the "minority interest" of $300 million has been included with the share capital. This is the value of outside holdings of shares in subsidiary companies.)

13.4 Debt

When a company uses debt to finance its activities, two things happen. First, because debt is less risky to the investor (i.e., the cost of debt is lower) and because debt interest is a tax-allowable expense for the borrower, the greater the debt, the greater the return on equity should be. Second, the greater the debt, the riskier the equity return becomes: both the variability of returns and the probability of default increase as a result of borrowing capital. Investors and creditors will want to measure the debt in relation to the equity (debt-to-equity ratio or debt-to-total-assets ratio), and will also want to measure the debt interest in relation to the income (interest cover ratio).

The two ratios, debt to equity and debt to total assets, are just different ways of measuring the same concept. It is redundant to consider both.

13.4.1 Debt-to-Assets (%)

Definition: (total debt ÷ total assets) × 100%

2005

$$\left(\frac{\$3,145}{\$5,956}\right) \times 100\% = 53\%$$

2004

$$\left(\frac{\$2,692}{\$5,243}\right) \times 100\% = 51\%$$

13.4.2 Debt-to-Equity (%)

Definition: (total debt ÷ shareholders' equity) × 100%

2005

$$\left(\frac{\$3,145}{\$2,811}\right) \times 100\% = 112\%$$

2004

$$\left(\frac{\$2,692}{\$2,551}\right) \times 100\% = 106\%$$

Analysis: Where debt is greater than 50% of assets (or greater than 100% of equity), the conclusion is that there is an unhealthily high level of borrowing. This is true of Canadian Tire in both years.

13.4.3 Interest Cover Ratio

Definition: operating income (income before taxes and interest)
÷ interest paid

This ratio measures the ability of the company to pay interest out of current earnings. The amount of interest expense is divided into the before-tax, pre-interest earnings.

2005

$$\frac{\$604}{\$84} = 7.2$$

2004

$$\frac{\$531}{\$78} = 6.8$$

Analysis: This is a generous level of interest cover. Income would have to fall by a factor of about 7 before there was insufficient profit to pay interest.

13.5 Efficiency

To be efficient can be thought of as getting a high level of sales out of a given set of assets, or, to put it the other way around, to use a small quantity of assets to support a given level of sales. Efficiency ratios examine this feature by relating the assets on the balance sheet to the sales revenue.

This can be done for all assets (total assets turnover) or individual asset classes (e.g., receivables turnover, inventory turnover). In each case a judgment may be made on whether the asset is well managed or not.

13.5.1 Total Asset Turnover

Definition: sales ÷ total assets

2005

$$\frac{\$7,774}{\$5,956} = 1.30$$

2004

$$\frac{\$7,154}{\$5,243} = 1.36$$

Analysis: For every $1 in assets in 2004, Canadian Tire generated $1.36 in sales revenue. In 2005, total asset turnover fell: for every $1 of total assets, $1.30 of revenue was made. This is slightly less efficient.

The total asset turnover ratio can be broken down into its component elements by looking at similar ratios for each of the assets. The two assets that are most commonly examined are the accounts receivable and the inventory.

13.5.2 Receivables Turnover Ratio and Number of Days' Receivables

Companies that let their customers buy goods on credit terms probably expect to increase their sales by doing so. There is a cost, however, in that the accounts receivable have to be financed. An efficient company is one that allows customers credit terms, but is then rigorous about collecting the amounts owing. Comparing receivables to sales revenue shows the turnover ratio. The more frequently these are turned over, the more efficiently the company is operating.

An alternative way of presenting the same information is the number of days' worth of sales that the receivables represent. It is unnecessary to calculate both ratios.

Receivables Turnover Ratio

Definition: sales ÷ receivables

2005

$$\frac{\$7,774}{\$1,425} = 5.5$$

2004

$$\frac{\$7,154}{\$987} = 7.2$$

Receivables Collection Period

Definition: receivables $\div$ (sales $\div$ 365)

2005

$$\frac{\$1,425}{(\$7,774 \div 365)} = 67 \text{ days}$$

2004

$$\frac{\$987}{(\$7,154 \div 365)} = 50 \text{ days}$$

Analysis: In 2005, the receivables are "turned over" 5.5 times, which is the equivalent of allowing trade credit to customers for a little over two months (67 days). This was significantly less efficient than in 2004.

13.5.3 *Inventory Turnover and Inventory Holding Period*

Inventory is clearly a necessary part of Canadian Tire's business activities. However, holding inventory is expensive. It has to be warehoused and moved around; it has financing costs, and it deteriorates. The less inventory the organization holds, all other things being equal, the more efficient the organization is.

Inventory turnover is measured by comparing it to sales, or (as with receivables) by calculating how many days' sales the inventory represents.

Inventory Turnover

Definition: sales $\div$ inventory

2005

$$\frac{\$7,774}{\$676} = 11.5$$

2004

$$\frac{\$7,154}{\$621} = 11.5$$

Inventory Holding Period

Definition: inventory $\div$ (sales $\div$ 365)

2005

$$\frac{\$676}{(\$7,774 \div 365)} = 32 \text{ days}$$

2004

$$\frac{\$621}{(\$7,154 \div 365)} = 32 \text{ days}$$

Analysis: In both years, Canadian Tire turned over its inventory 11.5 times, which is equivalent to holding it for 32 days. This is probably about average for a retail organization such as Canadian Tire. Any trend over time would indicate that they were becoming more efficient (if the holding period got shorter), or less efficient (if it got longer).

13.6 Market-Related Ratios

Ratios that shareholders will use in assessing the value of their shares include the earnings per share, the price-to-earnings ratio, and the dividend cover ratio.

13.6.1 Earnings Per Share

Definition: net income ÷ number of common shares

The higher the earnings, the better it is for the shareholders. Earnings will either be paid to shareholders now as a dividend, or they will get the benefit of capital growth through increased share prices if the earnings are ploughed back into the company to finance growth. Whatever the total earnings, they have to be shared among the shareholders, so the greater the number of shares, the lower each share's proportion of earnings.

Canadian Tire has an unusual capital structure. The official "common shares" number is 3,423,366. These are all held by members of the Billies family that started the company. Additionally, there is a large number of Class A non-voting shares. These shares carry the same rights to dividends as the common shares, but they have no votes. At the end of 2004, Canadian Tire had 81 million Class A shares in issue, and that had increased to 82 million by the end of 2005. We shall treat all these as common shares for the purpose of calculating earnings per share.

2005

$$\frac{\$330,000,000}{82,000,000} = \$4.02$$

2004

$$\frac{\$291,000,000}{81,000,000} = \$3.59$$

Analysis: The ratio has increased from $3.59 to $4.02 per share.

13.6.2 Price-to-Earnings Ratio

Definition: share price ÷ earnings per share

The relationship between the earnings of the company and the price of the shares is a judgment by the investing public on how well the company is regarded. A company with a high price-to-earnings ratio is looked on favourably, while a company with a low price-to-earnings ratio is looked on unfavourably.

Analysis: Suppose the price-to-earnings ratio for Canadian Tire was 12.5; earnings per share in 2005 was $4.02. The share price would be $4.02 × 12.5 = $50.25. That is, you could expect to either buy or sell shares at a price of $50.25 on the stock market.

The price-to-earnings ratio is actually the inverse, or reciprocal, of the return shareholders are getting on the market price of the share. A price-to-earnings ratio of 12.5 is equivalent to a return of $1 \div 12.5 = 8\%$. In other words, if you buy a Canadian Tire share for $50.25, and it earns $4.02 for you, your return on equity (or return on investment) is 8%.

13.6.3 Dividend Cover Ratio and Dividend Payout (%)

Definition: net income ÷ dividend

The dividend cover ratio shows the extent to which the earnings are being paid back to shareholders as current dividend and, by implication, the level of profits being ploughed back into capital growth. You can't have both!

2005

$$\frac{\$330}{47} = 7.0$$

2004

$$\frac{\$291}{40} = 7.3$$

The same information can be presented in a different form as the dividend payout percentage:

Definition: (dividend ÷ net income) × 100%

2005

$$\frac{\$47}{\$330} \times 100\% = 14.2\%$$

2004

$$\frac{\$40}{\$291} \times 100\% = 13.7\%$$

Analysis: The dividend is amply covered by the earnings in both years.

13.7 Summary

Canadian Tire is a solid but, perhaps, unexciting company from a financial perspective. Its liquidity is low. Its profitability is low. Its debt is on the high side. Its efficiency is greatly reducing. Its earnings per share and dividend payout ratios are largely unchanged.

Appendix 13.1
The Dupont Pyramid of Operating Ratios

Return on Assets

Way back in the 1920s, the Dupont Company developed a "pyramid" of operating ratios to help it analyze its business operations and to guide the company toward appropriate remedial actions if things went off-track.

The apex of the pyramid is the profitability ratio, return on assets (ROA). ROA is defined as operating income divided by total assets. At the operating unit level, this is seen as the main business objective. However, if the ROA has fallen below the expected level, it is not easy to pinpoint exactly what actions to take to raise it back to where it should be.

General Trading had ROA in 2002, 2003, 2004, and 2005 of between 12% and 14%, and the business was seen as doing just fine. In 2006, the ROA fell to 9%, and the owners became concerned that it was not profitable enough. Because the ROA was only 9%, the return on equity was lower than the company had expected. (Return on equity is net income, after tax and interest, divided by owners' equity, and is the main ratio for judging investors' returns.)

If the ROA is down to 9%, the owners should be telling the operating managers to increase it. The question is, how? Either increase the operating income or decrease the assets would improve the ratio, but what actions can the managers take? The answer is that the ROA ratio does not, by itself, identify any practical steps that managers can take to fix this situation. There is nothing obvious that can be done to magically increase operating profit, nor to decrease total assets.

Dupont broke the ROA down into two parts by relating each of the two terms in the formula to the sales revenue:

$$\text{ROA} = \text{operating profit} \div \text{total assets}$$

That is the same as:

$$= \text{return on sales} \times \text{total asset turnover}$$
$$= \left(\frac{\text{operating profit}}{\text{sales revenue}}\right) \times \left(\frac{\text{sales revenue}}{\text{total assets}}\right)$$

Thus, there are now two ratios to explain the ROA. The return on sales shows how much of every sales dollar is left over as profit after all the costs and expenses have been met. The higher the return on sales, the higher the ROA becomes. The total asset turnover tells us how many

Exhibit 13A.1: General Trading

Income Statements ($ '000)	2005	% to Sales	2006	% to Sales
Sales revenue	$500	100	$600	100
Cost of goods sold	250	50	330	55
Gross margin	$250	50	$270	45
Less: Expenses				
Rent, utilities, and taxes	50	10	54	9
Wages	100	20	132	22
Other expenses	40	8	48	8
Total expenses	$190	38	$234	39
Operating profit	$ 60	12	$ 36	6

Asset Turnover Ratios

For General Trading the assets on the balance sheet for 2005 and 2006 have been expressed as turnover rates in relation to the sales of those years as follows:

($ '000)	2005	Turnover Ratio	2006	Turnover Ratio
Sales revenue	$500		$600	
Cash	$ 50	10.0	$ 50	12.0
Accounts receivable	100	5.0	120	5.0
Inventory	250	2.0	130	4.6
Long-term assets	100	5.0	100	6.0
Total assets	$500	1.0	$400	1.5

The dramatic improvement in the total asset turnover ratio (from 1.0 to 1.5) can be attributed to a number of causes:

- The cash balance stayed the same ($50,000) but, because the sales were higher, the turnover ratio increased from 10 to 12.
- The accounts receivable increased from $100,000 to $120,000, but this exactly matched the rate of increase in sales revenue, so the turnover ratio stayed the same.
- A substantial drop in inventory level (from $250 to $130) means that the inventory turnover ratio has risen (from 2.0 to 4.6).
- The long-term assets having stayed the same ($100,000) and sales revenue having increased, the long-term asset turnover ratio has increased from 5.0 to 6.0.

times each dollar of assets creates its own value in sales revenue each year. The higher the asset turnover ratio is, the more times per year the return on sales is earned, and so the higher the ROA becomes.

For General Trading, the ROA of 12% in 2005 can be broken down into a return on sales of 12% and a total asset turnover of 1.0 (see Exhibit 13A.1. The 12% was earned 1.0 times, so the ROA is also 12% (12% × 1.0 = 12%).

In 2006, the return on sales fell to 6%, but the total asset turnover increased to 1.5. The 6% was earned 1.5 times, and that resulted in a ROA of 9% (6% × 1.5 = 9%).

Vertical Analysis of the Income Statement

The Dupont system does not stop at breaking the ROA into return on sales and total asset turnover. It takes each of these and breaks it down into its component parts.

Managing the elements of the income statement (the gross margin percentage, the percentage of sales spent on wages, etc.) is a route to increasing the ROA. By breaking down every element of the income statement and expressing it as a percentage of sales, we get a picture of where the sales revenue is disappearing to. By tracking changes in these percentages, we can see why the ROA has declined and, perhaps more important, we can identify management improvements that would put the organization back on track. This percentage analysis of the income statement is sometimes referred to as a "vertical analysis of the income statement". (To calculate the expenses as a percentage of sales, the dollar value of the expense is divided by the dollar value of sales revenue, and then multiplied by 100.)

The 2005 and 2006 income statements for General Trading are summarized in Exhibit 13A.1, and the expenses shown as percentages of each year's sales revenue. From the vertical analysis of the income statement, some of the reasons for the decline in the return on sales (and, hence, ROA) can be determined:

- The cost of goods sold as a percentage of sales has increased, as a result of which the gross margin has declined by five points, from a 50% gross margin to a 45% gross margin.
- The rent, utilities, and taxes have gone down by one percentage point.
- The wages have increased by two points.
- Other expenses have stayed at the same percentage level.

The management question at this point is: why did these changes occur? Then the next question is: were they deliberate? For example, the reduction in gross margin may be a deliberate decision to reduce selling prices in order to boost sales volume. If this was the case, it worked, as sales volume increased from $500,000 to $600,000. The additional wage expense may have been because of a deliberate decision to hire more staff or pay a sales-related bonus in order to boost sales. Again, if that was the case, it worked. On the other hand, it may be that the decline in gross margin was due to poor stock control or poor purchasing decisions, and it may be that the increase in wage expense was due to hiring unnecessary staff. Neither the accountant nor the accounting system can answer these questions; the managers responsible for the operation of the stores must address them. Once their input has been received, there may be a clear way to redress the situation, such as increasing selling prices, or reducing stock losses through theft, or reducing staffing levels.

Efficiency Analysis of the Balance Sheet Assets

Measuring the elements of the asset side of the balance sheet (inventory, receivables, long-term assets, etc.) in relation to sales also enables us to understand the dynamics of the change in ROA, and engage in practical ways to improve it.

The lower the dollar value of the asset base on which the organization operates, the more efficiently it is operating, all other things being equal. By reducing the value of receivables, inventory, or long-term assets, we can improve the asset turnover ratio, and so improve the ROA. Conversely, if we relax control over an asset such as inventory and let it build up to an unnecessarily high level, it makes the asset turnover ratio fall, and eventually reduces ROA.

As with the vertical analysis of the income statement, we must differentiate between what the accounting reports tell us (they tell us that the turnover ratios have changed) and what the causes of those changes were; only the managers concerned can explain why the changes happened.

It could be, for example, that the increase in sales revenue or the decrease in gross margin percentage was directly linked to the reduction in inventory levels because they had a sale to get rid of old, slow-moving stock. The reduction in inventory could also be an independent initiative in pursuit of greater efficiency and totally unconnected to sales volume or sales margins.

Whatever the reasons, the total asset turnover ratio has shown a substantial increase between 2005 and 2006 (see Exhibit 13A.1), so there is probably little that can be done to increase it further. However, if management did plan to make further increases in the total asset turnover ratio, this breakdown would show them where their actions would be felt most strongly. Informed by these individual asset turnover ratios, they would make decisions about whether to try to reduce receivables (by chasing poor-paying customers) or reduce inventories (by moving to a just-in-time inventory management system), or concentrate on long-term asset efficiency.

Summary

The Dupont Pyramid of Operating Ratios is a powerful way of using the financial accounting ratios (see Exhibit 13A.2). It takes the descriptive benefits of the ratios and moves them toward management applications by suggesting areas where managers can change business practices in ways that improve the return on assets.

Exhibit 13A.2   The Dupont Pyramid of Operating Expenses

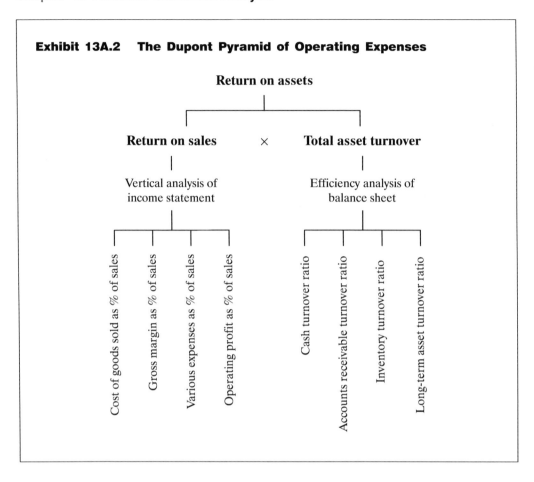

Self-Study Problem

1.

Randy the Retailer
Income Statement for 2008

Sales revenue		$5,000
Direct cost of sales		2,000
Gross profit		$3,000
Expenses		1,250
Operating income		$1,750
Interest	$250	
Income taxes	500	750
Net income		$1,000

Balance Sheet as at December 31, 2008

Current assets			Current liabilities		$2,000
Cash	$1,000				
Accounts receivables	1,400				
Inventory	2,600	$5,000	Long-term debt		500
			Total liabilities		$2,500
Long-term assets					
At cost	$6,000		Equity		
Amortization to date	3,500	2,500	Share capital	$1,000	
			Retained earnings	4,000	5,000
			Total liabilities		
Total assets		$7,500	and equity		$7,500

Required

Calculate appropriate accounting ratios and comment on the company's (a) liquidity, (b) profitability, (c) risk and (d) efficiency.

Solution

(a) Liquidity

Current ratio:

$$= \text{current assets} \div \text{current liabilities}$$
$$= \$5,000 \div \$2,000$$
$$= 2.5 : 1$$

Quick ratio:

$$= (\text{current ratio} - \text{inventory}) \div \text{current liabilities}$$
$$= (\$5,000 - \$2,600) \div \$2,000$$
$$= 1.2 : 1$$

Comment: This company is adequately liquid according to both these ratios.

(b) Profitability

Gross profit on sales %:

$$= (\text{gross profit} \div \text{sales revenue}) \times 100\%$$
$$= (\$3,000 \div \$5,000) \times 100\%$$
$$= 60\%$$

Return on sales %:

$$= (\text{operating income} \div \text{sales revenue}) \times 100\%$$
$$= (\$1,750 \div \$5,000) \times 100\%$$
$$= 35\%$$

Return on assets %:

$$= (\text{operating income} \div \text{total assets}) \times 100\%$$
$$= (\$1,750 \div \$7,500) \times 100\%$$
$$= 23.33\%$$

Return on equity %:

$$= (\text{net income} \div \text{total equity}) \times 100\%$$
$$= (\$1,000 \div \$5,000) \times 100\%$$
$$= 20\%$$

Comment: The gross profit ratio is 60% (it is not known whether or not this is what would be expected). Return on sales is 35%, return on assets is 23.33% and return on equity is 20%. None of these figures seems problematical.

(c) Risk

Debt to assets %:

$$= (\text{total debt} \div \text{total assets}) \times 100\%$$
$$= (\$2,500 \div \$7,500) \times 100\%$$
$$= 33.33\%$$

OR

Debt to equity %:

$$= \text{(total debt} \div \text{total equity)} \times 100\%$$
$$= (\$2,500 \div \%5,000) \times 100\%$$
$$= 50\%$$

Interest cover ratio:

$$= \text{operating income} \div \text{interest paid}$$
$$= \$1,750 \div \$250$$
$$= 7 \text{ times}$$

Comment: The amount of debt is reasonable (less than 50% of assets, less than 100% of equity) and interest is well covered. The company is low risk.

(d)   Efficiency

Total asset turnover:

$$= \text{sales revenue} \div \text{total assets}$$
$$= \$5,000 \div \$7,500$$
$$= .6667 \text{ times}$$

Receivables turnover ratio:

$$= \text{sales revenue} \div \text{receivables}$$
$$= \$5,000 \div \$1,400$$
$$= 3.6 \text{ times}$$

OR

Receivables collection period / Number of days' receivables:

$$= \text{receivables} \div \text{(sales revenues} \div 365)$$
$$= \$1,400 \div (\$5,000 \div 365)$$
$$= 102 \text{ days}$$

Inventory turnover:

$$= \text{sales revenue} \div \text{inventory}$$
$$= \$5,000 \div \$2,600$$
$$= 1.92 \text{ times}$$

OR

Inventory holding period:

$$= \text{inventory} \div \text{(sales revenue} \div 365)$$
$$= \$2,600 \div (\$5,000 \div 365)$$
$$= 190 \text{ days}$$

Comment: Receivables and inventory are turned over very slowly. As a result, total asset turnover is very low ($1 of assets does not even generate $1 of sales per year). This is very poor efficiency.

Note the relationship between efficiency and profitability:

Return on sales	×	Total asset turnover	×	Return on assets
35%	×	0.6667	×	23.33%

An increase in either the return on sales or the total asset turnover would increase the return on assets. This, in turn, would increase the return on equity.

Discussion Questions and Problem

Discussion Questions

1. Why are accounting ratios more useful than raw accounting data?
2. What is the objective of liquidity analysis?
3. What is the objective of profitability analysis?
4. What is the objective of debt analysis?
5. What is the objective of efficiency analysis?
6. How do market-related ratios increase our understanding of corporate performance?
7. Which is more important and why: the current ratio or the quick ratio?
8. Which is more important and why: the return on sales % or the return on assets %?
9. Which is more important and why: the return on assets % or the return on equity %?
10. How can efficiency ratios be used to increase profitability?

Problem

You are given the summarized financial statements of Shelburne Heating for 2006. Using financial ratio analysis, prepare a report on how well the company is doing.

Shelburne Heating
Statement of Earnings
and Retained Income for 2006
($ thousands)

Gross operating revenue		$5,374
Less: Cost of goods sold and operating expenses		
Various	$4,874	
Amortization	136	(5,010)
Operating income		$ 364
Less: Interest	$ 88	
Taxes	100	(188)
Net income		$ 176
Add: Retained earnings at start of year		860
		$1,036
Less: Cost of repurchase of shares	$ 32	
Dividends paid	31	(63)
Retained earnings at end of year		$ 973

Shelburne Heating
Balance Sheet
As At the End of 2006
($ thousands)

Current assets			
Cash		$ 579	
Accounts receivable		959	
Inventory		441	
Prepaid expenses		14	
Total current assets			$1,993
Long-term assets (net)			2,378
Total assets			$4,371
Current liabilities			$1,110
Long-term liabilities			1,357
Total liabilities			$2,467
Shareholders' equity			
Minority interest		$ 300	
Share capital	$622		
Retained earnings	973		
Foreign exchange adjustment	9	1,604	
Total shareholders' equity			1,904
Total liabilities and shareholders' equity			$4,371

4

Accounting for the Non-Profit Sector

Not-for-Profit and Governmental Organizations:

"A *nonprofit* activity is an integrated set of activities and assets that is capable of being conducted and managed for the purpose of providing benefits ... as a fulfillment of an organization's purpose or mission."

Financial Accounting Standards Board (U.S.), 2006

14

Accounting for Non-Profit and Governmental Organizations

Learning
Objectives

After studying this chapter, you should be able to:

→ Understand the nature of non-profit organizations

→ Understand the three basic characteristics of non-profit organizations

→ Explain the differences between non-profit organizations and governmental organizations

→ Understand how financial accounting for non-profit and governmental organizations differs from financial accounting for for-profit companies

→ Explain how financial statement analysis can be used by non-profit organizations

→ Explain the concepts of effectiveness and efficiency in the evaluation of non-profit organizations

→ Understand the role of budgeting and budgeting control in the management of non-profit organizations

14.1 Introduction

Up to this point this book has focused on accounting for business organizations, or what we will call in this chapter, *for-profit companies*. Despite the predominance of for-profit companies in the economy of Canada, non-profit organizations and governments represent a sizable share of economic activity. Though the objectives of these organizations differ from for-profit companies, accounting still plays an important role. This chapter surveys accounting principles and techniques for non-profit and governmental organizations.

14.2 Non-Profit and Governmental Organizations

14.2.1 *For-Profit and Non-Profit Organizations*

The principal objective of a business is to maximize profit — hence the term *for-profit company*, which we use to refer to business organizations in this chapter. There are, however, many activities for which self-interest and the profit-oriented form of organization is not appropriate. Organizations that are operated to provide goods or services rather than to make a profit are called *non-profit organizations* (*NPOs*).[1]

It is important to understand the distinction between for-profit companies and non-profit organizations. It is not the nature of the goods or services that they provide that distinguishes NPOs from for-profit companies.

---

[1] Non-profit organizations are also called *not-for-profit* organizations.

NPOs and for-profit companies can be found in all areas of economic activity. The essential difference between for-profit businesses and non-profit organizations is the motivation for their activities and the measure of their success. The assumption is that the objective of a for-profit company — to be more precise, the objective of the managers of a for-profit company — is to maximize profit on behalf of the owners. Whatever other personal motivations they may have, the common, basic interest of business owners, be they shareholders in incorporated companies, partners in partnerships or even sole proprietors, is financial self-interest. Profit — the growth of net worth from operations — is the measure of this objective, which explains the emphasis that accounting puts on the measurement of net income.

But not all economic activity is based on self-interest. Non-profit organizations exist to provide goods or services for some particular purpose rather than to maximize the profits of the business owners. There are various kinds of NPOs. Charities, for example, are organizations that raise money based on appeals to people's humanitarian feelings and then use the resources raised to carry out their mission of relieving poverty, encouraging the arts, finding cures for disease, etc. The pursuit of profit plays no role in their activities. Financial issues are important, primarily because what such organizations can do is limited by the amount of money and other resources they can raise. Put another way, financial considerations represents a *constraint* rather than any sort of objective. Since their expenditure is limited by their revenue, we can say that charities aim to *break even*. Operating to break even in the long run is in fact characteristic of non-profit organizations. Other activities that are operated on the same premises are hospitals, social service organizations, schools, and universities.[2] For some NPOs, the charitable aspect may not be present at all. Examples include clubs, unions, and other organizations, such as trade and professional associations, which offer services to their members, and co-operatives, which carry on business on behalf of their members. Non-profit organizations can be as small as personal charitable foundations or as large as national unions. What all of them have in common is the objective of providing services their revenue will support with no expectation of profit.

In a somewhat different category but still operating for the purposes of providing a service rather than making a profit are *governments* — in Canada, local, provincial, and federal governments. Governments are like NPOs in that profit is not an objective. But governments are unlike NPOs in that they have the *power to tax*. On the basis of various tax laws and, ultimately, the coercive power of the state, governments can compel individuals and companies to provide the money that is needed to carry out their activities.[3] The discussion that follows refers primarily to non-profit

---

[2] These examples are given for illustrative purposes; such activities are not necessarily carried out on a non-profit basis. For instance, although not very common in Canada, there are schools and hospitals that operate on a for-profit basis. These would be called *proprietary* schools or hospitals to distinguish them from non-profit organizations.

[3] Many hospitals, schools, and universities in Canada, while organized as NPOs, are effectively financed with public money and thus bear some of the characteristics of governmental organizations. Such organizations are sometimes referred to as *parapublic organizations*.

organizations but, in large part, applies to governments and government accounting as well. Significant differences between the characteristics or accounting of NPOs and governments will be highlighted.

14.2.2 *Characteristics of NPOs*

Non-profit organizations are defined by the presence of the following characteristics:

Service mission. The objective of an NPO is the provision of goods or services for a particular purpose rather than making a profit from its activities.

Break-even constraint. The long-run financial objective of the organization is to ensure that total expenses are equal to total revenues.

No beneficial ownership. Non-profit organizations have stakeholders and a governance structure, but do not have, as does a for-profit company, identifiable owners with an equity claim and the expectation of enjoying a financial return from the operation of the organization.

14.2.2.1 *Service Mission*

Every NPO has its own particular mission. For example, charities exist to help the poor or afflicted, or support the arts or research; schools and universities to educate students; hospitals to heal the sick; clubs and co-operatives to provide personal or business services to their members. Although the motivations differ, in all these cases the scope of the organization's activity is well-defined and resources are raised for that purpose. In some cases, such as charities, those that benefit and those that provide the resources are different; in others, such as clubs, associations, and co-operatives, they are the same. In many cases, such as schools and hospitals, there are elements of both: those that use the services (parents, students, patients) pay part of the costs, but funds are also provided by government or raised as charitable donations from alumni, friends, and others. In all cases, the objective of the NPO is to raise resources and spend them in a way that most effectively and efficiently serves the NPO's mission. This is its principal characteristic. See Focus Box 14.1.

14.2.2.2 *Break-even Constraint*

A second characteristic of an NPO is a financial one: the scale of its activities is limited by its revenue. In other words, over the long term, an NPO is constrained to break even. Of course, in a particular period it may happen that an organization raises more or less money than it spends. This "excess/(deficiency) of revenues over expenses" is called just that, rather than *profit*, and it is not normally sought for its own sake. It typically results from small, random variations of revenue and expense from budget; and, in the normal course of events, it will balance each other out over the longer term. Occasionally an NPO may budget for a series of excess revenues over expenses to accumulate capital for a future expansion of its activities; but again, this is not a case of maximizing prof-

---

Focus Box 14.1: Objective of the Canadian Red Cross Society

Excerpt from Notes to the Financial Statements

1. Purpose of the Organization
The Canadian Red Cross Society ["Society"] is a non-profit volunteer-based humanitarian organization dedicated to helping people in Canada and around the world with situations that threaten their survival and safety, their security and well-being, or their human dignity. The Society relies on continuing support from various levels of governments and fundraising from the United Way and other donors.

The Society, which is incorporated without share capital under the laws of Canada, is a registered Canadian charity and, as such, is exempt from income taxes under the Income Tax Act (Canada).

---

its for the benefit of the owners. (The law sometimes puts restrictions on the ability of an NPO to accumulate revenue in excess of expenses. For example, a charitable organization may lose its charitable status and the right to issue tax receipts if it does not distribute a substantial percentage of the donations it receives from the public.) Because non-profit organizations do not seek to make profits, they do not pay income tax.

14.2.2.3 *No Beneficial Ownership*

The absence of a profit motive brings out the third characteristic of NPOs: the absence of beneficial owners. NPOs are normally incorporated without share capital. The equity section of an NPO is usually very simple — just one line entitled "fund balance"[4] or "net assets". As corporations, they are legal persons or entities; they can own property and incur debt. As well, they have a governance structure that includes a board of directors and rules for determining who may elect the board and receive the financial reports. But although an NPO is a legal person that can own property, an NPO itself has no owners in the sense of persons who have a claim on the net assets of the organization or an expectation of enjoying a financial return from its operation. Rather, it has a membership or a community that contributes resources to the organization for the purpose of furthering its objectives.[5]

---

[4] An NPO using fund accounting would have a fund balance for each fund — see section 14.4.2.1, pp. 412–412.

[5] We can also speak of the potentially broader category of NPO *stakeholders*, which would include, in addition to the membership or community that contributes to the organization, those who are served by the organization. For non-profit organizations, the category of stakeholders can be very broad. *Creditors*, of course, have legal claims on the organization for interest and repayment of the loans they have extended, and they therefore have a stake. But governments, the press, and even members of the public at large can also have a say in how some non-profit organizations operate. The widespread public nature of the controversies that arose over the role of the Red Cross in blood collection is a case in point.

Clubs, co-operatives, and mutual societies are an exception to the no-beneficial-ownership principle. Though they have no profit objective, some clubs do issue shares to members who might then benefit from enhanced property values if the club is liquidated. Co-operatives and mutual societies have evolved in the non-profit tradition, but in many ways they have come to take on many for-profit characteristics, including shares, retained earnings, and profit maximization — see Focus Box 14.2.

Focus Box 14.2: Co-operatives and Mutual Societies

Co-operatives and mutual societies are organizations of a somewhat hybrid nature. They are an exception to the no-beneficial-ownership rule in that they carry on business on behalf of the members in addition to providing services to them. Co-operatives issue shares to members when they join and can pay dividends (usually based on the volume of business between the member and the organization). They pay taxes on undistributed income. Mutual societies, using different terminology, do much the same.

Historically, these organizations have not sought to maximize profits, although this is changing. Successful commercial activity carries with it pressure to conform fully to the business organizational model and has led some co-operatives and mutual insurance companies to operate effectively on a for-profit basis, and even in some cases to convert to the for-profit organizational form.

We can see an example of this pressure in the report of the chief executive officer in the 2004 annual report of the Mountain Equipment Cooperative (MEC). MEC was founded 33 years ago to serve hikers and mountain climbers in the Vancouver area. It has grown to be an organization with two million members across Canada and over $150 million in annual sales. The CEO makes the point that despite its commercial success, the Co-op has been able to maintain "a reputation for strong leadership in social and environmental matters". But he goes on to acknowledge that growth "has stretched and strained the business in ways the founders could not have envisioned". This has led to a "major restructuring of the organization" with the key priorities that include "... *planning for a modest annual surplus of 3–4%. This last goal sometimes seems incongruous, given that the Co-op is not about profit, but the size of the business dictates that we plan on achieving a surplus ... otherwise MEC has little flexibility to react to what is happening in the broader context* [emphasis added]". He feels it necessary to remind the members that the organization is still being run as a co-operative: "Any surplus at the end of the year, of course, goes back to members in the form of dividends to their share accounts."

It is difficult to avoid the conclusion that the more an NPO operates like a for-profit business, the more likely it is that it will become one. The main pressure has been the difficulty of access to capital when opportunities or threats arise. MEC deals with this by budgeting for a profit on a year-to-year basis. Will this be enough? Other large Canadian co-operatives have found it necessary to convert to the standard for-profit corporations. It will be interesting to see if the MEC can maintain its status as a co-operative.

14.2.3 Differences Between NPOs and Governmental Organizations

These three characteristics — service mission, break-even constraint, and no beneficial ownership — define the non-profit organization. Governmental organizations share these characteristics, but there are other important differences. Governments, like NPOs, have no beneficial ownership and pay no dividends. Governments pay no taxes (though they do collect them).

The biggest differences between governments and NPOs are in governance, mission, and financing. The differences in governance are generally understood and will not be pursued here. It is sufficient to note that governance in governmental organizations is essentially political and is based on constitutional law, whereas governance in NPOs is based on corporate law.

The mission of governments, even small municipal governments, is much broader in scope than most NPOs. Unlike an NPO, the service mission of government is multi-faceted, politically determined, and constrained only by constitution and convention. The break-even constraint is not so restrictive for governments. NPOs are primarily revenue-financed through a combination of voluntary contributions, sale of services, and grants and subsidies from other organizations, all of which can easily dry up. Governments' power to tax makes a big difference in their financial management. Even if taxes are not actually levied in the short run, sovereign governments normally have no problem financing deficits with debt. Even though long-term deficit financing by government raises economic questions beyond the scope of this book, deficits are more of an option for governments than they are for NPOs. Still, at some point, even sovereign governments are subject to a break-even constraint; it is just that they have a much longer time horizon over which they must balance revenue and expense than do any private sector NPOs.[6]

14.3 Accounting Techniques for Non-Profit Organizations

The focus in this book up to this point has been on the accounting principles and procedures of for-profit organizations. Many of the principles and most of the procedures of for-profit accounting are applicable to NPO accounting (and to a somewhat lesser extent to governmental accounting), so we will focus on the differences between them.

Accounting for NPOs grew out of the accounting practices of governments. Historically, government accounting has been heavily influenced by legal and political considerations. This is reflected in the use of fund accounting and, at least in the past, the use of cash-basis accounting in government accounting reports. Accounting for NPOs has evolved in the same tradition with its use of the cash basis recording of transactions, its

---

[6] Parapublic NPOs, such as hospitals, school boards, port and airport authorities, enjoy significant or full government support and, under certain conditions, can borrow money with a government financial guarantee that can allow them to operate with expenses in excess of revenues for relatively long periods of time.

Focus Box 14.3: Reporting Objectives and Accounting

It is helpful to consider differences in accounting for for-profit businesses, non-profit organizations, and governments in terms of the underlying reporting objectives. Communication of information to shareholders (both current and potential) is an underlying principle of accounting for business enterprises. Government accounting, on the other hand, has been influenced by the demands of political accountability and the constraints of the law with a focus on such questions as: How were revenues raised? Was expenditure within budget? Was spending in accordance with the law? Since accounting for non-profit organizations evolved in this tradition, it took on the basic form of government accounting, including the use of fund accounting and an emphasis on reporting cash transactions. In recent years, however, more of a measurement and information focus has been adopted, and NPO accounting has taken on many of the characteristics of business accounting. We can represent this as follows:

Informational Focus   **Political-Legal Focus**

Accounting for:

For-profits   NPOs   *NPOs*   **Governments**
                       (today)   (historically)

emphasis on fund accounting and stewardship reporting, and the importance given to control through budgets. This is changing, however. In the past few years, accounting standard setters have acted to bring accounting standards for non-profit organizations more in line with those of for-profit companies. Measurement of assets and liabilities, revenues and expenses using the principles of accrual accounting is the main focus of these changes. The fundamental differences in organizational objectives between for-profit and non-profit, of course, remain. Though in many ways they have moved toward business accounting, the use of fund accounting by NPOs (and governments) is a reflection of basic differences (see Focus Box 14.3). In addition there are differences in the areas of revenue recognition and the treatment of capital assets and, more generally, in accounting form and terminology. It is important to note, too, that because profit is neither sought nor measured, the use of accounting reports for scorekeeping in NPOs is much more limited.

14.4 Financial Accounting for Non-Profit Organizations

Broadly speaking, many of the principles of accounting used by for-profit companies apply to non-profit organizations as well. For this reason there is considerable similarity in accounting practice and terminology. There are at the same time important differences, and we will highlight the principal ones in the following areas:

- Financial statements
- Organizational entity
- Revenue and expense
- Amortization

14.4.1 *Financial Statements*

The general form of financial reports for both for-profit companies and non-profit organizations are the same, but there are differences in terminology reflecting their different objectives and legal structure. Both the balance sheet and the cash flow statement have the same names and same general form for for-profit companies and non-profit organizations. Both for-profit and non-profit organizations prepare operating statements, but what would normally be called an *income statement* or *earnings statement* by for-profit companies is a *statement of operations* or *statement of revenue and expense* by NPOs. Since NPOs are organized without share capital and do not earn profits, the equity change statement is much simpler and the terminology more appropriate to non-profit organizations: *statement of fund balances* or *statement of net assets* instead of the for-profit companies' *statement of retained earnings*. (The term *fund balance* will often be used even if there are no other features of fund accounting.) It is common for NPOs to combine the Statement of Operations with the Statement of Fund Balances as a Statement of Operations and Fund Balances.

Focus Box 14.4 compares the names of the financial statements of NPOs and for-profit companies. An example of combined statements of operations and fund balances and a multi-column balance sheet can be found in Appendix 14.1. It is worth pointing out that this organization, Centraide of Montreal, a large charitable fundraising organization (similar to United Way in other Canadian cities), does not prepare a cash flow

---

Focus Box 14.4: Financial Statement Terminology

Non-Profit Organization	For-Profit Company
Balance sheet	Balance sheet
Statement of operations (or revenue and expense)	Income statement (or Statement of earnings)
Statement of fund balance (or net assets)	Statement of retained earnings
Statement of cash flows	Statement of cash flows

statement. Lack of a cash flow statement is common among NPOs. Even though it is clear from this organization's balance sheet that the statements are prepared on at least a modified accrual basis, in a note to the financial statements the directors state that a statement of cash flows has not been presented as it would not provide any additional meaningful information. The auditors have accepted this assessment.

14.4.2 *Organizational Entity*

The basic notion of a business or organizational entity is the same for both for-profit companies and non-profit organizations. A difference arises, however, in the way in which the entity can be sub-divided. In a for-profit organization, these sub-entities are themselves legally independent incorporated companies and produce their own financial statements. For reporting purposes of the controlling parent, however, they are subsidiaries and their financial results are combined with those of the parent in consolidated statements (see Chapter 4, Appendix 4.3). Such parent–subsidiary relationships are not typically found in non-profit organizations. It is common, however, for the board of an NPO, especially a large NPO, to divide the entity internally by objective or by operating restriction. Thus, an NPO may contain two or more accounting entities, and they are called *funds*. This system of accounting is called *fund accounting*.

14.4.2.1 *Fund Accounting*

A fund is a self-balancing *accounting entity* within the legal entity that is the organization itself. *Fund accounting* refers to the accounting procedures underlying sets of self-balancing accounts in an organization, one for each fund established by law, contract, or policy. A fund will typically include a balance sheet (assets, liabilities, fund balance, or net assets), operating statement (revenues, expenses), and statement of fund balance (or net assets). The separation of resources in fund accounting is normally of an accounting nature only, although there may be physical segregation of some assets.

Fund accounting is characteristic of NPOs and governments, though not all such organizations use it. Fund accounting is found in organizations that have independent service objectives or administer segregated resources for which there are specific restrictions on how they are used. Fund accounting is never found in the for-profit sector. In a for-profit organization, the entity as a whole has the one overriding objective: to maximize the profits of the whole organization. Since a for-profit company's various activities are designed and operated with this goal in mind, any breakdown of these activities for reporting purposes is for information only — it is not a structural principle of the organization.

Every non-profit organization must have an *unrestricted* or *general fund*, although it may not be so named if it is a small organization with only one fund (and even in these cases, the term *fund balance* is frequently used in place of the term *net assets* now preferred by the standard-setters as the name of the equity section of the balance sheet). Other funds that are typically found in NPOs are the *restricted fund* (or funds), the *endowment fund*, and the *capital* or *plant fund*. In a very large NPO, the funds reported in the financial statements may in fact be groupings of smaller funds, since each legal or operating restriction will give rise to a separate fund. For example, each scholarship endowment in a university is accounted for in a separate fund, though for simplicity the numerous endowment funds would be grouped and reported together on the financial statements in one "endowment fund".

There are different ways of presenting the funds on the financial statements, but the multi-column format, which shows the funds in parallel columns, is the clearest accounting representation. When funds have transactions with one another (as is often the case) and there are balances owing/receivable at year-end, these balances will be shown on the financial statements. See Appendix 14.1 for an example of the financial statements of a charity that uses fund accounting.

14.4.3 *Revenue and Expense*

Traditionally, like governments, non-profit organizations operated on a cash basis rather that on an accrual basis. It was felt that accounting for cash was by far the most important responsibility of NPOs. Conversely, income measurement, which uses the accrual basis of accounting and is used to assess how much "better off" the entity is after each period of operations, was seen as inappropriate for a non-profit organization. This view has changed. Today, there is a consensus that, so far as possible, NPOs should follow the rules of accrual accounting, namely, that revenue and expenses be recognized when the event takes place rather than when cash changes hands. What this means is that there is an increasing use of accrual accounting procedures in NPOs, and we now see revenues and expenses are measured in a manner similar to that used in business accounting with corresponding accruals of receivables and payables. In addition, amortization accounting is often practised. (Because it is not always appropriate or even possible to apply all the principles of accrual accounting to NPOs, the method used is often described as "modified accrual-basis accounting".)

The purpose of using accrual accounting in NPOs is to measure real resource flows, not to determine income as such. Since an NPO does not have owners and there is no profit to account for, there must be a change in terminology. Instead of *net income*, the difference between revenues and expenses is normally labelled *excess/(deficiency) of revenue over expense* or just *net result*. The statement that corresponds to income statement in for-profit financial statements becomes, in non-profit terminology, the *statement of operations* or *statement of revenues and expenses*.

It should be noted that many NPOs, especially smaller organizations, feel that the advantages of using even modified accrual-basis accounting do not justify the additional bookkeeping cost. Such organizations would then do their reporting on a cash basis. In a pure cash-basis system, revenues are cash receipts and expenses are cash expenditures. Receivables and payables will not be recognized, nor will capital assets, which will be expensed fully and immediately when purchased. The balance sheet will have only two items: the asset (cash) and the equity (fund balance or net assets). There will be no statement of cash flows because it would be identical to the statement of operations.[7]

14.4.3.1 Revenue Recognition

By definition, revenue is the gross increase in net assets corresponding to the inflow of assets (or reduction of liabilities) from operations. The major issue in revenue recognition is timing: when do we recognize revenue in a particular series of transactions? Or to use the technical terms, *when is revenue realized?* Accountants have traditionally insisted that there should be a completed exchange before revenue can be considered earned. In other words, goods or services must be transferred to the buyer in exchange for cash or an enforceable claim to cash.

In the case of a typical for-profit company, realization is almost always directly linked to delivery, in other words to the provision of goods or services. The organization itself must fulfill its part of the contract, or at least a significant part of it, before revenue can be recognized. For non-profit organizations, however, this criterion must be interpreted differently because revenue is not based on an exchange. In fact, there is often no link between the supply of resources and the organization's provision of goods or services. This is most clearly the case for a charity with revenue coming from one group (e.g., the donors) and goods and services provided to a second group (i.e., the beneficiaries of the charity). Since there is no direct relationship between revenues and expenditures, the service-provision test is not really applicable. Thus, a non-profit organization normally chooses to recognize contributions as they are received. This is an exception to the general recognition rule, and the use of a fund accounting framework minimizes the possibility that it will be misinterpreted.

For NPOs, expenditure is the measure of service provided (even though it is not matched to revenue), but there remains the separate question of an enforceable claim. For a for-profit company, there must be a reasonable expectation that any money owed on a transaction will be collected. Because of the difficulty in enforcing charitable pledges, rather than treating it as an account receivable charities normally wait until the money is received before recognizing the revenue. (See Focus Box 14.5, Revenue Recognition Policy of Centraide of Greater Montreal.)

14.4.3.2 Fixed Assets and Amortization

Amortization is the measure of the use of long-term capital assets over time. It requires making a distinction between the capital expenditure at the time the capital asset was purchased and the subsequent series of amortization expenses. Traditionally, under the influence of governmental accounting where stewardship of cash was the principal concern, the financial statements of non-profit organizations measured the *expenditure* (payment) of funds. Amortization did not involve the expenditure of funds and

---

[7] As we can see from the sample financial statements in Appendix 14.1, even an NPO that uses modified accrual accounting with limited recognition of receivables and payables may not prepare a cash flow statement because it would add so little additional information to what is presented in the statement of operations.

Focus Box 14.5: Revenue Recognition Policy of Centraide of Greater Montreal

Excerpt from Accounting Policies, 2004

Cash donations are recorded when they are received, while subscription revenue is recognized when pledges are received.

---

consequently it was not recognized in the financial statements. According to this view, purchases of fixed assets must be accounted for in the period they take place. The transaction may be treated like all other current expenditures, and the asset is effectively "expensed" on purchase. An alternative treatment is to have the asset capitalized and then left on the balance sheet without any subsequent amortization. In either case there are no further transactions with respect to the asset. As far as NPOs are concerned, this did not represent a particular problem. An income measure was not needed to provide information to financial markets, nor for tax purposes or dividend purposes. Financial statements with a conventional measure of income including amortization might have been useful for presentation to a bank or other financial institution in support of a loan application, but in fact revenue guarantees from a government or a granting agency, or the security of mortgaged fixed assets would be worth much more. Moreover, some would argue that recording amortization would mislead statement users by recording a cost in the operating statement that was not properly a cost to operations since operating transactions and capital transactions should be kept separate.[8] To sum up, many preparers and users of NPO financial statements were of the opinion that amortization was unnecessary and even misleading.

The current view on amortization (by no means universally held) is more in line with the business income model with its focus on information for decision making. Preparing statements to show appropriable resources realized and disposed of (essentially a cash flow statement) does not preclude recognizing amortization. To ignore amortization throws away information. For all its faults, accounting amortization is the best estimate we have of asset consumption. Without it, expenses are an incomplete

---

[8] A clear distinction between operating transactions and capital transactions has a long tradition in government and NPO accounting. Finding the money to purchase the capital asset is one decision (and one basis of accounting), and getting the resources on a year-by-year basis to operate the service is another. For example, a hospital or university might finance the purchase of a new building by approaching a wealthy donor or organizing a capital campaign for that purpose. The building could be expected to last for a very long time, and in any case would presumably be replaced by mounting another capital campaign. In such circumstances, the cost of using the asset (i.e., amortization) was not an operating cost and should not be an expense in the statement of revenue and expense. In the same way, organizations that charge users fees should not include amortization as part of the cost of the service since to do so would be overcharging: both the donor and the user would be paying for the capital asset.

measure of the true economic cost of the organization's operations. The advantages of an amortization measure for costing should be self-evident, particularly where the operation is meant to be self-sustaining. It can be added that charges of "unfair competition"[9] from businesses operating in the same line will be more easily avoided if the NPO's fees are set on a full-cost basis including a fair measure of amortization.

Finally, there is a legitimate concern over the criticism that amortization would involve double charging if the assets were purchased with the proceeds of a capital campaign. If full-cost fees include amortization (assuming (1) that the amortization policy is appropriate, (2) that prices are stable, and (3) that all other costs are covered), break-even operations will imply that cash is accumulating for the replacement of the fixed asset at their original cost. Under these circumstances, it is true that a capital campaign to replace the organization's assets at the end of their expected useful lives would in fact be redundant. Thus, if amortization is charged in the accounts, capital campaigns should only be undertaken to expand or significantly upgrade an NPO's facilities.

In the past decade, full amortization accounting along the same lines as that used in for-profit accounting is required by NPOs in Canada. According to the CICA Handbook, *capital assets* should be carried at cost on the balance sheet and be *amortized*. If the amortization transactions are carried out in the operating fund, the effect will be essentially the same as conventional business amortization accounting. However, if the NPO uses fund accounting and segregates capital asset and related long-term debt in a capital asset fund, the result will be much different. Rather, it will appear in the statement of revenue and expense of the capital asset fund. See, for example, the revenue and expense statement (called *statement of operations…*) of the capital asset fund in Appendix 14.1 on p. 425.

14.5 Financial Statement Analysis

Compared to its use with for-profit companies, conventional financial statement analysis as summarized in Chapter 13 has limited usefulness in assessing non-profit organizations. Any ratio that uses a measure of profitability has no meaning for an organization that does not seek to make a profit, cannot pay dividends, and has no shares to trade on the market. This means that all the profit-based ratios (return on sales, assets, equity and the interest cover ratio) and all market-related measures (earnings per share, price-to-earnings ratio, dividend cover ratio, and dividend payout) have no application for NPOs. Similarly, debt ratios have limited usefulness. A debt-to-asset ratio might be helpful in assessing an organization's capacity to finance new capital assets with long-term debt, but finan-

---

[9] Complaints are sometimes made by for-profit health clubs and studios that feel the fees charged by neighbourhood YMCA/YWCAs and other NPOs unfairly undercut the commercial prices because they don't cover amortization of facilities (or pay a fair rent, which would include an allowance for amortization). Such arguments have validity if the NPO facility costing does not charge amortization.

cial management for the purpose of taking advantage of leverage (the debt-to-equity ratio) is meaningless for an NPO. All the same, interest on long-term debt is an ongoing commitment to make interest payments, and some measure of the relative burden of interest can be useful to readers. For an NPO, this could be measured by a variant of the interest cover ratio using revenue available for general operations instead of net income as the numerator. The higher the ratio, the lower the burden of interest.

Liquidity ratios — current ratio and quick ratio — can be useful, but only if the organization uses a full accrual basis that measures current assets and current liabilities in the same way that for-profit companies do. Since not all NPOs do so, one must ensure that a full accrual basis is used for the ratios to be meaningful. Similarly, some of the efficiency ratios may be useful with the right circumstances. If receivables arise out of revenue and are managed on a commercial basis, receivable turnover and collection period measures are applicable, but these conditions do not always exist. Readers of the financial statements of private schools and universities might find these measures useful, but there are not many other situations where they would apply. Even rarer in an NPO context are situations where inventory turnover and holding period measures could convey useful information. These measures could only be used for the rare NPO that carries and sells goods on a commercial basis and manages its inventory accordingly.

Financial statements of NPOs are used primarily to reveal the scale of the organization's operations and to check that it is satisfying the break-even constraint over the long run. To assess the success of the organization in carrying out its mandate in an effective and efficient manner, other tools are needed. These are discussed in the next section.

14.6 Evaluating Effectiveness and Efficiency in Non-Profit Organizations

How can we measure the success of a company or an organization? Consider the for-profit company first. In principle, the success of a for-profit organization is directly measured by net income. Net income is the difference between revenue (the value the market has paid for the goods and services produced and sold by the company, or the social value of its output) and expense (the cost of all the inputs used to produce the output). Net income thus is a measure of the value added by the company above and beyond all the measured inputs and represents the pure profit for the company owners. This profit can be compared to previous period's profit to give us a sense of how the company is doing over time. If the profit (net income) is compared to the owners' investment in the company (i.e., in accounting terms, the book value of shareholders' equity), we have a scale-free measure of rate of return, which can be compared to that of other companies of any size in the same line, or more generally, to any company. In general, the higher the net income, the higher the rate of return, and the more successful the company has been.

A similar assessment cannot be done for a non-profit organization. Making a profit is not an objective, and, in the long run, it is expected to be zero in any case. Even looking at revenue or expense alone as a measure of total output or total input is problematic. Revenue for most non-profit organizations is simply contributions, not a measure of what the organization produces, as for a for-profit company. Some NPOs, such as theatre groups, symphonies, and opera companies, do earn revenue from sales of tickets. But if prices are subsidized by other revenue from government and private donations, it would be inappropriate to take total revenue as a market measure of how much the public values what these organizations produce. Expenses are also not necessarily reliable measures of resources used. While some inputs of non-profit organizations are purchased at market price, other inputs, especially those of intrinsic value such as volunteer labour, are supplied at nominal or zero cost. In short, to the extent that there are outputs or inputs for which a market price has not been paid, there is no independent measure of the value of these resource flows. Consequently, conventional accounting measures and financial reports are of little help in evaluating the success of non-profit organizations.

As we have seen, conventional financial statement analysis has a very limited role in the assessment of non-profit organizations. Other tools and techniques do exist for this purpose. What follows is a brief overview of effectiveness and efficiency as principles for evaluating non-profit organizations. It must be emphasized that, unlike the concepts of financial accounting, there is not as yet a body of "generally accepted" evaluation criteria for NPOs. In certain industries, some indicators and measures might be widely used, but this does not mean that they are generally accepted. When a general standard of evaluation is accepted, it is most likely to come through the influence of governments, which have the power to mandate regulatory reports in fields such as health care (hospitals) and education (schools and universities).

14.6.1 *Effectiveness*

Effectiveness is solely concerned with *output* — how well does the organization do in what it has set itself to do. This involves a comparison between some desired, expected, or standard output on the one hand, and what is actually achieved on the other. There is no reference to inputs in the concept of effectiveness.

If the objective of a non-profit organization is to provide a single, well-defined service, then measuring the organization's effectiveness in providing that service is the most direct assessment of how well the organization has succeeded in its mission. Because effectiveness is an important measure, however, does not mean that it can be easily or unambiguously made. This is especially true for non-profit organizations that provide a range of services, or NPOs whose services are not easily identified or measured. Since for many large NPOs — hospital, universities, social service agencies, for example — there is no agreement on what they should be doing except in the broadest terms, it is easy to see that even identifying effectiveness measures will be fraught with difficulty. Listed below are some examples of effectiveness measures for common NPOs:

Hospitals: Number of patients served/cured/stabilized;
Number of emergency cases treated;
Measure of hospital-generated disease....

Schools: Percentage of eligible population served;
Percentage of students entering who complete the year;
Percentage of students placed in prestige colleges....

University: Percentage of eligible population served;
Percentage of students entering who graduate;
Size of library;
Number of library places;
Number of Nobel prize winners on faculty....

14.6.2 *Efficiency*

Efficiency is concerned with the *relationship of inputs to outputs*. This can be measured as a ratio of output to input, or as a difference between output and input. The ratio has more general application as there is no need for the numerator and the denominator to be in the same terms (for example, average annual graduates per full-time teacher). Still, if we want to compare two situations in terms of an efficiency ratio (for example, two different organizations or the same organizations at different times), we must be sure that in both situations the measure used as the numerator and the measure used as the denominator are the same. If, for example, the efficiency measure of a hospital is the number of patients per full-time nurse, we must be sure that the mix of patients is the same for the other hospital that is being compared. Otherwise, the measure must take that into account.

Consider another example. If we compare the efficiency of various universities by looking only at the number of full-time equivalent students per full-time faculty member, it will give very misleading results because some universities have medical schools and large graduate programs and others do not. For a meaningful comparison, one either weights the number of students in the different schools and programs in some unbiased fashion — which may be difficult to do — or avoids the problem by comparing only similar schools and programs rather than the university as a whole. In other words, it would be appropriate to compare undergraduate programs in two universities in terms of teaching efficiency (measured by number of students per faculty member); however, any *overall* comparison of the two universities would be invalid unless they had very similar structures.

Finally, efficiency and effectiveness are not unrelated. For example, the efficiency of public service in different jurisdictions is often compared. Take the case of garbage collection. If one city collects twice a week and the other only once, it would be quite surprising if the latter were not cheaper since the cost of garbage storage is largely borne by the households. From the municipality's point of view, cheaper generally means more efficient. But is it? Garbage collection costs per household are lower with once a week collection as compared to twice a week collection, but in fact they are different services even if there is no explicit measure of the storage costs to the householders of additional containers, loss of amenity, etc., of the less frequent service. This is not to say that less frequent garbage collection might not, on balance, be a wiser policy, but in making a proper judgment about efficiency, effectiveness must either be explicitly measured or held constant. It is for this reason that effectiveness and efficiency have to be dealt with together.

14.7 Budgeting and Budgetary Control

14.7.1 The Importance of Budgets for NPOs and Governments

Because, as a rule, non-profit organizations do not have measured output and do not sell their output in a market, management accounting techniques that focus on production (activity-based costing) or units sales (break-even analysis) have limited applicability to non-profit organizations or government. Budgeting and budgetary control are, however, widely used in the management of non-profit organizations. In fact because the discipline of the market is largely absent from non-profit organizations — and even more so for governments — budgeting and budgeting control are key management techniques for these organizations.

14.7.2 Techniques of Budgeting in NPOs

The mechanics of budgeting — operating budgets, cash (financial) budgets, and control — are much the same for NPOs as they are for for-profit organizations as described in Chapters 7 and 8. The differences lie in the objective. Unlike for-profit organizations that also use budgets for planning and motivating (target) purposes, the primary purpose of budgeting in NPOs is for organizational control. Selling, even when the organization does produce and sell some output, is very rarely a central activity of an NPO. The operating constraint for most NPOs is the revenue budget. The scale of activity of the organization and any financial planning and cash budgeting all flow from the organization's expectations of revenue. The objective of the budget is therefore to ensure — so far as possible — that expenditures are kept in line with expected revenues.

14.8 Summary

Non-profit and governmental organizations differ fundamentally in purpose from for-profit companies. The difference in purpose has historically affected the manner of accounting and the form of financial statements of both NPOs and governments. These differences have been narrowed in recent years, but the absence of profit as an objective requires that we use NPO and government financial statements as accountability reports rather than as the basis for analysis and prediction. Without the summary measure of efficiency that profit provides, concern for effectiveness and efficiency requires that accounting information from NPOs and governments be supplemented by non-financial measures, such as measures of frequency of service (e.g., case load for a social service agency, emergencies handled by an ambulance service) and measures of quality (percentage of graduates of an NPO school going on to university, dollar value of research grants held by medical staff at a hospital). Management accounting techniques have to be similarly adapted for use with NPOs and governmental organizations.

Appendix 14.1
Example of Financial Statements of a Not-for-Profit Organization Prepared Using Fund Accounting

This appendix presents excerpts of the 2003–2004 financial statements for Centraide of Greater Montreal, a large charitable fundraising organization.[1] Included are a description of the different funds, the combined statement of operations, and fund balance of the operating fund and the capital asset fund, as well as the balance sheets of all the funds in multi-column format. The published statements do not include a cash flow statement.

Excerpts from Accounting Policies

Fund accounting

The organization uses the restricted fund method to account for its activities:

i) Operating Fund

The Operating Fund comprises the current operating activities of Centraide of Greater Montreal. The annual net result, less interfund transfers, is applied against the Stabilization Fund.

ii) Stabilization Fund

The Stabilization Fund was created to provide financial stability to agencies financed by Centraide of Greater Montreal, to satisfy new initiatives and urgent needs of the community, and to answer needs considered urgent and approved by the Board of Directors. The Fund varies according to interest earned, the amount of unallocated funds, an annual contribution equal to 0.5% of the previous campaign, and the net result for the year. The balance of the Stabilization Fund must not exceed 10% of the amount of the previous campaign.

iii) Capital Asset Fund

The Capital Asset Fund comprises the depreciated cost of the building, furniture and equipment, and computer equipment. The Fund varies according to interest earned, amounts received for the purpose of acquiring fixed assets, depreciation, and an annual contribution equal to 0.5% of the previous campaign for updating and ongoing development of computer systems.

iv) 1,2,3 GO! Fund

The aim of the 1,2,3 GO! Fund is to provide disadvantaged children, up to three years of age, with conditions for optimal development by supporting local initiatives.

---

[1] Excerpts from Annual Report 2004, pp. 11–16. The complete set of statements can be found at **centraide-mtl.org/centraide/static/publications_e/default.htm**. © Centraide of Greater Montreal. Reproduced with permission of Centraide du Grand Montréal.

v) Development Fund

The Development Fund was created to fund research and development activities and pilot and other projects that are not considered as part of Centraide of Greater Montreal's usual activities and whose ultimate goal is to significantly increase the funds donated to Centraide of Greater Montreal over the coming years.

AUDITORS' REPORT

To the Members of Centraide of Greater Montreal

We have audited the balance sheet of Centraide of Greater Montreal as at March 31, 2004 and the statements of operations and fund balance of the Operating Fund, Stabilization Fund, Capital Asset Fund, 1,2,3 GO! Fund and Development Fund for the year then ended. These financial statements are the responsibility of Centraide of Greater Montreal's management. Our responsibility is to express an opinion on these financial statements based on our audit.

We conducted our audit in accordance with Canadian generally accepted auditing standards. Those standards require that we plan and perform an audit to obtain reasonable assurance whether the financial statements are free of material misstatement. An audit includes examining, on a test basis, evidence supporting the amounts and disclosures in the financial statements. An audit also includes assessing the accounting principles used and significant estimates made by management, as well as evaluating the overall financial statement presentation.

In our opinion, these financial statements present fairly, in all material respects, the financial position of Centraide of Greater Montreal as at March 31, 2004 and the results of its operations and its cash flows for the year then ended in accordance with Canadian generally accepted accounting principles.

Samson Bélair / Deloitte & Touche s.e.n.c.r.l.

Chartered Accountants
April 30, 2004

OPERATING FUND
Statement of operations and fund balance
YEAR ENDED MARCH 31, 2004

	2004	2003
	2002 Campaign $	2001 Campaign $
Revenues		
Subscriptions		
Pledges at beginning of year	37,333,301	36,970,605
Received during the year	3,265,642	1,695,131
	40,598,943	38,665,736
Uncollectible subscriptions	(1,315,289)	(1,313,333)
	39,283,654	37,352,403
Interest and other revenue	368,884	337,346
	39,652,538	37,689,749
Expenses		
Fundraising, communication and administrative costs	4,896,396	4,711,110
	34,756,142	32,978,639
Allocations and assistance to agencies		
Allocations to agencies (Note 5)	31,983,904	30,226,415
Assistance to agencies, social research and community services	2,465,810	2,393,785
	34,449,714	32,620,200
Net result	306,428	358,439
Fund balance, beginning of year	—	—
Interfund transfers (Note 7)	(365,200)	(349,000)
	(58,772)	9,439
Transfer from (to) Stabilization Fund (Note 2i)	58,772	(9,439)
Fund balance, end of year	—	—

STABILIZATION FUND
Statement of operations and fund balance
YEAR ENDED MARCH 31, 2004

	2004	2003
	$	$
Revenues		
Interest	89,665	76,989
Expenses		
Allocation to the Foundation of Greater Montréal	—	75,000
Net result	89,665	1,989
Fund balance, beginning of year	2,919,362	2,733,434
Transfer from 1,2,3 GO! Fund (Note 7)	145,803	—
Interfund transfers (Note 7)	182,600	174,500
Transfer (to) from Operating Fund (Note 2i)	(58,772)	9,439
Fund balance, end of year	**3,278,658**	2,919,362

CAPITAL ASSET FUND
Statement of operations and fund balance
YEAR ENDED MARCH 31, 2004

	2004	2003
	$	$
Revenues		
Contributions — Fondation Centraide du Grand Montréal	20,000	155,000
Interest	7,504	8,089
	27,504	163,089
Expenses		
Depreciation of fixed assets	286,300	258,264
Other expenses	18,691	1,560
	304,991	259,824
Net result	(277,487)	(96,735)
Fund balance, beginning of year	2,180,089	2,102,324
Interfund transfers (Note 7)	182,600	174,500
Fund balance, end of year	**2,085,202**	2,180,089

1,2,3 GO! FUND
Statement of operations and fund balance
YEAR ENDED MARCH 31, 2004

	2004	2003
	$	$
Revenues		
Contributions	—	46,238
Interest	4,050	5,899
	4,050	52,137
Expenses		
Support to neighbourhoods		
Allocations to neighbourhoods	45,587	149,442
Net result	(41,537)	(97,305)
Fund balance, beginning of year	187,340	284,645
Transfer to Stabilization Fund (Note 7)	(145,803)	—
Fund balance, end of year	**—**	187,340

DEVELOPMENT FUND
Statement of operations and fund balance
YEAR ENDED MARCH 31, 2004

	2004	2003
	$	$
Revenues		
Contributions — Fondation Centraide du Grand Montréal	250,000	250,000
Interest	6,468	4,040
	256,468	254,040
Expenses		
Training and research and development expenses	115,258	264,798
Net result	141,210	(10,758)
Fund balance, beginning of year	33,022	43,780
Fund balance, end of year	**174,232**	33,022

BALANCE SHEET
AS AT MARCH 31, 2004

	Operating Fund	Stabilization Fund	Capital Asset Fund	1,2,3 GO! Fund	Development Fund	Total 2004	Total 2003
	$	$	$	$	$	$	$
Assets							
Current assets							
Cash and temporary investments	20,156,140	3,278,658	238,701	—	174,232	23,847,731	23,105,744
Subscriptions receivable	14,438,358	—	—	—	—	14,438,358	12,911,207
Other assets	1,092,396	—	20,000	—	—	1,112,396	961,942
	35,686,894	3,278,658	258,701	—	174,232	39,398,485	36,978,893
Fixed assets (Note 3)	—	—	1,826,501	—	—	1,826,501	1,896,700
	35,686,894	3,278,658	2,085,202	—	174,232	41,224,986	38,875,593
Liabilities							
Current liabilities							
Accounts payable and accrued liabilities	980,780	—	—	—	—	980,780	1,879,739
Balance payable to agencies	130,250	—	—	—	—	130,250	134,648
Deferred revenues (Note 4)	34,575,864	—	—	—	—	34,575,864	31,541,393
	35,686,894	—	—	—	—	35,686,894	33,555,780
Fund balances							
Invested in fixed assets	—	—	1,826,501	—	—	1,826,501	1,896,700
Externally restricted	—	—	39,499	—	174,232	213,731	108,559
Internally restricted	—	3,278,658	219,202	—	—	3,497,860	3,314,554
	—	3,278,658	2,085,202	—	174,232	5,538,092	5,319,813
	35,686,894	3,278,658	2,085,202	—	174,232	41,224,986	38,875,593

Approved by the Board

Claire Richer Leduc, Chairman

Jean-Jacques Bourgeault, Treasurer

NOTES TO THE FINANCIAL STATEMENTS
YEAR ENDED MARCH 31, 2004

1.   Description of the organization

Centraide of Greater Montreal, a non-profit organization incorporated under Part III of the *Companies Act* (Québec), is recognized as a registered charity within the meaning of the *Income Tax Act*. Centraide of Greater Montreal collects public donations to promote community involvement through sharing and voluntary activities.

2.   Accounting policies

These financial statements are not prepared on a cumulative basis and do not include the accounts of the Fondation Centraide du Grand Montréal.

The financial statements have been prepared in accordance with Canadian generally accepted accounting principles and include the following significant accounting policies:

Fund accounting

The organization uses the restricted fund method to account for its activities:

i)   Operating Fund

The Operating Fund comprises the current operating activities of Centraide of Greater Montreal. The annual net result, less interfund transfers, is applied against the Stabilization Fund.

ii)   Stabilization Fund

The Stabilization Fund was created to provide financial stability to agencies financed by Centraide of Greater Montreal, to satisfy new initiatives and urgent needs of the community, and to answer needs considered urgent and approved by the Board of Directors. The Fund varies according to interest earned, the amount of unallocated funds, an annual contribution equal to 0.5% of the previous campaign, and the net result for the year. The balance of the Stabilization Fund must not exceed 10% of the amount of the previous campaign.

iii)   Capital Asset Fund

The Capital Asset Fund comprises the depreciated cost of the building, furniture and equipment, and computer equipment. The Fund varies according to interest earned, amounts received for the purpose of acquiring fixed assets, depreciation, and an annual contribution equal to 0.5% of the previous campaign for updating and ongoing development of computer systems.

iv)   1,2,3 GO! Fund

The aim of the 1,2,3 GO! Fund is to provide disadvantaged children, up to three years of age, with conditions for optimal development by supporting local initiatives.

v)   Development Fund

The Development Fund was created to fund research and development activities and pilot and other projects that are not considered as part of Centraide of Greater Montreal's usual activities and whose ultimate goal is to significantly increase the funds donated to Centraide of Greater Montreal over the coming years.

Fixed assets

Acquisitions of fixed assets are recorded at cost. Depreciation is calculated under the straight-line method over the following periods:

Building	40 years
Furniture and equipment	8 years
Computer equipment	4 years

Temporary investments

Temporary investments include Treasury bills, bankers' acceptances and commercial paper of recognized businesses and are shown at cost, plus accrued interest receivable.

NOTES TO THE FINANCIAL STATEMENTS
YEAR ENDED MARCH 31, 2004

2.   Accounting policies (continued)

Revenue recognition
The annual fall campaign is conducted to raise funds for Centraide of Greater Montreal and its agencies for the subsequent fiscal year. Consequently, the available net proceeds from the current campaign (2003), i.e. subscriptions less deferred fundraising, communication and administrative costs, are shown as deferred revenues on the balance sheet.

Cash donations are recorded when they are received, while subscription revenue is recognized upon receipt of pledges.

Expenses
Expenses are accounted for in the statement of operations of the Operating Fund and are allocated as follows:

	Fundraising, communication and administrative costs	Assistance to agencies, social research and community services
Annual campaign and major donors	100%	—
Allocation and social research	—	100%
Communications	85%	15%
General management	60%	40%
Administration	75%	25%

The financial statements do not include the cost of services rendered by individual volunteers and staff loaned to Centraide of Greater Montreal by businesses and public institutions.

Use of estimates
The preparation of financial statements in conformity with Canadian generally accepted accounting principles requires management to make estimates and assumptions that affect the reported amounts of assets and liabilities and disclosures of contingent assets and liabilities at the date of the financial statements and the reported amounts of revenue and expenses during the reporting period. Actual results could differ from these estimates.

3.   Fixed assets

	Cost	Accumulated depreciation	2004 Net book value	2003 Net book value
	$	$	$	$
Building	2,187,447	811,242	1,376,205	1,430,724
Furniture and equipment	461,516	299,126	162,390	160,539
Computer equipment	1,393,291	1,105,385	287,906	305,437
	4,042,254	**2,215,753**	**1,826,501**	1,896,700

During the year, the purchase of fixed assets totaled $216,101 ($345,438 in 2003).

NOTES TO THE FINANCIAL STATEMENTS
YEAR ENDED MARCH 31, 2004

4. **Deferred revenues**

	2004	2003
	$	$
Available net campaign proceeds	2003 Campaign	2002 Campaign
Subscriptions	40,552,736	37,333,301
Provision for uncollectible subscriptions	(1,475,494)	(1,395,665)
	39,077,242	35,937,636
Deferred fundraising, communication and administrative costs	(4,501,378)	(4,396,243)
	34,575,864	31,541,393

During 2003–2004, the 2003 campaign proceeds announced by Centraide du Grand Montréal totaled $43,056,964. Of this amount, $40,552,736 was recorded in the books as at March 31, 2004. The balance of campaign proceeds should be received during the subsequent year. The amounts raised in the 2003 campaign will be presented as revenues in the 2004–2005 financial year.

5. **Allocations to agencies (Schedule)**

	2004	2003
	$	$
Support for neighbourhood life	9,008,850	8,605,699
Support for families and youth	7,245,124	6,883,262
Support for the improvement of living conditions	6,200,402	5,924,100
Support for social inclusion	5,221,279	4,983,372
Support for volunteering	1,795,800	1,719,711
Support for community development (representatives)	1,429,250	1,087,595
Support for the development of community action	437,000	412,527
United Way of Canada	291,665	276,890
Special projects	239,604	249,554
Designated contributions	114,930	83,705
	31,983,90	430,226,415

6. **Related party transactions**

Fondation Centraide du Grand Montréal, a related organization, is a registered charity incorporated under Part III of the *Companies Act* (Québec) whose goal is to collect donations, legacies or other contributions, manage its assets and give to Centraide of Greater Montreal all net proceeds generated by the capital without expending any portion thereof. The net assets of Fondation Centraide du Grand Montréal are $18,844,789 as at March 31, 2004 ($18,865,532 as at March 31, 2003).

Fondation Centraide du Grand Montréal contributes to the fundraising campaign of Centraide of Greater Montreal on an annual basis. During the year, the Foundation pledged an amount of $280,000 ($350,000 in 2003). In addition, the Foundation contributed an amount of $20,000 ($155,000 in 2003) to the Capital Asset Fund and an amount of $250,000 ($250,000 in 2003) to the Development Fund of Centraide of Greater Montreal. Finally, the Foundation paid $9,000 ($9,000 in 2003) in administrative fees to Centraide of Greater Montreal; this amount is presented in deduction of fundraising, communication and administrative costs.

NOTES TO THE FINANCIAL STATEMENTS
YEAR ENDED MARCH 31, 2004

6. Related party transactions (continued)

Subscriptions receivable include an amount of $280,000 ($350,000 in 2003) from Fondation Centraide du Grand Montréal. An amount of $372,664 ($338,661 in 2003) in the other assets balance is receivable from Fondation Centraide du Grand Montréal. In addition, an amount of $124,039 ($847,768 in 2003) in the balance of accounts payable and accrued liabilities is due to Fondation Centraide du Grand Montréal.

7. Interfund transfers

The Board of Directors approved an annual contribution transfer to the Stabilization Fund for an amount of $182,600 ($174,500 in 2003). The Capital Asset Fund also received a contribution for an amount of $182,600 ($174,500 in 2003) in order to acquire computer equipment. In addition, the balance of $145,803 from the 1,2,3 GO! Fund has been transferred to the Stabilization Fund at the end of the start phase of the project. Financing of neighbourhoods is now done directly from the allocations to agencies.

8. Pension plan

Centraide of Greater Montreal participates in a multi-employer contributory defined benefit pension plan. The benefits are capitalized in the pension fund for all participants of the pension. The employer's contribution paid for the year ended March 31, 2004 is $263,645 ($252,892 for the year ended March 31, 2003). Based on the last actuarial valuation performed December 31, 2001, there are no unfunded liabilities with respect to the plan.

9. Statement of cash flows

A statement of cash flows has not been presented as it would not provide any additional meaningful information.

Self-Study Problem

1. Refer to Appendix 14.1 for the financial statements of Centraide of Greater Montreal for the year ended March 31, 2004, and answer each of the following questions.

   (a) Since charities are based on appeals to humanitarian feelings and non-profit organizations are based on self-interest, why should a charitable organization such as Centraide find it necessary to have its financial statements audited?

   (b) Evaluate Centraide's (short-term) liquidity position. How does its liquidity position at the end of March 2004 compare to that of a year previously?

   (c) What does the account Deferred Revenues represent? What is the relationship between Deferred Revenues and Revenues?

   (d) What was the depreciation expense for the year ended March 31, 2004? Why does depreciation expense not show on the statement of operations and fund balance of the operating fund?

   (e) What is the point of having separate funds, such as operating fund, stabilization fund, etc.?

2. The Faculty of Management at Holywell University offers a special intensive summer program for senior managers in the non-profit sector. Because it is a non-credit program, the program is not eligible for government grants and thus must be self-financing. Unfortunately, on account of shrinking enrolments, the program has been experiencing financial difficulties. Last summer, for example, the program attracted only 30 participants and lost money.

   Fees and costs are as follows:

Per participant	
Revenue: Tuition fees	$ 6,000
Expense: Books, residence rooms, meals, and other costs	$ 2,000
General program costs	
Teaching honoraria (10 courses @ $5,000)	$50,000
Office (including office salaries)	$60,000
Advertising and promotion	$30,000

   Required

   (a)   i. Calculate the current break-even level of participants.
         ii. How much money was lost last year?

   (b) The dean of the faculty is convinced that the class size can be increased to more economic levels without compromising the quality of the program. To this end she is prepared to authorize an additional $10,000 per year in promotional and other support expenses.

         i. If this strategy is followed, what would the new break-even level be, as measured in numbers of participants?

         ii. How many participants would be needed to generate an annual surplus of $60,000?

(c) The program director agrees that promotion is important but feels that pricing is the critical factor. He argues that a $1,000 reduction in tuition fees combined with just $5,000 in promotion will attract 80 participants. Of course, to maintain program quality the class would have to be split, doubling the number of sections offered.

    i. If the program director is right about the number of participants, what would the annual program surplus be?

    ii. What would be the new break-even point for the program?

(d) The associate dean of the faculty argues that a program of this nature should be required to contribute 15% of its tuition revenue toward general faculty and university overhead.

    i. How does this affect the break-even point? Recalculate for the original situation in part (a).

    ii. In general, is the requirement that such programs make a contribution to the general overhead reasonable? Briefly discuss.

Solution

1. (a) The short answer is that an audit is legally required — still, we should understand why this is so. The readers of the financial statements want to know that the charity's financial statements present fairly the results of its operations and its financial position in accordance with generally accepted accounting principles. Giving such assurance is an auditor's job. This is not primarily a question of looking for fraud or other kinds of malfeasance. Even if everyone who works for Centraide behaves in the most disinterested and high-minded fashion, errors in accounting procedure or policy can occur. It is the auditor's job to uncover them. Malfeasance can occur. Even if a charity's appeal is to higher motives, this does not mean that we can ignore self-interest on the part of those who work for charities or indeed any individual or organization that deals with a charity. For example, although charities rely to a great extent on volunteers, they do have permanent employees. These people may earn less than those who do similar jobs in the for-profit sector, but they do not work for nothing. This is a reflection of self-interest. Self-interest may rarely lead to malfeasance, but it can; and we can never assume that nobody who deals with a non-profit organization will take advantage of his or her position to advance his or her own interest. Financial scandals have occurred in every kind of NPO, including charities, hospitals, and religious organizations. An audit does not ensure that every incidence of malfeasance will be uncovered, but it will usually reveal the material ones.

(b)   Short-term liquidity is evaluated using the current ratio —
current assets ÷ current liabilities. Centraide's current ratios
for 2003 and 2004 are as follows:

31 March 2004	31 March 2003
(39,398,485 ÷ 35,686,894 =)	(36,978,893 ÷ 33,555,780 =)
1.104	1.102

These ratios — almost identical for the two year-ends —
are just above 1, which is not considered very strong. However, most of the current liabilities represent deferred revenues
which, if the future unfolds as it should, do not represent
external debts that must be paid (see (c) below). It might
be more useful to exclude these liabilities as well as the corresponding subscriptions receivable (and other assets) and calculate a version of the quick ratio, cash, and temporary
investments to accounts payable and accrued liabilities:

31 March 2004	31 March 2003
(23,847,731 ÷ 980,780 =)	(23,105,744 ÷ 1,879,739 =)
24.3	12.3

Using this test, Centraide is twice as strong at the end of
fiscal 2004 than it was a year earlier. However, ratios in both
years are extremely high, and by any standard, the organization was very liquid at both balance sheet dates.

(c)   As explained in note 2, "Accounting Policies", on p. 428, the
annual fall campaign for donations raises funds for the following year. Accordingly, the pledges received are recognized as
assets on the one hand (cash or subscriptions receivable as the
case may be), but they are accounted for as deferred subscriptions (shown as a current liability) rather than being taken
into revenues in that year. We can see the details in note 4,
Deferred Revenues", on p. 430: the liability — an obligation to
distribute to member charitable agencies — is reduced by an
allowance ("provision for uncollectible subscriptions") and the
associated fundraising costs ("deferred fundraising … costs").
In the following year, the deferred revenues are "realized" as
revenue along with any late cash subscriptions. Thus deferred
revenue as at March 31, 2003, less amounts uncollected, plus
late cash collections related to the fall 2002 campaign, is
recognized as revenue in the 2003–2004 financial year.

Debits and credits can make the explanation clearer. When
pledges are made, Centraide debits subscriptions receivable
and credits, not revenue, but deferred revenue. As the subscriptions are collected, cash is debited and subscriptions
receivable is credited. This will happen throughout the fall
campaign, the following winter, and into the next financial
year. The deferred revenue account can only increase through
the fall as new pledges are made; moreover, collection of
subscriptions has no effect on this account because there was

a policy decision not to recognize these subscriptions (or cash received) until the following year. After March 31, 2003, however, 2002–2003 pledges are now recognized as revenue, and there is an entry debiting the deferred revenue account and crediting (transferring the deferred revenue balance) to subscriptions revenue for 2003–2004.

(d) Depreciation expense (amortization) for the year ended March 31, 2004 was $286,300. This is shown on the statement of operations and fund balance of the capital asset fund rather than on the statement of operations and fund balance of the operating fund because, as in most NPOs using fund accounting, capital assets are accounted for in a separate fund.

(e) The objective of using separate funds is to keep separate the accounting of operations or activities, which have their own objectives, restrictions or are in some other way (such as capital assets) independent of other operations. This allows the readers of the financial statements to evaluate each activity on its own criteria.

2. (a) i. Break-even is
unit fixed costs ÷ unit contribution margin
= ($50,000 + $60,000 + $30,000) ÷ ($6,000 – $2,000)
= $140,000 ÷ $4,000
= 35 participants

Check:	Revenue	35 @ $6,000	=	$210,000
	Variable expenses	35 @ $2,000	=	70,000
	Contribution margin	35 @ $4,000	=	$140,000
	Less fixed costs			140,000
	Net contribution			$ 0

ii. Last year's results

Revenue	30 @ $6,000	=	$180,000
Variable expenses:	30 @ $2,000	=	60,000
Contribution margin	30 @ $4,000		$120,000
Less fixed costs			140,000
Net contribution			($ 20,000)

(b) i. New break-even with $10,000 additional fixed costs would be ($140,000 + $10,000) ÷ $4,000
= $150,000 ÷ $4,000
= 37.5 or 38 participants

ii. Target net contribution of $60,000:
($140,000 + $10,000 + $60,000) ÷ $4,000
= $210,000 ÷ $4,000
= 52.5 or 53 participants required

(c) New unit contribution margin is $5,000 – $2,000 = $3,000.
New fixed costs (note that the number of courses is doubled):

Teaching honoraria (20 courses @ $5,000)	$ 100,000
Office (including office salaries)	60,000
Advertising and promotion ($30,000 + $5,000)	35,000
Total	$ 195,000

i. Profit with 80 participants:

Fees	80 participants @ $5,000	$ 400,000
Books, etc.	80 participants @ $2,000	160,000
Contribution margin	80 participants @ $3,000	$ 240,000
Fixed costs		195,000
Net contribution		$ 45,000

ii. New break-even
$195,000 ÷ $3,000 = 65 participants
(If the number of classes were not doubled, the new break-even would be $145,000 ÷ $3,000 = 48.33 or 49 participants.)

(d) i. A 15% overhead charge comes off the top (since it is a percentage of the fee, it is incorrect to add it directly to variable unit expenses):

Fees	$6,000
Overhead charge @ 15%	900
Net fees	$5,100
Variable expenses	2,000
Unit contribution margin	$3,100

Break-even is fixed costs divided by unit contribution margin: $140,000 ÷ $3,100 = 45.16 or 46 participants, i.e., an increase of 11 participants or 31%.

ii. The discussion up to this point is in terms of break-even or target profit of the program. These two outcomes take into account the direct costs of the program, but they do not take into account the general fixed costs of the university. Every university program draws on the general resources of the university and should, in fairness, make a contribution toward general operations. Another way of looking at this is to consider that the general operations of the university cost typically from 25% to 40% of total costs, and these can only be supported to the extent that fee- and grant-attracting programs generate a surplus, on average, of 33% to 67% of direct costs. If this sort of cost structure is the case at Holywell, the proposed 15% contribution to university overhead is far too low.

Discussion Questions and Problems

Discussion Questions

1. How does a non-profit organization differ from a for-profit company?
2. How do governments differ from NPOs?
3. What are the three defining characteristics of NPOs?
4. Since NPOs are organized for the purpose of providing a service rather than for making a profit for their owners, why should there be any concern for financial considerations in their operations?
5. Why don't NPOs present income statements?
6. What is a "fund" in NPO accounting?
7. List the financial statement analysis ratios that have no application to NPOs.
8. Why are effectiveness and efficiency ratios particularly useful in the assessment of NPOs?
9. Why are budgets of such great importance for NPOs and governments?

Problems

1. The exhibit presented on the following pages contains excerpts of financial statements from Inter Pares, an international charity headquartered in Canada.[1] Answer the following questions using the information provided:

   (a) In the balance sheet you will see a section entitled Net Assets. What are net assets? What is the corresponding balance sheet section of a for-profit company and how does that differ from Net Assets? Why are there divisions in the net asset section?

   (b) Refer to the statement of revenue and expense. How does this statement differ from the income statement of a for-profit company? Why does it have multiple columns?

   (c) Refer to the statement of changes in fund balances. What is the corresponding statement for a for-profit company and how does that differ from this statement?

   (d) Evaluate
   - (i) the organization's liquidity
   - (ii) its ability to pay interest on its debt
   - (iii) the proportion of revenue used for (1) fundraising and (2) administration

---

[1] From Inter Pares — Publications — 30th Anniversary Special Report **www.interpares.ca/en/publications/ar-2004/page6.php**. Reprinted with permission of Inter Pares, Ottawa, Ontario.

30th Anniversary Special Report
AUDITOR'S REPORT TO THE MEMBERS, INTER PARES

We have audited the statement of financial position of Inter Pares as at December 31, 2004 and the statement of revenue and expense and changes in fund balances for the year then ended. These financial statements are the responsibility of the organization's management. Our responsibility is to express an opinion on these financial statements based on our audit.

We conducted our audit in accordance with Canadian generally accepted auditing standards. Those standards require that we plan and perform an audit to obtain reasonable assurance whether the financial statements are free of material misstatement. An audit includes examining, on a test basis, evidence supporting the amounts and disclosures in the financial statements. An audit also includes assessing the accounting principles used and significant estimates made by management, as well as evaluating the overall financial statement presentation.

In our opinion, these financial statements present fairly, in all material respects, the financial position of the organization as at December 31, 2004 and the results of its operations and its cash flows for the year then ended in accordance with Canadian generally accepted accounting principles.

Ottawa, Ontario
February 17, 2005
Ouseley Hanvey Clipsham Deep LLP
Chartered Accountants

STATEMENT OF FINANCIAL POSITION
As At December 31, 2004

	2004	2003
ASSETS		
CURRENT		
Cash	$ 873,411	$ 644,790
Accounts receivable	46,751	67,257
	920,162	712,047
INVESTMENTS (note 1)	418,719	356,350
CAPITAL ASSETS (note 2)	760,260	781,767
DEFERRED CHARGE (note 3)	—	8,000
	$2,099,141	$1,858,164
LIABILITIES		
CURRENT		
Advances on projects	$ 524,037	$ 512,796
Accounts payable and accrued liabilities	27,241	52,086
Current portion of mortgage payable (note 4)	24,973	15,815
	576,251	580,697
SEVERANCE PLAN PAYABLE (note 3)	86,283	83,342
MORTGAGE PAYABLE (note 4)	279,560	403,503
	942,094	1,067,542
NET ASSETS		
Unrestricted	(76,132)	(50,360)
Invested in capital assets	455,727	362,449
Bequest fund (note 5)	280,657	—
Reserve fund (note 6)	305,190	297,725
Endowment fund (note 7)	191,605	180,808
	1,157,047	790,622
	$2,099,141	$1,858,164

STATEMENT OF CHANGES IN FUND BALANCES
For the Year Ended December 31, 2004

	Invested in Unrestricted Net Assets	Capital Assets	Bequest Fund	Reserve Fund	Endowment Fund	2004 Total	2003 Total
FUND BALANCE— BEGINNING OF YEAR	$(50,360)	$362,449	$ —	$297,725	$180,808	$ 790,622	$729,494
Excess of revenue over expense	19,006	—	329,157	7,465	10,797	366,425	61,128
Purchase of capital assets	(11,255)	11,255	—	—	—	—	—
Amortization of capital assets	32,762	(32,762)	—	—	—	—	—
Principal repayment of mortgage	(114,785)	114,785	—	—	—	—	—
Interfund transfers (note 5)	48,500	—	(48,500)	—	—	—	—
FUND BALANCES—END OF YEAR	$(76,132)	$455,727	$280,657	$305,190	$191,605	$1,157,047	$790,622

STATEMENT OF REVENUE AND EXPENSE
For the Year Ended December 31, 2004

	General Operations	Bequest Fund	Reserve Fund	Endowment Fund	2004 Total	2003 Total
REVENUE						
Donations	$1,255,049	$329,157	$ —	$ 250	$1,584,456	$1,275,771
CIDA-VSP	1,335,985	—	—	—	1,335,985	1,053,323
CIDA — other projects	2,614,082	—	—	—	2,614,082	3,679,685
Project generated grants	77,965	—	—	—	77,965	200,057
Interest and other	3,785	—	7,465	10,547	21,797	31,572
	5,286,866	329,157	7,465	10,797	5,634,285	6,240,408
EXPENSE						
Program						
Projects	3,742,166	—	—	—	3,742,166	4,588,973
Operations	935,404	—	—	—	935,404	974,488
	4,677,570	—	—	—	4,677,570	5,563,461
Administration	285,025	—	—	—	285,025	323,386
Fundraising	305,265	—	—	—	305,265	292,433
	5,267,860	—	—	—	5,267,860	6,179,280
EXCESS OF REVENUE OVER EXPENSE FOR THE YEAR	$ 19,006	$329,157	$7,465	$10,797	$ 366,425	$ 61,128

NOTES TO FINANCIAL STATEMENTS — DECEMBER 31, 2004

1. SIGNIFICANT ACCOUNTING POLICIES

a) **Organization:** Inter Pares works overseas and in Canada in support of self-help development groups, and in the promotion of understanding about the causes, effects and solutions to underdevelopment and poverty. Inter Pares was incorporated without share capital under Part II of the Canada Business Corporations Act. The Corporation is a registered charity under Section 149(1)(c) of the Income Tax Act and as a result is not subject to income taxes.

b) **Revenue Recognition:** Inter Pares follows the deferral method of accounting for contributions. Restricted contributions are recognized as revenue in the year in which the related expenses are incurred. Donations are recorded as revenue when received.

c) **Investments:** Investments consist primarily of government bonds and other loans receivable and are recorded at cost which approximates market value.

d) **Capital Assets:** Capital assets are recorded at cost. Amortization is provided on a straight line basis over 5 years for office equipment. Computer equipment is amortized 50% in the first year and 25% in the remaining 2 years. The building is amortized on a straight line basis over 40 years.

2. CAPITAL ASSETS

	Cost	Accumulated Depreciation	2004 Net	2003 Net
Land	$200,000	$ —	$200,000	$200,000
Building	582,230	37,000	545,230	559,980
Computer & office equipment	151,373	136,343	15,030	21,787
	$933,603	$173,343	$760,260	$781,767

During the year, depreciation of capital assets amounted to $32,762 (2003 — $29,623).

3. PENSION AND SEVERANCE PLAN

During 1998 a pension plan was implemented to contribute to staff Retirement Savings Plans. In addition, an institutional staff severance plan was established. The cost to establish these plans was estimated to be $128,000. This cost is being amortized over a seven year period. During the year the amount amortized to expense was $8,000 (2003 — $20,000).

4. MORTGAGE PAYABLE

	2004	2003
Royal Bank of Canada — mortgage payable at $3,945 monthly including interest at 7.75%, due July 1, 2007, secured by 221 Laurier Avenue East.	$304,533	$419,318
Less current portion	24,973	15,815
	$279,560	$403,503

5. BEQUEST FUND

During the year a bequest fund was established. Bequests received are recorded as revenue in this fund. During the year $48,500 was transferred to unrestricted net assets.

6. RESERVE FUND

Inter Pares maintains an unrestricted operational reserve to assure that obligations are honoured in the event of unanticipated changes in external funding.

7. ENDOWMENT FUND

The Margaret McKay Endowment Fund receives gifts whose principal is invested and held for a minimum of ten years. In addition to such externally restricted gifts, the Endowment Fund contains transfers from Inter Pares which are subject to the same restrictions. As at the year-end, the Endowment Fund includes $70,850 (2003 — $70,600) in externally restricted gifts.

2. The bookkeeper of the Langford Municipal Arena has prepared the following statement for the month of November, which he calls the Statement of Financial Results:

Langford Municipal Arena
Statement of Financial Results
for the month of November 2005

Receipts

Revenue from ice rentals	$84,000	
Revenue from admissions	36,000	
Borrowings from bank	30,000	$150,000

Expenses

Payment for supplies purchased	$13,400	
Payment for equipment purchased	31,000	
Payment for a one-year insurance policy	12,400	
Wages paid in cash	32,950	
Miscellaneous cash expenses	9,760	
Deposit on ice cleaning machine to be delivered in January	20,000	119,510

Net $ 30,490

Required

The bookkeeper wants advice on how to prepare an accrual-based statement of revenue and expense (SRE). Review the wording of each italicized caption in the statement above and specify, with explanation, (1) which would be likely be included in an SRE, (2) which would be included if appropriately modified, and (3) which would be excluded.

Example
Payment for supplies purchased: (2) Included with modification: Supplies used, with the caption "Supplies" or "Supplies expense", is an appropriate expense item, but not cash paid to purchase supplies as indicated above.

3. Activity at the Dryden Point Hospital reaches a peak in the second quarter of the year (April–June). The hospital catchment area includes a range of mountains greatly favoured by climbers. Unfortunately, many novice climbers cannot resist the temptation of climbing in the spring, the prime avalanche season. The lucky ones end up in the hospital's emergency wards and operating rooms, often for extended periods of time (the unlucky ones are never found).

The hospital prepares quarterly cash budgets over the calendar year. The forecasted grants from the provincial medicare office for the current year are as follows:

1st quarter	$390,000
2nd quarter	$750,000
3rd quarter	$390,000
4th quarter	$390,000

In general, grants are collected two-thirds in the quarter that they are made and one-third in the following quarter. The opening balance of accounts receivable are expected to be collected in the first quarter. These grants account for 100% of hospital revenue.

Hospital supplies costing $360,000 will be purchased evenly over the first quarter, none in the rest of the year. Payment will be made thirty days after purchase.

Nursing salaries are $150,000 in the first, third, and fourth quarters, $250,000 in the second. Payment is made in the quarter that the cost is incurred. General hospital overhead costs are $100,000 in the first, third, and fourth quarters, $300,000 in the second quarter, including $50,000 amortization each quarter. Payment lags behind the cost by approximately one month.

The hospital maintains an operating line of credit with its bank and pays interest on borrowings at an annual interest rate of 7%, payable quarterly. The hospital plans to maintain a minimum cash balance of $8,000 at all times. It will borrow in multiples of $5,000 when necessary to maintain this minimum. All borrowings are made at the beginning of the quarter where the deficiency is predicted, and any repayments will be made at the end of the quarter.

The hospital plans to purchase new medical equipment in the second and fourth quarters in the amounts of $150,000 and $50,000, respectively.

The closing balance sheet from the previous year shows a balance of cash on hand of $23,000 and accounts receivable of $128,000.

Required

Prepare a cash budget for the hospital for the first two quarters of the current year in a recognized format. Be sure to show operating cash flow, ending cash balance before financing, amounts borrowed/repaid, interest payments, and final cash balance.

4. Consider the following statistics about non-profit ambulance services in four districts: Arbury, Bellevue, Cardborough, and Darbton in a recent year:

		Districts			
Characteristics		**A**	**B**	**C**	**D**
1	Population	124,000	487,000	542,000	1,700,000
2	Population density	0.8	3.9	5.6	8.7
3	Pickup time (min.)	23	13	9	15
4	Cost per patient ($)	27.30	23.6	19.5	26.15
5	Cost per mile ($)	2.60	2.75	2.35	3.85
6	Cost per 1,000 pop. ($)	11,500	9,430	8,650	10,750

Explanatory notes:

Row 2 Population density per acre
Row 3 Average time from call to pickup of patient
Row 4 Total cost of service divided by number of ambulance calls
Row 5 Total cost of service divided by number of vehicle-miles
Row 6 Total cost of service divided by population in thousands

Required

(a) Review, in turn, each of the six measures of the districts and their ambulance services. Indicate what each measure tells us about the district or its ambulance service. In particular, evaluate each one as a measure of effectiveness and/or a measure of efficiency.

(b) On the basis of your answer to part (a), give a summary ranking of the four districts as to
   (i) their effectiveness
   (ii) their efficiency

Indicate in what ways this ranking may be inadequate. Identify the key pieces of additional information you would need to refine it.

(c) The ambulance services described above are non-profit organizations. Performance evaluation of profit-oriented companies would be handled differently. Identify the main difference between performance evaluation of non-profit organizations and of profit-oriented companies. Do we get a clearer appraisal of organizational success in one case or the other? What are the implications for public policy?

5. The board of governors of the Bullstrode Museum of Fine Arts, concerned about cutbacks to its operating grant from the provincial government, is considering a proposal from its executive director that would, if successful, make the museum a little less dependent on government financing.

The proposal involves devoting a section of the museum's art restoration workshop that is not currently being used to the production of miniature copies of the most renowned piece of sculpture in its collection, Koppelheim's *The Hug*. These reproductions would then be sold in the museum's retail shop to contribute toward the museum's revenues.

Expected unit costs have been estimated by an industrial engineer as follows:

Direct materials (plaster, wood, paint)	$20.00
Direct labour	$10.00
Other variable costs (including selling)	$ 5.00

In addition, there would be fixed costs related to this operation of $140,000 per annum. The engineer further estimates that such an operation could produce a maximum of 10,000 units a year.

The museum hopes that it could generate around $50,000 a year from this activity. The members of the board, however, are a little concerned at the risks involved, especially the $140,000 in fixed costs, most of which would have to be committed at the beginning of the year. Finally, nobody has yet given serious thought to the selling price of the model when it goes on sale in the museum shop.

Required

(a) If the price of the model were set at $70, what volume would have to be sold to break even? To make a contribution of $50,000 to museum revenues?

(b) If the price of the model were set at $50, what volume would have to be sold to break even? To make a contribution of $50,000 to museum revenues?

(c) Advise the board on this proposal. Should the museum go ahead with the project or not? Indicate what additional information you would need to be able to give better advice.

6. Consider the following information drawn from the financial statements of Cavendish University and Dalrymple University:

	Cavendish	Dalrymple
	in thousands of dollars	
Balance Sheet		
ASSETS		
Operating fund		
Cash	$ 3,000	$ 2,500
Student fees receivable	3,000	3,000
Total	$ 6,000	$ 5,500
Capital fund		
Fixed assets	$ 25,000	$ 21,000
LIABILITIES AND FUND BALANCES		
Operating fund		
Current liabilities	$ 5,000	$ 3,000
Fund balance	1,000	2,500
Total	$ 6,000	$ 5,500
Capital fund		
Mortgage payable	$ 20,000	$ 10,000
Fund balance	5,000	11,000
Total	$ 25,000	$ 21,000
Operating Fund —		
Statement of Operations and Fund Balance		
REVENUE		
Student tuition fees	$ 24,000	$ 15,000
Government grant	76,000	53,000
Total	$100,000	$ 68,000
EXPENSES	99,500	70,000
Excess of revenue over expense		
(expense over revenue)	$ 500	($ 2,000)

Required

Compare Cavendish and Dalrymple under each of the following headings. Support your conclusion with quantitative evidence and make a judgment in each case as to which university is in a stronger position:

(a) Liquidity

(b) Risk

(c) Management of receivables

Glossary of Important Terms

Glossary

Absorption cost (full cost): the valuation of a product or service, including its flexible (unit-variable) cost and an allocation of fixed overhead.

Account: a financial record where transactions of a similar nature are recorded. All the accounts together constitute the *general ledger*.

Accounting: the process of recording, organizing, and communicating financial information.

Accounting cycle: the sequence of accounting procedures from identifying transactions, recording journal entries, posting to general ledger, adjusting and closing the books, and preparing the financial statements.

Accounting equation: recording transactions in terms of their effect on the assets, liabilities, and equity of the organization — i.e., assets = liabilities + equity.

Accounts payable: amounts owed by the company to suppliers of goods and services.

Accounts receivable: amounts owed to the company from customers.

Accrual concept: the recording of revenues and expenses in the time period when the economic flow occurs, rather than when the cash is received or paid.

Accrue: to record revenue or an expense that has occurred even though the related cash flow may not have happened.

Accumulated amortization: a contra-account. The total amortization taken over the lifetime of an asset or an asset group since its purchase. Presented as a deduction from the corresponding asset on the balance sheet.

Acid-test ratio (quick ratio): a measure of liquidity — i.e., (current assets less inventory) ÷ current liabilities.

Activity: a unit of work carried out to achieve an objective and that incurs a cost.

Activity-based costing: analysis of cost and cost behaviour using activities as the drivers of costs.

Activity-based management: use of activity-based costing information to make decisions.

Actual cost: the (historical) cost of an asset or expense.

Adjusting journal entry: an end-of-period journal entry made to bring the books up to date or to correct an error.

Allowance account: a *contra-account* that is used when the valuation is revised periodically, such as an *allowance for doubtful accounts (doubtful debts)*, or an *allowance for inventory decline*.

Allowance for bad and doubtful debts: an amount deducted from accounts receivable to provide for debts that will, eventually, be discovered to have been bad debts.

Amortization: the systematic allocation of cost of a long-term asset to the time periods during which the business should benefit from it (also called depreciation).

Annuity: an amount of money received each year for a specified period of time.

Appraisal cost: (in quality management) a cost incurred in inspecting products or services to assess their quality conformance.

Asset: an economic resource that is expected to benefit a future accounting period.

Asset turnover: an efficiency measure of assets and how they are employed to generate sales: sales ÷ total assets.

Attention directing: the role of accounting in bringing significant events to the notice of managers or shareholders.

Audit: the examination of a company's records and financial statements by an outside body.

Auditor: a professional accountant who carries out an audit.

Avoidable cost: a cost that, subject to a decision being taken, may be avoided.

B

Bad debt: an expense, the loss due to a customer's failure to pay for goods or services.

Bad debt allowance: an amount deducted from accounts receivable for potential bad debts, reducing them to their net realizable value.

Balance: in an account, taking the difference between total debits and credits, the net value of the account, debit, or credit as the case may be.

Balance sheet: a list of the company's assets, liabilities, and equity at a point in time.

Balanced scorecard: a systematic process for reporting on operations that bases its contents on the company strategy; it balances the past against the present and the future, and balances financial results against the perspectives of the customer, internal process improvements, and learning and growth objectives.

Batch-related costs: costs incurred by running a batch of production (rather than unit-driven variable costs).

Benchmarking: using the results of comparable organizations as the standard of performance.

Book value: (of an asset) the historical cost, less accumulated amortization to date (also: written-down value); (of a company) the balance sheet totals of all assets, less all liabilities (i.e., the balance sheet value of the equity).

Books: an informal term for all the accounting records of the company — in particular, the journals, general ledger, and financial statements.

Break-even: a situation where revenues equal expenses.

Break-even (a.k.a. cost/volume/profit) analysis: use of the contribution margin to see how many units must be sold (the break-even point) to cover fixed costs.

Budget: a list of revenues and/or costs that are expected for a future control period.

Budgetary slack: a discrepancy between the budget and what the budget would be if set to "tight" standards of performance.

Business entity concept: each business enterprise is considered separate and distinct from its owners.

Business-sustaining activity (or cost): an activity or its related cost incurred for the benefit of the business as a whole and not traceable to units, batches, products, customers, etc. (formerly known as fixed costs).

C

Canadian Institute of Chartered Accountants (CICA): the main organization of professional accountants and auditors in Canada.

Capacity-related costs: costs incurred to give a company the capacity to carry out activities such as manufacturing, customer service, research, etc.; once committed, total capacity costs do not change in the short term — the capacity may be used, or left idle, but the cost remains.

Capital asset: an asset that is held over a long period of time for its value in use, such as a *fixed asset* (property plant and equipment) or an *intangible asset.*

Capital budget: a budget for spending large amounts of money on long-term assets.

Capital budgeting: a decision process for assessing the viability of capital spending (*see also* payback, return on investment, and net present value).

Capitalize (verb): to recognize that an expenditure creates or increases a *capital asset* rather than an *expense.*

Cash budget: a forecast of cash inflows and outflows and, hence, cash balances for a specified future time period.

Cash flow statement: a financial statement that summarizes the sources and uses of cash under the following headings: Cash From/Used in Operations; Cash From/Used in Financing Activities; Cash From/Used in Investing Activities; Change in Cash. (Also called Statement of Changes in Financial Position.)

Cash from/used in financing activities: cash flow resulting from borrowing or repaying loans, issue, or repayment of shares.

Cash from/used in investing activities: cash flow resulting from the purchase or sale of long-term assets.

Cash from/used in operations: cash flow resulting from the operating activities of the company: it is calculated as operating income plus amortization, plus the decrease (or minus the increase) in non-cash working capital.

Centralized (decision making; organization; responsibility): a system where all major decisions are made by senior management (*see also* decentralized...) on the basis that only senior management can see the big picture.

Certified General Accountants' Association (CGA): a body of professional accountants.

Change in cash: the difference between cash resources at the beginning and end of a time period.

CICA: *see* Canadian Institute of Chartered Accountants.

Closing the books: the process of transferring the balances of the revenue and expense and dividend accounts to retained earnings.

Committed cost: a cost that is legally committed even if the event has not taken place; a cost that will still be incurred even if the project is terminated.

Common cost: the cost of an activity or resource that is used by more than one responsibility unit.

Common share: the basic ownership units of a company: they have a residual interest in the assets of the company. (Also called common stock; ordinary shares.)

Competition; competitive market: a situation where there are many suppliers and many customers, and no supplier or customer can affect prices through their own actions.

Compound interest: interest earned being reinvested so that both principal and interest can then earn interest.

Conservatism concept: a systematic process for not overstating profits; expenses are recognized whenever they possibly may occur; revenues are not recognized unless they are highly likely.

Consolidation: aggregation of the financial results of companies that are linked through ownership or control.

Constant dollar: an accounting concept that assumes dollars are directly comparable whatever time they arose.

Continuity concept: the assumption that an organization will continue to exist and operate unless there is evidence to the contrary (also called going concern concept).

Continuous improvement: a philosophy of regular reductions in costs through increased efficiency.

Contra-account: an account that adjusts an asset account to the correct valuation at the balance sheet date, such as *accumulated amortization* or an *allowance account*.

Contribution margin (unit): the difference between the selling price and the unit-variable cost: the benefit of selling one additional unit (*see* break-even).

Control: the set of procedures used to assess how well the organization is achieving its objectives.

Controllability: a cost is controllable by a manager if its level is determined by the actions of that manager; the manager can be held responsible for costs he/she controls.

Controller: a senior accounting manager of a company (occasionally known as comptroller).

Conversion cost: the cost of transforming raw materials into finished goods; traditionally, conversion cost consisted of labour and overhead, but would now be defined with respect to whatever conversion activities have occurred.

Cost: a monetary value placed on a resource (*see* actual c., full c., historical c., standard c., variable c.); costs become expenses when they are used up.

Cost accounting: techniques and reports that deal with the cost and profitability of products and processes.

Cost accumulation: collecting and classifying costs according to their functional nature.

Cost allocation: tracing costs to cost pools or cost objects; allocation of cost pools to other cost objects through cost allocation rates.

Cost allocation base: a measure of use or activity (such as labour or machine hours) used to allocate cost (e.g., overhead), which cannot be traced to cost objects directly.

Cost behaviour: the analysis of the causes of costs (*see* flexible cost, fixed cost, activity-based cost) so that forecasting and control are made possible.

Cost centre: a control unit that is expected to carry out an activity, and incur costs to do so (*see also* revenue c., profit c., investment c.).

Cost concept (historical c.c.): that an asset should initially be valued at its original cost to the enterprise.

Cost driver: an activity that gives rise to a cost.

Cost driver rate: the rate of cost incurred per activity unit.

Cost function: a mathematical function relating a firm's or an industry's total cost to its output and factor costs.

Cost leadership: a business strategy based on minimizing costs through efficiency (*see also* differentiation).

Cost object: a product, service, process, etc., of which the cost is being calculated.

Cost of capital: (*see also* weighted average cost of capital) the minimum rate of return required to pay the providers of debt and equity capital; it is used in capital budgeting to assess the viability of investment proposals.

Cost of goods sold: in retailing, the direct (unit variable) costs of making a sale; in manufacturing, the direct costs will also include a proportion of (fixed) manufacturing overhead.

Cost of quality report: a systematic process for reporting on the costs incurred to achieve and monitor quality levels.

Cost of unused capacity: a capacity cost incurred, but not utilized.

Cost-plus pricing: an approach to pricing by reference to the cost of a product or service and the addition of a markup (a dollar amount or a percentage).

Cost pool: an account where the costs that are driven by a single cost driver are accumulated.

Cost/volume/profit analysis: *see* break-even.

Cr: *see* credit.

Credit (1): as a verb, to make credit entry.

Credit (2): entry on the right side of a double-entry bookkeeping system that represents the addition to a liability, equity, or revenue, or the reduction of an asset (*see* debit).

Credit (3): to buy or sell goods on delayed payment terms.

Creditor: a person or company that has lent money to the company.

Current asset: an asset that is likely to be recycled within one year (e.g., cash, accounts receivable, inventory).

Current liability: an amount owed that is due for payment within one year.

Current ratio: a measure of liquidity: current assets ÷ current liabilities.

Customer profitability analysis: use of activity-based costing information to assess the relative profitability of customers.

Customer-sustaining activity/cost: an activity carried out (with a cost incurred) to maintain a customer.

Cycle time: for repetitive activities, the time taken to go through one complete iteration of the process.

D

Debenture: a formal written notice of a long-term debt, specifying terms such as interest and repayment.

Debit: entry on the left side of a double-entry bookkeeping system that represents the addition of an asset or expense, such as an increase in dividends, or the reduction of a liability or revenue, or a reduction in shareholder's equity (*see* credit).

Debt ratio (debt-to-equity ratio; debt-to-assets ratio): a measure of relative indebtedness.

Decentralized (decision making; organization; responsibility): a system where major decisions are made by lower level management on the basis that the people near to the decision are best informed to decide.

Decision (making): choice between alternative courses of action for the future.

Depletion: the process similar to amortization that allocates the cost of using up a wasting asset, such as mineral or timber rights, to the appropriate accounting period.

Depreciation: *see* amortization.

Differentiation: a strategy based on the provision of goods or services that are very well suited to customers' needs and that may be sold at a premium price.

Direct cost: a cost that can be traced directly to a cost object (e.g., materials, labour).

Direct manufacturing cost: a cost that can be traced directly to the manufacture of a product.

Disclosure concept: an obligation to provide additional information wherever it is needed to allow a full appreciation of the financial reports.

Discounting: (in capital budgeting) the restatement of a future cash flow to its present value by eliminating (discounting) the interest opportunity.

Discretionary cost: a cost incurred as a result of management's (discretionary) decision about an activity (*see also* engineered cost).

Distribution cost: a cost incurred in distributing a product or service to a customer.

Dividend: a payment to shareholders (especially common shareholders) as a distribution of profit.

Dividend cover ratio/dividend payout ratio: a measure of the sustainability of dividends: Dividend cover ratio = net income ÷ dividend paid; Dividend payout ratio = (dividend ÷ net income) × 100%.

Double entry: a recording system that recognizes that every transaction must be recorded in accordance with the accounting equation (assets = liabilities + equity); the assumption that every asset has had a source, etc.

Doubtful debt: an amount that is set aside for the possibility that some customers may not pay the amounts they owe (also bad debt allowance).

Dr: *see* debit.

E

Earnings: (also net earnings) net income.

Earnings per share: net income divided by the number of shares in issue.

Earnings per share (diluted): net income divided by the number of shares in issue, plus any additional shares committed to be issued.

Economic flow: a change in a company's assets or liabilities. Also referred to as resource flow.

Economic value added: a measure of the difference between the return and the cost of an asset, and it can be calculated as operating income – interest charged for the use of the assets (formerly known as residual income).

Effectiveness: the extent to which organizational objectives have been achieved.

Efficiency: carrying out an activity without wasting resources.

Efficient capital market: a market in which share prices fully and immediately reflect all relevant public information.

Engineered cost: a cost that is unavoidable in supplying a product or service.

Entity: *see* business entity.

Equity: the residual interest in a company (shares and retained earnings).

Expenditure: the payment of cash.

Expense (1): cost expired or liability incurred to earn income. A sub-account of retained earnings.

Expense (2): used as a verb — to recognize an expenditure as an expense, used often in contrast to *capitalize*.

External failure (cost): costs encountered after delivery or shipment to customers resulting from products or services not conforming to requirements or customer needs. External failure costs result from errors detected after the output or product is delivered to a customer. These costs are incurred because the appraisal system failed to detect and remove all errors in the system.

F

Financial accounting: the process of preparing and disseminating general-purpose reports, such as the balance sheet and the income statement, for shareholders and external users.

Finished goods inventory: goods that have been manufactured but not yet sold.

First-in-first-out (FIFO): an inventory flow model that assumes items sold are those that have been in inventory longest (*see also* weighted average, last-in-first-out, and specific identification); in a time of rising prices, FIFO is relatively unconservative.

Fixed asset: a long-term asset with a physical presence (e.g., property, plant, equipment).

Fixed cost: a cost that does not change as a result of changes in units of activity (*see also* flexible cost); many fixed costs are period costs.

Flexible budget: a budget based on the same costs and efficiencies in the original (master) budget, but flexed (variable items are increased or decreased) to reflect changes between budgeted and actual activity levels.

Glossary

Flexible budget variance: a measure of the difference between the actual costs incurred and the budgeted costs for the actual activity level projected by a flexible budget.

Flexible costs (unit-variable costs): costs that increase or decrease in proportion to changes in numbers of units produced or sold (also called variable cost).

For-profit company: an organization that seeks to maximize profit for benefit of its owners (*see* non-profit organization).

Full cost: *see* absorption cost.

Fund: a fund is a self-balancing accounting entity within the legal entity that is the organization itself.

Fund accounting: the set of accounting procedures and self-balancing accounts in an organization, one for each fund established by law, contract, or policy.

G

General ledger: the collection of all the regular accounts in which assets, liabilities, equity, and transactions are recorded.

Generally accepted accounting principles (GAAP): a set of allowable methods for calculating and reporting financial reports for external users.

Goal congruence: a situation where the achievement of individual objectives is aligned with the achievement of corporate objectives.

Going concern: the assumption that the business will continue indefinitely.

Goodwill: the excess of the purchase price of an acquired entity over the fair market value of its assets and liabilities.

Gross book value: the cost of an asset before deduction of amortization (*see also* net book value).

Gross margin (gross profit): the excess of sales revenue over the direct cost of sales (it may be a dollar figure or a percentage of sales).

H, I

Historical cost: the original cost of an asset to the company.

Imposed budget: a situation where a budget is imposed on an operating unit without consultation or agreement.

Incentive compensation: a system in which the monetary rewards are tied to achieving unit or corporate objectives.

Income statement: a financial accounting report of the revenues, expenses and income for a period of time.

Incorporated company: a company that has received a charter as a legal person under the Canada Business Corporations Act, or the Corporation Act of a province. Shareholders in incorporated companies enjoy *limited liability*. Almost all companies incorporated in Canada (federally or provincially) have the words *limited* or *incorporated* (or an abbreviation) in their names.

Incremental budgeting: a budget based on a previous budget, possibly incorporating some changes (*see* zero-based budget).

Incremental cost/revenue: the additional cost or revenue of making or selling one additional unit (*see also* sunk cost); or the additional cost or revenue caused by taking a decision.

Indirect cost: a cost that cannot be uniquely traced to a cost object (*see also* direct cost).

Input: a resource used up in the course of a company's or NPO's operations. For example, expenses are inputs to the earnings process for a company, and in the operations process for an NPO.

Intangible asset: a long-term asset that has no physical form (e.g., goodwill, patents, trademarks).

Interest: a regular payment for the use of money.

Interest cover ratio: a measure of the sustainability of interest payments: operating income (income before taxes and interest expense) ÷ interest expense.

Internal failure (cost): costs encountered prior to delivery or shipment to customers resulting from products or services not conforming to requirements or customer needs. Internal failure costs result from errors detected within the enterprise before the output or product is delivered to a customer. These include all the costs associated with errors detected and removed by the appraisal system (e.g., re-inspection and retesting all outgoing goods).

Internal rate of return: (in capital budgeting) the discount rate that results in a net present value of zero.

Inventory flow: an assumption about which units of inventory are represented by goods sold (*see* FIFO, weighted average, LIFO).

Inventory holding period: length of time inventory is held before it is sold; inventory × 365 ÷ sales revenue (equivalent to inventory turnover ratio).

Inventory turnover ratio: the number of times per year inventory is sold (turned over); sales revenue ÷ inventory (equivalent to inventory holding period).

Investment: (in capital budgeting) the initial amount of money spent on a capital project.

Investment centre: an organizational unit that has responsibility for costs, revenues, and investment decisions, and that can, therefore, be controlled through the return on investment ratio.

Job cost: a system that traces and assigns all costs incurred for a unique product, product line, job, or project. The costs must be directly attributable to the job.

Journal: the book in which all transactions are recorded in chronological order.

Journal entry: an entry recording a transaction in the journal. It includes at least one debit entry and one credit entry.

Just-in-time inventory management: an approach to organizing operations so that inventory of raw materials and finished goods is unnecessary, and inventory of work-in-process is substantially reduced.

K, L

Kaizen costing: *see* continuous improvement.

Last-in-first-out (LIFO): an inventory flow model that assumes items sold are those that have been most recently purchased (*see also* weighted average, first-in-first-out, and specific identification); in a time of rising prices, LIFO is relatively conservative.

Ledger (account): the collection of accounts in which assets, liabilities, equity, and transactions are recorded.

Liability: an amount owed by a company to an outside party.

Limited liability: the legal fact that a shareholder's liability for the debts of a company is limited to the amount the shareholder has invested in the shares.

Liquidity: whether or not a company has cash and other liquid resources available to pay its debts.

Liquidity ratio: *see* current ratio.

Long-run costs: the costs incurred to carry out an activity in the longer term.

Long-term debt: debt due to be repaid more than one year in the future.

Lower of cost or market price: an application of the conservatism concept in which inventory is valued either at cost or at market price if the market price is less than cost; market price may mean net sale proceeds or replacement cost.

M

Make or buy decision: analysis of choices between carrying out an activity internally and sub-contracting it to an outside agency.

Management accounting: the set of accounting activities that supports the internal processes and decisions of an organization.

Management by exception: the philosophy that things that have gone according to plan need not be investigated, but exceptions should be investigated and give rise to corrective action as necessary.

Management by objectives: a process whereby reasonable objectives are agreed on between a manager and his/her superior, and progress toward achieving them is monitored through measurement and feedback.

Management control: use of accounting and other information systems to assess the performance of operating units and their managers.

Margin: the markup on costs to recover unallocated costs and profit.

Marginal (revenue/cost): *see* incremental revenue/cost.

Market share: the sales of a company expressed as a percentage of total sales for that market.

Markup: *see* margin.

Master budget: the budget set originally, based on forecasted sales/ production levels (*see also* flexible budget).

Matching concept: the relating of sales revenues to the economic effort expended in achieving them: the relationship of expenses to time periods.

Materiality concept: the convention that trivial items need not be reported.

Minority interest: where financial reports are consolidated but where less than 100% of the shares are owned by the parent company, the share of ownership held by outside shareholders.

Mixed cost: a cost that is made up partly of variable cost and partly of fixed cost.

Motivation: the tendency of an individual to behave in a particular way.

N

Net income: revenues minus expenses, interest, and taxes; income available for the shareholders.

Net present value (NPV): (in capital budgeting) the cash flows arising from a project, discounted (*see* discounting), and added together; positive NPV implies an acceptable project.

Net worth: owners' equity.

Neturality: it means to present information free from any bias (see also conservatism).

No par value: a share that has no stated monetary value.

Non-profit organization: an organization that has a service mission, is constrained to break even (in contrast to a *for-profit company*, which seeks to maximize profit), and has no beneficial ownership (*see* for-profit company).

O

Objectivity concept: a philosophy that accounting values should not be systematically biased or distorted.

Operating budget: the part of the budget that forecasts revenues, expenses, and operating profit.

Operating income: revenues less operating expenses (but before deduction of interest expense or tax expense) (*see also* net income).

Opportunity cost: the monetary value of a sacrifice incurred by taking one decision in preference to another.

Output: product or service, the provision of which is an object of an organization's or company's activities.

Outsource: to arrange to purchase a product or service from an external supplier rather than supply it internally.

Overapplied overhead: a situation where the overhead allocated to products is greater than the overhead incurred; it arises either because overhead spending is less than budgeted or because the overhead application base is greater than what was budgeted.

Overhead: expense other than direct materials and labour.

Overhead recovery: the use of a measure of activity, such as labour hours, to allocate budgeted overhead to products or processes through an overhead recovery rate.

Owners' equity: the amount of the shareholders' investment in the company; the assets less the liabilities; common shares plus retained earnings.

P

Par value: the legal or stated monetary face value of a share or a bond (*see also* no par value).

Parent company: a company that owns all the shares, or a majority of the shares, of another company (normally called the subsidiary company).

Participative budgeting: an approach to budget setting in which all levels contribute their inputs, and where the budget is not finalized until all parties agree to it (*see also* imposed budget).

Partnership: two or more individuals working together and sharing the profits of an enterprise, though not incorporated as a limited liability company.

Payback: (in capital budgeting) the point in time when future cash flows will have repaid the initial investment.

Perfect competition/perfectly competitive market: *see* competition.

Period cost: a cost that is incurred through the passage of time, rather than the level of output.

Periodicity concept: the assumption that the life of a business can be meaningfully divided into shorter (usually annual) periods for reporting to owners and managers.

Personal financial planning: application of accounting and finance concepts to individual situations (e.g., insurance, savings, investments, pensions).

Post: to copy a journal entry into the corresponding accounts.

Preferred dividend: the dividend paid to the owner of a preferred share.

Preferred share: a share that has some priority (e.g., being paid dividends) over the common shares.

Prepaid expense: an amount paid for an expense for which value has not yet been used (e.g., rent paid in advance).

Present value: a (future) cash flow after discounting to remove the opportunity cost of interest (*see* also net present value).

Prevention cost: (in quality control) a cost incurred to ensure conformance to quality standards.

Price setter: a company that can determine product price in a market.

Price taker: a company that must accept market prices for its products.

Process re-engineering: the radical rethinking and redesign of any business process to improve its performance.

Product cost: the cost associated with making/selling a product.

Production department: a functional unit that is responsible for transforming raw materials into finished products.

Product-sustaining activity: an activity and its related cost incurred in respect of a product or product line (as opposed to unit-variable cost, batch cost, or business-sustaining cost).

Profit centre: an organizational unit that is responsible for revenues and expenses and, hence, profits, and that can therefore be controlled by comparison of actual profit with budgeted profit.

Profitability ratios: measures of profit in relation to the resources used to sustain them: profit as % of sales; operating profit as % of assets (or return on assets); net income as % of equity (or return on equity).

Q

Quality control: the activities and costs associated with quality conformance, including prevention, appraisal, and internal and external failures.

Quick ratio: *see* acid-test ratio.

R

Rate of return: *see* return on investment and internal rate of return.

Raw material inventory: materials on hand that have not yet been put into production.

Receipt: the collection of cash.

Recognition concept: the rules governing the point at which a transaction (especially a sale) will be recognized.

Re-engineering: *see* process re-engineering.

Relevance concept: (in relation to information) how useful information is for decisions, control processes, or beliefs.

Relevant cost/revenue: a cost or revenue that changes as a result of a decision.

Glossary

Reliability concept: *see* objectivity.

Residual income: *see* economic value added.

Required rate of return: *see* cost of capital.

Responsibility centre: an organizational unit for which a manager is held responsible (*see* cost centre, revenue centre, profit centre, investment centre).

Retained earnings: profits made by a company since its date of incorporation (or reorganization) but not distributed to shareholders as dividends.

Return on assets: *see* profitability ratios.

Return on equity: *see* profitability ratios.

Return on investment (ROI): the profit from an operation expressed as a percentage of the investment in that operation.

Return on sales: *see* profitability ratios.

Revenue: the proceeds of sale of goods or services. Alternatively defined as the gross increase in owners' equity from operations.

Revenue centre: an organizational unit that has the responsibility to make sales; its performance can be judged by the variance between budgeted sales revenue and actual sales revenue.

Risk: the inherent uncertainty of the future.

S

Sales: revenue earned by providing goods in contrast to revenue from providing a service.

Sales forecast: a prediction of the sales level at a given price.

Scorekeeping: use of financial accounting information to assess how well assets have been utilized.

Security: an asset pledged to ensure repayment of a debt.

Sensitivity analysis: analysis of the effect of changes in input assumptions on the outcome of a decision.

Share: *see* common shares and preferred shares.

Share capital: the accounting value of all the shares, common and preferred, issued and outstanding.

Shareholders' equity: share capital, retained earnings, and all other equity accounts.

Short-run: examination of the effect of decisions, costs, revenues, etc., in the very near future.

Society of Management Accountants: an organization of professional accountants whose members specialize in management accounting and strategy.

Sole proprietorship: an individual operating an unincorporated business.

Specific identification: an inventory flow model where uniquely identified units are recognized as being sold individually (*see also* weighted average, first-in-first-out, and last-in-first-out).

Stakeholder: any person or organization with a legal, moral, or organizational interest in the activities of a company or non-profit organization. Includes shareholders (if any), creditors, managers, employees, governments, members of the public, etc.

Standard cost: a pre-determined cost at which a product is expected to be made, a service rendered, etc.

Statement of changes in financial position: *see* cash flow statement.

Statement of retained income: a financial accounting report that shows the retained income at the start of the year, its increase due to the addition of net income, its decrease due to the payment of dividends, and the balance of retained income at the end of the year.

Step fixed costs: a cost that is fixed within a given range, but then moves abruptly to a higher level when that range is exceeded.

Strategy: the process of choosing a basis for competing in the marketplace.

Subsidiary: a company of which all, or a majority, of the shares are owned by another (parent) company.

Sunk cost: a cost that was incurred in the past and that has, therefore, no relevance to decisions about the future.

T

T-account: a visual representation of a ledger *account*, with *debits* on the left-hand side and *credits* on the right-hand side.

Target cost: an appropriate cost that generates the target profit, given the target volume, target selling price, target quality of the product.

Target costing: a market-driven strategy with a method of determining the appropriate cost of a product, and then designing and producing the product to meet this cost.

Time value of money: (in capital budgeting) the interest opportunity in respect of a future cash flow.

Total asset turnover: *see* asset turnover.

Transaction: an event that changes the assets, liabilities, or equity of a company, and according to generally accepted accounting principles, must be recorded in the books of a company.

Transfer pricing: the organizational rules that govern the setting of prices for the internal transfer of goods or services.

U

Underapplied overhead: a situation where the overhead allocated to products is less than the overhead incurred; it arises either because overhead spending is greater than budgeted, or because the overhead application base is lower than budgeted.

Glossary

Unearned revenue: collected sales revenue for which goods or services have not yet been supplied.

Unit-related activities: *see* flexible cost.

V

Value chain: the set of interrelated activities that delivers a product or service to the customer; each element of the value chain should add more value than it adds cost.

Variable cost: *see* flexible cost.

Variance (analysis): the difference between the budget and the actual cost, and its associated analysis and management.

W, Z

Weighted average: an inventory flow model that assumes commingling of assets for sale (*see also* first-in-first-out, last-in-first-out, and specific identification).

What-if analysis: *see* sensitivity analysis.

Work-in-process (work-in-progress) inventory: inventory of goods that have begun the manufacturing process but have not yet completed it.

Working capital: current assets less current liabilities.

Zero-based budget: a budget based on radical reassessment of the objectives of a functional unit and the most efficient and effective ways of achieving them.

Index

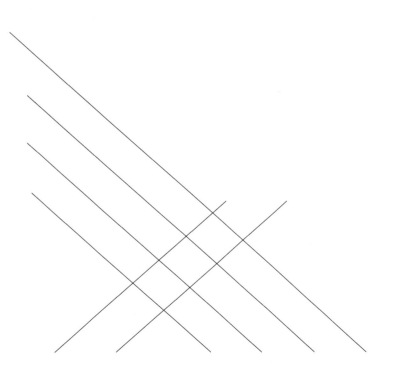

Index

A

accounting *see also* accrual accounting
   attention directing 6
   basis for business decisions 2–4
   cash-basis 413–414
   concepts 28–30
   decision making 6–7
   financial 7
   fund 412–413
   management 8
   personal financial planning 8
   role of 5–7
   scorekeeping 5–7
accounting cycle
   balancing the general ledger 32–33, 34
   correcting, adjusting, and closing the
     books 33–35
   financial statement preparation 35
   posting journal entries to the general
     ledger 32
   steps in 31
   transaction identification 31–32
   transaction recording 31
accounting equation 136–138
   described 18–19
   effects of transactions on 19–23
accounting information
   characteristics of 25–28
   relevance of 25–27
   reliability of 27
accounting ratios *see* ratios
accounts payable 37
accounts receivable 37, 140–141
accrual accounting 413
   defined 78
   resource flow 79–80
accrued expenses 172
accumulated depletion 184
activity-based costing 230
   customer profitability analysis 295
   overhead costs under 290–291
   product costing 293–294
adjusting journal entries 35, 58–61
allowance for doubtful debts 118–120, 141
allowance method 118–120
amortization 85–88
   buildings 146–147
   and capital cost allowances (CCAs) 99
   CICA Handbook 416
   declining balance method 96–97
   GAAP requirements 96
   intangible assets 184–185
   methods 96–98
   in non-profit organizations 414–416
   plant and equipment 147–148
   straight line method 96
   transactions 116–118
   units of production method 97–98
amortization expense 199
   payback and 356

annuities 368–370
asset turnover ratio 150, 150–151
assets *see also* intangible assets
   on balance sheet 138
   depletion 184
   described 138
   fixed 37
   realization 139
   total 150
   valuation of 138
attention directing 6
audit 138
auditor 7–8

B

bad debt expense 80, 88, 89, 141
   transactions 118–120
balance sheet
   accounts of 137
   in cash-basis accounting system 413–414
   common shares 327
   consolidated 157–159
   debt 334
   defined 18, 23
   efficiency analysis of 393
   example of 152
   inventory 83
   overview of 136–138
balance sheet equation *see* accounting
   equation
balanced scorecard 271–273
bank loans 37, 186–188
batch level costs 291
benchmarking 230
Bill 198 182
bond market 175
break-even model
   break-even point 286–287
   and change analysis 288–290
   contribution margin 286
   defined 286
   and profit 287–288
break-even point 286–287
budgetary control
   in cost centres 265–267
   explained 260–262
   in investment centres 269–271
   in profit centres 267–269
   in revenue centres 264–265
budgeting 198
   see also cash budget; operating budget
   activity-based costing 230
   behavioural aspect of 273–274
   benchmarking 230
   case against 247
   characteristics of 227
   compromise budget 230
   for governmental organizations 420
   imposed budget 245, 262

Kaizen system *230*
master budget *233–234*
for nonprofit organizations *420*
padded budget *229–230*
participative budget *245, 262–263*
for a production department *231–233*
purposes of *226*
for a service department *227–231*
zero-based budget *229*
budgets *see* budgeting
business entity *28*
business organizations
forms of *5–6*
business-sustaining costs *290*

C
Canada Business Corporations Act *16*
Canadian Institute of Chartered Accountants
financial statements objectives *17*
Canadian Red Cross Society *407*
Canadian Tire
cash from financing activities *203*
cash from investing activities *203*
cash from operations *201*
financial statements
retained earnings *330*
sales forecasting for *236–238*
statement of cash flows *214*
statement of changes in financial
position *203*
statement of retained earnings *93*
summarized financial statements *381*
capacity issues *314–315*
capital budgeting *354*
capital budgeting techniques *326*
see also present value
payback *356–358*
return on investment (ROI) *358–361*
capital cost allowances *99–100*
capital growth *328*
capital sources *see also* debt
common shares *326–327*
equity *331–332*
net income and dividends *327–328*
preferred shares *330–331*
retained earnings *330*
cash
account *37*
balance sheet presentation *139*
cash-basis accounting *413–414*
cash budget
background of *242*
cash payments *243*
cash receipts *242–243*
defined *226*
importance of *198*
preparation of *243–245*
cash flow statement *see* statement of cash
flows

cash flows
annuities and *368*
and balance sheet account changes *206–208*
discounting and *364–365*
from financing activities *201–202*
from investing activities *202*
net present value (NPV) and *365–367*
from operations *199–201*
in payback *357*
and return on investment (ROI) *359–361*
cash payments *243*
cash receipts *242–243*
Centraide of Montreal *414–415*
financial statement samples *422–431*
CICA Handbook *17*
amortization
co-operatives *408*
Coca-Cola trademark *184*
committed costs *316*
common shares *326–327*
compound interest *362–363*
compromise budget *230*
conservatism *29, 144*
consolidated financial statements
described *157*
goodwill *159*
minority interest *157–159*
consolidation *see* consolidated financial
statements
constant dollar *30*
contra asset account *88*
contribution margin *286*
control process *260*
corporations
financial reporting *16–18*
cost behaviour *see also* activity-based costing;
break-even analysis
defined *284*
fixed costs *285–286*
mixed costs *286*
variable costs *284–285*
cost centres
production departments *266–267*
service departments *265–266*
cost-flow approaches *see* inventory valuation
cost of capital *332, 336–337*
cost of goods sold *82–84*
transactions *51–52, 55, 110–114*
costing *see* product costing
costs *see also* cost behaviour; expenses;
overhead costs
batch level *291*
business-sustaining *290*
committed *316*
differential *312–314*
fixed *285–286*
full *317*
product-sustaining *291*
sunk *316*
variable *142–143*

Index

credit sales *79, 140–141*
creditor *5*
credits *45–48, 52–54*
current assets
    accounts receivable *140 141*
    cash *139*
    described *139*
    inventory *141–144*
    other *144–145*
    prepaid expenses *145*
    short-term investments *139–140*
    total *145–146*
current liabilities
    accrued expenses *172*
    defined *170*
    short-term debt *172–173*
    trade payables *171–172*
current ratio *173–174, 382*

D

days' sale in inventory *145*
debentures *174–175*
debits *45–48, 52–54*
debt
    defined *186, 175, 333*
    financial leverage *335–338*
    interest on *334*
    level *333*
    repayment of *334*
    reporting *335*
    security *335*
debt ratios *175–176, 333, 385*
debt-to-assets ratio *176, 333, 385*
debt-to-equity ratio *176, 333, 385*
decision making *6–7*
    see also long-term decision making; short-
    term decision making
declining balance amortization method *96–97*
deferred revenue *186*
deferred taxes *99–100*
depletion *184*
depreciation *see* amortization
differential costs *312–314*
disclosure *29*
discount rate
    described *364–365*
    determination of *370*
    in risk analysis *370*
discounting *364–365*
dividend cover ratio *328, 388*
dividend payout ratio *92, 93, 388*
dividends
    account *40*
    defined *178*
    distribution of *328*
    payment of *92, 178*
    stock dividend *329*
double-entry accounting system *see also*
    transactions

accounts of *37–40*
balanced general ledger *33*
closing the books *62–64*
debits and credits *45–48, 52–54*
described *36–37*
importance of *54*
important points of *40–41*
Dupont Pyramid of Operating Ratios
    efficiency analysis of balance sheet
        assets *393*
    illustrated *394*
    return on assets (ROA) *390–392*
    vertical analysis of the income
        statement *392–393*

E

earnings per share *94, 388*
efficiency ratios *386–387*
equity *331–332*
    see also owners' equity; shareholders' equity
    described *176*
    dividends *182*
    of nonprofit organizations (NPOs) *407*
    preferred shares *179*
    retained earnings *179*
    shares *177–178*
ethical standards *355–356*
expense(s) *see also* costs
    account *38–40*
    accrued *172*
    amortization *85–88, 199*
    bad debt *80, 88, 89, 140–141*
    cost of goods sold *82–84*
    defined *38, 81–82*
    prepaid *85, 145*
    tax *99–100*
    transactions *102–105, 110–120*
ExxonMobil *355–356*

F

Fayol, Henri *226*
financial accounting *7*
financial leverage *175, 336–338*
    impact on retained earnings *338*
financial reporting
    objectives of *16–18*
financial statements *see also* balance sheet;
    income statement; statement of cash
    flows; statement of retained earnings
    auditing of *7–8*
    preparation of *35, 64–66*
    and profitability assessment *24–25*
    publication of *24*
    types of *16, 23–24*
first-in-first-out (FIFO) model *154, 155*
fixed assets *37*
fixed costs *285–286*
full costs *317*

fund accounting *412, 412–413*
funds *411, 412–413*
future value *363, 364*

G

GAAP *see* generally accepted accounting
    principles (GAAP)
general ledger *see also* transactions
    adjusting and closing *33–35, 62–64*
    balancing *32–33, 34, 63*
    defined *32*
    T-account *104*
General Motors *150*
generally accepted accounting principles
    (GAAP) *19*
    and amortization *96*
    inventory *113–114*
    tax expense *99–100*
    transaction identification *31*
    transaction recording *31*
goal congruence *273–274*
going concern *28*
goodwill *149–150*
    on consolidation *159*
governmental organizations
    accounting practices of *409–410*
    budgetary importance *420*
    versus business organizations *404–405*
    financial management of *409*
    versus nonprofit organizations *409*
gross margin *90*
    and cost of goods sold *83*
    gross profit on sales *383*
gross profit ratio *see* gross margin

H, I

historical cost *28*
historical cost approach
    problems with *136–138*
impairment loss *184–185*
imposed budget *245, 262*
incentive-based reward system *273*
income statement
    defined *23, 78*
    example of *95*
    vertical analysis of *392–393*
inflation adjustment *228–229*
intangible assets
    defined *148*
    finite life *184*
    goodwill *149–150*
    indefinite life *184–185*
    patents *149*
    trademarks *149*
    transactions *184–185*
interest *334*
    compound *362–363*
    simple *362*
interest cover ratio *385*

inventory *see also* inventory valuation
    account *37*
    cost of goods sold *82–84*
    described *141*
    GAAP requirements *113–114*
    and planned production *235*
    transaction *113–114*
inventory flow *see* inventory valuation
inventory holding period *387*
inventory of finished goods *141*
inventory of raw material *141*
inventory turnover ratio *144, 387*
inventory valuation *83, 141–142*
    described *153*
    first-in-first-out (FIFO) model *154, 155*
    full cost versus variable cost *142–143*
    last-in-last-out (LIFO) model *154–156*
    lower of cost or market price rule *144*
    overhead costs *142–143*
    specific identification *153, 154*
    weighted average model *156*
investment centres *269–271*
investment risk *341–344*
investor *5*

J, K

journal *32*
journal entries *32*
    see also transactions
    adjusting *35, 58–61*
Kaizen system *230*

L

labour planning *239–240*
last-in-last-out (LIFO) model *154–156*
leverage *175*
liabilities *see also* current liabilities; long-term
    debt
    deferred revenue *186*
    defined *170*
    total *175*
limited liability *180–181*
limited liability company *5*
liquidity ratios *173–174, 382*
long-term assets
    balance sheet presentation *146*
    buildings *146–147*
    land *146*
    plant and equipment *147–148*
long-term debt *188–189*
    bank loans *186–188*
    debentures and notes *174–175*
    defined *170*
    mortgage loans *174*
long-term decision making *see also* capital
    budgeting techniques
    described *354–355*
    strategic analysis *355–356*
    uncertainty *370–371*

Index

loss 78
lower of cost or market price rule 144

M

make or buy 315–316
management accounting 8
management by exception 6, 260–262
management theories
    management by exception 6, 260–262
    responsibility and control 263–264
market model 340–344
market-related ratios 387–389
master budget 233–234
matching concept 29
matching principle 78
materiality 29
minority interest 157–159
mixed costs 286
Morgan Car Co. 235
mortgage loans 174
Mountain Equipment Cooperative (MEC) 408
mutual societies 408

N

net income 90
    defined 25, 38, 78, 417
    and dividend payments 327–328
net income to sales ratio 90
net present value (NPV) 365–367
neutrality 29
nonprofit organizations (NPOs)
    accounting practices of 409–410
    amortization 414–416
    break-even constraint 406–407
    budgeting practices of 420
    versus business organizations 404–405
    characteristics of 406
    effectiveness measures 418–419
    efficiency measures 419–420
    evaluating success of 417–420
    financial statement analysis 416–417
    financial statements of 410
    fund accounting 412–413
    versus governmental organizations 409
    organizational entity of 412
    revenue and expense 413–414
    revenue recognition 414–416
    service mission 406
    stakeholders of 407–408

O

one-write system 32
Ontario Brewery 238–241
operating budget
    background of 235–236
    defined 226
    labour planning 239–240
    preparation of 240–241
    production forecasting 238–239

sales forecasting 236–238
operating income 88–90
    accounts 24
    and cash flow 199–200
overhead costs 84–85
    defined 290
    fixed 142–143
    over and under recovered 296, 297
    production overhead 290–291
    transactions 114–116
overhead recovery rate 292–293, 296
owners' equity
    accounts in three types of business
        organization 37
    changes in 180

P

padded budget 229–230
par value shares 177–178
participative budget 245, 262–263
patents 149
payback 356–358
payments 243
periodicity 28
personal financial planning 8
planned production
    and inventory 235
preferred shares 179, 330–331
prepaid expense 85, 145
present value
    annuities 368–370
    described 361
    discounting 364–365
    net present value (NPV) 365–367
    simple and compound interest 361–363
    weighted average cost of capital
        (WACC) 336, 337, 343, 370
present value table 366
price-to-earnings ratio 388
principle of revenue recognition 107–110
private companies 5
product costing
    activity-based costs 293–294
    background of 290–291
    traditional cost allocation 292–293
product-sustaining costs 291
production forecasting 238–239
production overhead 290–291
profit see also net income
    and break-even point 287–288
profit centres 267–269
profitability assessment 24–25
profitability ratios 26, 91, 382–384

Q, R

quick ratio 173–174, 382
ratio analysis
    debt ratios 333, 385
    efficiency ratios 386–387

liquidity ratios *173–174, 382*
market-related ratios *387–389*
profitability ratios *26, 91, 382–384*
ratios *88–94, 382–389*
purpose of *380*
realization *139*
receivables *see* accounts receivable
receivables collection period *140, 387*
receivables turnover ratio *140, 141, 386*
recognition *29*
resource flows *39–40*
responsibility and control *263–264*
retained earnings *92, 178–179, 330*
account *37*
and dividend distribution *179*
and financial leverage *338*
return on assets (ROA) *25, 26, 90, 383, 390–392*
return on average investment *359*
return on equity (ROE) *25, 26, 90, 384*
return on investment (ROI) *358–361*
return on sales *90, 383*
returns *107–109*
revenue
account *38–40*
defined *38*
other *80*
sales *78–80*
transactions *50–52, 102–105, 109–110*
revenue centres *264–265*
revenue recognition *79–81, 414–415*
described *105*
principle of *107–110*
risk
financial leverage *175, 337*
investment *341–344*
in long-term decision making *370–371*
versus returns *341–344*
risk assessment
debt analysis *175–176*
liquidity ratios *173–174*
Rogers Communications Inc. *236*

S
sales forecasting *236–238*
sources for *235*
sales revenue *78–80*
transaction *51, 54–55*
Sarbanes Oxley Act *182*
scorekeeping *5–7*
security *335*
sensitivity analysis *371*
share capital account *37*
shareholders
and financial statements *24*
limited liability of *180–181*
residual status of *327*
rights of *177, 330*
role of *17*

shareholders' equity
defined *38*
transaction *189–190*
shareholders' return *340–341*
shares *177–178*
common *326–327*
contributed surplus *331*
foreign exchange adjustments *331*
in limited liability company *5*
par value *177–178*
preferred *179, 330–331*
price increase of *179*
in private company *5*
retained earnings *330*
stock dividend *329*
stock splits *329*
short-term debt *172–173*
short-term decision making
capacity issues *314–315*
differential costs and revenues *312–314*
effects of timeframe on *316–317*
make or buy *315–316*
short-term investments *139–140*
simple interest *362*
specific identification *153, 154*
statement of cash flows *207*
and balance sheet account changes *206–208*
cash from financing activities *201–202*
cash from investing activities *202*
cash from operations *199–201*
change on cash balance *202*
defined *24, 198–199*
example of *205*
interpretation of *203*
T-account method *208–214*
statement of changes in financial position *see* statement of cash flows
statement of retained earnings *178*
defined *23–24, 92*
example of *101*
illustrated *93*
stewardship concept *17–18*
stock dividend *329*
stock splits *329*
straight line amortization method *96*
strategic analysis *355–356*
sunk costs *316*

T
T-account *104*
T-account method for statement of cash flows *208–214*
tax expense *99–100*
total asset turnover *386*
trade credit *171*
automated payments of *171*
trade payables *171–172*

Index

trademarks *149*
    Coca-Cola *184*
traditional cost allocation *292–293*
transactions
    adjusting journal entries *58–61*
    amortization *116–118*
    bad debt expense *118–120*
    balance sheet accounts *183*
    bank loans *186–188*
    cost of goods sold *51–52, 55, 110–114*
    deferred delivery *109–110*
    effects on accounting equation *19–23*
    examples of *42–45, 48–58*
    expense *102–105, 110–120*
    identification of *31–32*
    intangible assets *184–185*
    long-term debt *188–189*
    measurement of *7*
    overhead expenses *114–116*
    recording of *7, 31–32, 41–42*
    returns *107–109*
    revenue *50–52, 102–105, 107–109*
    sales revenue *51, 54–55*
    shareholders equity *189–190*
treasury bills (T-Bills) *342*

U, V

uncertainty *370–371*
units of production amortization method *97–98*
variable costs *142–143, 284–285*

W, X, Z

weighted average cost of capital (WACC) *336, 370*
weighted average model *156*
Wendy's International Inc.
    consolidated balance sheet *152*
    consolidated cash flow statements *205*
    consolidated statement of retained
        income *101*
    consolidated statements of income *95*
"what-if" analysis *288–290*
work-in-process inventory *141*
working capital management *326*
Xerox Corporation *149*
zero-based budget *229*

Student Self-Study Resource

to accompany

Accounting for Non-Financial Managers

The first purchaser of this book is provided access* to additional interactive multiple-choice tests for self-assessment and review. Available online, the tests can be accessed using the following information:

Access http://www.captus.com/anfm/student

Login: anfm-student09w
Password: vuromu
Valid until 2010-08-31

* Access to this site is subject to change without notice. Contact sales@captus.com if you have problem accessing the site.